THREE THEOLOGICAL MISTAKES

THREE THEOLOGICAL MISTAKES

How to Correct Enlightenment Assumptions
about God, Miracles, and Free Will

Ric Machuga

CASCADE *Books* • Eugene, Oregon

THREE THEOLOGICAL MISTAKES
How to Correct Enlightenment Assumptions about God, Miracles, and Free Will

Copyright © 2015 Ric Machuga. All rights reserved. Except for brief quotations in critical publications or reviews, no part of this book may be reproduced in any manner without prior written permission from the publisher. Write: Permissions, Wipf and Stock Publishers, 199 W. 8th Ave., Suite 3, Eugene, OR 97401.

Cascade Books
An Imprint of Wipf and Stock Publishers
199 W. 8th Ave., Suite 3
Eugene, OR 97401

www.wipfandstock.com

ISBN 13: 978-1-62564-757-3

Cataloging-in-Publication data:

Machuga, Ric.

Three theological mistakes : how to correct Enlightenment assumptions about God, miracles, and free will / Ric Machuga.

xviii + 276 p. ; 23 cm. —Includes bibliographical references and index.

ISBN 13: 978-1-62564-757-3

1. Philosophical theology. 2. Philosophy and religion. 3. Religion and Science. I. Title.

BT 40 .M1 2015

Manufactured in the U.S.A.

To Christy and Matt, Michael and Speri

Contents

Preface | ix

—1—
The Collapse of Mechanistic Philosophy | 1

—2—
What Logic Can Never Do | 24

—3—
No Logical Bridge | 46

—4—
Two Views of God | 66

—5—
God, Miracles, and Good Reasons | 86

—6—
In Defense of Particularity | 109

—7—
The Ethics of Grace | 127

—8—
The Politics of Stewardship | 151

—9—
Free Will and Predestination | 173

—10—
The Goodness of God | 200

—11—
Augustine's Conception of Hell | 224

—12—
God's Gracious Wrath | 244

Bibliography | 263
Index | 271

Preface

This book addresses five big questions.
- Is the existence of God a matter of faith or knowledge?
- Does God sometimes act miraculously or are there physical causes for everything?
- Is morality absolute or relative?
- Are humans truly free or does God's sovereignty determine everything?
- When bad things happen, is God the cause or are they the fault of humans?

Too frequently Christians answer these questions with a Yes to one side and a No to the other side. Thomas Aquinas and Karl Barth answer Yes to both, in all cases. Following their model, I will defend a "third way" which transcends the dichotomies of fideism versus rationalism, supernaturalism versus naturalism, relativism versus absolutism, free will versus predestination, and God's justice versus his mercy.

Our difficulties came to a head in the seventeenth century. Though the Enlightenment was responsible for much that is fine, just, and good, it also promoted three bad ideas: mechanism, universal quantification, and mono-causation. Mechanism is the claim that physical causes always have predictable effects fully determined by the laws of nature. This led to the assumption that the laws of cause and effect are logically clear and mathematically precise. So we must, as Galileo advised, "Measure everything, and that which you cannot, measure it anyway." Finally, since causal relations are always clear and precise they must be exclusive—if something is physically caused, then it was not caused by God, and conversely, if something is caused by God, then it cannot be physically caused. This sort of mono-causation produced a rigid natural/supernatural divide and the search for an "empirically detectable" God.

These three assumptions are demonstrably false, both philosophically and scientifically. In their place I articulate and defend three good ideas:

- Not all causes are mechanistic.
- All quantities are ultimately qualities.
- Full understanding requires dual-causation.

First, while every effect has a cause, many effects are not, and never will be, humanly predictable. Causation, predictability, and determinism are distinct ideas that must never be conflated. Second, while many things can be quantitatively measured, such measurements are ultimately based on qualitative human judgments about *what* something is. Every number is an iteration of the number one. But there is nothing "measurable" that one baseball game, one table, one person, one corporation, one nation-state, one essay, and one poem have in common except a *qualitative* integrity and unity. Third, when God employs humans to achieve his intended goal, the question "Who did that?" cannot be answered on the assumption of mono-causation. Instead, the answer requires dual-causation, or what Thomas Aquinas referred to as primary and secondary causes and Karl Barth the divine accompanying.

Thus, my central theme is that these three "good ideas" answer questions about God, miracles, and evil in a way which is scientifically, philosophically, and theologically satisfying, without resorting to false dichotomies.

Chapter 1 considers the assumption that physical causation and predictability are one and the same. No one cognizant of twentieth-century science believes that this is true. All physical actions have physical causes, but most of these are not even in principle predictable. Chapters 2 and 3 complete the philosophical case for this third category of the "physically caused but not predictable." These chapters do little to build an affirmative case for the alternative position. But until we throw away our old glasses and get a new prescription, we will never realize how much mechanistic philosophy masquerading as science has distorted our vision.

Chapters 4 and 5 will begin to flesh out the alternative to an Enlightenment conception of God. Isaac Newton's theory of universal gravity was the foundation of the mechanistic philosophy that virtually defined the Enlightenment, roughly the period beginning with the publication of his *Mathematical Principles of Natural Philosophy* (1687) to the publication of Immanuel Kant's *Religion within the Limits of Reason Alone* (1793). Newton was neither a materialist nor an atheist. But his conception of God was quite different from the pre-Enlightenment conception of God as the Author of creation. Newton pictured God as one who was "very well skilled in mechanics and geometry." A century later, William Paley famously compared God to a skilled watchmaker. And today many Christians think in terms of an Intelligent Designer who acts in a scientifically detectable fashion. Instead of a divine Author who *speaks* the universe into existence, creates all things through his *Word* and is the "*author* and finisher of our faith," we now have a supernatural Craftsman who has fashioned an incredibly complex machine, capable of pretty much running on its own, except when God miraculously intervenes to suspend the "laws of nature" or when humans, with their God-given free will, make autonomous choices, independent of all antecedent physical causes.

These two competing conceptions of God assume different ideas about how God acts vis-à-vis his creation. The Craftsman model assumes a theory of mono-causation, while the Authorship model assumes a theory of dual-causation. Mono-causation assumes that everything has *either* a natural cause *or* a supernatural cause. Thus, when we come across things which are either too complex and/or improbable for science to explain in terms of natural causes, the justifiable inference is that they must have a supernatural cause. Dual-causation, on the other hand, assumes that God is the primary cause of *everything's* existence. Nonetheless the created order is informed so that the agency of real secondary causes is also responsible for what happens. Thus, nothing happens without a physical cause. However, as we will explore later, this does *not* justify the inference that God is absent, irrelevant, or uncaring. As the cause of our very being, God is closer, more involved, and more solicitous of our good than anyone else, including ourselves.[1]

The simplest way to understand the difference between mono-causation and dual-causation is to consider two distinct ways people can cooperate to achieve a goal. If a rock is too heavy for any single person to move, then two people might tie a rope to it so that they can both pull on the rope to exert a sufficient force to move the rock. In such a case, each person might contribute 50 percent of the force necessary to move the rock.

But there is a quite different way two people can work together to achieve a goal. Many years ago a friend and colleague said he was going to make an exquisite pasta dish for dinner and asked if I would like to join him. I immediately accepted the offer, though I was very puzzled. You see, my friend is a quadriplegic—how, I wondered, was *he* going to cook for me? When I arrived at his house, it soon became clear how he would do this. After the standard chit-chat, my friend politely began giving me instructions—"get two cloves of garlic from the pantry, three tablespoons of

---

1. "Because in all things God himself is properly the cause of universal being which is innermost in all things, it follows that in all things God works intimately." Aquinas, *Summa Theologica*, I 105.5; see also *Summa Theologica*, I 8.1.

olive oil, finely chop three leaves of basil . . . ." It continued like this for about thirty minutes, in part, because many of the ingredients and techniques he employed I had never heard of before, and hence, my friend was forced to give extremely detailed (and to his mind, elementary!) instructions. Yet when we finished, the pasta was truly exquisite.

So here's the question: who made the pasta—me or my friend? While in one sense we "cooperated," it would be wrong to describe this as a case where he and I each did 50 percent of the work. No, in the most important sense, my friend did *everything* because I was only the set of hands he used to prepare the pasta. While my hands did the physical work, they would have been utterly useless without his detailed instructions. Nonetheless, there was a real dignity in what I did and the words "well done, good and faithful servant" would have made perfect sense.

Besides thinking in terms of mono-causation, Enlightenment thinkers had a penchant for *universal* laws. Newton's "laws of nature," after all, were applicable to *everything*. So too, when Kant described a religion that functioned "within the limits of reason alone" this meant forming a conception of God under which everyone would be treated equally and fairly. Like the "laws of nature," the "laws of morality" must be universal. A God who failed to meet these criteria, Kant thought, would ipso facto be immoral, and hence, unworthy of our worship.

This made it extremely difficult, perhaps impossible, for Kant to reconcile himself to the irreducibly *particular* claims of Christianity. It was the Jews, not the Egyptians, Assyrians, or Babylonians, to whom God said: "I will make of you a great nation, and I will bless you, and make your name great, so that you will be a blessing" (Gen 12:2); and it was Jesus, not Confucius, Lao-tzu, or Buddha, who died on the cross to reconcile the world unto himself. Such particularity is scandalous if one begins with Enlightenment assumptions. Chapter 6 examines these assumptions and finds them wanting.

Chapter 7 considers a third issue that arises from the Enlightenment penchant for the universal. What makes a house good in Alaska and what makes a house good in Hawaii are quite different. So it would be silly to search for the *universal* laws of constructing good houses. But the Enlightenment credo that *everyone* has a right to life, liberty, and the pursuit of happiness remains at the center of our moral and political philosophies. And this means that much contemporary ethical philosophy is focused on resolving ethical dilemmas, i.e., what should we do when different people's rights conflict? Lying is wrong because everyone has a right to have their questions answered truthfully. But when the Gestapo asks, "Have you seen any Jews?", should we still answer truthfully, even when it means almost certain death for someone else? Solving puzzles like this has become a central issue for those who begin by assuming that ethics is all about discovering, protecting, and promoting universal rights.

The ethics of Aquinas and Barth take a very different approach. For them the crucial moral question is not *knowing* what to do in difficult cases, but *doing* what one already knows should be done in the most ordinary cases. When St. Paul wrote "For I do not do the good I want, but the evil I do not want is what I do," he had no difficulty knowing what was good; his only problem was finding the power to "just do it."

Aristotle had much to say about the virtues and habits that are developed through good instruction and lots of practice. These provide one source of "power" for doing good. And we will not belittle these. But St. Paul, Aquinas, and Barth all argued that though virtues and habits are real secondary sources of power for doing good, the primary power is the work of the Holy Spirit that proceeds from the Father and the Son. In the end, Christian ethics *is* Christian theology and Christian theology *is* the theology of grace.[2]

In chapter 8 we move from the ethics of grace to the politics of stewardship. We do this to highlight the radical difference between an ethic focused on universal *rights* versus one focused on what we have been *given*. It is John Locke, perhaps the most important Enlightenment political philosopher, who is primarily responsible for this misstep. His influence is clearly visible in our Declaration of Independence and his central argument still convinces many Christians and non-Christians alike.

Locke argued that prior to a social contract that brought governments into existence, the whole of creation was God's and God's alone. In this primitive state, God's bountiful creation supplied more than enough to meet everyone's needs, so the lack of government was not a significant problem. Nonetheless, Locke thought that for people to gather more food than they could use before it rotted and went to waste would be morally wrong and insulting to the Creator. But with the invention of money all this changed. Humans had now invented a way to turn the fruits of their labors into something that would never rot, and hence, would never go to waste. So from here on, when humans freely "mixed" their labor with the land, they acquired an individual *right* to the fruits of their labor which had no limits. No longer were individuals limited in how much they could accumulate and call their own. A couple of generations later, David Hume argued

---

2. "It is the Christian doctrine of God, or more exactly, the knowledge of the electing grace of God in Jesus Christ, which decides the nature of theological ethics." Barth, *Church Dogmatics*, II.2, 543.

that this right to property was not only unlimited, but that the protection of private property was *the* central purpose of government.³

Enlightenment political theory had moved a great distance from the political thought which preceded it. Though a theory of "natural law" had already been formulated and defended by Aquinas, there is only a superficial connection between it and the Enlightenment theory of "natural rights." One indication of the breadth of the divide is Aquinas's clear and adamant insistence that property law is *not* part of the law of nature, but instead, a part of positive law (i.e., man-made law) which is neither universal nor absolute. Thus, he would argue that, "It is not theft, properly speaking, to take secretly and use another's property in a case of extreme need: because that which he takes for the support of his life becomes his own property by reason of that need."⁴ We agree with Aquinas. Since God is the primary cause of all we are or have, being good stewards (cooperating, secondary causes) of what we are given precludes any absolute and unlimited *right* to property.

Chapters 4 through 8 all, in one way or the other, invoke the idea of dual-causation. But how can humans truly be free and responsible agents if God is the primary cause of everything? Doesn't free will require that our actions are wholly our own? On the other hand, if God is the Author of *all* of creation, then how can we be anything more than mere characters in a play or drama who do exactly what the script says we will do? In short, how can free will and predestination possibility be reconciled? And isn't this the ultimate either/or choice? Isn't it logically impossible to say Yes to both?

Chapter 9 will address these questions head on. In it I argue that there are two distinct conceptions of freedom. The first, which we will call autonomous freedom, cannot logically be reconciled with a robust understanding of predestination. The second can. When Jesus said to his disciples, "You shall know the truth and the truth shall set you free," he had in mind a very different conception of freedom. Moreover, not only is the sort of freedom that Jesus promised logically compatible with predestination; it *requires* predestination.

A still greater problem remains—the problem of evil. One consequence of the Enlightenment's emphasis on human autonomy that many Christians still find very attractive is that it seems to provide an explanation for pain and suffering. If we, and not God, are ultimately responsible for our free choices, then the pain and suffering caused by humans is *our* fault, not God's. And conversely, if on the assumption of dual-causation we are *only* secondary causes, then doesn't God bear the ultimate responsibility for all

---

3. MacIntyre, *Whose Justice*, chapter 15.
4. *Summa Theologica*, II-II 66.7.

the pain and suffering caused by humans? So without a robust doctrine of free will understood in terms of human autonomy, it seems that the problem of evil is philosophically insoluble.

While there is no denying the appeal of the "free will defense" to the problem of evil, chapter 10 articulates and defends an alternative approach. In this pre-Enlightenment approach, God's transcendent existence is the ultimate good and evil is the ultimate privation. Evil is the "impossible possibility" that God permits, but does not cause. This is not a philosophical *explanation* of evil. Aquinas and Barth have no philosophical solution to the problem of evil. Instead, they remain content to *describe* evil's effects on God's good creation. Our utterly inexplicable turning away from all that brings joy and happiness toward that which brings only sorrow and destruction cannot be explained. Yet our fallen foolishness also makes fitting the incarnation with the great and glorious salvation found in Christ's death and resurrection.

Nevertheless, no theologically adequate description of demonic evil can ignore the fact that it *deserves* the wrath of God. In the final two chapters, we will explore three distinct ways of understanding God's wrath. Since the time of Augustine, many Christians have thought of it in wholly punitive terms. In this view, God's wrath is the everlasting punishment experienced by those in hell. However, there has always been a second understanding of hell. Though it has clearly been a minority position in the history of the Church, a few Christians have argued that the wrath of God is always restorative and ultimately redemptive. While some people will have to go *through* hell, in this second view, God's wrath ultimately succeeds in bringing *all* humans first to repentance and then to redemption.

The final chapter outlines yet a third view of hell. It follows Barth and says Yes to *both* the punitive and the redemptive aspects of God's wrath. On the cross Jesus suffered the wholly *punitive* wrath of God; for everyone else, God's wrath is ultimately *redemptive*, though it does include a punitive aspect. Yet Barth insists that he is not a universalist. Is he being subtle or simply slippery?

If we assume an Enlightenment conception of freedom in terms of autonomy, then Barth is clearly being slippery. Given this assumption our eternal destiny is wholly in our own hands and the choice for or against God is ultimately our own. No matter how much God *desires* that all will be saved, there is no way that he can *assure* that this will be the case. But if by "freedom" we mean the freedom Jesus promised to his disciples, then Barth's position is subtly defensible. The bottom line is that we must neither affirm nor deny that all will be saved, but we must also unceasingly hope and pray that hell will be emptied. As Edith Stein once said, "Human freedom can be neither broken nor neutralized by divine freedom, but it may well be, so to speak, outwitted."[5]

Now, a note on heroes and villains. Thomas Aquinas and Karl Barth are clearly the heroes of this book. So who are the villains? That's not nearly as obvious. Rene Descartes, Isaac Newton, David Hume, John Locke, and Immanuel Kant are all frequently mentioned, and rarely in a positive light. But I wouldn't consider them villains. And I would certainly never suggest that there isn't much to be learned by reading them. Nor would I suggest that there isn't much to learn from the Enlightenment to which they all contributed. Of course, given the subtitle of the book, the reader can rightfully expect that the Enlightenment will receive some serious criticism. But my goal is not to find and punish villains.

A Thomist of the previous generation, Etienne Gilson, frequently compared the history of philosophy to the scientist's laboratory. When science is working as it should, no one criticizes individual scientists just because their theory is proven false in the laboratory. Coming up with good scientific ideas and theories is hard work that only great minds can do well. And the fact that a scientist's idea or theory doesn't work in the laboratory does not belittle the scientist. The only scientists who deserve criticism are those whose ideas are too vague or inchoate to permit rigorous testing. So too, Gilson argued, coming up with good ideas and theories in philosophy is hard work which only great minds can do well. And while scientific ideas are frequently tested by expensive tools, philosophical ideas can only be tested by history. Given the interconnection and resonances of philosophical ideas, it takes centuries for all the implications of a great philosopher's ideas to become clear. Descartes, Newton, Hume, Locke, and Kant were all great philosophers. But now, two-and-a-half centuries after they died, even mediocre philosophers are able to put their fingers on mistakes and implications that were invisible at the time they were first proposed.

What's more, the great philosophers we discuss sometimes had vague intuitions of future difficulties that would arise when their ideas were simplistically and perfunctorily applied to ethical, political, or theological problems. A great tool only produces great results in the hands of a skilled craftsman. So great philosophers frequently qualify and nuance their big ideas with numerous fine distinctions.

And while fine distinctions have their place, this book is not one of them. My goal is not a careful exegesis of past philosophers. Instead, I assume with Thomas Aquinas that "the study of philosophy has as its purpose to know not what people have thought, but rather the truth about the way

---

5. Quoted in Balthasar, *Dare We Hope*, 221.

things are."⁶ If historical scholars can point to more nuanced and qualified statements which demonstrate that these great philosophers did not really endorse mechanism, universal quantification, and mono-causation, then so much the better!

Finally, a note on reading this book. The book focuses on big ideas about God, miracles, and free will. But the conclusions I reach are not deductions from alternative "presuppositions." Instead, I try to build a case based on a wide range of issues and specific examples for a decidedly "unmodern" approach to these questions. While my goal is to study the forest, doing this requires much time looking at individual trees. So to make sure the "big picture" is not lost, each chapter begins with a short abstract. These should keep the forest more clearly in focus.

I have also included fairly extensive footnotes, many of which include quotes (some fairly long) from both primary and secondary sources. These can easily be ignored without substantial loss. The primary purpose of the footnotes are twofold. First, to make clear the utter unoriginality of my arguments. Second, to provide interested readers with references to my decidedly unmodern way of thinking.

Of course, I am speaking loosely when I refer to *my* thinking. "Thoughts" are not *owned* like cars or pieces of property. A book like this is the product of countless hours of discussion with friends and colleagues. Here are a few that immediately come to mind and deserve my heartfelt thanks: Dan Barnett, Greg Cootsona, John Wilson, Dave Montoya, Bill Martin, Scot Hoiland, Michael Machuga, Matt Caldwell, Michael Fitzpatrick, Andrew Lavin, Justin Gilley, Jay Gallangher, Robin Parry, David Yeago, James Madden, Gary Deddo, and David Opderbeck. And finally I must acknowledge the computer skills of my wife, Kathy—without her my frustration level with all things technological could have easily prolonged this project beyond the useful life of my neurons.

---

6. Aquinas, *Commentary on De Caelo [On the Heavens]*, I.22, quoted in Stump, *Aquinas*, 9.

—1—

The Collapse of Mechanistic Philosophy

> *A small error at the beginning of something,"* said Thomas Aquinas, *"is a great one at the end."* One such error is the common failure to distinguish between causation and predictability (i.e., determinism). While every action or event has a cause, most actions and events are not even "in principle" predictable. Our failure to make this distinction permits mechanistic philosophy to masquerade as science.

TIME AND CHANCE HAPPEN TO THEM ALL

Common sense assumes a real difference between things that happen by chance and things that happen in a predictable or mechanical fashion. Things that happen by chance can only be *described* after the fact. Things that happen in a predictable or mechanical fashion can also be *explained* in terms of natural laws.

An ordinary tennis ball illustrates this difference. We can all predict that when we throw or hit a tennis ball across the net, it will soon hit the ground somewhere on the other side. An excellent tennis player can predict with pretty fair accuracy precisely where the tennis ball will land. And if the tennis ball is being shot out of a ball machine, any high school physics student could predict when and where the ball would land just by measuring the force imparted and the angle and direction in which the ball was aimed. Students today can do this because three centuries ago Isaac Newton discovered the mathematical laws of mechanics and gravity. Since these laws explain what is and isn't relevant to the motion of any given object, they allow us to predict what will happen.

More specifically, Newton's laws tell us that the mass of the ball, the force imparted, and the direction and angle it is aimed fully determine (and hence, predict) where and when the ball will land. Well, not exactly: if this were posed as a problem for college physics majors they might be asked to add factors such as air resistance and wind direction to their predictions. But because of Newton, they would never need to know the color of the ball, the time of day, whether the ball machine was manufactured in the United States or China, or countless other identifiable factors in the immediate proximity. Once we have accurately measured a handful of relevant factors, we have all the information necessary for an accurate prediction of where and when the ball will hit the ground.

Now let us change the situation slightly. Think of the same ball machine shooting the tennis ball down a fairly steep dirt road strewn with rocks, several switchbacks, and drop-offs. Once again, we can predict where the ball would first hit the ground. But where it would come to rest as it rolled and bounced down the road, perhaps careening over the edge of a rocky cliff, is an entirely different matter. This time a college degree in physics would be of little help. Why? It is not because there are gaps in the causal chain or other "supernatural" forces acting on the bouncing ball. No, the causal forces here are no different from those in the first situation.

The critical difference is that in the first example, a small error in the initial measurements will have a small consequence in the final outcome, whereas in the second example, a small error in the initial measurements will have an unpredictably large consequence. The difference between the two is that every rock and switchback in the second example constitutes a threshold or "tipping point."

In the first example, a sudden gust of wind might cause the ball to land slightly to the left of our prediction, but it would not completely invalidate our prediction. However, in the second example, the tiniest of errors at the beginning of our calculations would totally invalidate our prediction. A tennis ball careening down an irregular, rocky dirt road is like a ball in a pinball machine. While there are no magical or mystical elements in either case, in both cases there are cascading chain reactions. If the tennis ball hits a rock or the pinball hits a pin ever so slightly to the right of center, one causal sequence will be initiated. But if it hits ever so slightly to the left of center, another entirely different sequence will emerge. In one case, it may send the tennis ball sharply to the left and then into a smooth culvert running all the way to the bottom of the road. But in another case, it may send the tennis ball sharply to the right and then over a cliff. And even if the ball only moves slightly to the right or left when it hits the first rock, each and every rock in the road constitutes a threshold or a "tipping point" just as capable of initiating a sequence of events with equally unpredictable results.

Contemporary scientists call these sorts of examples nonlinear systems. The name may be new, but the idea is ancient. If Tom and Harry are being chased by a bear and their only option is to leap twenty feet over a very deep chasm, and if Tom can jump precisely twenty feet, while Harry can jump precisely nineteen feet, eleven inches, this slight difference in jumping abilities will produce radically different results—Tom lives and Harry dies! When tennis balls are careening down mountain roads, the extremely large number of relevant factors (the precise location, size, and shape of every rock) coupled with numerous thresholds (nonlinear events) makes it humanly impossible to predict where the ball will come to rest. Yet, while it would be impossible to predict what happens in such cases, anyone with a good slow-motion camera could easily record, and then describe, every step in the cascading chain of events.

Of course, the unpredictability of a tennis ball bouncing down a rocky dirt road is of little significance. But the havoc caused to human plans by thresholds and tipping points is not always trivial. Here are two examples.

In the 1980 presidential election, Jimmy Carter was challenged by Ronald Reagan. During the campaign, Reagan and many others had repeatedly characterized Carter's foreign policy as being "weak" and criticized him for being too willing to sacrifice our national honor when faced with challenges from abroad. The Iranian revolutionaries' seizure of diplomatic hostages in Tehran became the prime example of Carter's inaction and (apparent) weakness. And for many, it seemed to confirm everything Reagan was saying about Democrats.

However, we now know that Carter had set in motion a rescue mission and was only biding his time. By April of 1980, American intelligence agents posing as European businessmen had infiltrated the ranks of the Revolutionary Guards holding the hostages, and they had detailed information about precisely where in the embassy the hostages were being held and other important information about their daily routines. There were even reports that some members of the Revolutionary Guards had been "flipped" (changed sides) and were ready and willing to assist the Americans in their escape.

On April 24, after all the groundwork had patiently been laid, Carter gave the order to begin the rescue. Though the carefully planned and practiced rescue would only require six helicopters to fly all the captives to safety, eight helicopters took off from an aircraft carrier just in case something went wrong. But even these precautions were insufficient. Shortly after take-off, one of the eight helicopters developed a rotor problem and was forced to turn back. Halfway through the flight, the helicopters were caught in a haboob, a rare meteorological phenomenon in which winds generated by a thunderstorm create clouds of dense dust many miles away without any warning. This caused the loss of one more helicopter. Still, the mission had the six helicopters needed for a successful rescue, and success here would have made the "wimp" charge look ridiculous; all the negative predictions about Carter's chances of reelection would be out the window. But success was not to be had. The mission was aborted when a hydraulic pump on one of the six remaining helicopters failed—the result of a crack in a ten-cent aluminum nut!

About two millennia earlier, Virgil's description of the founding of Rome rested upon perfectly understandable but equally unpredictable events. Though Virgil was more of a poet than a historian, his story rings true. It begins when Aeneas's son innocently goes hunting and the nostrils of his hounds catch the scent of a stag sacred to the Rutulians. When Aeneas's son lets an arrow fly, it reaches its target, but not in such a way as to kill the stag there and then, but in a way that would allow the fatally injured animal to "creep moaning into his stall . . . all stained with blood." The hardy country folk immediately take up arms to seek vengeance.

But why did the hounds happen to catch the scent of this particular stag and not one of the countless others that inhabited the forest? Why did the arrow fatally wound, but not immediately kill, the sacred stag? Why did the stag have just enough life left to make it back to his stall rather than die during the journey, thereby masking the identity of its assailant? We might agree on a description of how the battle for Rome began. But on the morning of Aeneas's son's hunting trip, no one could have predicted the prodigious consequences that would follow.

And how did it end? Weary of war, the two armies agreed to settle the dispute with one-on-one combat between two champions, Aeneas for the Romans and Turnus for the Rutulians. When both saw level ground, they ran swiftly toward one another, each throwing his spear, but neither managed to down his opponent. Then they clashed in close combat. They were evenly matched in skill and strength, but when their swords met, Turnus's sword shattered "like brittle ice, and now its fragments gleamed back at him from the yellow sand."[1]

But why did Turnus's sword shatter? Virgil says it was because Turnus mistakenly grabbed his charioteer's sword as he ran to meet Aeneas, not his

---

1. Virgil, *Aeneid* XII.735–65.

father's sword that he had used in all of his previous battles. Of course, the cascading chain of events didn't begin there. Why did he grab the wrong sword? Did his charioteer misplace the proper sword? When he reached for his father's sword, was Turnus distracted by the flight of a bird (i.., an evil omen)? Did the fast and rocky ride of the chariot knock Turnus's sword from its scabbard, forcing him to grab his charioteer's sword instead?

All of these questions define crucial tipping points (thresholds) that, as Virgil said, make it "hard to distinguish chance and prowess in the fight's confusion."[2] The Preacher in Ecclesiastes agrees: "Again I saw that under the sun the race is not to the swift, nor the battle to the strong, nor bread to the wise, nor riches to the intelligent, nor favor to the men of skill; but time and chance happen to them all" (Eccl 9:11).

A common sense understanding of each of these examples—a tennis ball bouncing down a rocky dirt road, the 1980 presidential election and the founding of Rome—would include at least three points. First, some events can be fully *described*, but never *explained*. Second, even though there is a *cause* for everything that happens, in these cases the final outcome was neither *determined* nor *predictable*.[3] Third, each of the outcomes *could have been otherwise*. However, many Enlightenment thinkers challenged all of these commonsense points. The next section will consider their arguments and what we will call "mechanistic philosophy."

LAPLACE'S DEMON

"Time and chance happen to them all," said the Preacher. But, then, the Preacher lived a long time ago, back in the days when people believed that the sun orbited a stationary earth in the center of a two-thousand-year-old universe. Today we know so much more. "Sure," objectors would say, "no one living a thousand years ago imagined that we would be able to predict the paths of comets, much less be able to instantaneously communicate with people halfway around the world or even with space ships passing by Saturn. So before adopting the three points of 'common sense,' think of all that we

---

2. Ibid.

3. "The theory of natural selection can describe and explain phenomena with considerable precision, but it cannot make reliable predictions, except through such trivial and meaningless circular statements as, for instance: 'The fitter individuals will on the average leave more offspring.' Scriven (1959) has emphasized quite correctly that one of the most important contributions to philosophy made by the evolutionary theory is that it has demonstrated the independence of explanation and prediction." Mayr, *Toward a New Philosophy of Biology*, 31–32.

have learned! We now know that the earth revolves around the sun, which is on the outer edge of a medium-sized galaxy, which is but one of billions of galaxies in a universe that is billions of years old, and in which *everything* is strictly determined by the laws of nature. So while it may still be difficult to precisely predict the outcome of many events, *in principle* these predictions are fully within the capabilities of modern science."

In 1814 Pierre-Simon Laplace, a mathematician and physicist, famously formulated this objection to the three points of common sense:

> We may regard the present state of the universe as the effect of its past and the cause of its future. An intellect which at a certain moment would know all forces that set nature in motion, and all positions of all items of which nature is composed, if this intellect were also vast enough to submit these data to analysis, it would embrace in *a single formula* the movements of the greatest bodies of the universe and those of the tiniest atom; for such an intellect nothing would be uncertain and the future just like the past would be present before its eyes [emphasis added].[4]

According to this view, all of reality is fully determined, and therefore the unpredictability that we commonly attribute to "time and chance" is *in fact* due wholly to our lack of knowledge. While the relevant causal factors determining the winners of elections and wars (or even the precise resting place of a tennis ball bouncing down a rock-strewn mountain) may be too complex for human calculation, in fact, everything is mechanistically determined. According to Laplace, what the Preacher called "chance" is not a permanent part of reality, but only the (temporary) result of our lack of scientific understanding. Since every action is caused, our inability to predict an event's outcome is wholly the result of human ignorance because nothing in reality takes place by chance. Or as philosophers like to say, "chance" names an epistemological category, not an ontological category. If we knew enough, we would understand that given the same initial conditions, nothing could have been otherwise.[5]

Not surprisingly, many people reject Laplace's deterministic vision since it seems to call into question much that we all hold dear, including human freedom. And Christians have their own objections. Without freedom, humans would not have the unique dignity of being created "in the image of God." And some have even worried about the implicit idolatry

---

4. Laplace, *A Philosophical Essay on Probabilities*, 4.

5. "The word 'chance,' then, expresses only our ignorance of the causes of the phenomena that we observe to occur and to succeed one another in no apparent order." Quoted in Gillispie, *Laplace*, 51.

The Collapse of Mechanistic Philosophy

of transferring the traditional attributes of God—omniscience and omnipotence—to Science (with a capital S). Nonetheless, many Enlightenment thinkers think that the arguments in favor of a mechanistic philosophy are more powerful than these objections.

Their first argument is based on history. Many events which were once attributed to supernatural causes or transcendent human freedom are now explicable in terms of perfectly ordinary and "natural" causes. The Greeks prayed to Neptune for safe passage across the Aegean in their triremes (warships); today we check for storms on images from satellites. In New Testament times the Jews attributed epileptic seizures to demons; today we explain them in terms of brain lesions. Fifty years ago school teachers scolded restless and disruptive children; today we treat them with Ritalin, which is far more effective. Though some people still pray for divine intervention to solve their problems, now scientists using fMRI (functional magnetic resonance imaging) can locate the specific area in the brain that "prays." And while it is not yet possible to explain why some people pray to Jesus and others to Allah, the "spiritual peace" they experience is explained by the dopamine in their brain.

And even the "free will" to choose one's own religion is now coming under scrutiny by brain scientists. Again, using fMRI, scientists are able to predict a person's decision up to seven seconds prior to the subject's consciousness of his or her own "choice."[6] Of course, the decisions being considered are rather trivial (e.g., hitting a flashing button with either the left or right hand), but these experimental studies are still in their infancy. So there is every reason to believe that in the future our so-called "significant" decisions will become explicable in terms of brain functions. And when that happens, scientists will be able to *explain* why some people pray to Jesus, while others pray to Allah, or at least, that's the updated version of Laplace's first argument.

The second argument in favor of mechanism is more philosophical and goes like this: Only uncaused events are in principle unpredictable. But to say that something is uncaused is to say that it came from nothing. Yet by definition "nothingness" doesn't exist. Nothing simply "poofs" into or out of existence. Despite our lack of any definitive medical research, we know that if someone gets cancer there must be a cause, even if scientists have yet to discover what the cause is.

Try to imagine a senator arguing before Congress, "We have spent billions of dollars looking for the cause of cancer. Yet in many cases we are no closer to discovering its cause than we were thirty years ago. Therefore,

---

6. See Callaway, "Brain Scanner Predicts Your Future Moves."

the only reasonable conclusion is to stop wasting money looking for causes where none exist." The senator's argument is a classic non sequitur. His premises may both be true. But his conclusion—"these cancers have no cause"—does not follow. Instead, what follows from the senator's premises is that "these cancers have causes that are *yet to be discovered.*"

Before responding to these arguments for mechanism, a brief digression concerning motives is in order. Francis Bacon famously said that knowledge is power. And he was at least in part correct: the kind of knowledge that allows us to explain and predict also gives us control and power. When and if we discover the biological laws that govern the growth of cancers, those cancers will no longer be under the control of Providence; instead, they will be under *human* control.

But we must not be too hard on the Enlightenment. There is nothing wrong with using our God-given talents to mitigate human pain. In many cases it is meek, right, and proper to seek power and control over nature. The Bible itself enjoins humans to tend, cultivate, and steward God's good creation. And as Thomas Aquinas (the great medieval philosopher and theologian to whom we will refer frequently throughout this book) said: "the dignity of causality is imparted even to creatures."[7] While God is the primary cause of all that exists and happens, humans are real secondary causes who are able to control much of their environment. We will say much more about this in later chapters, but for now we happily acknowledge that we live in a world where we should not only *pray* for those who are ill, but we should also *work* on their behalf building hospitals, educating and training doctors, and supporting research institutions in their search for the causes of cancer. And as we work to bring cancer and other effects of the fall under the control of modern science, we must not begrudge the Enlightenment thinkers rightful praise for their achievements.

Of course, some attempts to obtain mastery over God's creation are acts of rebellion and faithlessness. But this gives Christians no right to impute impure motives to Laplace. Perhaps in part he was seeking to "play the role of God." But, then, this is true of all of us at various points in our lives. And it would be contrary to a major theme of this book to pretend we were able to quantifiably measure, and then compare, Laplace's faulty motivation with our own more godly motivation. Humans will never be in a position to

---

7. *Summa Theologica* I.22.3. Barth approvingly quotes this same passage from Aquinas in *Church Dogmatics* II.2, 512. Again, God gives independence to creatures "not by a lack of power but by an immensity of goodness; he has wished to communicate to things a resemblance to him in that they would not only exist but be the cause of others." Aquinas, *Summa Contra Gentiles* III.70.7. See also the whole of ibid., III.69.

explain why most things happen, including why Laplace was motivated to defend universal determinism. The only prudent course is to pray that our *own* motives are those of good stewards, not those of faithless rebels.

THE DEMISE OF LAPLACE'S DEMON

In scientific quarters, things have changed since the time of Laplace; science with a small "s" has slain the demon of universal determinism. The mechanical clockwork of Newtonian physics has given way to quantum mechanics. Absolute space and time have given way to general relativity. And Newton's geometrically precise parabolic curves have given way to the chaos of double pendulums. One contemporary scientist puts it like this:

> To summarize, no man can go faster than the speed of light; no man can make simultaneous measurements of two conjugate variables with infinite precision; and no man can compute or measure any continuum variable precisely. In consequence, we can no longer disguise the fact that deterministic Newtonian dynamics has been dealt a lethal blow. Relativity eliminated the Newtonian illusion of absolute space and time; quantum theory eliminated the Newtonian dream of a controllable measurement process; and chaos eliminates the Laplacian fantasy of deterministic predictability.[8]

While it took both genius and persistence to undo the philosophical assumptions that were attached to Newtonian physics, at this point it is not difficult to understand why contemporary physics has returned to the commonsense distinction between describing and explaining, caused and determined/predictable, and acknowledging that many things could have been otherwise.

Quantum mechanics is full of surprises that we will not even begin to consider here. But its fundamental point is no more mysterious than the echolocation of bats or the sonar of submarines. Imagine that you are blind, but also that your hearing is very good. In fact, it is so good that like a bat you can "see" by listening for echoes. (While in college I knew a blind student who by snapping his fingers was able to find his way around campus without ever bumping into walls or closed doors.) Now as long as the physical force of the sound waves sent out are sufficiently small relative to the objects one is "observing," then there is theoretically no limit to what even a blind person can "see."

---

8. Ford, "What is chaos," 354.

But as the force of sound waves sent out approaches the mass of the objects one is attempting to observe, one's "vision" quickly deteriorates. To make our point less abstract, imagine a person who "saw" by throwing out thousands upon thousands of Ping-Pong balls, waiting for their rebound, and then calculated the shape and location of the objects from which the balls rebound. Certainly "vision" by Ping-Pong balls would be rather crude when compared to "vision" by echolocation," and even more crude when compared to "vision by photons (light). But if we imagine the balls becoming smaller and smaller and we also imagine a steady increase in the rapidity and precision with which the balls are dispensed, then there is no conceptual reason that Ping-Pong-ball vision couldn't rival the echolocation of bats.

However, there is one purely conceptual limit to all kinds of "vision"—whether by Ping-Pong ball, sound, or light. Determining whether a door is open or closed by throwing Ping-Pong balls is not difficult. But imagine trying to determine the location of another object of comparable size, that is, imagine a person using Ping-Pong-ball vision to locate another Ping-Pong ball. If a person could approach absolute precision in the direction and force with which the Ping-Pong balls were thrown, then at least theoretically we could locate another Ping-Pong–ball-sized object with one very big caveat—*our information would always be out-of-date*. The reason is obvious—one Ping-Pong ball bouncing off another Ping-Pong–ball-sized object will significantly alter the location of the object we are trying to "see." By the time our outgoing balls return, the location of our target ball will have changed.

At this point, a stubborn Laplacian may object: "But wait. Since we know the velocity with which the Ping-Pong balls are being thrown ,by timing how long they take to return we can calculate the distance of the rebound. And by measuring where the balls strike our detectors, we can determine whether the struck object will move in a straight line or at an angle. From these two pieces of data, like a good billiards player, it is a simple calculation to determine where the object we hit will be at any specified time in the future. Therefore, our observations need *not* be out-of-date after we make the proper corrections!"

Oh, how hard old assumptions die! The Laplacian argument begs the crucial question by assuming that the observer already knows the shape and mass of the object they are trying to "see." True, if we imagine a highly skilled billiards player shooting at billiard balls he is not in a position to see, by watching for rebounds of the visible cue ball he could calculate where the invisible ball was, both before and after it is struck. But this assumes that he already knows the mass and shape of the object that is causing the rebound. However, if the mass and shape of an invisible object a person is trying to locate by this "echo" method is *unknown* (and not orders of magnitude bigger than the cue ball), then the rebounding cue ball will tell him nothing about the present location of the unknown object.

In other words, if a billiards player *already knows* the shape and mass of the objects at which he is taking aim, then from the rebound it is possible to calculate the future location of the object hit. However, if the object struck is of an *unknown* shape and mass, then the rebound tells us nothing about the future location of the struck object.

Simply, but in no way disparagingly, put, one of the things quantum mechanics does is apply the commonsense truths concerning Ping-Pong-ball vision to ordinary vision by light. Humans cannot see in the dark. The only time we can see if a door is open or closed is when light is bouncing off the door and into our eyes. This much is obvious. But what we and Newtonian physicists usually forget, and what quantum scientists remember, is the second prerequisite for seeing to be accurate and up-to-date—namely, the object being observed must be orders of magnitude larger than the light with which we make our observations.

Though physicists tell us that in some experimental contexts light behaves like a material object (a photon) and in other experimental contexts it behaves as a wave, we will keep things simple by picturing photons as extremely small Ping-Pong balls. When we try to gather accurate and up-to-date information[9] about an electron "orbiting" the nucleus of an atom, our attempts will always be frustrated by the fact that the very source of our information (photons from the observer's light source bouncing off of electrons) significantly alters the location of what is being observed. Unless physicists discover something significantly smaller than photons, it will always be conceptually incoherent to claim that *everything* is predictable.

The behavior of photons, electrons, and other subatomic particles is unpredictable because we cannot make an observation without altering the data in unforeseen ways. And even if we suppose that scientific progress continues indefinitely into the future so that scientists discover (or make) something a fraction of the size of photons, one class of events will still remain unpredictable—namely, the behavior of these newly discovered and/or humanly constructed miniphotons.

---

9. Physicists tell us that by properly arranging an experiment it is possible to accurately locate the position of a photon, but in so doing we disturb its momentum. On the other hand, it is possible to rearrange the experiment so that we can accurately determine the momentum of a photon, but then we cannot locate its position. What cannot be done is to set up an experiment where we accurately determine *both* the location and momentum of a photon.

"Seeing" what we use to *see with* is as impossible as a swimmer catching her own waves. As Gilbert Ryle[10] pointed out over a half century ago, the problem with the claim that everything is *in principle* predictable is not merely empirical; it is also conceptual. We do not need to make careful observations of Olympic-class swimmers to figure out that they will never be able to swim so fast as to catch their own waves—the faster they swim, the faster their waves will proceed!

There is little controversy about what has thus far been said about quantum mechanics. But there is significant disagreement about how it should be interpreted. The majority opinion (called the Copenhagen interpretation) argues that events or behaviors are in principle unpredictable *because* they are uncaused.

The minority opinion (we will call it the Realist interpretation) argues that we must never conflate what can be humanly *known* with what *is* the case. Even though we will never be able to know what caused an electron to "jump" from one orbit to the next, we know that nothing comes from nothing. Just as common sense assumes that no one gets cancer without a cause (even though that cause is not and may never be known), so too electrons don't "jump" without a cause (even though, for reasons we'll consider momentarily, we will never know what that cause is).

We'll consider the Copenhagen interpretation first.

Though the Copenhagen interpretation was first formulated by Neils Bohr and other scientists, their arguments are really philosophical and are grounded in their answer to that old conundrum: If a tree falls in the forest and no one hears it, does it make a sound? Copenhagen scientists assume that the answer is No. Following Berkeley, a famous eighteenth-century philosopher and bishop, they assume that "to be is to be perceived."

Suppose a scientist says that he has discovered that on April 15, 2001, the entire universe doubled in size. Not only did we suddenly become twice as tall, but all the measuring instruments by which we measure people became twice as big. And lest anyone try to measure their increase in height by timing how long a beam of light takes to travel from their head to their foot, included in this scientist's discovery is the claim that the speed of light has become twice as fast. Should anyone take such a theory seriously? Since Einstein, the answer has been No.[11] A difference that by stipulation can

---

10. Ryle, *Concept of Mind*, 197.

11. Prior to Einstein, many scientists and some philosophers believed in what Newton called absolute space and time. We will consider Newton's ideas in more detail in chapters 4 and 5. But for now, it is not controversial to say that Einstein's theories have completely undercut the "scientific" support for an idea of absolute space and time in

never make a difference is not a *real* difference! Or, to put the issue in the affirmative—if it walks like a duck, flies like a duck, smells like a duck, etc., then it's a duck! So too Copenhagen scientists argue that if we agree (as all physicists do) that it is in principle impossible for us to ever *know* the cause of an electron's jump, then it is meaningless to claim that it *has* a cause. In short, to be unknowable is to be nonexistent.

Philosophical realists disagree. There is now good reason to believe that other galaxies contain stars with planets orbiting them just as the earth orbits our sun. There is also good reason to believe that some (if not all!) of these extraterrestrial planets will never be explored by humans. Does that mean that on the back side of these planets (which by supposition humans never observe) nothing exists—no rocks, water, or molecules? If we start with Bishop Berkeley's assumption—that to be is to be perceived—then that's precisely what we are forced to conclude.[12] Philosophical realists are unwilling to grant assumptions that do great violence to common sense. So too, physicists who are philosophical realists are unwilling to conclude that the jump of electrons from one orbit to the next *has* no cause just because we can never *observe* the cause. What *exists* and what can be *known*, they say, must never be conflated.[13]

Yet, it is reasonable to ask: Why cannot the cause of an individual electron's jump be known? Again, Copenhagen physicists answer: Because no cause exists. Realists, on the other hand, answer: Because the universe is so intertwined and interconnected that when we consider things as small as electrons, we would have to know precisely the state of *everything* in the physical universe before we would be able to predict when a particular electron would make its jump. Similar problems arise inside the nucleus of an atom. As Heisenberg argued, an alpha particle will never be emitted without a cause, but we can never predict when it will "jump" because

> the forces in the atomic nucleus that are responsible for the emission of the *a*-particle . . . contain the uncertainty which is brought about by the interaction between the nucleus and the rest of the world. If we wanted to know why the *a*-particle was emitted at that particular time we would have to know the microscopic structure of the whole world including ourselves, and that is impossible.[14]

---

comparison to which the rest of the universe could be said to have doubled.

12. Berkeley himself did not draw this conclusion because he argued that God "saw" everything.

13. The physicist/theologian Stanley Jaki is just one example.

14. Heisenberg, *Physics and Philosophy*, 89–90. See also F. S. C. Northrop's introduction to this book, where he distinguishes between determinism and causation—"every

Here's some indication of the magnitude of the problem. One mathematician calculated that even when considering things as relatively large as billiard balls, attempts to predict the outcome of a chain reaction nine collisions long would require us to factor in the gravitational pull of a man standing next to the table. And if we tried to predict the outcome of fifty-six billiard ball collisions, we would have to factor in the gravitational pull that an electron at the edge of the universe exerts.[15]

We've come full circle. Why is it, we asked at the beginning, that Jimmy Carter lost the 1980 election? The proximate cause of mission failure was a ten-cent nut in one of the hydraulic pumps: If it had not been for *that* particular flawed nut finding its way into *that* particular helicopter at *that* particular time, there is good reason to think that the general perception of weakness and indecisiveness in the Carter White House would have been radically altered.

But if we should then ask about the cause of the proximate cause, the answer is lost in the darkness of history. After a point, all we can conclude is that "time and chance" happen to us all. In other words, at some point we will be forced to tell a story that goes something like this: Five years ago when *this* nut was riding down the conveyer belt, a fly landed on the nut inspector's left shoulder, causing the inspector to momentarily turn his attention to the left at the precise moment the fateful nut was to be inspected. Had that particular fly landed on the nut inspector's right shoulder, his keen eye would have spotted the defective nut—which would have then become as historically insignificant as the hundreds of other defective nuts in the rejection bin. But it was not to be! The neurons in that fly's tiny brain caused it to go left rather than right, and the fateful nut continued to its destiny, down a path marked with countless additional thresholds and tipping points, any of which (from a purely human perspective) *might* have defeated destiny.

Of course, no human will ever know the actual history of this fateful nut. But such a story rings true to many, especially to Christians who believe that the hairs on their head are numbered.

THE CHAOS OF A DOUBLE PENDULUM

At the start of the nineteenth century, Laplace and scientists in general assumed that small mistakes in measurement at the beginning of an experiment would have small effects at the end of the experiment. But as we

---

deterministic system is a causal system, but not every causal system is deterministic." *Physics and Philosophy*, 11.

15. Taleb, *Black Swan*, 178.

already noted, consequences can be hugely disproportional to the size of an initial error. The fact that observations and measurements will never be precisely accurate means that in a world riddled with thresholds and tipping points, the old saying is true: close only counts in horseshoes and hand grenades!

But there is a second problem with the dream of Laplace, which is a uniquely modern discovery. It is called the three-body problem. The problem is nicely illustrated by a very simple machine whose actions are utterly unpredictable. It's called a double pendulum, and numerous simulations and real examples of such machines can be found on the Web with a simple Google search. Double pendulums are nothing more than one pendulum attached to the bottom of a second pendulum. Though the behavior of a single pendulum is quite predictable, a double pendulum is not, and the reason is purely mathematical.

Remember Laplace's boast—with sufficient data we would be able to calculate the future position of everything *in a single formula*. But we now know that there is no single formula for calculating the gravitational interactions of three bodies, let alone the 10^{80} interacting bodies that make up our universe.

Newton famously (or infamously, depending upon one's theological perspective) believed that the modern astronomy for which he was primarily responsible proved the existence of God. Newton's formulas flawlessly predicted the motion of a single planet around the sun. Furthermore, these predictions could be extended as far into the future as one cared to extend them because the elliptical orbit of a single planet is stable—that is, it indefinitely repeats itself after each orbit.[16] But astronomical observations at the time showed that the orbits of Jupiter and Saturn were not stable—that is, after each orbit they were moving closer to each other, and other things being equal, they would eventually collide. So why hasn't this happened? Newton argued that the only reason Jupiter and Saturn had not and would not collide was that God occasionally intervened to "fine tune" his clock.[17]

When Napoleon and Laplace met a little over a century later, Napoleon asked him about the place of God in his astronomical theories. Laplace

16. Mercury is an exception. The axis of its elliptical orbit rotates slightly. This is called the precession of Mercury's perihelion.

17. "Leibniz charged that Newtonian views were contributing to a decline of natural religion in England. The implication that God occasionally intervened in the universe, much as a watchmaker has to wind up and mend his work, derogated from his perfection. Clarke admitted that God had to intervene in the universe, but only because intervention was part of his plan. Indeed, the necessity of God's occasional reformation was, for Newtonians, proof of God's existence." Hetherington, *Planetary Motions*, 169. See also Koyre, *Closed World to Infinite Universe*, chapter 11.

famously replied: "Sir, I have no need of that hypothesis." And why was he able to eliminate God from Newtonian astronomy? Again, the problem for Newton was the gravitational interaction of the sun, Jupiter, and Saturn. While Newton discovered the formula for predicting the motion of either the sun and Jupiter *or* the sun and Saturn, he did not discovered a single formula for predicting the gravitationally entangled motion of the sun, Jupiter, *and* Saturn.

Now we might guess that Laplace, the father of the imaginary demon who was going to predict everything with a single formula, had made mathematical progress and discovered an elusive single formula for predicting the motion of three interacting bodies. But that is *not* what Laplace did. Instead, with prodigious patience, he used paper, pen, and Newton's own formula to show why the planets in our solar system don't eventually collide with one another. First, based on the known positions of the sun and Jupiter, he calculated their centers of gravity. Then he used this calculated center of gravity to determine the future position of Saturn. Based on this, he calculated the mutual center of gravity of Saturn and the sun. With this second calculated center of gravity, he then returned to calculate the future position of Jupiter. Reiterating this tedious process over and over and over, Laplace discovered that the orbits of Jupiter and Saturn were themselves on a cycle of 929 years of first moving toward each other and then away from each other.[18] Thus, Laplace mathematically demonstrated the stability of the solar system without the need for divine intervention.

Laplace's debunking of Newton's notion of a "fine-tuning" God deserves our praise. (We will say much more about the Enlightenment conception of God in chapter 4.) Additionally, had he reflected upon the laborious iterations involved in calculating his 929-year cycle, he might have realized that only *some* systems with three interacting gravitational bodies are stable. The orbit of a single planet around the sun is mathematically derivable; the orbit of two planets around the sun is *not* mathematically derivable, even though their orbits are wholly caused by gravitational forces. We can perfectly describe where they have been; but we cannot predict where they will be *with a single formula.*

Double pendulums exacerbate this mathematical limitation by introducing countless thresholds ("bifurcation points") where the second pendulum may or may not have sufficient energy to swing over the top. (If my verbal description is hard to follow, I suggest looking at one of the many videos of double pendulums on the Internet.) At each of these thresholds—like a tennis ball bouncing down a rocky road—the slightest miscalculation

---

18. Gribbin, *Deep Simplicity*, 13–16.

produces radically different results. So with sufficient energy the behavior of a double pendulum becomes chaotic and unpredictable, *but not because there are mystical or nonphysical forces involved.*

With a single planet orbiting the sun or a single pendulum, there is a single equation such that once the initial conditions are known, we can pick any time in the future, plug the data into the equation, and come out with the answer. However, when there are two planets in orbit or with a double pendulum, all we can do is to reiterate the equations. The further in the future our prediction, the more times we will have to iterate our calculations. So, as Joseph Ford said, "a chaotic orbit is its own briefest description and its own fastest computer: it is both determinate and random."[19]

A DEMON-SLAYING STAR

We have made two points thus far, either of which is lethal for Laplace's demon: 1) Quantum mechanics means that infinitely precise measurements are impossible, and the fact that our universe is riddled with thresholds means that little mistakes in the beginning will, at unpredictable points, have huge consequences in the end; and 2) there is no single formula for predicting the future location of three interacting bodies—so in these cases (like those involving double pendulums) all we can do is watch and wait.

We will now make a third point. Einstein's theory of relativity establishes that nothing can move faster than the speed of light. For example, if our sun exploded "right now,"[20] it would be about eight minutes before anyone on earth would know. Eight minutes doesn't sound like much, so let's think about a star a thousand light-years from earth—we will call it the "demon-slaying" star. To see why, let's transfer Laplace back in time to

---

19. Ford, "What is chaos," 354. See also Gribbin, *Deep Simplicity,* 49–50. Though here a confirmed Laplacian may object that "It is simply not true that the thing itself is its own fastest computer—after all, Laplace himself was able to calculate and predict, long in advance, when Jupiter and Saturn would repeat their cycles of expansion and contraction." True, but incalculable problems remain. Many paths taken by double pendulums are stable and regularly repeat themselves. So these, like the orbits of Jupiter and Saturn, *are* predictable. But other paths taken by double pendulums are not stable and do not regularly repeat themselves. It is in these cases that the thing itself is its own fastest computer. So strictly speaking, it is the point where chaotic systems like double pendulums become unpredictable that the thing itself is its own fastest computer. So again, while this transition point can always be *described* after the fact, it cannot be predicted or *explained.*

20. The scare quotes are necessary because "right now" only makes sense if we assume a Newtonian notion of absolute space and time, and this is precisely what Einstein will not allow.

ancient Rome and the Preacher of Ecclesiastes forward in time so that they can meet to discuss the "time and chance" thesis. Everything else we know about ancient Rome remains the same: in particular, it remains a time and place famous for both its legal, organizational, and military skills, *and* its superstitious fear of omens.

And to make clear the problem the finite speed of light creates for the determinist's thesis, we will ignore for the sake of the argument quantum mechanics and grant Laplace knowledge of the *precise* location and momentum of every electron in the observable universe. We will also ignore the three-body problem. Under these very generous conditions, what will Laplace be able to predict? More specifically, will he be able to predict on January 1 that three days later the Roman legions will still be at peace? The Preacher of course will say that he cannot since "time and chance happen to them all," and Laplace will disagree. So who's right—Laplace or the Preacher?

Twenty-first-century science (science with a small "s") gives the nod to the Preacher. Laplace's problem, even granting our incredibly generous assumptions, is that his database is incomplete. The observable universe does not and cannot include what happens outside Laplace's "light cone." Imagine that exactly 999 years 364 days before the fateful meeting we have described, our "demon-slaying" star (located exactly 1,000 light-years from earth) exploded in a supernova. On January 1, not even Laplace with his postulated superhuman knowledge could have known that on January 2, the light from the "demon-slaying" star would finally reach earth and be visible to *everyone*—including the Roman legions, who might well be spooked into war![21]

THE INCOHERENCE OF "SELF-PREDICTION"

Finally, there is a fourth source of unpredictability; it's the predictor.[22]

By definition a prediction involves three factors. First, every prediction by definition includes two events separated in time. It is not a prediction when a person describes what is happening *now*. Second, a prediction is public, that is, someone has to announce at t1 that some *specific event*[23]

---

21. For a more scholarly presentation, see Popper, *The Open Universe*, 57–61.
22. See MacIntyre, *After Virtue*, 95–97.
23. Closely connected to the conceptual problems involved in the idea of self-prediction is the idea of predicting future human inventions. To predict the invention of the wheel, someone would have had to *specify* what a wheel is. However, to specify what a wheel *is* is to ipso facto invent the wheel. Of course, one can, like Jules Verne, make

will happen at t2. Third, the predictor's prediction must be based on reason, evidence, and/or arguments. Simply making a lucky guess about the future does not count as a prediction.

Now we have already discussed the problem of getting up-to-date information about very small objects—any observation we make is going to affect the object so that we can only know where the object *was* and never where it *is*. But here, we will ignore that problem. We also discussed the problem caused by the finite speed of light. At t1 our prediction will, at best, be based on all that can be observed within the light cone at t1. So what is predicted to happen at t2 might always be falsified by events which, at the time of the prediction, were outside the light cone of the predictor. But once more, we will ignore this problem.

The final problem with mechanism concerns the predictor's *own* effect on the prediction. All human predictors are a part of the universe they are trying to explain, and as such, they necessarily interact with it. Without this interaction they could never obtain the evidence and data they need to make their prediction. Now in many cases, the interaction is nil. Bouncing photons off of planets to determine their mass and momentum has no significant effect on them. Thus, their orbits are as predictable as a good clock. That's why at least one of the planets—the earth—*was* the standard clock for millennia.

But the dream of mechanists is not that one day *some* parts of our universe will be predictable. That's not a dream; that's been true for ages. No, the dream is that one day *all* parts of our universe will become predictable—both those parts that presently exhibit clocklike behavior (such as the motion of the planets) and those parts that presently exhibit cloudlike behavior (such as the weather).[24] And it is a dream that is half fantasy and half nightmare. The fantasy is that one day those parts of the natural world to which we today can only submit—hurricanes, earthquakes, cancer cells, etc.—will have to submit to us! The nightmare is that "we" will turn into a "them"—that is, you and I will one day come under the complete control of a "them."

Mechanist philosophers will protest that their thesis is wholly philosophical, not political, so it cannot be refuted by the nightmarish scenarios of a "Big Brother." After all, why should we simply assume that humanity's

---

certain vague "predictions" about the invention of electric submarines or lunar modules. But then, I can, without any scientific training, "predict" the weather six months from today at my home in Northern California—it will be colder!

24. The contrast between clouds and clocks is an allusion to a famous essay by Karl Popper that first developed the argument which follows. Appropriately, his essay is entitled "Of Clouds and Clocks" and is now available online.

newfound power to control their own destiny will be put to nefarious use? Why not assume that in addition to controlling the forces of nature which bring us harm, we will also learn to control the "inner forces" that bring harm to both ourselves and others?

Fair enough. Our concern in this section is wholly philosophical, and the fact that power and control over "nature" is always a two-edged sword (since nature includes us!) is irrelevant. Even if the dream turns into a nightmare, we are here discussing the *truth* of mechanism, not evaluate the *desirability* of its consequence. Again, fair enough. So let us only consider the truthfulness of the claim that one day we might "learn to control our 'inner forces' that bring harm to both ourselves and others."

"Inner forces" can be understood in two distinct ways. First, they can be understood to refer to what Plato called the "leaden weights" of gluttony, sensual pleasures, and their more sophisticated refinements that drag people down so that they can only focus their attention on that which they can see or feel[25]—in short, what Christians call sin. But these are not the sorts of things that mechanists are referring to when they speak of "inner forces." For mechanists, the "inner forces" are processes in the brain that are themselves wholly determined by antecedent physical and chemical factors.

So let us test the thesis that one day these brain processes will themselves be predictable. And again, we are going to grant for the sake of the argument that (1) mechanists will one day be able to observe other people's brains with the same clarity and precision that physicists and chemists now observe our inanimate world *and* (2) they will be able to do so without significantly affecting what they are observing so as to make their data out-of-date. Even granting both of these scientifically dubious assumptions, there will always remain at least one set of brain processes that will remain *in principle* unpredictable, namely, the brain processes of the person making the prediction.

The problem, once again, is that no swimmer can catch his own waves. Suppose there is a neat and one-to-one correspondence between what a human thinks or says and particular states of that person's brain.[26] This means that when Fred, our super scientist, makes a prediction at t_1, his brain is in some corresponding state that we will label BS_1. And suppose further that his prediction is that at t_3 Sally will uninhibitedly start singing "The

---

25. Plato, *Republic* VII.519.

26. We are deliberately being quite colloquial here. While there appears to be an intuitively obvious *meaning* to the idea of "neat and one-to-one correspondences," it hides a critical ambiguity. We discuss this ambiguity between type/type and token/token correspondences in chapter 7 of *Life, the Universe, and Everything*. But here we will grant the mechanist all his assumptions and metaphors.

Star-Spangled Banner" at the top of her voice. The problem is that as soon as Fred announces his prediction, Fred also knows that at t3 Sally will make a fool of herself, *unless he acts to prevent Sally's embarrassment*. But whether he will or will not act to save Sally from embarrassment is something that Fred doesn't (and cannot) know at the time he makes his announcement. Perhaps hearing his own announcement will remind him of one of his own embarrassing moments in the past and what it did to his self-esteem. So at t2, in a moment of pity, Fred warns Sally about what she is about to do, and hence, his original prediction is now out-of-date.

The problem with his first prediction is that he didn't factor in his own BS_1, which included sympathetic thoughts toward Sally making a fool of herself. And the problem is insoluble. No one can observe the glasses they themselves are using to make observation. So too, the brain that Fred is himself using to make predictions cannot be observed while he is using it. The moment he announces his prediction concerning Sally's embarrassing behavior, his prediction is in danger of being falsified *by his own brain*.

Fred's self-reflection begins an escalating series of self-reflections that can never, so to speak, be "out-swum." If mechanism is true, Fred's moment of pity at t2 also has a cause, call it BS_2. After warning Sally at t2 and having to make a second prediction, Fred will also *know* that he has been forced to make a new prediction. This in turn might cause Fred to worry about his own embarrassment. So once again, Fred will be forced to announce yet a third prediction saying that his t2 prediction is out-of-date because he forgot to factor in his own BS_2. But if mechanism is true, Fred's third prediction at t2.5 also has a cause, call it BS_3. Obviously, there is no end to the regression.

If this seems hopelessly convoluted, it is! The self-reflection of which all humans are capable is like standing between two mirrors and looking at the reflection of your reflection of your reflection of your reflection—it never ends. Likewise, self-prediction will always fall prey to the famous example from Gilbert Ryle.

> A singing-master might criticize the accents or notes of a pupil by mimicking with exaggeration each word that the pupil sang; and if the pupil sang slowly enough, the master could parody each word sung by the pupil before the next came to be uttered. But then, in a mood of humility, the singing-master tries to criticize his own singing in the same way, and more than that to mimic with exaggeration each word that he utters, including those that he utters in self-parody. It is at once clear . . . that at any given moment he has uttered one noise which has yet to be mimicked . . . and it makes no difference how rapidly he chases

his notes with mimicries of them. He can, in principle, never catch more than the coat-tails of the object of his pursuit.[27]

The problem is that one's own behavior can never be *predicted*; it can only be *chosen*. The instant one tries to predict one's own behavior *on the basis of evidence*, an endless series of self-reflections begins. We become like the swimmer trying to catch his own wave or the singing-master parodying his own song. This means that not only is one's own behavior *in principle* unpredictable, but everything that happens inside of your own sphere of influence is also in principle unpredictable.

And somewhat ironically, as our power to control nature *increases*, the sphere of the predictable *decreases*. Right now it is quite possible for scientists to predict the future location of the planets years in advance because there is nothing humans can do to change their orbits. We can also predict the future location of many asteroids. But in the foreseeable future (or perhaps the time is already here) the orbits of small asteroids will come within the sphere of human influence. When that time arrives, the orbits of small asteroids will no longer be *predictable*; instead, they will be *chosen* and something that *could have been otherwise*.

Ancient wisdom and common sense both understood that our universe includes things whose behavior is as predictable as a finely made clock and things whose behavior is no more predictable than a tennis ball bouncing down a rocky dirt road. The growth of modern science in the seventeenth century[28] led people to begin questioning ancient wisdom and common sense. And toward the end of the nineteenth century, to many scientists it appeared that common sense had been vanquished. Contrary to our romantic sensibilities, it appeared that science had proven that the universe was one gigantic machine. However, as we have seen in this chapter, by the end of the twentieth century, science—more specifically, quantum

---

27. Ryle, *Concept of Mind*, 195–96.

28. We have deliberately focused on the physical sciences in this chapter since, if anywhere, it is there that Laplace's case is the strongest. But if we turn to the biological sciences, the case for universal predictability becomes even less plausible. Stephen Jay Gould, in his magnum opus, put it like this: "Finally, my general love of history in the broadest sense spilled over into my empirical work as I began to explore the role of history's great theoretical theme in my empirical work as well—contingency, or the tendency of complex systems with substantial stochastic components, and intricate nonlinear interactions among components, to be unpredictable in principle from full knowledge of antecedent conditions, but fully explainable after time's actual unfolding." *Structure of Evolutionary Theory*, 46.

mechanics, the three-body problem, and general relativity—had undercut the arguments for mechanistic philosophy.

Of course, what science gives, science can take away. It is minimally conceivable that one day quantum mechanics, the three-body problem, and general relativity will themselves be corrected and made deterministic just as these modern theories corrected and made indeterministic Newton's theory of gravity. Still, the incoherence of self-prediction remains. Valid predictions presuppose up-to-date data. But no one can observe their very act of observing. Thus, no humans will ever be able to predict either their own behavior or any other event they are capable of affecting.

—2—

What Logic Can Never Do

Rene Descartes thought that pure logic could produce infallible knowledge in all disciplines. But logic can only tell us what is not the case; it can never tell us what is the case. To reduce philosophy to logic is a second error with huge implications.

The Enlightenment was in part a reaction against the political, economic, and religious chaos of the sixteenth century. At the beginning of the seventeenth century, a French mathematician and philosopher, Rene Descartes, sought to create order out of chaos. Already famous for his mathematical unification of algebra and geometry (he invented "Cartesian coordinates"), Descartes believed that the only way to restore order to the world of ideas was to find an absolutely firm foundation—one that could not be doubted—upon which to build a philosophy. That foundation for Descartes was the same logic that grounded mathematics.

As we saw in the last chapter, mechanistic philosophy is not science ,and in this chapter we will see that logic is not philosophy. Good philosophy requires more; it requires the ability to understand analogies.

GOOD ANALOGIES

But before we can understand how analogies work, we must first consider the prior distinction between "vague" and "ambiguous."

Since speed varies continuously, there are no two points on the continuum of speed between which there is not a third point. In this regard, all continuums are like a series of fractions—1 ¼, 1 ½, 1 ¾, etc. Between any two fractions, we can specify a third. For example, 1 ⅜ lies between the first two in the previous series and between 1 ¼ and 1 ⅜ lies 1 ⁵⁄₁₆. This series includes an infinite number of fractions. Thus, the statement "Bill is running fast" is always going to be a little vague. On the other hand, "Bill left his keys in the room" is ambiguous. Are we talking about his car keys, the keys he uses to grade student's tests, the keys he replaced on his piano or even the keys that are the legends of maps? "Keys" is ambiguous because there is no significant and systematic connection or relation between any of these uses of the word "key."

However, while the words *vague* and *ambiguous* have distinct meanings, occasionally a term can be *both* vague and ambiguous. The word *right* is an example. In one context, "right" refers to a direction. "Turn right at the next stop sign." In another context, "right" refers to the appropriate, morally correct, or good thing to do. "You must always do the right thing, even if you don't want to." In other words, "vague" and "ambiguous" are related like "purple" and "heavy"—while they mean something different, it is possible for a word to be both vague and ambiguous in the same way that a ball can be both purple and heavy.

Medieval philosophers took this distinction one step further. They distinguished three kinds of words or terms. First, they spoke of equivocal terms. These were words which "spoke with many voices," that is, they were ambiguous though not necessarily vague. Univocal terms were the opposite. These were words which "spoke with one voice," or, in our language, they are not ambiguous, though they might be vague. But between equivocal and univocal terms they identified a third kind of term, namely, words that were analogical. The standard example was "health" and it came from Aristotle. We can say of a person, a color, or an activity that it is healthy. For example: 1) "Sam is healthy"; 2) "Samantha's color is healthy"; and 3) "Walking is healthy." While "healthy" means something different in each of these three sentences, they are nonetheless related. Skin color is a sign of a person's health and walking is a contributory cause of a person's health.[1]

---

1. The term *analogy* is itself vague and ambiguous, and the literature unpacking its philosophical implications is huge. An excellent place to begin is Torrance's *Persons in Communion*, chapter 3. See also White, *Analogy of Being*, for a collection of essays by contemporary followers of Aquinas and Barth. For a more historical treatment of the Enlightenment insistence that all terms be univocal, see Placher, *Domestication of Transcendence*, and the first chapter of Gregory, *Unintended Reformation*.

Philosophers like Descartes seeking infallible conclusions, however, cannot countenance the use of analogical terms for at least two reasons. First, they are vague. How "related" do two terms have to be to be analogical as opposed to merely equivocal? Everything is "related" to everything else in *some* sense, if only in the sense of being to its left or right. Or again, we previously said that "Turn right at the stop sign" and "Always do the right thing" were equivocal. Yet, even here there may be some connection between the "directional" and the "ethical" use of the term "right." For example, when sanitation is poor a culture might require that all ceremonial and religious functions be performed with the right hand, since only the left hand is traditionally used for wiping oneself. In this way the right hand becomes the "good" hand and the left becomes the "unclean" or "bad" hand, which makes the "directional" and "ethical" use of the word "right" at least minimally analogical. Since there is no clear line separating analogical and equivocal terms, Descartes concluded the criteria for their use must be wholly subjective. Therefore, analogical terms must never be used in philosophical arguments aspiring to the high standards set by logic and mathematics.[2]

But according to Thomas Aquinas, philosophy cannot be based on pure logic. While logic may demonstrate that both halves of a contradiction cannot be true, logic by itself is powerless to determine which half of a contradiction is true and which is false. While logic may tell us what is *not* the case, it can never tell us what *is* the case. So there must be something more to philosophy than logic. Reasoning by analogy is part of that "something more," even though Aquinas would happily grant that *analogy* is a vague term—sometimes analogies are quite strong, other times they are quite weak.[3] Since "strength" and "weakness" are terms that vary continuously

---

2. "A renewed commitment to an unequivocal language of science—[for] every science, including theology—was the mark of the fourteenth century as it was again that of the seventeenth." Funkenstein, *Theology and the Scientific Imagination*, 26. Furthermore, "After Descartes it has become necessary to distinguish Aristotelian '*syllogismus*' and '*demonstratio*' from a Cartesian, rationalist 'deduction.' Aristotle and St Thomas do not begin with self-evident principles and derive conclusions from there in a rationalist-deductive mode (even though *Posterior Analytics* is often interpreted this way); rather, they begin with a statement to be justified (it will become the 'conclusion' only in a formal restatement of the argument) and 'reduce' it back to its ultimate explanatory principles." Paul Durbin, quoted in Stump, "Aquinas on the Foundations of Knowledge," 154.

3. "This led us to discover one of the most remarkable and distinctive features of analogous concepts, especially the ones of broadest range: it is in fact impossible to define what we mean by an analogous concept, to grasp the similarity involved, except by actually running up and down the known *range* of cases to which it applies, by actually calling up the spectrum of *different* exemplifications, and then *catching the point*. . . .

on a continuum, there will always be a certain amount of vagueness in the distinction between good and bad analogies.[4]

Furthermore, he would happily grant that only good judgment (not pure logic) can determine which is which.[5] And though the precision of logic is a virtue in many cases, logical precision is not the only virtue of good arguments. Instead, we must take seriously Aristotle's dictum that it is a measure of a wise person to seek only as much precision as the object of study permits.[6] In mathematics, deductive logic, and computer programming, all terms must be absolutely precise and univocal; but in the repair of jet engines and the building of good houses absolute precision is impossible. Good airplane mechanics and good carpenters learn to tolerate a certain

---

It can be *seen*, and *shown forth* by our meaningful linguistic behavior, as Wittgenstein would say, but it cannot be said or expressed clearly by itself." Clarke, *Explorations in Metaphysics*, 126–28.

4. "Aquinas is perhaps best known for his theory of analogy. But if by 'theory' you mean a systematic, mathematical and logically interconnected set of propositions, then on closer inspection it turns out that he never had one." Burrell, *Aquinas: God and Action*, 55. Barth, on the other hand, is not known for his theory of analogy. Nonetheless, it permeates the *Church Dogmatics*. "But the object itself—God's truth in His revelation as the basis of the veracity of our knowledge of God—does not leave us any option but to resort to this concept [analogy]. . . . And, pressed again by the true revelation of God, we are pushed on to the word 'analogy.'" Barth, *Church Dogmatics* II.1, 225, 226. And again, "But at this point we must take up again and complete a statement that we have made already. We have stumbled again on the co-existence and co-inherence of veiling and unveiling in God's revelation. That God also veils Himself in His revelation certainly excludes the concept of parity [univocality] as a designation of the relationship between our word and God's being. And that God also unveils Himself in His revelation excludes the concept of disparity [equivocality]. We are therefore forced to avail ourselves of the concept of analogy by the fact that in God's revelation both His veiling and His unveiling are true." Ibid., II.1, 235–36. Finally, "It is true, of course, that although there is no identity of the divine and creaturely operation or *causare* [causing], there is a similarity, a correspondence, a comparableness, or analogy. In theology we can and should speak about similarity and therefore analogy when we find likeness and unlikeness between two quantities." Ibid., III.3, 102.

5. Aquinas "never tried to domesticate analogical notions by finding a univocal thread of meaning linking the various identifiable uses. What seems to most modern writers to be the only way to offer analogy respectability would have rendered it superfluous for Aquinas. . . . What makes analogical expressions at once respectable and invaluable to Aquinas is our use of judgment. For it is judgment—of the same sort that selects an apt metaphor—which identifies the paradigm sense, and can discern how the other uses are 'proportionally' related to that principal use. Moreover, the paradigm sense need never be fixed, so that discernment requires an active exercise of judgment. Nor can we expect to find an algorithm in recognizing 'proportional' relatednesses, since *proportio* merely translates *analogia* here, and mathematical proportions are but a special subclass." Burrell, *Knowing the Unknowable God*, 112.

6. *Nicomachean Ethics* 1.3.1094b22.

degree of imprecision. And even the amount of imprecision that is tolerable varies with the kind of work that is being done—good airplane mechanics work to tolerances of a thousandth of an inch; good carpenters do not.

But the vagueness of analogies is more than a necessary evil; it is a positive good. Consider, for example, an imaginary child named Fred. He is a child prodigy in mathematics who was born and raised in an environment devoid of animals. How could you define, explain, or describe for him what a dog is? Dogs, you might begin by saying, are living creatures like humans, but they look very different and cannot understand mathematics. They have eyes and noses like humans, but their noses are much larger. And though their eyes look like human eyes, when they are looking for something they don't use their eyes, but instead they use their noses. Of course, Fred would have many questions. Even so, a back-and-forth dialogue of describing how a dog both is and is not like a human could go on for days, months, and years without a mathematical prodigy like Fred understanding what a dog is as well as an ordinary five-year-old born and raised in an environment with dogs, cats, and all sorts of other of animals.

While Thomists never argue that analogical descriptions are as good as firsthand experience, when we are forced to think about things of which we have no firsthand experience, analogical reasoning is our only alternative, and in some cases, it is quite a good alternative. Compare Fred with an ordinary five-year-old. Fred's mathematical abilities may even hinder him (rather than help him) in understanding back-and-forth descriptions of how a dog *both* is and is not like a human being. In mathematics X is either equal to or not equal to Y. "Like" is not a word that mathematicians employ in their work. The sort of back-and-forth explanations that an ordinary five-year-old is quite familiar with would be foreign to Fred. Not only is Fred (by supposition) unfamiliar with dogs, but he is also (by his talents and dispositions) unfamiliar with the only language we can use to describe what a dog is. The mathematical language of equations—x *equals* y—would be totally useless. What's needed to understand a world with dogs and humans is the language of analogy—x is *like* y.

Normal five-year-olds don't understand differential equations, but they do understand the word "like," and hence adults can explain to them all sorts of things that they have never before seen. "What's a camel?" asks Sally. Her father responds, "A camel is *like* a horse, but it has a big hump on its back." But it is precisely this word "like"—very simple to five-year-olds, but very puzzling to philosophers too enamored of logic—that causes Fred such grief. Without a willingness to engage in a back-and-forth dialogue there are huge regions of reality that remain totally opaque to mathematical geniuses.

Here's another analogy for understanding how analogies work. Suppose we lived in a three-dimensional, temporal universe in which there was no gravity. While it would take the skills of a good science fiction writer to flesh out what life would be like in such a universe, a good place to start would be to imagine life in a gigantic "space shuttle," wherein astronauts float about weightlessly while performing their work. By definition, such a three-dimensional universe would be picturable, and hence, much would be univocally describable.

Of course, in a universe in which everyone is born, raised, and dies without gravity, the term "weightless" would be as mystifying as the term "wet" to a community of rational fish. Yet, as long as Cartesian prejudices against analogical reasoning were overcome, it would not be impossible for inhabitants of this gravity-free universe to speculate about an invisible force attracting everything to everything else. Even in a gravity-free universe, people would know what it feels like to be pushed to the back of their seat as they are accelerating in a rocket ship.

Finally, suppose a group of weightless philosophers asked the question: Could someone be "fully human" and yet not be "weightless"? Such a question may well land these philosophers in a Kantian antinomy where equally good arguments could be given for both affirmative and negative answers. Yet that doesn't mean that a group of weightless theologians would be forced to give the same answer. The difference is that theologians are like SETI scientists listening for evidence of extraterrestrial life.

So imagine that our weightless SETI theologians one day receive extraterrestrial communications that are humanly intelligible. Included in these communications are images of creatures that look remarkably like them. Yet, in the verbal descriptions there are references to a universal force called "gravity" that allows these extraterrestrials to sleep in beds without being strapped down and to walk on floors without Velcro on their shoes. Now this is not an analogical argument for the existence of divine revelation; but it is the beginnings of an analogical argument for the proposition that *if* there is divine revelation, then it *must* be understood analogically.[7]

---

7. To think scientifically, says T. F. Torrance, "It is better not to operate with images and symbols, or similar terms, but rather to operate with the concept of analogy—but analogy must be understood in a rather different way from its traditional use, which had its roots in a Pythagorean doctrine of proportions. In scientific operations, analogical relations are not relations in which we compare things with one another on one and the same level, but are relations in which the pattern of thought or image on one level is semantically significant which it refers beyond itself to a correlate on a higher level, which may very well not be picturable at all, but may instead be inherently unobservable, as in quantum or relativity theory." *Ground and Grammar*, 116.

CLEAR AND DISTINCT IDEAS

Descartes's quest for infallible certainty, however, will always have a strong appeal. Consider how frequently we dismiss someone else's arguments by saying something like: Are you *sure* you're right? You've been mistaken plenty of times in the past. So why should we believe you this time? Since you are not one-hundred percent certain that you are correct, you cannot really claim to *know* that your conclusion is true.

True knowledge, Descartes argued, is knowledge that can *never* deceive because it is the kind of knowledge that is based on an absolutely firm foundation. Such knowledge must be grounded in "clear and distinct ideas." Ideas are "clear," according to Descartes, only when they cannot be doubted. He explained what he meant by asking us to imagine an evil genius with supernatural powers and a single goal—to deceive humans. Such an evil genius could easily deceive me about what I am now doing. While I *believe* that I am currently sitting at my laptop computer working on a manuscript, I might in fact be in bed and only *dreaming* that I am writing about an evil genius.

Okay, then what about the waking belief that I am a human being with two legs and two arms? Could an evil genius deceive me about this? Sure he could: just imagine the nefarious computer program in *The Matrix*. By manipulating the electrical impulses coming to our brains an evil genus could create *any* sort of false beliefs he so chose—including belief that we each have two legs and two arms, when in fact we are nothing more than brains in vats. "But not so fast," said Descartes. Not even a supercomputer controlled by an überprogrammer could deceive me about my own existence as a thinking being since to deceive *me* I must exist as a thinking being who can be deceived. Pure logic assures us of this, Descartes argued, because it is self-contradictory to think that an evil genius can deceive someone who doesn't exist.

And if, argued Descartes, we don't beg the question in favor of a purely materialistic conception of reality, then even a brain is unnecessary. Perhaps "I" don't even exist as a brain in a vat; perhaps I am a pure spirit. Nonetheless, no evil genius can deceive me about my existence as a being that has *ideas*. The reason is logically indubitable: if I didn't exist as a being with ideas, there would be no one to be deceived. By starting with *ideas* we rid ourselves of all doubts.

So my "idea" of myself as a thinking being is *clear*; it cannot be doubted. What makes it *distinct*? According to Descartes, the first characteristic of ideas is that they are absolutely distinct from all that is *material*. My idea of "the first prime number after five" (i.e., seven) is totally independent of any physical representation of the number seven. And second, an idea is distinct only if its boundaries are sharp and there can be no confusion between it and anything else. In other words, my idea of myself as a thinking being is distinct only in so far as my idea is *not* analogical. All analogical terms are vague, and hence by definition they are not distinct.

Descartes's insistence that philosophers *only* use univocal terms led inexorably to a mind/body dualism. Ideas have no length, breadth, height, or weight. Yet by definition material substances have length, breadth, height, and weight. So from the very beginning we know that the ideas in our *minds* are absolutely distinct from anything going on in our *brains*. This "clear and distinct" division of all of reality into two (and only two) kinds of substances—the immaterial and the material—constituted a radical break from the much more commonsense philosophy of Thomas Aquinas.

THE GREAT CHAIN OF BEING

Aquinas thought that it was a mistake to start one's philosophy with *ideas*. True, God is a spirit and hence not material. But the rocks and stars, plants and animals, apes and humans that he created are *not* ideas. Rocks, stars, plants, animals, apes, and humans are all material objects with height, breadth, width, and weight that we come to know through observation, not logic. (Philosophers classify Descartes as an idealist because he begins with *ideas* and they classify Aquinas as a realist because he begins with observable *things*.) Furthermore, rather than dividing reality into only two categories—the material and the immaterial—Aquinas thought that at least six different categories[8] were required to actually describe reality:

1. The living God who is the uncreated pure spirit (intellect and will) and the creator of everything else;

2. Angels who are created, living, immaterial beings (intellect and will) that serve as God's messengers;

3. Humans who are created, living, material beings with intellect and will made in the image of God;[9]

---

8. According to Mortimer Adler, it is unclear whether or not Aquinas thought there were only a "small handful" of distinct and different categories of naturally existing species or whether each biological species should count as distinct and different (see *Problems for Thomists*). Either way, were Aquinas living today, given the overwhelming evidence demonstrating that biological species are not "fixed and immutable," we are confident that Aquinas would opt for something like the "small handful" of species that we will discuss.

9. "The human being is a kind of boundary line of spiritual and corporeal creatures,

4. Animals who are created, living, material beings with consciousness, but without intellect and will;

5. Plants which are created, living, material beings devoid of consciousness, will, and intellect; and

6. Rocks, stars, planets, etc. that are created material beings devoid of life, consciousness, will, and intellect.

And though Aquinas spoke of "different *kinds* of things," he was not philosophically committed to these being absolutely distinct. Rather, he thought of a "Great Chain of Being"[10] in which the hierarchy of created beings was arranged in such a way that the lower always "touched" the higher so that there was never a great gap between one and the other. Aquinas cheerfully followed Aristotle and acknowledged that "nature precedes little by little from things lifeless to animal life in such a way that it is impossible to determine the exact line of demarcation."[11] Seeking only to *describe* God's good creation, Thomists have no need of the kind of precision required in mathematics and logic.[12]

---

existing in a horizon of eternity and time, reaching from the lowest realm and approaching the highest." Aquinas, *Summa Contra Gentiles,* 2.81.12. And again, "The human intellect holds a middle course between the angelic and the animal." Aquinas, *Summa Theologica* I.85.1.

10. Lovejoy's *The Great Chain of Being* traces this idea from its beginning in Plato down to the nineteenth century. It is a good place to start an investigation on this notion, but like any work of such a grand scope, Lovejoy's is not always to be trusted on individual philosophers. Robert Pasnau is only slightly excessive when he says "Lovejoy's reading of Aquinas is absolutely appalling" (*Thomas Aquinas on Human Nature,* 463). Lovejoy formulates the principle of plentitude like this: everything that can be made, will be made. He grants this strict doctrine is only implicit in Plato's *Timaeus.* He also notes that Aristotle explicitly denies it. "It is not necessary that everything that is possible should exist in actuality; . . . it is possible for that which has potency not to realize it" (Lovejoy, *Great Chain of Being,* 54–55). But what he fails to say is that Aquinas too explicitly rejects the principle of plentitude: "God can make something else better than each thing made by Him" (*Summa Theologica* I.25.6). Lovejoy thereby has created a false dichotomy: either God is logically forced to create all possible species and thus create the *best* of all possible worlds or God is left envious because he did not create all the good things possible. The only example he can cite of this alleged contradiction is Abelard (*Great Chain of Being,* 71). We will return to this issue in chapter 12.

11. Aristotle, *History of Animals* VIII.1.588b, 4–22. See also Aristotle, *Parts of Animals* IV.5.681a.

12. "Often it is rather difficult even to distinguish external from internal factors [in biological thought]. The Great Chain of Being (*scala naturae*) was a philosophical concept which clearly had an impact on concept formation in the case of Lamarck and other early evolutionists. Yet, Aristotle had developed this concept on the basis of empirical observations of organisms." Mayr, *Growth of Biological Thought,* 4.

But as we've already said, Descartes insisted on logical certainty. He begins his famous *Meditations on First Philosophy* with the firm resolution "that I should withhold my assent no less carefully from opinions that are not completely certain and indubitable than I would from opinions that are patently false."[13] But while we might all prefer certainty to doubt, Thomists insist that humans are not angels, and hence, we were not created with their intuitive and indubitable knowledge. That is not our place in the order of creation.

Even though Descartes was a good Catholic, dedicating his work to the Pope, the affect of his "firm resolution" was to belittle both common sense and God's good creation. No one who has lived around dogs, cats, or horses can doubt that they are conscious—that they have feelings, affections, wants, and desires. But remember Descartes's first premise: mind is absolutely distinct from matter. Given this initial assumption, we are left with only two options when it comes to animals: first, Fido is a purely material being, without wants, desires, and feelings, essentially indistinguishable from a machine; or second, Fido is a conscious being who has precisely the *same* kind of wants, desires, and even ideas as humans. But because Descartes was a Christian and believed that only humans were created in the "image of God," he was logically committed to the first option. So Descartes claimed that Fido, who yelps and bleeds after cutting his paw on a piece of glass just *like* we do, in fact feels no more pain than a watch that has cracked its crystal.

Aquinas would have nothing to do with such a radical break from common experience. Unlike Descartes, he worked in the tradition of the Great Chain of Being. His categories closely followed common sense and thus he assumed that there are at least three distinct kinds of animating principles (what translators frequently call "souls")—"vegetable souls" that unconsciously seek to reproduce; "animal souls" that reproduce and consciously seek other things like food and drink; and "human souls" that reproduce, consciously seek food and drink, and are able to *conceive* of things that they have never seen, heard, tasted, touched, or smelled.[14] Examples of humans' conceptual abilities range from being able to think about "tomorrow" to

---

13. See also his *Rules for the Direction of the Mind*, where he says in #2, "Thus, in accordance with the above maxim, we reject all such merely probable knowledge and make it a rule to trust only what is completely known and incapable of being doubted."

14. "The will is the power to have wants which only the intellect can frame. It does not take any intellectual ability to desire a plate of meat in front of one; but only an intellectual being can want to worship God or square the circle. If we leave aside the question whether there are non-human intelligences, we can say roughly that the human will is the power to have those wants which only a language-user can have." Kenny, *Aquinas on Mind*, 59.

being able to worship "the immaterial creator of the physical universe." (I will say much more about these uniquely human abilities in subsequent chapters.) As we have already noted, though the "divide" between plants and animals might not be perfectly distinct; nonetheless Aquinas understood that "hard cases make poor laws" and would not sacrifice the distinctions of common sense for the precision of the logician.

And, at least from Descartes's point of view, Aquinas's classifications are even messier. According to Aquinas, the "souls" of humans, animals, and plants are not to be conceived of as distinct substances. Instead, the various kinds of "souls" are to be thought of as different kinds of abilities or principles that are inseparable from the bodies that they animate. That means that plants, animals, and humans are all composed of *both* material and immaterial principles. While there is an absolute distinction between the Creator and the created, in all other cases, we must remember that the lower will always "touch" the higher as a tangent touches a circle. Animals can do things that plants cannot do; but when comparing the highest of plants with the lowest of animals, the difference is minimal. Think of a venus flytrap that *moves* to catch its prey and coral reefs that, though classified by biologists as a collection of tiny animals, never *move*.

WORDS ARE BOTH "MATERIAL" AND "IMMATERIAL"

So, while Descartes's division of the universe into two absolutely distinct substances, material and immaterial, makes for neat and clean *logic*, it demands we sacrifice common sense. Aquinas, on the other hand, was content to *describe* what he saw, namely, three relatively distinct animating principles—vegetable "soul," animal "soul," and human "soul." And here the scare quotes around "soul" are crucial. To many moderns, and to most Christians, "soul" carries strong religious connotations and is frequently thought of as that which separates from the body at death but lives on in heaven. But Aquinas never thought like this; in none of these cases is "soul" conceived as a distinct and separable immaterial substance. If forced to talk in modern terms, Aquinas would insist that plants, animals, and humans—in ways which are both alike and not alike!—are composed of *both* material *and* immaterial causes or principles.

(Now this raises an obvious question: How could Aquinas be a Christian if he didn't believe in the immortality of the soul? The full answer will have to wait, but the short answer is this: while Aquinas believed that the "soul" had a shadowy sort of existence after death and independent of the body, his understanding was that we are not fully human until our "soul" is reunited with the body at the resurrection.)

But let us return to the contrasting philosophies of Descartes and Aquinas. It is common to compare, with various degrees of disparagement, Aquinas's medieval and enchanted worldview with our own modern and disenchanted worldview. Now it was Descartes who was largely responsible for "disenchanting" (i.e., removing "spirits") from everything in the world except humans. His insistence that all our ideas be "clear and distinct" turned the observable world of rocks and dirt, pansies and pine trees, and dogs and cats into a world essentially indistinguishable from the world of machines designed and built by humans. Only humans and God were "enchanted," i.e., animated by something more than the material principles of cause and effect. Everything else ran like a finely crafted watch. Again, while our *emotions* may say that Fido's wagging and prancing means he's happy, Descartes argued that *reason* (pure logic) knows that Fido's actions are no more indicative of happiness than a cuckoo clock's "crowing" at the top of the hour is indicative of its happiness. Both are disenchanted machines, devoid of "spirit." (Here we see that it was not only Newton's laws of universal gravity but also, somewhat ironically, Descartes's idealism, which led to the mechanistic philosophy of the Enlightenment.)

But the logic of disenchantment doesn't stop there. Remember, our goal in this chapter is to draw out the implications of Descartes's assumption that philosophy and theology must be conducted with mathematical precision, and hence only employ "clear and distinct" ideas in their reasoning. So let us again focus on the word *distinct*.

Descartes argued that since mind and matter are *distinct*, there can be *absolutely no overlap* between mind and matter. But if this is the case, then in which category should we put the word *tool*? In one sense, the word *tool* is extended and physical. It has a specifiable size, shape, chemical composition, and even weight. (We can imagine a forensic scientist in a training exercise being required to remove from a blackboard the chalking "tool" and weigh it in grams.) But clearly there is nothing about a word's size, shape, chemical composition, or weight that *makes* it a word. What makes a word a word is not material in Descartes's sense. A word is a word only because a community of human language users *intended* something physical to be a word, whether it is chalk, ink, or even smoke in the sky.[15]

15. "Aquinas took Aristotle's distinction between actions entailing change and those which do not to demarcate a set of actions called intentional, and to characterize a domain called spiritual. This region is set off from that of material substances by the simple fact that a spiritual power does not need to be changed to be activated. And since matter names the substratum present in every alteration, properly so-called, the

In a pre-Cartesian world, or even in today's commonsense world, there is no difficulty in understanding *what* makes something a word. And we certainly do not think that what turns ink or chalk into a word is some sort of immaterial substance that mysteriously resides in between the ink or chalk molecules. No, the "material" aspect and "immaterial" aspects of words exist in an inseparable, but distinguishable, unity. In this respect, words are like smiles. We can distinguish a smile from a face, but we would never dream of separating them into distinct substances. So if by "enchanted," we mean a world in which there is *more* than that which can be placed in piles of stuff to be measured and weighed, then any world that contains *words* is enchanted.[16]

CORRELATION IS NOT CAUSATION

But once we move away from Descartes's logical world of "clear and distinct" ideas, "enchantment" is everywhere. Consider sodium, one of the naturally occurring elements. Scientists are able to measure the weight of a single sodium atom. They can also describe the number and position of electrons in their orbits. But until we know that sodium reacts violently when it comes into contact with water, we really do not know *what* sodium is. Medieval philosophers called the "whatness" of sodium its quiddity; Aristotle called it the "form" of sodium. Either way, the quiddity or form of a thing is that which specifies its "final cause," or what it is *meant* to be or do. Contrast this with Descartes's solemn pledge: "The entire class of causes which people customarily derive from a thing's 'end' [i.e., final cause], I judge to be utterly useless in physics [i.e., the scientific study of material objects]."[17]

And with regard to final causes, Descartes's pledge has become widely accepted. Real scientists, it is commonly assumed, only deal with that which can be objectively measured and weighed. Vague notions of quiddities, forms, and final causes are thought to be nothing more than the speculations of outdated philosophers. Yet, chemists today have no problem speaking of chemical *agents*, some of which react *violently* when they are exposed to water! And while many try to obviate the irony by putting quotes around

---

domain of activities which do not involve change is fittingly called immaterial or spiritual." Burrell, *Aquinas: God and Action*, 147.

16. And here we also see the beginnings of Galileo's bad idea that only that which can be precisely measured is of scientific interest. We will say much more about this in chapter 4, in the section entitled, "Quantitative vs. Qualitative Arguments." The argument in these last two sections is fleshed out in more detail in my *In Defense of the Soul*.

17. Descartes, *Meditations*, #4.

"agents" and "violently," it's worth asking: Is this more than a fig leaf to cover philosophical naiveté?

Descartes's descendants are right about one thing: quiddity, form, and final causation are not the sorts of things that can be counted or measured. Yet why should we assume that *everything* real must first be observed with the tools of science, then physically isolated, and finally counted and weighed?[18] The "whatness" of a word is simply its meaning, but *meaning* is not something that can be physically isolated and then observed under a microscope. Besides, what today's scientists call "information" is simply a different name for what Aristotelians called "form." Notice that even our word in*form*ation contains Aristotle's idea of "form." Of course, information is not *in* a word the way water is *in* a bottle. Again, no scientists will ever physically isolate the information in a word. But then, no Aristotelian ever supposed they would.

And even if we ignore the fact that the very *words* scientists and philosophers use to refute a pre-Cartesian understanding of the world presuppose the very thing they seek to eliminate (in*form*ation), Descartes's attempt to disenchant the world is still in conflict with itself. Many modern philosophers have tried to explain the origin of a word's information wholly in terms of human conventions. And while Thomists believe that all of these attempts have been unsuccessful,[19] the reduction of a word's meaning to a set of human conventions doesn't solve the scientific problem of explaining the origin of the information in DNA molecules. It certainly isn't the product of *human* conventions. After all, the DNA in dinosaurs existed long before humans intended or agreed on anything. And even before animals with DNA existed, sodium atoms existed, and they too contain a kind of information.

The information in a sodium atom consists of its natural properties, which allow scientists to both explain and predict its behavior—for example, the fact that it explodes ("reacts violently") *whenever* it comes into contact with water. Now it is tempting, but mistaken, to think that "natural properties" are directly observable. Some people assume that we can observe the properties of sodium simply by repeatedly placing sodium in water and watching it explode. Since such experiments have been conducted countless times, and since, without fail, the sodium has exploded, some scientists and philosophers have assumed that they are thereby *observing* the natural properties of sodium.

---

18. "For to proceed from causes to effects or the reverse is not an activity of the senses but only of the intellect." Aquinas, *Commentary on Aristotle's Metaphysics* VI.10. 1146.

19. See my *In Defense of the Soul*, chapter 9.

But as any statistician will correctly point out that correlation does not equal causation. Just because B always follows A, that doesn't mean that A causes B or that B is a "natural property" of A. Consider Sam, a Native American born in Alaska and raised speaking Inuit, and Sally, a Harvard statistician compiling examples of *mere* correlations to use in her classes. One of Sally's examples goes like this: for the last hundred years, well over ten thousand students have walked through the doors of Emerson Hall at Harvard University and not one of them could pass a simple test conjugating Inuit verbs. She then asks her students, "If Sam wins a scholarship to Harvard and takes a statistics class from me in Emerson Hall, do you suppose that he will be able to pass a simple test conjugating Inuit verbs? Why or why not?" The correct answer is obvious. Just because none of the thousands of previous students have been unable to conjugate Inuit verbs in Emerson Hall, there is no reason to believe that when Sam walks through the doors of Emerson he will suddenly be unable to speak and understand his native language. And we know this is true *because correlation does not equal causation*.[20]

But let us now ask the further question: What *makes* this the correct answer? Is it something that we have *observed* or is it something that we know in some other way? As David Hume, another Enlightenment philosopher, pointed out three centuries ago, causation itself is never directly observable, nor is a "natural property." We all know that alcohol and many drugs impair linguistic abilities, but doors do not. And here's the crucial point: the students in Sally's class knew this "fact" about the doors of Emerson Hall *prior to* and *independently of* their teacher's announcement that a perfect correlation existed between the doors of Emerson Hall and an inability to conjugate Inuit verbs. So, at least in this case, observed correlations *cannot* be the source or ground of our understanding of "natural properties."

But if observation is not the source or ground of our understanding of "natural properties," what is? A good answer to this question would require a book of its own, though we will say more in the next chapter. For now, suffice it to say that in addition to observed correlations, some plausible story or theory is required to produce an explanation. Brain scientists today can give a fairly detailed and plausible story about how alcohol and many drugs

---

20. It is sometimes said that while "correlation does not *imply* causation," causation does imply correlation, i.e., before we can establish a cause we must first *observe* a correlation. But this is a mistake. Consider the meteorite that struck the earth sixty-five million years ago near the Yucatan Peninsula and *caused* the death of the dinosaurs. There is no *correlation* between this event and the death of the dinosaurs because this only happened *once*. In other words, it is not true that every correlation implies causation *and* it is also not true that every cause implies some kind of correlation. We will say more about this in chapter 5 when we discuss the "scandal of particularity."

affect those portions of the brain that are required for linguistic understanding. Without this plausible story or theory we may be able to *observe* what's happening, but we cannot *explain* what we are observing. And note: it is the story or theory that justifies the language of "natural properties" and "laws of nature," *and not vice versa*.

Today it is biologists who tend to be the touchiest about the language of final causes. A biologist colleague of mine would frequently remind students that when thinking "scientifically," they should never say things like "the turtle came ashore *to* lay her eggs." Instead, they must always say "the turtle came ashore *and* laid her eggs." My daughter's graduate advisor told her the same sort of thing. The word "to," these biologists seem to think, was "unscientific" because purposes, goals or ends are essentially unobservable, and hence unmeasurable. The only thing that can be observed and measured is that the turtle came ashore *and* laid her eggs.

Okay, we cannot directly measure *why* female turtles come ashore the way we can precisely measure *when* they come ashore to lay their eggs. But, again, to observe that in over three thousand instances B (laying eggs) follows A (a female turtle comes ashore) is a mere correlation that tells us nothing of scientific interest. There are many other things that always follow a female turtle's coming ashore besides egg laying, e.g., kicking some sand and crawling over driftwood. Obviously the sand kicking and driftwood crawling behaviors of turtles are of no interest to biologists. Why? Because biologists study life, and the "whatness," "form," and "end" of life is to reproduce. Without implicitly assuming that the essential nature of a turtle is different in kind from the essential natures of nonliving things—dirt, rocks, driftwood, etc.—biological science is impossible.[21]

21. No biologist has been more insistent on the distinction between biology and the physical sciences than Ernst Mayr, founder of the neo-Darwinian synthesis and arguably one of the most important biologists in the last one hundred years. Here are a few quotes from *What Makes Biology Unique?*:

"Furthermore, all biological processes differ in one respect fundamentally from all processes in the inanimate world; they are subject to *dual causation*. In contrast to purely physical processes, these biological ones are controlled not only by natural laws but also by *genetic programs*. This duality fully provides a clear demarcation between inanimate and living processes" (30).

"Reductionist philosophers usually have tried to support their case in favor of reduction by attempting to reduce Mendelian genetics to molecular genetics.... It is not only the untranslatability of biological terms and concepts that makes theory reduction impossible but also the fact that very few biological generalizations can be connected with any of the laws of physics or chemistry" (79).

"It was Darwin who contributed the concept of biopopulation, one of the fundamental differences between the living and the inanimate world. Another one, equally exclusive to the living world, the genetic program, could not be conceived until cytology, genetics, and molecular biology had matured. It is responsible for the dual causation

Three centuries before Descartes, Aquinas made all this clear in one of his first works, *Principles of Nature*. This was really nothing more than his "senior thesis" and it made no pretension of being a piece of "original" research. Instead, he was simply summing up those principles about which all his professors would agree. One of these principles was that "the cause of the causality of the efficient cause is the final cause."[22] Though the English seems stilted and redundant (I'm told it reads much better in the original Latin), the point Aquinas was making is the same as a statistician insisting that correlation is not causation.

In medieval philosophy the term "final cause" meant nothing more than that which turned a mere correlation into a *lawful* cause-and-effect relation.[23] An efficient cause is that which *makes* something happen. In other words, to say that A *makes* B happen is to say that there is something about the essential nature of A that explains *why* B happens as opposed to saying merely *that* it happens. We may know *that* in a thousand previous instances, walking through the doors of Emerson Hall is followed by an inability to

---

of all activities of and in living organisms" (89).

In an earlier book, *The Growth of Biological Thought,* Mayr wrote: "The formation of constitutive hierarchies is one of the most characteristic properties of living organisms. At each level there are different problems, different questions to be asked, and different theories to be formulated. Each of these levels has given rise to a separate branch of biology: molecules to molecular biology, cells to cytology, tissues to histology, and so forth, up to biogeography and the study of ecosystems. . . . For a full understanding of living phenomena every level must be studied but, as was pointed out above, the findings made at lower levels usually add very little toward solving the problems posed at the higher levels. When a well-known Nobel laureate in biochemistry said, 'There is only one biology, and it is molecular biology,' he simply revealed his ignorance and lack of understanding of biology" (65).

In sum, "It is embarrassingly recent that biologists have had the intellectual strength to develop an explanatory paradigm that fully takes into consideration the unique properties of the world of life and yet is fully consistent with the laws of chemistry and physics" (96–97).

22. Aquinas, *Principles of Nature*, ch. 4. The language is my own paraphrase. Aquinas's own source is Aristotle's *Metaphysics.* "The efficient cause is related to the final cause because the efficient cause is the starting point of motion and the final cause is its terminus. There is a similar relationship between matter and form. For form gives being, and matter receives it. Hence the efficient cause is the cause of the final cause, and the final cause is the cause of the efficient cause. The efficient cause is the cause of the final cause inasmuch as it makes the final cause be, because by causing motion the efficient cause brings about the final cause. But the final cause is the cause of the efficient cause, not in the sense that it makes it be, but inasmuch as it is the reason for the causality of the efficient cause. For an efficient cause is a cause inasmuch as it acts, and it acts only because of the final cause." Aquinas, *Commentary on Aristotle's Metaphysics* V.2.775.

23. Veatch, *Aristotle*, 48.

conjugate Inuit verbs. And even if we assume that this correlation is *never* violated (suppose that Sam decides to go to Yale instead of Harvard), observations by themselves will not distinguish between real causation and mere correlation. We say, "Correlation is not causation." Thomas Aquinas and his peers said, "The cause of the causality of the efficient cause is the final cause," i.e., what makes a correlation "lawful" is that which explains *why* something happens.

Since Descartes's time, many people have mocked the notion of final causes. Mocking what one doesn't understand is easy. Why do bunnies have white tails? So that hunters have a target *to* aim at! Why do people have noses? So that eye doctors have something on which *to* hang their prescriptions! Isn't it obvious, assumes the satirist, that only *conscious people* are able to do things "on purpose" or "to reach a goal"? Sodium does not explode in water to achieve an end, but *only* in conformity to the laws of nature. To apply such human attributes to inanimate nature, say the mockers, is a misguided and hopelessly outdated anthropomorphism; it is a sign of an "enchanted" worldview that is only slightly better than primitive animism.

But the charge of misguided anthropomorphism cuts both ways. Mocking the talk of "*laws* of nature" is no more difficult than mocking final causes. The language of "laws of nature" is just as "anthropomorphic" as the language of Aristotle and Aquinas. When did *nature* convene its (her?) legislative session to propound these laws? Did the laws of nature receive a clear majority of the ballots cast or only a simple plurality? Does "nature" decide such questions with a written constitution like the United States or with a "virtual" constitution like the British? Mocking the talk of "*laws* of nature" is no more difficult than mocking final causes. And just as seriously as scientists today don't believe that "laws of nature" were established in a legislative session convened in the murky prehistory of our universe, so too, serious followers of Aristotle and Aquinas never believed that sodium's violent reaction to water was *consciously* intended.

AN EXCURSUS ON LOGISTIC MAPS

Chapter 1 described the demise of mechanism. While there are no scientific limits to what can be described after the fact, there are clear scientific limits to what is mechanically predictable. Now in one sense, there is nothing more orderly and predictable than the mathematical reasoning upon which Descartes sought to ground his philosophy. Two always comes after one, and three always comes after two. And while we find it hard to believe that anyone has ever counted up to 2,347,698,235,108, we can all "predict" what number will come next.

But recent discoveries have called into question the "predictability" of even mathematics. One of these is an iterative function called a "logistic map." It is a very simple function where the solution to the first equation becomes the starting point for the same equation repeated a second time. This process is then repeated over and over and over. In this respect, logistic maps are a lot like compound interest. Suppose a person deposits $100 in a bank at 5 percent annual interest. At the end of the year, that person would have $105. But, today, banks typically offer compound interest. While some banks compound their interest daily, to keep the example simple, we'll only "compound" it quarterly at an annual rate of 5 percent. This works out to a quarterly rate of 1.25 percent. In other words, $100 deposited on January 1 will be worth $101.25 at the end of the first quarter. But when we calculate our earnings for the next quarter, we do not multiply our initial deposit of $100 by 1.25 percent; rather, we multiply *$101.25* by 1.25 percent. In other words, the "multiplier" (function) stays the same, but our second starting point is the result of our previous calculation. This means that our starting point is continually changing. Expressed in a simple formula, 1.25 percent interest compounded quarterly for one year looks like this:

(Rate times Principal) plus Principal, repeated four times

First calcualtion where Principal is $100.00 = (1.25% x $100.00) + $100.00 = $101.25

Second calcualtion where Principal is $101.25 = (1.25% x $101.25) + $101.25 = $102.52

Third calcualtion where Principal is $102.52 = (1.25% x $102.52) + $102.52 = $103.80

Fourth calcualtion where Principal is $103.80 = (1.25% x $103.80) + $103.80 = $105.10

This process of repeating a simple calculation is called iteration. Both compound interest and logistic maps are simple calculations which are iterated. But not all iterated functions are predictable. Here is the formula for a logistic map:

$$(R \times P) \times (1-P)$$

(P is any number between zero and one and R is any number between zero and four). It looks quite simple. But at a specific point, which is itself unpredictable, the results become chaotic. To keep our examples simple, let us first iterate the function with .5 as our value for P and 3.5 as our value for R. Here are the first four iterations of this logistic map to compare with the above figure for compound interest:

$$(R \times P) \times (1-P)$$

First Calculation where P is .5 = 3.5 x .5 x (1 - .5) = .875
Second calculation where P is .875 = 3.5 x .875 x (1 - .875) = .3828
Third calculation where P is .3228 = 3.5 x .3828 x (1 - .3828) = .8269
Fourth calculation where P is .8269 = 3.5 x .8269 x (1 - .8269) = .5009

Both look equally simple and unsurprising. And the unsurprising nature of this first logistic map with P equal to .5 and R equal to 3.5 is confirmed when we look at the first thirty iterations:

1	.5	11	.3828	21	.5
2	.875	12	.8269	22	.875
3	.3828	13	.5	23	.3828
4	.8269	14	.875	24	.8269
5	.5	15	.3828	25	.5
6	.875	16	.8269	26	.875
7	.3828	17	.5	27	.3828
8	.8269	18	.875	28	.8269
9	.5	19	.3828	29	.5
10	.875	20	.8269	30	.875

In this first table where we used 3.5 as our value for R, there were no surprises—every fourth iteration repeated itself so that a clear and predictable pattern emerges. And this will be true for any value of R up to about 3.57. However, at 3.58 a radical change occurs—all predictable patterns disappear; instead the results become "random," as is obvious when looking at the first thirty iteration of a logistic map with the same value for P of .5, but this time we assign a value of 3.67 to R.

1	.5	11	.396	21	.3654
2	.9175	12	.8778	22	.851
3	.2778	13	.3937	23	.4652
4	.7363	14	.8761	24	.9131
5	.7126	15	.3985	25	.2913
6	.7516	16	.8797	26	.7577
7	.6851	17	.3884	27	.6738
8	.7918	18	.8718	28	.8066
9	.6051	19	.4101	29	.5724
10	.877	20	.8878	30	.8982

Here there is no orderly pattern; instead, chaos reigns. Furthermore, there is no mathematical formula which "predicts" the disappearance of predictable patterns when the value of R reaches 3.58. (Imagine how surprised and angry you'd be if at 3.57 percent interest your principle always increased, but for some inexplicable reason, when the bank increased the rate to 3.58 percent you *lost* money!)

Descartes's "clear and distinct ideas" were supposed to "disenchant" the material realm, making it mechanistic and predictable. Yet, even the mathematical reasoning that Descartes assumed would domesticate nature, can, at unpredictable times, turn quite wild. There is nothing except time that prohibits a precise calculation of the numerical value for any logistic map a thousand iterations out. We can precisely *describe* what happens after the fact; there are no "mathematical" demons or spirits that are mucking up our calculations. Even so, mathematical reasoning cannot predict when a certain function will become unpredictable. While the actions of machines are mathematically predictable, mathematics itself is not.

In chapter 1 we considered Laplace's dream of a future where capital "S" Science might one day be able to *explain* everything and make us humans masters of our universe. But "science" turned on Laplace. Today it rests content with an increasingly accurate description of the created order, which in many cases is anything but mechanistic. In this chapter we considered Descartes's attempt to ground a philosophy on his "firm resolution" to only trust capital "L" Logic. But Descartes's project faced three insurmountable obstacles. First, as we just saw, the mathematical logic of a simple iterated equation defeats the whole premise of his project. Second, as we saw earlier, Descartes's "Logic" does extreme violence to common sense by forbidding the use of the word "like," and hence, all analogical reasoning.

Third, Descartes's "Logic" itself undercuts science by making it impossible to distinguish between causation and correlation.

But if logic *by itself* cannot explain our universe and make us the masters of our own destiny, perhaps logic *together* with "the scientific method" will prove successful. This was the hope of the dominant philosophical movement of the first half of the twentieth century called "logical positivism." It will be our topic in the next chapter.

—3—

No Logical Bridge[1]

Descartes craved certainty. Yet his attempt to explain all things in terms of logic alone ended in failure. Something more is needed; something like a logical bridge between observation and reality. Many scientists (but almost no philosophers) believe that "the scientific method" and its reliance on quantifiable measurements provides such a bridge. But this too is an error.

Almost everyone knows *how* to ride a bicycle. Yet, if you asked them to explain how they were effortlessly able to balance their body on two thin wheels, very few could explain the inertial physics of revolving wheels. So too, by definition, scientists know *how* to do a scientific experiment or *how* to make scientific observations. But that doesn't mean that they are also good at explaining *what* they are doing and *how* they reach their conclusions. This is not said as a criticism—no one can or should try to know

---

1. I borrowed this phrase from T. F. Torrance. "In any case there can be no logical bridge between the universe and God, any more than there can be a logical bridge between the theoretic concepts of natural science and the ontic structures of the empirical world disclosed to science through its inquiries." *Divine and Contingent Order*, 112. Torrance appears to have picked this up from Einstein. "The supreme task of the physicist is to arrive at those universal elementary laws from which the cosmos can be built up by pure deduction. There is no logical path to these laws; only intuition, resting on sympathetic understanding of experience, can reach them. . . . [So] there is no logical bridge between phenomena and their theoretical principles." Einstein, *Essays in Science*, 4.

everything. It is only to point out that scientists, just like people in general, are able to *do* many things well prior to self-consciously reflecting on *what* they are doing.

True, most scientists today explain what they are doing by describing the five steps of something called "the scientific method." But among those who make it their job to self-consciously reflect on what scientists do—philosophers and historians of science—there is widespread agreement that there is no such thing as "*the* scientific method."

Now in one sense, this is hardly surprising. In the sport of bicycle racing, Lance Armstrong is among the best; in the sport of tennis, Roger Federer is among the best. But does anyone believe in something called "*the* method of sports" that would make Lance Armstrong a skilled tennis coach? So too, the various "scientific" disciplines from, physics to paleontology, all have radically different objects of study, so why should anyone think that they all use the same method of investigation?[2]

At this point a defender of the Enlightenment is likely to object: "True, being a good bicycle racer does not mean that you will be a good tennis coach. But at a more general level, there *is* something that sports announcers call 'athleticism' that transcends the differences among individual sports and describes something common to them all. Likewise, there *is* a 'scientific way of knowing' that is essentially distinct from the 'subjective' methods of the philosophers, moralists, and theologians."

This was a common philosophical argument in the first half of the twentieth century put forward by those calling themselves logical positivists. They understood that Descartes's philosophy was a failure; something more than logic was needed to build a bridge between observation and theory. If such a bridge could be constructed, then the Enlightenment's goal of replacing the "metaphysics" of philosophers and the dogmas of the theologians with the pure reason of a scientific understanding of reality might be given new life, even after the previous failures of Descartes and Laplace.

However, today it is clear that logical positivism is itself a failure and that there is no logical bridge connecting observations and scientific theories. It is also clear that the demise of logical positivism was the third and fatal blow that finally killed the Enlightenment dream of a mechanistic, wholly quantitative and mono-causal explanation of the universe.

But before we do a postmortem, we must first say more about the nature of the problem; in particular, we must be clear about the meaning of

---

2. No scientist defended the autonomy of the individual disciplines in the "sciences" better or more vociferously than Ernst Mayr. All of his books listed in the bibliography at some place make this case, though none do it as overtly as *What Makes Biology Unique?*

the term *logical*. Out on the street, "logic" refers to any sort of reasonable argument. But in this dispute all sides are using the term in a much more narrow sense to refer *only* to valid deductive arguments.

DEDUCTIVE AND INDUCTIVE ARGUMENTS

A valid deductive argument is formally structured so that *if* the premises are true, then it is totally, 100-percent, cross-your-heart-and-hope-to-die *impossible* for the conclusion to be false. Here is a paradigm for a valid deductive argument which goes all the way back to Aristotle:

> All humans are mortal.
> Socrates is a human.
> Therefore, Socrates is mortal.

Yet, no logician believes that this argument *proves* that Socrates is mortal because we do not know with complete certainty that the two premises are true. Perhaps some human beings don't die but are instead miraculously carried up to heaven like Elijah, or perhaps Socrates wasn't really a human, but instead some kind of demigod like the Egyptian kings were thought to be.

The reason logicians are absolutely confident that valid arguments with true premises absolutely guarantee the truth of their conclusions is because valid deductive arguments never assert more than is already asserted in the premises. Ultimately all valid deductive arguments are as boring and obvious as:

> Roses are red.
> And violets are blue.
> Therefore, roses are red.

It is inconceivable that these two premises could be true and the conclusion false because the conclusion merely repeats the first premise. That's not to say that very complex deductive arguments will not produce surprising results. The best example of this is the "logistic map" we considered at the end of the last chapter. No one thought the simple iterative function would turn chaotic at a value of approximately 3.57. Nonetheless, the entire history of deduction, from Aristotle to logistic maps, has never produced a single example of a valid argument with true premises producing a false conclusion.

So it is easy to see why a mathematician and philosophical idealist like Descartes liked deduction. If one can find an absolutely firm foundation upon which to base a deductive argument, then no deception is possible because not even an evil genius can make both sides of a contradiction true. So the only problem is: How or where can we find true premises about which we are absolutely certain? Descartes looked inward and examined his own ideas. But as we have already argued, the real world is not nearly as "logical" as Descartes supposed or as quantifiable as Galileo hoped. Something more than mere logic and counting is required. So logical positivists looked to *inductive* arguments to provide what's missing.

So what's an inductive argument? Here there is disagreement. Philosophical realists like Aristotle and Aquinas insist that inductive arguments can only be defined negatively, that is, they are any arguments which are *not* deductive. Positively, all we can say is that good inductive arguments are reasonable and their analogies "make sense." In so doing, realists happily admit that it is impossible to specify in advance a set of logical rules to define the meaning of "reasonable" and "good analogy." All we can say is that through much experience "good judgment" can be developed.[3] In this regard, good inductive arguments are like pornography—neither can be defined, but we know both when we see them.

Of course, not all would agree. Positivists, and Enlightenment thinkers in general, argue that "good judgment" is far too subjective. What's required, they say, is a set of "objective" rules for the evaluation of inductive arguments. In this regard, they attempted to do for induction what Aristotle had done for deduction.

In the next section, we will consider this strong disagreement between realists and positivists about the possibility of finding "objective" rules for the evaluation of inductive arguments. But first we need to consider the one point where there is complete agreement: the validity of deductive arguments is dependent only on their *form*, whereas the strength or weakness of inductive arguments is largely dependent on their *content*. Consider, for example, these two inductive arguments:

- Fred has a VW Rabbit with a diesel engine, a five-speed manual transmission, and radial tires, and it consistently gets over fifty miles per

---

3. In Aristotle's language, "good judgment" encompasses (1) experience and (2) dialectic, i.e., discussion. First, "it is by induction that we have to get to know the first things. For that is how perception too implants the universal in us." *Posterior Analytics* II.19.99b34. Second, dialectic "is useful for the philosophical sciences, because if we fully examine the puzzles on each side, we will more easily see what is true or false. And it is also useful for finding the first principle of each science. For we cannot say anything about them from the proper first principles of the science in question, since the first principles are prior to everything else. Hence it is necessary to discuss them through the common beliefs on each subject. And this is proper to dialectic alone, or to it more than to anything else; for it has a road towards the first principle of all disciplines." Aristotle, *Topics* 101a26-b4. See also *Metaphysics* III.1.995a27, and *Heavens* I.10.279b5.

gallon of fuel. So, if I purchase a VW Rabbit with a diesel engine, a five-speed manual transmission, and radial tires, I too will get over fifty miles per gallon of fuel.

- Fred's car is red, with a racing stripe down its side, a moon roof, a CD player, and a radar detector, and it consistently gets over fifty miles per gallon of fuel. So if I purchase a Ferrari, as long as I make sure that it is red, with a racing stripe down its side, and has a moon roof, CD player, and radar detector, then I too will get over fifty miles per gallon of fuel.

No philosopher or logician thinks that the first argument is conclusive. Perhaps the VW that I purchase will turn out to be a "lemon." Nonetheless, everyone agrees that the first argument is a whole lot better than the second argument. Why? It has nothing to do with the arguments' *formal structure*, since this structure is the same in both—that is, they both argue that since the two cars are the same in five known respects, it is likely that they will also get similar gas mileage. The difference concerns the *content* of the two arguments. In the first argument, the make and model of a car, and its engine, transmission, and tires are all *relevant* factors when it comes to gas mileage. However, in the second argument, the color, racing stripes, moon roof, and CD player are *irrelevant* factors when it comes to gas mileage. On this we can all agree.

Disagreements, however, begin to appear when we try to explain what *makes* a factor relevant. According to Aristotle and Aquinas relevancy is determined by a factor's *fittingness* in the overall consistency, coherence, and comprehensiveness of a bigger theory. John Stuart Mill, a nineteenth-century polymath strongly attracted to the Enlightenment, wanted more; something less vague, something more "scientific." His *A System of Logic* (1843) was one of the first attempts to supply more formal—and hence, "objective"—criteria for the evaluation of inductive arguments.

MILL'S EARLY ATTEMPTS TO FORMALIZE "SCIENCE"

Suppose Sally and Samantha get sick after a picnic, but not Tom, Dick, and Harry. We want to know why. Mill tells us to formulate a hypothesis and gather information. He formulated five methods for establishing causation. In the picnic case, the most obvious hypothesis is that Sally and Samantha got sick because of something they ate. Suppose Sally had some fried chicken, potato salad, and lemonade. Samantha had a hamburger, lettuce salad, and lemonade. Using what Mill called the "method of agreement," the most obvious source of the illness is the lemonade. Our suspicions would be confirmed if we then discovered that Tom, Dick, and Harry all had canned soda instead of lemonade. Here we have employed what Mill called the "method of difference." Putting these two "methods" together (Mill called it "the joint method of agreement and difference") we have constructed a pretty strong case for the lemonade as the cause of the girls' illness.

The last two of Mill's rules are also fairly obvious. The "method of concomitant variation" states that if both C and E increase or decrease together, then C and E are probably causally connected. For example, suppose that while driving north on Interstate 5 into a strong headwind, Dick gets twenty-five miles per gallon in his pickup truck. Then, on the way home, driving the same truck at the same speed, he gets twenty-eight miles per gallon. The only difference is that on the return trip there was no wind. Here we have a case where gas mileage varies proportionally with the variation of wind. In this case, it is reasonable to assume that lack of a headwind was the cause of Dick's improved gas mileage.

Finally, there is the "method of residues." Its procedure is a simple process of elimination. If we know that A is not the cause of E, and that B is not the cause of E, and C is not the cause of E, etc., then there must be some other cause of E. Suppose Harry is feeling unusually tired. He tries going to bed earlier, but that does not help. So he then tries eating a more balanced diet, but that doesn't work either. Finally, he tries getting more exercise. But still he feels uncharacteristically tired. Therefore, Harry concludes that there must be some other factor causing his tiredness—perhaps the stress from working with a new boss.

Like the other four rules, Mill's fifth rule sharpens common sense. But unlike the first four rules, it is a misnomer to call this a "method" for discovering causes. Instead, it is a reformulation of a fundamental principle of philosophical realism—nothing comes from nothing. And to conclude in the above example that Harry's tiredness is caused by stress is really nothing more than a shot in the dark until it is tested by one of the other four methods.

Now most of the work scientists do is simply a careful, rigorous, and patient application of these commonsense ways for discovering causes. In this sense, there is no denying that scientists have a "method," though it is misleading to call it "*the* scientific method," as if it was some scientist's discovery or in some other way uniquely a method *of* scientists. No, it is every sane person's method.

And it is even more than misleading to suggest the "scientific method" is itself a rigorous rule or algorithm that guarantees correct results. Logicians and mathematicians have rules without exceptions; everyone else, including scientists, has to settle for something less. A common barroom ditty illustrates the problem with conceiving of Mill's Methods (or anything else scientists do) as an algorithm. It's entitled *Liquor and Longevity*.

> The horse and mule live thirty years
>   And know nothing of wines and beers.
> The goat and sheep at twenty die
>   And never taste of scotch or rye.
> The cow drinks water by the ton
>   And at eighteen is mostly done.
> A dog at fifteen cashes in
>   Without the aid of rum or gin.
> The cat in milk and water soaks
>   And then in twelve short years it croaks.
> The modest, sober, bone-dry hen
>   Lays eggs for nogs, then dies at ten.
> All animals are strictly dry;
>   They sinless live and swiftly die.
> But sinful, ginful, rumsoaked men
>   Survive for three-score years and ten;
> And some of them, a very few,
>   Stay pickled til they're ninety-two.

If we mechanically applied Mill's Methods to the facts adduced in the ditty, then the conclusion is clear: liquor increases longevity. Horses and mules, goats and sheep, dogs, cats, and cows drink no liquor and die relatively young; men drink liquor and live relatively long.

A defender of Mill might retort that liquor is not a relevant factor. True, but how did we learn this? Mill's methods only work if we *assume* what philosophers call "background knowledge." Without this assumed knowledge, we have no way of determining what is or is not a relevant factor in any causal sequence. Again, correlation is *not* causation.

Other philosophers attempt to circumvent the problem by defining "relevancy" in terms of temporal and spatial proximity. Only those antecedent circumstances that are near in either time or space will be considered relevant. But this hardly narrows the field.

Suppose you wake up one morning with a terrible headache and want to know its cause. It is impossible simply to list all the "circumstances" that precede the headache and then, going through them one by one using the method of agreement and difference, locate the cause. Try making a complete list of all the "circumstances" involved in the hour of your life immediately preceding this one; obviously the list would include things like: ate breakfast, took a shower, drove my car to school, etc. But unless we beg the question by *assuming* a criterion of relevancy, the list must include things like: opened a brown door with my left hand while a mosquito was sucking blood from the top portion of my right ear during which time I was kissing my wife's left cheek and grabbing my lunch with my right hand, etc. The truth of the matter is that when we try to determine the cause of a headache we rule out as irrelevant literally billions and billions of temporally and spatially proximate "circumstances" as not worth worrying about *prior to applying the methods of agreement and difference*. How do we do this? How do we know that certain "circumstances" are irrelevant prior to formulating a hypothesis? These are questions for which Mill has no answer.[4]

Mill's methods work well *within* an established theoretical framework. This framework can be as simple as the "background knowledge" that opening a door with the left (as opposed to the right) hand is not a causally relevant factor in getting a headache. Or it can be quite sophisticated, like Newton's theory of universal gravitation or Darwin's theory of evolution by natural selection. Once these "big questions" are decided, working scientists' questions about relevancy are narrowed down to a workable field.

For example, *after* Newton's theory of universal gravity was well established, astronomers who observed slight irregularities in the orbit of Uranus never even considered the color of Saturn's rings as a possible cause. Only quantities of mass and distance were deemed to be relevant causal factors when calculating orbits of planets. Why? Because the Newtonian framework was an assumed part of scientists' background knowledge. But, again, this "background knowledge" was not itself *proved* by Mill's Methods. Only *after* the "big question" of Newtonian verses Aristotelian understandings of gravity is decided do questions concerning irregularities in a planet's orbit become relatively "small questions" where Mill's methods are more workable.[5]

---

4. Arthur David Ritchie tells a cute story about just how "blind" observations are apart from a criterion of relevancy. "Lord Russell has said that the Greeks were good at devising hypotheses but not much good at observation; and has cited Aristotle as one of the culprits. In his *Unpopular Essays* (1950, 135), he returns to the attack: [Aristotle] 'could have avoided the mistake of thinking that women have fewer teeth than men by the simple device of asking Mrs. Aristotle to keep her mouth open while he counted. He did not do so because he thought he knew.' . . . [But] from what we know of the life of Aristotle, we can infer that he married in his thirties or later, as indeed was customary then, certainly after his own wisdom teeth irrupted. . . . His wife on the other hand will probably have been in her 'teens on marriage, as was customary, and almost certainly her wisdom teeth would not have irrupted. Aristotle might well have counted his own teeth and his wife's and found that she had four less than he had." *Studies*, 18–19.

5. I flesh this out in some detail in chapters 2 and 3 of *Life, the Universe, and Everything*.

THE INTERTWINING OF OBSERVATION AND THEORY

So how are these "big questions" answered? Positivists argued that the premises in all arguments must be strictly limited to those that could be positively observed and measured apart from any subjective judgments or intuitions by humans. The ideal "observer" for positivists was some kind of machine. Instead of relying on humans to determine whether the liquid in test tube A was more or less red than the liquid in test tube B, positivists would build some sort of instrument with a dial and a pointer (there were no digital readouts in their day!). All humans would have to do is to read off the number to which the pointer was pointing, thereby reducing human "subjectivity" to an absolute minimum. Instead of making qualitative judgments concerning good or bad analogies, scientists would only make quantitative observations. After all the quantitative, and hence, *totally objective* data were gathered, they believed that only deductive logic would be required to make sense of the data—thus positivism was frequently called *logical* positivism. In short, they hoped to build a logical bridge between observations and scientific theories.

However, as we already said, today there is widespread agreement among philosophers that the movement was a failure. The positivist's hopes were dashed by the simple fact that the quantifiable observations scientists use to verify a theory and the theory itself are hopelessly intertwined.[6] The rest of this chapter will be a bare-bones description of one of the problems with positivism. (In the next chapter we will consider another problem, namely, the positivists' attempt to eliminate all qualitative judgments in both science and philosophy.)

With the expansion of trade in the early seventeenth century, it became economically profitable to dig deeper and deeper mines. However, the deeper miners dug, the more important it became to find an efficient way to remove the water from the bottoms of mines, since the best suction pumps, for some unknown reason, would only "lift" the water about thirty-four feet; after that, no matter how much suction was created by a pump, the water would mysteriously stop rising. So instead of having one pump at the top of the mines with a long pipe extending to the bottom, they were forced to have a series of pumps, each with a pipe around thirty feet long.

---

6. The most serious attempt to turn Mill's common-sense methods into an algorithm was carried out by Rudolf Carnap. Hilary Putnam is hardly exaggerating when he says, "To put it very briefly, Carnap wanted to reduce theory choice to an algorithm. . . . Today no one holds out any hope for Carnap's project." *Collapse of the Fact/Value Dichotomy*, 141.

An Italian named Torricelli was puzzled. The cutting-edge, "big" theory of the day was that "nature abhorred a vacuum"—that's why when a pump sucks the air from the top of a pipe, water from the bottom of the pipe rushes up to fill the vacuum. The puzzling question was why nature should only abhor a vacuum at least thirty-four feet long.

Torricelli thought he had an answer. He argued that suction pumps don't really "suck" the water up, instead, there is a "Sea of Air" around the water that is *pushing* the water up the tube. By removing the air from inside the pipe, the pressure of the air outside the pipe pushes down on the pool of water at the bottom, thus forcing up the water inside the pipe. And since the height of the atmosphere is limited, the amount of pressure exerted by the air outside the pipe is also limited. This means that the weight of the water being "pushed up" can't be more than the weight of air pushing down on the water outside the hose. When the weight of the air pushing down equals the weight of the water being pushed up, the water will rise no more. That's Torricelli's theory, and his "proof" was demonstrated in a couple of experiments.

Since mercury is fourteen times heavier than water, Torricelli reasoned that the air pushing down on a pool of mercury at the bottom of a tube of mercury will only support a column about one-fourteenth the height of an equal column of water; that's about thirty inches. And when he performed the experiment, the results were exactly as he predicted. He also reasoned that if he took his "thirty-inch column of mercury" (he had just invented the barometer) up a mountain, the amount of air pushing down would decrease, so the column of mercury should also decrease in height. Once again, when he performed the experiment, the results were exactly as predicted.

Formally, Torricelli argued like this:

Argument #1

Hypothesis: If there is a "Sea of Air," then mercury will only rise about thirty inches.

Observation: Experiments show that mercury only rises about thirty inches.

Conclusion: There is a "Sea of Air."

Argument #2

Hypothesis: If there is a "Sea of Air," then mercury will rise less than thirty inches on top of a mountain.

Observation: Experiments show that mercury rises less than thirty inches on top of a mountain.

Conclusion: There is a "Sea of Air."

Both of these arguments are of the form:

1) If A, then B
2) B
Therefore, A

But there is a *huge* problem with these arguments—they are both logically *invalid*! As logicians say, they commit the fallacy of "affirming the consequent."

The logical fallaciousness of "affirming the consequent" is obvious when we consider another argument with a logically identical structure to Torricelli's arguments.

Argument #3

If any person is beheaded (A), then they will be dead (B).

George Washington is dead (B).

Therefore, George Washington was beheaded (A).

It is obvious that the third argument doesn't *prove* its conclusion for the simple reason that we know its conclusion is false. Since both its premises are true, the problem with argument #3 can *only* reside in its logical form or structure. And since argument #3 and both of Torricelli's arguments are logically identical in form/structure, his arguments are also logically invalid, and hence, they do not *prove* their conclusion either.

Of course, we are not saying that Torricelli's conclusion is false; we are only saying that his quantitative observations do not provide a "logical bridge" between his experimental observations and his "Sea of Air" hypothesis.

The same point is illustrated by the "raven paradox." Suppose one wonders whether the proposition "All ravens are black" is true. How might I confirm such a statement? Since I am currently at my desk writing, and since there are no birds in my study, it *seems* that I would have to go outside and actually observe some birds. But logic proves otherwise! By a procedure permitted by the rules of deductive logic called contraposition, "All ravens are black" is *logically* equivalent to "All non-black objects are non-ravens." This equivalency is no more controversial than saying that 2 + 2 = 4.

So here's the paradox. If science is simply a matter of making logical deductions from careful observations, then *logically speaking* there can be no objection to doing armchair ornithology. From where I now sit, I can clearly observe a red book, brown lamp, gray speakers, blue water bottle, and countless other non-black objects. Furthermore, I can clearly observe that each of these non-black objects is *not* a raven. Therefore, *if* logic and observation is all that is necessary to confirm a scientific proposition, then *each* of these observations confirms the proposition "All ravens are black" because *each* of them confirms the logically equivalent proposition "All non-black objects are non-ravens." Since armchair ornithology is the very antithesis of real science, it follows that real science is *more* than mere logic and careful quantitative observations.

Sophisticated positivists responded to both these problems—the problem of "affirming the consequent" and the "raven paradox"—by arguing that even if there is no logical bridge between quantifiable observation and the *proof* of a scientific theory, there is a logical bridge between quantifiable observation and the *disproof* of a scientific theory. For example, we can easily disprove with observation and logic alone the Flat Earth theory. On a clear day, when we can observe tall ships coming in from sea, we can see the tops of the ships before we see their bottoms. This is because the curvature of the earth blocks our line of sight. So we can logically prove that the earth isn't flat. Put more formally, the argument looks like this:

Argument #4

Hypothesis: If the earth is flat, then we should see the tops and bottoms of ships coming in from sea at the same time.

Observation: We see the tops of ships *before* we can see their bottoms.

Conclusion: The earth is not flat.

Here the positivists are partially correct: the logical form of argument #4 is a perfectly good modus tollens argument. No logician doubts its validity. Nonetheless, there is still no logical bridge connecting observation and theory, because theories never come in discrete, unitary packages. They always include auxiliary assumptions, what we previously called "background knowledge." For example, the first premise of argument #4 is only true *if* we assume that light always travels in a straight line. If light should sag (because of gravity) over long distances like a piece of nylon string pulled tight, then the first premise is not true. (And in point of fact, relativity theory has demonstrated that light is bent in the presence of a strong gravitational field.) Thus, argument #4 must be amended to read:

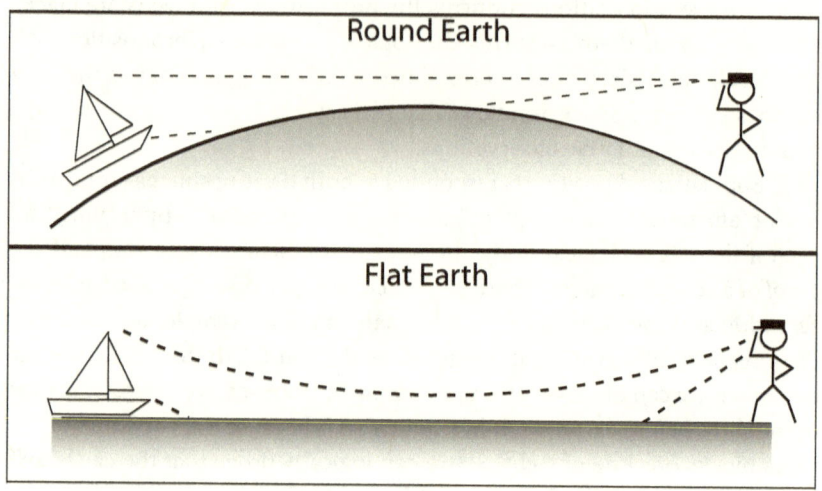

Argument #4a

Hypothesis: If (a) the earth is flat *and* (b) light always travels in a straight line, then we should see the tops and bottoms of ship coming in from sea at the same time.

Observation: We do not see the tops and bottoms of ships coming in from sea at the same time.

Conclusion: Either (a) earth is not flat *or* (b) light does not always travel in a straight line.

And notice: amending the first premise means that logically speaking we *must* also amend the conclusion. There is nothing in the "logic" of argument #4a which requires us to think that the earth is not flat. Any stubborn Flat-earther is fully within his logical rights to conclude that the earth really is flat, it is just that light doesn't always travel in a straight line.

Now the point of argument #4a is *not* that there is some real doubt about the shape of the earth. It is only to deny the positivist's claim that logic and quantifiable observation *by themselves* allow us to falsify bad theories. The problem with the Flat-earther's auxiliary assumption is that it comes out of nowhere to save the day like a deus ex machina in a bad B movie. Out on the street, we correctly call such a move "silly," "implausible," "ridiculous," "desperate," far-fetched," etc.; in the academic world, we call it ad hoc, a violation of Ockham's razor, unparsimonious, etc. But whatever we call the Flat-earther's defense, it violates no rule of deductive *logic*. This is why Einstein says, "Every attempt at a logical deduction of the basic concepts and postulates of mechanics from elementary experience is doomed to failure."[7]

7. Einstein, *Essays in Science*, 4.

And here it is important to note that Copernicus's heliocentric theory and Newton's theory of gravity were initially faced with similar counterarguments. For Copernicus, it was the parallax problem. A parallax is simply a change in the apparent location of an object when the observer changes his point of view. A very simple way to demonstrate this is to focus on an object across the room with only one eye open; now focus on the same object with only the other eye open. Notice how the object appears to change its position. So too, Copernicus's critics argued that if the earth really did revolve around the sun, then when we focus our instruments on a particular star on January 1 and then again on July 1, we ought to observe a measurable parallax. This is because, according to Copernicus's theory, the earth will have moved halfway around the sun. And here there was no disagreement; no measurable parallax was observable. In short, his critics (using a perfectly valid modus tollens argument) reasoned:

Argument #5

Hypothesis: If the earth revolves around the sun, then we ought to observe a measurable stellar parallax.

Observation: We do not observe a measurable stellar parallax.

Conclusion: The earth does not revolve around the sun.

Copernicus had in fact anticipated this objection (which goes all the way back to Aristotle) by arguing that the stars are so far away that our instruments are not sufficiently powerful to observe the parallax.[8] In short, he responded with argument #5a:

Argument #5a

Hypothesis: If (a) the earth revolves around the sun *and* (b) the stars are not too far away, then we ought to observe a stellar parallax.

Observation: We do not observe a stellar parallax.

Conclusion: Either (a) the earth does not revolve around the sun *or* (b) the stars are too far away.

---

8. "But that there are no such appearances [i.e., observable stellar parallax] among the fixed stars argues that they are at an immense height away, which makes the circle of annual movement or its image disappear from before our eyes since every visible thing has a certain distance beyond which it is no longer seen, as is shown in optics. For the brilliance of their lights shows that there is a very great distance between Saturn the highest of the planets and the sphere of the fixed stars. It is by this mark in particular that they are distinguished from the planets, as it is proper to have the greatest difference between the moved and the unmoved. How exceedingly fine is the godlike work of the Best and the Greatest Artist!" Copernicus, *Revolutions*, bk. 1, 529.

Obviously, Copernicus chose to believe the second half of the conclusion, i.e., that the stars were too far away.[9]

Now to those who would mistakenly belittle the observational skills of Copernicus's critics, we must remember that the Ptolemaic astronomers (those who argued that the earth was at the center) were just as accurate in their predictions of the seasons, eclipses, and location of the planets as those who followed Copernicus's heliocentric theory. Observationally, both theories were both accurate to one-sixth a degree of arc.[10] Quantitatively Copernicus made no improvement. All he could argue was that his theory was simpler and more elegant than the Ptolemaic theory. And while "simplicity" may be quantifiable *if* we already agree on what is worth counting (a big "if" as we will see in the next chapter!), "elegance" is clearly a qualitative judgment. Here are Copernicus's own words to explain the problem with the Ptolemaic astronomers who resorted to complex geometrical devices (epicycles, eccentric circles, and equants[11]) to explain the motion of the heavens: "They are in exactly the same fix as someone taking from different places hands, feet, head, and other limbs—shaped very beautifully but not with reference to one body and with correspondence to one another—so that such parts made up a monster rather than a man."[12] Of course, Coper-

---

9. "Physics is not a machine which lets itself be taken apart; we cannot try each piece in isolation and, in order to adjust it, wait until its solidity has been carefully checked. Physical science is a system that must be taken as a whole; it is an organism in which one part cannot be made to function except when the parts that are most remote from it are called into play, some more so than others, but all to some degree. If something goes wrong, if some discomfort is felt in the functioning of the organism, the physicist will have to ferret out through its effect on the entire system which organ needs to be remedied or modified without the possibility of isolating this organ and examining it apart. The watchmaker to whom you give a watch that has stopped separates all the wheelworks and examines them one by one until he finds the part that is defective or broken. The doctor to whom a patient appears cannot dissect him in order to establish his diagnosis; he has to guess the seat and cause of the ailment solely by inspecting disorders affecting the whole body. Now, the physicist concerned with remedying a limping theory resembles the doctor and not the watchmaker." Duhem, *Aim and Structure*, 188.

10. "Finally, because Copernicus used the ancient Ptolemaic observations as his fundamental base, his own predictive system was not substantially more accurate than Ptolemy's, and, if accuracy of prediction were the criterion, then Copernicus's work must be deemed a massive failure." Gingerich, "The Copernican Revolution," 96. And again, "In Copernicus's time, however, no startling new astronomical observations refuted Ptolemaic astronomy. Nor did Copernicus's heliocentric system provide a better match between theory and observation than had Ptolemy's geocentric system. Copernicus, himself, acknowledged that Ptolemy's planetary theory was consistent with numerical data." Hetherington, *Planetary Motions*, 93.

11. See chapter 2 of my *Life, the Universe, and Everything* for more details.

12. Copernicus, *Revolutions*, "Preface and Dedication to Pope Paul III," 507.

nicus was correct; the earth really does move. But the distinction in beauty between a monster and a man is not something we learn through quantitative observations and logic *alone*.

Newton's theory of universal gravity is a wonderful synthesis of the mathematical astronomy of Copernicus, the slightly elliptical orbits of the planets observed by Kepler, and the quasi-inertial physics of Galileo.[13] Yet, Newton also appealed to an auxiliary hypothesis to save his theory from immediate falsification. At the heart of his theory was the claim that every body always exerts a gravitational pull on every other body even though there is *no physical connection* between them. Many of Newton's critics thought that this sort of "action at a distance" was a return to medieval superstition. But besides name-calling, they argued that if everything is always exerting a gravitational pull on everything else, then the entire universe ought to collapse into one massive ball. Put formally, they argued:

> *Argument #6*
>
> *Hypothesis:* If (as Newton argued) gravity acts instantaneously at a distance, then the universe will collapse into a single massive ball.
>
> *Observation:* The universe has not collapsed into a single massive ball.
>
> *Conclusion:* Gravity does not act instantaneously at a distance.

Newton's response is so counter to our popular understanding of how science operates that I will quote him directly: "And lest the systems of fixed stars should, by their gravity, fall on each other, he [God] hath placed those systems at immense distances from one another."[14] In other words, it is God who keeps the universe from collapsing in on itself! Put formally,

> *Argument #6a*
>
> *Hypothesis:* If (a) gravity acts instantaneously *and* (b) God permits it, then the universe will collapse into a single massive ball.
>
> *Observation:* The universe has not collapsed into a single massive ball.
>
> *Conclusion: Either* (a) gravity does not act instantaneously at a distance *or* (b) God prevents the collapse of the universe.

---

13. Since Galileo lacked a theory of universal gravity, he was still committed to the older Aristotelian idea that *circular* motion was perfect, and hence, that the planets naturally revolved in a circle around the sun. It was Newton who argued that all bodies, once in motion, continue to move in a *straight line* unless acted upon by some other body.

14. Newton, *Principles*, 370.

For those not familiar with the history of science, Newton's response appears to be highly ad hoc. Yet the rest of his theory was so mathematically elegant and powerful that throughout the eighteenth and nineteenth centuries Newton himself had a status in both the scientific world and in popular culture only slightly lower than God himself. Furthermore, it was not until the 1930s when Hubble discovered evidence suggesting a Big Bang that scientists had a viable alternative to Newton's "God hypothesis."

If scientists are limited, as the positivists argued, to making logical deductions from quantifiable observations, then there is no way to distinguish reasonable auxiliary assumptions from ad hoc auxiliary assumptions. There is no logical criterion which makes the Flat-earther's auxiliary assumption in argument #4a—"light always travels in a straight line"—ad hoc, which does not also make Copernicus's assumption in argument #5a—"the stars are too far away"—and Newton's assumption in argument #6a—"God prevents it"—equally ad hoc. The history of science[15] demonstrates that scientists working on big, cutting-edge theoretical problems are not limited to making logical deductions from observation. Instead, they rely on *qualitative* judgments to distinguish between good and bad analogies and these judgments always include more than logic and *quantifiable* observations.

THE THREE C'S OF COMPREHENSIVENESS, CONSISTENCY, AND COHERENCE

Good stories, good philosophical explanations, and good scientific theories have the same characteristics.[16] First, they are comprehensive. That is,

---

15. When we move from the physical sciences to the biological sciences the positivists' project becomes even more implausible. For example, Stephen Jay Gould writes, "I first learned about August Weismann in high school biology as the man who 'disproved' Lamarckism by cutting off mouse tails for numerous generations and noting the fully retained tails of all offspring (a good example of terrible teaching based upon the myth of crucial experiments as the source of all insight in science). Weismann did perform these experiments, but they (by his own admission) did little to combat Lamarckism, which is, as supporters parried, a theory about the inheritance of functional adaptations, not of sudden and accidental mutilations." *Structure of Evolutionary Theory*, 201. Is or isn't the auxiliary assumption that Lamarckism is "a theory about the inheritance of functional adaptations, not of sudden and accidental mutilations" an ad hoc assumption?

16. Ernst Mayr, the formulator of the neo-Darwinian synthesis and arguably one of the most important biologists of the twenty century, was blunt and to the point: "the sharp break between science and the nonsciences does not exist." *The Growth of Biological Thought*, 77. Here's one of his examples: "When a biologist tries to answer a question about a unique occurrence such as 'Why are there no hummingbirds in the Old World?' or 'Where did the species *Homo sapiens* originate?' he cannot rely on universal laws.

they have a richness of detail that accounts for and encompasses a large amount of data. Second, they are consistent. That is, they don't contradict themselves. And third, they are coherent. That is, they have an integrity that unifies the data and "makes sense" of it.

Consistency is a purely logical criterion; coherence is not. While all coherent explanations are consistent, not all consistent explanations are coherent. As we demonstrated in the previous section, there is nothing *logically* inconsistent in affirming (1) that the earth is flat and (2) that we see the tops of ships before we see the bottoms. All we have to do is to add a proposition, namely, (3) that light bends in the presence of a strong gravitational field. And, of course, if someone shows a stubborn Flat-earther pictures of the earth taken from the moon, they will write off the pictures as a secret plot by the "government" to deceive the public! What makes all "conspiracy theories" so maddening is that, judged solely by the criterion of deductive logic, they are perfectly consistent.

But good stories, explanations, and theories must be more than logically consistent; they must also be coherent in a way that is inexpressible, yet recognizable to humans who are capable of "seeing" more than can be quantified. Moreover, the fact that we cannot define "coherence" shouldn't bother us. It is impossible to *define* what one table, one person, one game, one corporation, one rainbow, one fishing trip, one joke, or one story have in common.[17] All we can say is that they exhibit a unifying *quality* that we can recognize when we see it. There is an inexpressible quality that makes a good story or theory hang together with integrity that we can all recognize without a set of "objective" criteria.

Crossword puzzles provide a nice illustration of what we are calling the three Cs of comprehensiveness, consistency, and coherence. When solving a crossword puzzle the solution must first be comprehensive, that is, all the "boxes" must be filled. If the clue for "one across" requires a six-letter word, and you fill it with a five-letter word, then even if your word makes sense of the clue and its letters are consistent with the letters of words which cross it vertically, it is still not a good solution.

Second, good solutions are consistent, that is, when horizontal and vertical words cross, the *same* letter is at their intersection. These first two

---

The biologists has to study all the known facts relating to the particular problem, infer all sorts of consequences from the reconstructed constellations of factors, and then attempt to construct a scenario that would explain the observed facts of this particular case. In other words, he constructs a historical narrative." *This Is Biology,* 64.

17. We will say more about this "transcendental" (i.e., indefinable) property of unity in chapter 10.

criteria for a good solution to a crossword puzzle are, so to speak, "machine gradable"—every box has one letter in it and no box has two letters in it.

But the third criterion (coherence) is not machine gradable. Logic and math will never answer the question: does the word selected *fit* the clue provided? Consider a very simple crossword puzzle composed of one five-letter word going across and one five-letter word going down, crossing at the third letter. The clue for "1 across" is: "Describes reality." The clue for "1 down" is: "makes something happen." Now there will be many ways of solving such a simple puzzle which satisfy the first two criteria of comprehensiveness and consistency. For example:

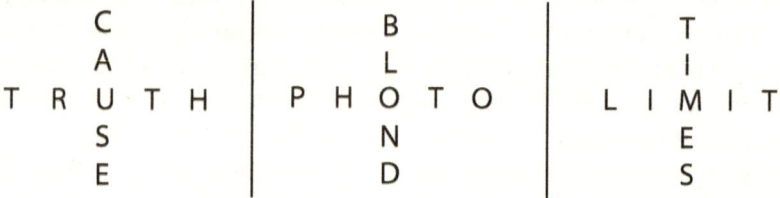

All three of these solutions are comprehensive and consistent. But the solution on the left is better than the other two because both words selected *fit* the clues provided: "Truth" describes reality and a "cause" makes something happen. In the middle solution, while it makes some sense to say that a "photo" describes reality, it make very little sense to say that "blond" makes something happen, though certainly a creative wag could tell a story where a "blond" makes something happen! And the right-hand solution would require even greater "creativity" to make the words selected *fit* the clues provided.

The three philosophies we've considered thus far—Drescartes's idealism, logical positivism, and the realism of Aristotle and Aquinas—can roughly be defined with respect to the three Cs. For Descartes, logical consistency was the be-all end-all. Since he wouldn't trust any of the data from our five senses, logical consistency was the only criterion for truth.

Logical positivists have room for quantifiable observational data, though they prefer to reduce the "human" element to the bare minimum and let machines do most of the "observing" and data gathering. Thus, they will also consider the criterion of comprehensiveness. What they will not include is the criterion of coherence because they say that it is far too "subjective."

Philosophical realists consider all three criteria and have no problem with the "subjectivity" of coherence. "Of course," they say, "coherence can't be reduced to mere logic; it requires the good judgment of *humans* (not mere machines or computers) developed over time and employing much experience. Furthermore, coherence is an absolutely essential element in any scientific understanding of the world since without it there is no reason to prefer the Copernican theory of a spherical earth revolving around the sun to a conspiracy theorist's flat earth resting on a tortoise."

In short, science gives us insights into the nature of reality that can be obtained in no other way. But it does not work as idealist philosophers would like it to—by logic alone. Nor does it work as positivist philosophers said it did—with a logical bridge connecting quantifiable observations to theories. Instead, it works the way a good story works: it gathers together a wide range of observations and events and then weaves them together into a single narrative (a theory) that is *largely* consistent and *fairly* coherent.[18]

The qualifications "largely" and "fairly" are crucial. No scientific theory is *perfectly* consistent with everything that we know or think we know. For example, relativity theory and quantum mechanics are mathematically inconsistent because the former assumes that the universe is a continuous whole while the latter assumes that the universe is composed of discrete "quanta."

The idea of *perfectly* coherent stories, theories, or explanations assumes that one day humans will be able to fit *everything* into a single story. We know many things, but we *infallibly* know nothing, because we can never know what we don't know. And it is not merely "scientifically" subtle things that we can't know, like what's happening outside our light cone. It is also the seemingly trivial things that turn out to have profound effects, like why Turnus grabbed the wrong sword and why a ten-cent nut failed in Carter's rescue mission. Only God's knowledge is infallible because only God knows everything.

Thus far, our conclusion is simple: Demanding that all explanations be mechanistic and that all observation be quantifiable are both bad ideas. The third bad idea of the Enlightenment—mono-causation—will be examined in the next two chapters.

---

18. In an endnote Torrance says: "This is not, of course, to depreciate logic or logical argumentation, but to be strictly logical about logic, for logic has to do with the interrelations between ideas or statements, not with the relation between ideas or statements and empirical reality, where we have to reckon with what Einstein called an 'extra-logical' relation ... If there were a logical relation between knowing and what we know there would be a logical way of deriving knowledge and a logical way of verifying it—but the strange notion of logical induction dies hard! Popper and Polanyi have contributed no less than Einstein to destroying that idea." *Divine and Contingent Order*, 150–51.

—4—

Two Views of God

There are two distinct conceptions of God. The older view, which we will defend, thinks of God as the One who speaks the universe into existence, creates all things through his Word, and is the "author and finisher of our faith." This changed with the advent of mechanistic philosophy. Newton described God as one who was "very well skilled in mechanics and geometry." A century later, William Paley famously compared God to a skilled watchmaker. And today many Christians think in term of an Intelligent Designer who acts in a scientifically detectable fashion. Instead of a divine Author, we now have a supernatural Craftsman.

Mono-causation is the assumption that if A is the cause of Z, then necessarily B is not also the cause of Z. For example, mono-causation is the assumption that if archaeologists one day demonstrate that during the reign of Hezekiah (715–686 BCE) 185,000 Assyrians camped outside the walls of Jerusalem were suddenly killed by an outbreak of cholera, then the prophet Isaiah's statement that "the angel of the Lord went forth, and slew a hundred and eighty-five thousand in the camp of the Assyrians"(Isa 37:36) must be false. Given the assumption of mono-causation, the reasoning is simple: if *cholera* was the cause of death, then the "angel of the Lord" was not the cause of death, since every event has one and only one *real* cause.

Mono-causation is the third bad idea of the Enlightenment. By the time Newton had more or less brought the Copernican Revolution to its conclusion, it was widely believed that the assumption of mechanism and the need to reduce *all* qualitative judgments to quantifiable measurements were the defining characteristics of all true science. Mono-causation is a corollary of these two assumptions. After Newton, most thinkers came to assume that as science discovered more and more about the *true* causal explanation of how things work, then the older, essentially philosophical and theological explanations of how things work would become obsolete.

Now Newton himself, and many other scientists of the Enlightenment, never believed that mono-causation would make God obsolete. As we will see later in this chapter, Newton was adamant that there was still much for God to do in his mechanistic universe. But what Newton meant by the word *God* was very different from what Aquinas meant by the same word.

Prior to the Enlightenment, the typical analogy for God was of a Being who *speaks* the universe into existence, who creates all things through his *Word* and is the "*author* and finisher of our faith" (Heb 12:2). After the Enlightenment, the typical analogy for God was of a very skilled craftsman. Newton described God as one who was "very well skilled in mechanics and geometry."[1] A century later, William Paley famously compared God to a skilled watchmaker. And even today many Christians think of God as an Intelligent Designer who acts in a scientifically detectable fashion.[2] Instead of a divine Author, we now have a supernatural Craftsman.

There is a significant difference between these two conceptions of God. This chapter and the next will flesh out those differences. But first, we will make some broad-brush opening comments comparing and contrasting two ideas about "existence" itself. In philosophy, much depends on what you mean by "is."

NOUNS AND VERBS

Ancient Christians sometimes spoke of "thin places." These were times and places where the presence and power of God were especially evident. Today many Christians speak more frequently of God's miraculous interventions that change the course of nature. This is not an insignificant difference.

---

1. Newton, Letter to Bentley, December 10, 1692.

2. To be clear, the alternative to a "scientifically detectable" God is not a God for whom there are no good reasons. As we will argue later in this chapter, an Author of creation is a necessary assumption for doing science, not a conclusion drawn from science. So if there are good reasons for doing science, there are good reasons for believing God exists.

"Thinness," like the series of fractions we discussed in chapter 2, varies continuously and is always a "more-or-less" affair. There are no hard-and-fast lines in a single, continuous whole. *All* of creation is God's; it is just that in some places the veil between the Creator and the creature becomes more transparent. It is in these thin places that we see God's creative activity more clearly than in other places. And in those places where we do not clearly see God's activity and ownership, the problem is with us, not with God.

The picture today has changed. Miraculous "intervention" is an all-or-nothing affair that assumes a theory of mono-causation. It is like the series of whole numbers. Not all numbers are prime. "Primeness" exists at eleven, but not at ten or twelve. So too, the language of intervention inevitably leads to a division of universe into two distinct realms—the supernatural and the natural. In this picture, most of the universe can be understood in natural terms of cause and effect. But two sorts of cases require a supernatural explanation. The first are the miracles of the Bible where, for example, water is turned into wine or Jesus commands a storm to be still. The second are things like the human brain or the bacterial flagellum that are thought to be so mathematically (i.e., quantitatively) complex that they could not have come about by random chance, and hence, they can only be understood as a direct intervention of God. In both sorts of cases—the biblical miracles and the scientifically inexplicable miracles of complexity—the veil is lifted and the hand of God becomes empirically detectable. Why? Because given the assumption of mono-causation, what cannot be explained scientifically must ipso facto be explained theologically.

The contrasting metaphors of "interventions" and "thin places" are also reflected in grammar. When an "interventionist" metaphor is assumed, "supernatural" becomes a noun. But when a "thin place" metaphor is assumed, "supernatural" becomes an adjective or adverb. In the pre-Enlightenment world, Christians did not use "supernatural" as a noun to name a distinct realm or place. Of course, when the town skeptic suddenly confessed faith in Christ or a plague-infested child laying on her deathbed was suddenly made well, they most certainly would have described such occurrences as supernatural events. But in doing so, they were describing *how* an event took place, not the *event* itself.

The use of "supernatural" as an adverb or adjective, as opposed to a noun, is illustrated by the way we distinguish between a wind-powered schooner and a nuclear-powered submarine. They are both kinds of *things* (ships). But being wind powered and being nuclear powered are not themselves things; they are distinct descriptions of *how* ships are propelled. When we speak of a "nuclear-powered submarine" we are not suggesting or thinking that there is a distinct "realm of nuclear-poweredness" that somehow became attached to the submarine. Likewise, when pre-Enlightenment Christians spoke of a "supernatural event" they were not suggesting or thinking that there is a distinct "realm of the supernatural."[3] To do so would imply that "the realm of nature" is something that can and does exist apart from God's sustaining grace. And this is precisely what happened with Newton and Descartes; the observable universe, i.e., the realm of nature, became an independent, self-sustaining realm of its own. And "supernatural" became its mirror image—distinct from and "better" than the realm of nature, but nonetheless, one of the two categories of *things that exists*.

The alternative is to insist that the Creator and the creature *exist* in radically distinct ways; they are *not* to be conceived of as members of a single category called "things that exist." Aquinas frequently said that existence is not a genus (category) that God and creatures share. Barth concurred,[4] and frequently spoke of an infinite *qualitative* distinction between God and everything else. So what does this mean?

We'll begin with a simple illustration. Consider the following series:

- Triangle, square, pentagon, hexagon, decagon, chiliagon, and circle.

Between which two of these geometrical figures is there the greatest gap? In a quantitative sense, the "gap" between a decagon and a chiliagon is the

---

3. The analogy comes from N. T. Wright, though several other scholars have made the point. "Even in the premodern West, as Nicholas Lash points out, there was no concept of nature and supernature as two ontologically distinct realms. Until the seventeenth century, supernatural was used adverbially or adjectivally to indicate someone acting above what is ordinarily expected of them, for example, a human being acting justly and truthfully through the gifts of God's grace. The term supernatural, therefore, could never be applied to God." Cavanaugh, *The Myth of Religious Violence*, 87; see also 99–100, 104. Paul Helm makes the same point with regard to the biblical understanding: "To begin with, it is important to note that the Bible does not employ a rigid distinction between the natural and the supernatural." *Providence of God*, 106. And finally, "Henri de Lubac's landmark deconstruction of baroque Christian theology, *Surnaturel*, showed us just how anthropomorphic a picture governed . . . theology's insistence on distinct 'natural and supernatural orders,' whereby creation is deemed a given arrangement into which God intervenes to inaugurate something new. Since we must affirm the oft-told story to represent our temporal perspective on God's eternal intent, the language which better respects both that intention and our perspective would speak of a 'fresh initiative' or a 'fuller disclosure' of God's providential care. In that way, the creator is affirmed to be active throughout, and we will be less tempted to use the metaphor of 'intervening' to describe God's action in history. Regarding this tendency of Jewish as well as Christian thinkers to canonize the perspective of 'salvation history' into a two-stage theology, Karl Barth issued a characteristically forthright corrective: 'the covenant is the goal of creation and creation is the way to the covenant.'" Burrell, *Freedom and Creation*, 142.

4. See chapter 10 for references and a fleshing out of the claim that God is not in a genus.

greatest—the first has only ten sides while the second has a thousand sides. But in a qualitative sense, the "gap" between a circle and all the other figures is the greatest—each of the other figures had sides and angles; circles have neither. No matter how many sides we add to a chiliagon, it will never become a circle. So too, the difference between God's existence and our existence is not one of degree (i.e., number of sides), but a difference in kind—one has sides; one does not.

In philosophical terms, this means that *existence* itself (not just the term) is analogical. To understand what this means, we need to connect the concept of analogical terms with the Great Chain of Being (see chapter 2). For Descartes, there were only two kinds of things—material substances and immaterial substances. For Aquinas, there were at least four, maybe five, kinds of things: 1) nonliving things (dirt and minerals); 2) living things (plants); 3) living things with consciousness (cats and dogs); 4) living things with both consciousness and intellect (humans). Finally, there is God, but again, Aquinas hesitates to think of God as something else that "exists."

One of the ideas that is so hard for post-Enlightenment people to understand is that when Aquinas speaks of the three different kinds of "souls"—"plant soul," "animal soul," and "human soul"—he is not talking about different kinds of substances that are added to dirt and minerals to turn them into plants, animals, and humans. Rather, the different "souls" merely name the distinct *abilities* of different kinds of things. For example, humans can reproduce like plants, and consciously experience the world like animals, but they can also *conceive* of things that they have never observed, like a chiliagon.

Or again, by the time children reach the age of three or four, they are all capable of understanding the concept of tomorrow. Now a smart dog can be taught to do all sorts of things, like going outside to fetch a newspaper.[5] But no dog can be taught to forego a short walk around the block *right now* and wait patiently for a much longer hike and a swim in the mountains *tomorrow*. And the problem is not that "tomorrow" is an especially complex notion, like the ones rocket science employs. Instead, the problem is that "tomorrow" is abstract, and thus, cannot be "pictured." It is this ability to think conceptually that enables humans to *do* things that no other animal

---

5. "But, given Aquinas's view of being and actuality, an increment in capacity or potentiality constitutes an increment in being; and, because of the supervenience of goodness on being, a species or genus with more capacities of the sort that show up in the differentiae will have potentially more goodness than one with fewer. So, other things being equal, the goodness of a human life is greater than that of a dog's just because of rationality, the incremental capacity." Stump, *Aquinas*, 75.

can do.⁶ It was these abilities to which Aquinas was referring when he said that humans *exist* at a higher level.

Contemporary self-help books frequently hint at something like this when they promise readers that if they faithfully put into practice what they read, then they will "be living at a higher level" or that they will be able to "transcend mundane existence." Even if we think that such language is a bit grandiose, the suggestion that there are various *degrees* of existence is not unintelligible. Both in self-help books and in Thomistic philosophy, "existence" is more like a light bulb with a dimmer switch that shines with various degrees of intensity, rather than one with a simple on/off switch.⁷ Or again, "existence" is like the many different kinds of polygons, from triangles to chiliagons. All of them are geometrical figures that enclose a definable area. But chiliagons do this "better" than triangles (because they can define a greater area with the same perimeter).

Now this last analogy is admittedly something of a stretch. But it helps explain why Aquinas would not attribute "existence" to both the Creator and the created. Circles not only enclose definable areas better than any other polygon; they do so in a *totally different way*—without using either sides or angles. So while Aquinas and Barth are willing to say in some loose sense that both humans and God "exist," they both insist that there is a radical difference in *how we* exist and *how God* exists, a difference so great as to warrant the description of "an infinite qualitative difference"—like the difference between a circle and a chiliagon.

Here's a final analogy. When we say, "Ric Machuga exists," and when we say "Barack Obama exists," we all acknowledge that there is a huge

---

6. Of course, this is a highly controversial claim. But notice what two of the most important evolutionary biologists say. In the context of evolutionary psychology explanations for altruism in nonhuman species, Stephen Jay Gould said that such arguments must fail because "all other species lack this special mental mechanism for spreading *abstract ideas* against the thrust of natural selection." *Structure of Evolutionary Theory*, 135, emphasis added. Mayr is even more direct: "Even though we often use the word 'language' in connection with the information transmittal systems of animals, such as the 'language of bees,' actually all of these animal species have merely systems of giving and receiving signals. To be a language, a system of communication must contain syntax and grammar. Psychologists have attempted for half a century to teach language to chimpanzees, but in vain. Chimps seem to lack the neural equipment to adopt syntax. *Therefore, they cannot talk about the future or the past.*" *What Evolution Is*, 253, emphasis added. I discuss the philosophical significance of these sorts of arguments in *In Defense of the Soul*, especially in chapter 9.

7. "The idea that something 'either exists or not,' without degrees of intensity of existing, is impossible for Aquinas, as it must still be for theology, since it implies a neutral, inert, meaningless, and uncreated existing as belonging to a thing in its own right." Milbank and Pickstock, *Truth in Aquinas*, 29. See also Miller, *Most Unlikely God*, 44.

difference in the power, authority, and honor between me and the president of the United States. But in another sense, there is no difference in the *existence* we share as human beings. He may be one of the most powerful persons in the world, but he and I are both people who exist.

But now consider the propositions: "Barack Obama exists," and "God exists." How do we think about the predicate ("exists") that is being applied to both Obama and God? Does it mean the same thing in both cases? Aquinas and Barth are adamant that it does not. The difference between the way God exists and the way Obama exists is a difference in kind, not degree. In fact, the difference is greater (infinitely greater) than the way Shakespeare exists and the way his most famous character, Hamlet, exists. Even though Shakespeare is a real historical figure and Hamlet is only a fictional character, both exist in space and time with observable height, facial features, hair color, etc.; and both could have learned to ride a bicycle. However, when we compare God's "existence" and Obama's "existence" the scare quotes are absolutely necessary. Only Obama exists in space and time; only Obama has an observable height, facial features, hair color, etc.; and only Obama can ride a bicycle. These contrasts between God's "existence" and Obama's "existence" are what Exodus 3:14 is signaling when it describes God as the great "I am"—all creatures *have* existence, but only God *is* existence; he does not share our existence; rather, he is the *source* of our existence.

The problem with thinking in terms of two distinct "realms"—the natural and the supernatural—is that no matter how many superlatives we add to our description of God, he and we will always share one common feature, namely, existence. Instead of focusing on the *existence* of God, we should focus on what God *does*, namely, create and sustain the entire universe. And he does this at all times and in all places, not just when and where he performs a miracle. In fact, it would be nice if we could ban the use of "existence" as a noun to describe one of God's attributes. The Author of creation doesn't *have* existence; he *does* existence. Unfortunately, talk about proving or disproving the existence of God (in the same way we talk about scientists proving the existence of black holes or the nonexistence of phlogiston) has become so ubiquitous that no linguistic prohibition will turn back the clock.[8]

---

8. Kant famously argued that the cosmological arguments for the existence of God (one version of which we consider in the final section of this chapter) ultimately reduces to Anselm's and Descartes's ontological argument. The fallacy of both, says Kant, was that they both mistakenly assume that "existence is a predicate." The irony here is that no philosopher was more insistent that "existence" is not a predicate (i.e., property) than Aquinas. See Davies, "Aquinas, God, and Being."

GOD AS AUTHOR OR CRAFTSMAN?

Descartes invented analytic geometry and Newton invented calculus, so it is not surprising that they both assumed that mathematics was the key to understanding the natural realm. Though there was a serious disagreement between followers of Descartes and followers of Newton about *what* a mathematical understanding of nature revealed, they both had theories of gravity. Descartes's theory assumed that a theory of gravity must provide an *understandable* model of how gravity worked. He did this by likening the action of gravity to the action of vortexes in water or air where all motion is by direct contact, one thing "pushing" something else. Newton, on the other hand, admitted up front that *how* gravity worked was mysterious. While many would mock the idea of "action at a distance," in essence he replied: "But my math works!" Newton's only goal was to *predict* how gravity affects everything from apples falling from trees to planets circling the sun. Largely because Newton's theory of gravity gave us more predictive power over nature than Descartes's vortex theory, Newton's theory is still studied in elementary physics courses while Descartes's has gone the way of phlogiston and phrenology.[9]

But power over nature was not all that Newton's theory provided. It also provided two arguments for the existence of God. First, while his theory of gravity precisely predicted everything from the motion of cannonballs to the elliptical orbit of the planets, there was nothing in the theory that could explain who set the planets on their initial course. Unless each planet were precisely placed and pushed, they would either crash into the sun or fly off into space. We already said that Newton described God as "very well skilled in mechanics and geometry." And we know that such a being must exist because only a divine Craftsman could make the necessary calculations "of the several distances of the primary planets from the sun and secondary ones from Saturn, Jupiter and the earth, and the velocities with which these planets could revolve at those distances about those quantities of matter in central bodies."[10] We will call this the "complexity" argument for the existence of God.

Newton's second argument for a supernatural Craftsman arose from a paradox that we have alluded to previously. Newton conceived of space as an infinite "container" with nothing in it. (We'll say more about this in the next chapter.) He also conceived of gravity as "instantaneously acting at a

---

9. The classic discussion of this difference is Koyre, *From the Closed World to the Infinite Universe*. For a textbook discussion, see Hetherington, *Planetary Motions*, 159-60.

10. Newton, Letter to Richard Bentley, December 10, 1692.

distance." This meant that every particle was exerting a "pull" on every other particle, even though there was no physical contact between particles and there was no lapse of time between the "pull" of one particle and the effect on the other particle. But if this is so, then shouldn't the entire universe collapse into a single gigantic mass? As we already mentioned, Newton's answer was Yes, but "least the system of fixed stars should, by their gravity, fall on each other, he [God] hath placed those systems at immense distances from one another."[11] While his critics thought such a response ad hoc, Newton thought that the "scientifically" inexplicable fact that the universe did not collapse was further evidence for a divine Craftsman. We'll call this the "gap" argument.

When you combine the complexity argument and the gap argument you get an Enlightenment conception of God, and with it comes the natural/supernatural distinction we've been discussing. Those characteristics of our universe that can be explained scientifically are natural. Those highly improbable features of our universe (like the precise placement of the planets and the irreducible complexity of the bacterial flagellum) and those rare events that cannot be explained scientifically (like the biblical miracles) were the Enlightenment's justification for belief in a supernatural God.

Now there is an obvious weakness with the gap argument: what is scientifically inexplicable in one decade or century frequently becomes scientifically explicable in the next decade or century. We saw one example of this in the first chapter. Newton's own inability to explain the stability of the orbits of Jupiter and Saturn was followed by Laplace's prodigious calculations of a stable, 926-year cycle of contraction followed by expansion. And today we have no problem explaining in a wholly scientific fashion why the universe doesn't collapse. Hubble's discovery of the red shift in the light coming from distant stars is best explained by an expanding universe, which in turn establishes a Big Bang in the distant past. And today we know that it is the force of the Big Bang (not divine intervention) that prevents the universe from collapsing on itself. The "god" that is established by the science of one generation is the same "god" that is disestablished by the science of the succeeding generation.

On the other hand, we shouldn't make too much of such an objection. It is true that science frequently explains today what it couldn't explain yesterday. But the converse is also true. Just as science explains one set of problems, new problems inevitably arise. For example, in Aquinas's generation the origin of life was "scientifically" unproblematic. The ability of the sun to spontaneously generate new life from the earth was taken for granted. But

---

11. Newton, *Principles*, 370.

in the nineteenth century Louis Pasteur demonstrated that "spontaneous generation" is in fact only the development of visible life out of microscopic life. Today the origin of that microscopic life—life itself—is much *more* problematic than it was in Aquinas's day.

And here's a second example. Prior to Newton, scientists believed that the celestial and terrestrial realms were governed by two distinct sets of laws—in the heavens, objects naturally moved eternally in perfect circles; here on earth, things naturally moved toward or away from the center of the earth until they came to their natural place of rest. One of the great triumphs of Newton's theory was its ability to unify these two distinct and unconnected explanations into a single unified theory.

But now scientists have a new problem: general relativity is very good at precisely predicting the motions of things which are very big and quantum mechanics is very good at describing the motions of things which are very small. Yet mathematically, the two theories are as distinct and unconnected (some even say incompatible), just as in the ancient theory of distinct celestial and terrestrial realms. It seems that as fast as some scientific "gaps" are closed, new "gaps" are opened. Aquinas would not have been surprised by the closing and opening of "gaps" in our understanding. In one of his popular expositions of the Apostle's Creed, he wrote: "If we were able by ourselves to know perfectly all things, visible and invisible, it would be foolish for us to believe what we do not see. But our knowledge is so imperfect that no philosopher has ever been able to discover perfectly the nature of a single fly."[12] In this comment, he is like the professor who tells his students: "I am absolutely confident that 90 percent of everything I'm teaching is true; it is just that I don't know what is included in the remaining 10 percent."[13] No one can know what they don't know. So until history ends, there will be no end to the opening and closing of scientific, philosophical, and theological gaps.

Let us now pivot and consider the older metaphor for God as the Author of creation.[14] It is common knowledge that Aquinas had "Five Ways" to prove the existence of God and that his fifth way concerned the teleological

---

12. Aquinas, *Three Greatest Prayers*, 13. And again, "the essence of a thing remains unknown to us." Aquinas, *On Truth*, 10.1. See also Josef Pieper, *In Defense of Philosophy*, 71.

13. In the jargon of contemporary philosophers, Aquinas was an epistemological externalist. That is, the justification of belief can not be found solely within the knower. There is nothing in consciousness (e.g., a "feeling" of certainty or seeing something "clearly and distinctly") that by itself can justify a belief. We will say more about this in chapter 12.

14. "God's knowledge stands to all created things as artists' to their products." Aquinas, *Summa Theologica* I.14.8.

ordering of nature. In his words, "We see that things which lack knowledge, such as natural bodies, *act for an end*.... Hence it is plain that they achieve their end not by chance, but by design [emphasis added]."[15] Aquinas's teleological argument is frequently (though mistakenly) thought to be the same as the "watchmaker argument" that William Paley made famous at the very beginning of the nineteenth century.

Paley argued that if one found a complex piece of machinery like a watch in the desert, even someone who had previously never seen a watch would have no doubt that it was designed. Things like watches are simply too *complex* to come about by chance. But the human eye is at least as complex and intricate as a watch. So who can rationally doubt that it, too, has an intelligent designer? The only difference in the two inferences is that the designer of the human eye is not another human, but rather a superhuman God. (Though Paley's name is frequently associated with the watchmaker argument, Newton deserves equal credit, since Paley merely took Newton's complexity argument for astronomy and applied it to biology.)

But in point of fact, Aquinas's argument is quite different from either Paley's or Newton's. There are two distinct kinds of *order* or *design*. First, there is the artist's ordering of paint on a canvas.[16] Second, there is the tile layer's ordering of tiles on a floor. Both of these require great skill, but the skills involved are quite different and are differently evaluated. It is not easy to order hundreds of tiles on a floor according to a preconceived pattern and have the spacing between tiles precisely the same. Nor is it easy to paint the Mona Lisa. But the expertise required is quite different.[17]

15. Ibid., I.2.3.

16. Here are Aquinas's own words: "God is the cause of things through his intellect and will just as an artist is the cause of things made. The artist works through an idea conceived in the intellect and through the love of his or her will related to something; so God the Father works in creatures through his Word, the Son, and through his love which is the Holy Spirit." *Summa Theologica*, I 45.6. And again, "... just as man the artist in the conception of his intellect comprehends the essences of all the products of art. Thus, then, all creatures are nothing but a kind of real expression and representation of those things which are comprehended in the conception of the divine Word; wherefore all things are said (John 1:3) to be made by the Word." Aquinas, *Summa Contra Gentiles* IV.42.3.

17. Here I am borrowing from Arthur Peacocke. "So when, loosely, entropy is said to be a measure of 'disorder' or 'randomness' it is... the kind of order exemplified by a perfect wall-paper pattern rather than that of an original painting." The rest of the quote will also be quite interesting to the scientifically inclined reader: "Such 'order' [i.e., of a wallpaper pattern] is therefore scarcely adequate as a measure of the complexity and *organization* of biological systems. Nevertheless it could be affirmed that the kind of *dis*order measured by entropy is incompatible with biological complexity and organization and, indeed, the state of maximum entropy, of maximum disorder in the sense defined, is equivalent to biological death. Thus, we may say that a state of low entropy

So too, the kind of order Aquinas sees in nature is quite different from the kind of order that Newton and Paley see in nature. Aquinas's argument is based on the *ordering* of means to an end (in this regard it is like a fine painting); Newton's and Paley's argument is based on mathematical *complexity* (in this regard it is like skillfully laid tiles). There is a crucial difference here. Aquinas's argument is based on irreducibly *qualitative* judgments; Newton's and Paley's arguments are based on mechanically *quantifiable* measurements. Their arguments also have distinct conclusions. Newton's and Paley's arguments concludes with a supernatural Craftsman; Aquinas's argument concludes with a divine Author. But before we flesh out and evaluate their respective arguments, we need to say more about our frequently invoked distinction between quantities and qualities.

QUANTITATIVE VS QUALITATIVE ARGUMENTS

Enlightenment thinkers love to count. Galileo famously admonished scientists "to measure what can be measured and to make measurable what cannot be measured."[18] If we can quantifiably measure something, then we think it is objectively real; if we can only describe something's qualities, we tend to dismiss it as merely a subjective fact about the preferences of the person doing the describing—or at least, that was the assumption of the logical positivists we considered in the previous chapter.[19]

---

is a necessary but not sufficient condition for biological complexity and organization to occur.... But the picture that is emerging in more recent thermodynamic analyses of dissipative systems and of living organism has a different tenor. Certainly the stream as a whole moves in a certain general, overall direction which is that of increasing entropy and increasing disorder, in the specific sense I have defined. However, the movement of the stream itself inevitably generates, as it were, very large eddies within itself in which, far from there being a decrease in order, there is an increase first in complexity and then in something more subtle—functional organization." Peacocke, "Chance and Law," 129, 143.

18. Quoted in Mayr, *Growth of Biological Thought*, 95. Unfortunately Mayr fails to cite his source and I have been unable to run down the reference. Nonetheless, I have no doubt that it is the sort of thing Galileo might well have said in his brasher moments. And it certainly captures in a succinct and memorable fashion the sentiment behind his famous words in the *Assayer*: "But the book [of nature] cannot be understood unless one first learns to comprehend the language and read the letters in which it is composed. It is written in the language of mathematics, and its characters are triangles, circles, and other geometric figures without which it is humanly impossible to understand a single word of it; without these, one wanders about in a dark labyrinth." Galileo, *Discoveries*, 238.

19. "The champions of quantification tend to consider the recognition of quality as something unscientific or at best as something purely descriptive and classificatory.

Aristotle, Aquinas, and pre-Enlightenment common sense all assumed the opposite.[20] As we said in chapter 2, it makes no sense to ask someone to count the number of keys in a room unless we first *specify* what is meant by "keys." Are we talking about keys to open locks, keys on a piano, keys on maps, or even pictorial representations of geographical formations like the Florida Keys? It makes even less sense to ask someone to count the number of *things* in a room. What counts as a "thing"? A desk is a thing, but so is each of its legs. So does a desk count as one thing or five things? Three marbles on a floor are things. But how many "things" are they? If we are counting round physical objects, then there are three things. But if we are counting triads, dyads, and monads, then there is one triad, three dyads, and three monads, a total of seven things. And of course, if we are counting molecules, then there are far more things.

It is hard to think of a word that is more equivocal than *thing*. It is only after we *specify* what we are to count that counting becomes possible. So what does it mean to speak of specific things?

"Specific" is a cognate of "species," and "species" is commonly used in reference to different kinds of plants and animals. This brings us back to our discussion in chapter 2 concerning *what* something is. We distinguish different species of animals because we assume they have different "what-nesses" or forms. Aristotle and Aquinas couldn't say much more about a thing's "whatness" or form other than there are irreducibly *qualitative* properties of rocks, plants, and animals that make them distinct *kinds* of things. Though these qualitative differences can be humanly recognized, they cannot be mechanically measured.

They reveal by this bias how little they understand the nature of biological phenomena. Quantification is important in many fields of biology, but not to the exclusion of all qualitative aspects." Mayr, *Growth of Biological Thought*, 55.

20. In this, Aristotle and Plato were in full agreement. "The true craftsman does nothing at random, but imposes upon his behavior a 'certain orderly arrangement,' [*Gorgias*, 503 E 4] which he 'has in view' from the very beginning. This constitutes the standard or measure, [*Statesman*, 284] by reference to which he measures his work at every stage. In the lower arts which deal with physical things, this measurement takes a quantitative form, as in building and stonecutting, where the work is done according to specifications of size, weight, length, etc. In the higher arts, which deal with non-physical structures (as education for example), measurement is qualitative, and the work is measured by the 'mean,' the 'fit,' the 'seasonable,' and 'what is required.' [*Statesman*, 284 E] It is a great mistake to suppose that these latter arts are therefore less 'exact' than those subject to quantitative measurement. [*Statesman*, 285] The form of the state, with reference to which the statesman measures his procedure, is not less 'exact' than the blueprint of the architect, though the former exacts a qualitative order of temporal acts rather than a quantitative order of spatial materials." Wild, *Plato's Theory of Man*, 47.

Enlightenment thinkers would balk. Different species of animals are specified by differences in their DNA, and DNA is something that *can* be "measured" by gene-sequencing machines. A simple Google search will turn up machine-produced pictures showing the genetic differences between species. And we can now literally count how many genes different species have in common and hence quantify their similarities.

Contemporary Aristotelians and Thomists, while in no way denigrating the wonders of modern technology, will argue that talk of "counting genes" misunderstands the problem. DNA is a code, and no code can be *understood* merely by taking its picture. Ernst Mayr, one of the principal formulators of the modern synthesis of genetics and evolution, put it like this: "Aristotle's *eidos* (Greek for 'form') is a teleonomic principle which performed in Aristotle's thinking precisely what the genetic program of the modern biologist performs."[21]

Codes, like words, are physical objects (or events, if the words are spoken) that convey meaning or information. (Notice again the root: in*form*ation.) What talk of "counting genes" misses is this: the meaning or information in a word or code can never be *reduced* to the physical properties of the object or event which embodies its meaning.[22] Consider, for example the following:

- Tool
- Instrumento
- Werkzeug

Though physically different, each conveys the same concept in English, Spanish, and German respectively. And while they each reflect photons quite differently and thus would produce quantitatively distinct results in any scientific instrument taking their measure, their *form* is the same, that is, they convey the same information.

Now in one sense, "information" is quantifiable. Every time someone sends an email or data file over the Internet we see a number quantifying how much "information" has been sent. But the "information" that Internet programs measure has nothing to do with the in*form*ation that specifies and makes something what it is, e.g., a word conveying the concept "Tool." And we know this for a very simple reason: while "Tool," "Instrumento," and "Werkzeug" all convey the same piece of in*form*ation, their "information"

---

21. Mayr, *Growth of Biological Thought*, 88.
22. See footnote 21 in chapter 2.

measured in bytes is not the same. "Tool" has four letters, "Instrumento" has eleven letters, and "Werkzeug" has eight letters.[23]

THE COMPLEXITY ARGUMENT FOR A DIVINE CRAFTSMAN

We can now bring the discussion back to Newton's and Paley's "complexity" arguments. "Complexity" and "information" as measured in bytes refer to the same thing; "complexity" and "in*form*mation" as the specification of *what* something is do *not* refer to the same thing. The premises of the argument for a supernatural Craftsman concern the statistical improbability of a highly complex object coming about by random chance. And there are standard quantifiable measurements for this sort of complexity, either in terms of the algorithmically compressible size of a file or in terms of entropy. So once we know how complex something is, then we can easily determine the probability of such an object coming to exist by random chance—the more complex something is, the less likely it is a product of random chance. That much seems intuitively obvious, and even a little boring.

What's exciting to contemporary Christian defenders of Newton and Paley is that modern science is discovering how astronomically complex our universe really is. If the initial explosion of the Big Bang had differed in strength by as little as 1 part in 10^{60}, the universe would have either quickly collapsed back on itself, or expanded too rapidly for stars to form. If gravity had been stronger or weaker by 1 part in 10^{40}, then life-sustaining stars like the sun could not exist. If the neutron were not about 1.001 times the mass of the proton, all protons would have decayed into neutrons or all neutrons would have decayed into protons, again making life impossible. The precise value of these numbers is not important. What is important is that by any estimation there are at least six (some scientists say up t twenty-five)

---

23. The argument of this paragraph is highly compressed. In chapter 7 of *In Defense of the Soul* I flesh it out in much more detail with respect to evolutionary biology. One of the reasons we must not confuse bytes with in*form*ation is that the concept "tool" is itself a product of human conventions; it does not describe a category in nature like DNA. Linguistic anthropologists can produce hundreds of examples of cultures with widely divergent concepts. My favorite is *ilunga*, a Bantu word, which means something like "a person who is ready to forgive any abuse for the first time, to tolerate it a second time, but never a third time." How are we supposed to quantify or measure the information conveyed by this single six-letter word? When biologists cracked the DNA code, they learned to read the information that was already *in* nature; when computers measure the bytes in a data file, they are merely counting symbols, not measuring information, since the symbols are themselves meaningless apart from the linguistic conventions of their particular culture.

universal constants which had to be *precisely* what they are for life as we know it to be possible.[24]

And even after a universe arises in which life is *possible*, the incredible complexities of even a single-cell organism, much less something like the human brain, make it astronomically improbable that humans evolved by random chance. Rather than being a foe of Christianity, it seems that modern science is turning out to be one of its greatest allies.

But can science really do the work of philosophy and theology? One of the standard objections to the complexity argument is that statistical probabilities say nothing about individual cases. The odds against any particular person living to be 122 are astronomically high. But Jeanne Calment (1875–1997) did it. In fact, the odds against *any* historical event being *just what it is* are astronomically high, yet history happens every day. So are we to say that the astronomically improbable happens every day?

Of course not, because probability statements are always about a class of events, not individuals within the class. No individual object or event considered *by itself* is probable or improbable.[25] Individuals are only probable or improbable relative to a class. It is only when we compare Jeanne Calment to the billions of other people who died before their one-hundred-and-twenty-second birthday that we look on her as being "special." But when we say that our universe is highly improbable, and thus "special," to what are we *comparing* it? The universe by definition is one, and hence, like any historical event, its probability is exactly 100 percent.[26]

The other standard objection to the complexity argument is that there is no scientific way to know how many *attempts* the universe had to develop

---

24. http://www.discovery.org/a/91.

25. "It is in fact one of the paradoxical features of probability laws that, while we have to derive the probabilities from the observation of sequences of occurrences, any occurrence is compatible with any postulated probability, for probability laws determine nothing whatever about any individual instance within their ambit." Mascall, *Importance of Being Human*, 16.

26. Some modern philosophers talk about "possible worlds," i.e., worlds that do not actually exist, but are in some sense "possible." If these philosophers are correct, then we could compare our *actual* universe with the class of all *possible* universes, and thereby assign a mathematical probability to the one and only actual universe. Our response is twofold: First, talk of "possible worlds" is a *philosophical* theory, and hence, it will not be modern *science* with its quantitative measurements that establishes the existence of a divine Craftsman. Second, talk of "possible worlds" is typically unpacked in terms of that which is *logically* possible. But then the number of possible worlds, like the number of whole numbers, will be infinite. That means that our actual universe will be not just highly improbable, but infinitely improbable. But wait! If the number of possible universes is infinite, then *any* universe will be infinitely improbable, including an utterly *simple* universe composed of a single undividable fundamental particle!

"by random chance." True, science can make quite good estimates about how long ago the Big Bang occurred. But it can say nothing about what, if anything, preceded it. Was the Big Bang the origin of *everything*, or, as many Hindus believe, was *our* particular Big Bang merely one of an infinite series of Big Bangs followed by a "Big Crunch"? This is a question that is beyond science, so no scientist can tell us anything about the statistical odds of our universe coming about by random chance. Again, if we are considering an infinite number of "attempts" (as Hindus believe), then the probability of our astronomically fine-tuned universe happening "by chance" is exactly 100 percent, i.e., it is statistically certain.

Though Aquinas never used the language of statistical probability, we can be quite certain that this is how Aquinas would have argued, because this is not a new debate. Saint Bonaventure, one of Thomas Aquinas's thirteenth-century contemporaries, argued that it was philosophically demonstrable that the universe was *not* infinitely old, but rather that it had a beginning. On the other hand, Averroes, an Islamic Aristotelian of the previous century, agreed with Aristotle that it was philosophically probable that the universe *was* infinitely old. Aquinas argued that both positions are mistaken. He argued that human reason and experience can neither prove nor disprove a beginning point for the universe; only divine revelation can speak to this question.[27]

However, our primary point here is not to refute Newton's and Paley's complexity argument—or its contemporary equivalent, i.e., the intelligent design movement—but to contrast it with what we'll call Aquinas's "divine In-former argument."

THE DIVINE IN-FORMER ARGUMENT

We have implicitly been pretty hard on Newton in this chapter. But in addition to his newly formulated "complexity argument," Newton also made mention of the much older argument for a divine In-former that goes back at least to Aquinas. Newton writes:

> Whereas the main business of natural philosophy [i.e., science] is to argue from phenomena without feigning hypotheses, and to deduce causes from effects, till we come to the very first cause, which certainly is not mechanical; and not only to unfold the mechanism of the world, but chiefly to resolve these and such like

---

27. "The newness of the world is known only by revelation; and therefore it cannot be proved demonstratively. . . . Hence it cannot be demonstrated that man, or heaven, or a stone did not always exist." Aquinas, *Summa Theologica* I.46.2.

questions... Whence is it that Nature doth nothing in vain; and whence arises all that order and beauty which we see in the world? ... And though every true step made in this philosophy brings us not immediately to the knowledge of the First Cause, yet it brings us nearer to it, and on that account is to be highly valued.[28]

The sentiments expressed here would have received a hearty "amen" from Aquinas. But Newton's language is slightly archaic and Aquinas's can be quite technical, so here we will engage in a "creative retrieval" of their arguments.[29]

We have already referred to the fact that DNA is a code containing information. About this there is little disagreement. But we must not equivocate on the meaning of "information." We are not here talking about the kind of "information" that can be measured in bytes. If we were, the "information" contained in Mt. Lassen would be orders of magnitude greater than the "information" contained in a DNA molecule, for the simple reason that Mt. Lassen is composed of trillions of times more atoms than any DNA molecule. So to specify the precise location of each and every atom in Mt. Lassen would take up much more space on the hard drive of a computer than to specify the precise location of each and every atom in a molecule of DNA. Instead, when we are talking about the "information" in DNA we are referring to the essentially *qualitative* property that DNA has when it is considered as a *code* or set of *instructions*.

Second, we assume that the information contained in any word, code, or set of instructions must be the product of a *mind*. As Michael Polanyi said,[30] it is not irrational to believe that over eons of time, rocks have randomly been rolling down the hillsides around South Wales in such a way that they look like:

WELCOME TO SOUTH WALES

But it is irrational to believe *on the basis of these rocks* that we are about to enter South Wales. If these rocks "tell us something," then they didn't get there by chance. And, conversely, if they got there by chance, then they don't "tell us" anything. Only minds, whether human or otherwise, can produce the kind of information conveyed by words, codes, and instructions.

Putting these two together, we have a very simple, yet decisive (if only hypothetical) argument for a divine In-former. It goes like this:

1. The DNA of dinosaurs contains information.

28. Newton, *Optics* III.1.28, 528–29.

29. "Creative retrieval" is Norris Clarke's description of his own way of reading Aquinas. I have learned much from him.

30. Polanyi, *Personal Knowledge*, 33.

2. Information requires a mind.

3. The information in the DNA of dinosaurs is not the product of human minds.

4. Therefore, it must be the product of a divine In-former.[31]

The logical validity of this syllogism is incontestable, so the only question is the truth of its premises. The truth of the first premise is assumed by all biology. And without this assumption, the fact that dinosaur eggs always produced dinosaurs—and never produced elephants—would be utterly mysterious and inexplicable. The truth of the second premise is simply the universal assumption of common sense illustrated by Polanyi's example of rocks rolling down the hillside. And the third premise is also an assumption of all modern biology, geology, and paleontology, if for no other reason than humans and dinosaurs never existed at the same time.

There are only two alternatives: we can (1) believe in science *and* a divine In-former or (2) we can disbelieve in science and disbelieve in a divine In-former. (Whether this second alternative is rational we will leave to the reader to decide.) But we cannot rationally believe in science and *not* believe that there is an Author of creation who in-formed DNA.

So here we have a very old argument for a divine In-former that is both simple and decisive. But it is not *logically* decisive, as a philosophical idealist like Descartes demands. Nor is it "scientifically" decisive as the logical positivists demand. It is only *hypothetically* decisive. That is, if we assume that the information in DNA is a good scientific explanation of how living organisms function, then we must also assume that there is a divine In-former. As we said earlier, science does not *prove* the existence of a divine Craftsman, but science does *assume* the existence of a divine Author capable of in-forming DNA.[32] So to be clear, we are not using the discoveries of modern science as premises in a philosophical argument. But we are making a philosophical argument about the conditions that make science possible.[33]

---

31. I defend this conclusion against numerous philosophical and scientific objections in chapter 10 of *Life, the Universe, and Everything*.

32. Actually, the divine In-former argument isn't tied to DNA—the fact that sodium *must* react violently when it comes in contact with water is all we need for the divine In-former argument. As we argued in chapter 2, causation is more than correlation. That "something more" is ground in the "whatness," quiddity, or form of sodium. Without these, all we could justifiably say is that there is a 100 percent *correlation* between sodium coming in contact with water and sodium reacting violently.

33. There is a large and interesting set of sources that argue *historically* for the connection between belief in God and the origins of modern science. Whitehead's *Science and the Modern World* is one of the first. Stanley Jaki's *Science and Creation* is one of

Finally, we must also be absolutely clear about how *little* this argument says about the God of the Bible. Returning to the chiliagon/circle analogy at the beginning of this chapter, we can say that the series from triangles to squares, to pentagons, ... to chiliagons, and, finally, to the circle is a *progression* pointing in a particular direction.[34] But if we lived in a world in which there were no curves, only lines and angles, then it would be extremely difficult to understand what a circle might be. Only if one were given a "new life" in a world with lines, angles, *and* curves, and only *after* we had acquired this "new life" could we with hindsight fully understand the qualitative "jump" from chiliagons to circles.

This chapter has been wholly philosophical; the next will be more theological.[35] Philosophical knowledge relies only on first-hand experience that is equally available to everyone. Theological knowledge relies primarily on the testimony of those few who have been given a glimpse into another way of existing—a new way of existing, so to speak, which includes lines, angles, *and* curves.

---

the most detailed. And many of T. F. Torrance's books are among the most theologically informed arguments for the historical connection between "faith" and "science." His *Divine and Contingent Order* is a good place to begin.

34. "But the object itself—God's truth in His revelation as the basis of the veracity of our knowledge of God—does not leave us any option but to resort to this concept [analogy]. . . . And, pressed again by the true revelation of God, we are pushed on the word 'analogy.'" Barth, *Church Dogmatics* II.1, 225, 226. Neither we nor Barth are herein talking about the "analogy of being" as a "point of contact" between God and humans. See the "Excursus on Natural Theology" in the next chapter for further details.

35. "It is one thing to amass reason why someone might be constrained to acknowledge his [God's] existence. Such activity is neither religious nor properly theological for it does not pretend to deal with God in himself. Rather it is a means of leading to a point whence a person will have to entertain the subject seriously." Burrell, *Aquinas: God and Action*, 12.

—5—

God, Miracles, and Good Reasons

Though mechanistic philosophy has been largely discredited, many Christians still view the world in surprisingly mechanistic terms. Like Newton, they assume that most of what happens is explainable with "laws of nature," it is just that God occasionally "suspends" these laws. Miracles are thus thought of as supernatural interventions that make things happen that otherwise wouldn't. Aquinas and Barth reject this natural/supernatural dichotomy. Instead of thinking in terms of mono-causation, they think in terms of dual-causation.

C. S. Lewis was once asked how an intelligent man like himself could believe in the devil. He said that he couldn't, at least, if by "devil" one meant someone who dresses in red, carries a pitchfork, and is permanently surrounded by fire. It seems that something similar has happened with belief in God, and we are not just referring to God pictured as a grandfatherly figure, with a long white beard, who lives on top of clouds. A divine Author is not the same as a divine Craftsman. Believing in a divine Craftsman *and* modern science has its difficulties; believing in a divine Author *and* modern science does not.

GOD IS NOT A PART OF THE UNIVERSE

One of the problems associated with belief in a divine Craftsman is that such a belief is surprisingly dependent on a mechanistic understanding of how the world works. Like Newton, those who believe in a divine Craftsman implicitly assume that most of what happens in the world is explicable according to the "laws of nature," but occasionally God intervenes to "suspend" these laws. Though they would be the first to insist that "supernatural" and "natural" do not refer to something like the upper and lower floors of a house, they nonetheless insist that God's acts *change* nature to make things happen that otherwise wouldn't.

Answers to prayer, the miracles of the Bible, the "fine tuning" of the universe, and God's empirically detectable hand in the evolutionary process are all cited as examples where God's actions "make a difference." Without this sort of *interaction* between God and his creation, it is argued, we would be left with the aloof gods of pagan Greece and Rome or perhaps even the deistic God of many Enlightenment thinkers. If God makes no difference in the realm of nature, then what good is he? And the converse is also true. If our prayers and worship "make no difference" to God, then what good are they?

This is probably the majority conception of God within the church today. It is also the conception of God that is the target of the New Atheists. It is not hard to understand why. Today's scientists—whether or not they are professing Christians—assume what is called "methodological naturalism." This is the working assumption that while it is logically possible that God occasionally "suspends" the laws of nature, divine intervention is *not* a solution to a scientific question. When Newton invoked "God" as the guarantor of a stable universe he violated this principle. It is precisely this sort of violation that Sidney Harris famously satirized in his cartoon "Then a Miracle Occurrs."

Of course, defenders of a divine Craftsman will correctly point out that not all questions are scientific. So the fact that there are no *scientific* reasons to believe in such a God says nothing about the philosophical or theological reasons for believing that God occasionally intervenes in the natural realm. There is nothing unreasonable in thinking that a God who *creates* the laws of nature might temporally suspend these same laws if it suits his purposes.

But such a God is not the God of either Aquinas or Barth. Nor, as we argued in the last chapter, is this the sort of God that is *presupposed* by science.[1] The Author of creation is the kind of God who, in one sense, *never*

---

1. Again, to say that a divine In-former is presupposed by science is not to say that it is *consciously* presupposed. Riding a bicycle would be impossible were it not for the angular momentum of its spinning wheels—just try balancing on a bike when it is not moving! However, children learn to ride bicycles long before they know anything about the physics of bike riding. So too, many people learn how to *do* science without ever giving a moment's thought to the philosophical presuppositions for what they are doing.

"makes a difference" in the realm of nature. But, then, in another sense, he *always* "makes a difference." And this is not as paradoxical as it initially sounds. Shakespeare the author never appears in *Hamlet* as a character to "make a difference." But at the same time, though in a different sense, Shakespeare the author makes all the difference in the world, since without him, the world of *Hamlet* would not exist. An intervening divine Craftsman makes a difference *in* the world; a divine Author makes a difference *to* the world.

Here's another way of putting it: When a divine Craftsman *makes* something happen, pre-existing things change. But when the divine Author *creates* the universe, there is nothing to change! Aquinas puts it like this:

> God's action, which is without pre-existing matter and called creation, is neither a motion nor a change, properly speaking.... In the action which is creation, nothing potential pre-exists to receive the action.... Again, in every change or motion there must be something existing in one way now and in a different way before.... But where the whole substance of a thing is brought into being, there can be no same thing existing in different ways, because such a thing would not itself be produced, but would be presupposed to the production. Hence creation is not a change.[2]

Even though the act of creation changes nothing, the Author of creation is the very antithesis of the aloof gods of Greece and Rome or the deistic God of some Enlightenment thinkers. One of Newton's own thought experiments will help sort out the difference.

Newton asks us to imagine that the entire universe is composed of a single indivisible particle. In one sense this is difficult, but in another sense it is easy. Scientists tell us that our universe is composed of about 10^{80} fundamental particles. That's a big number, so in some sense it is difficult to "think away" most of the universe by pretending that it is composed of a single particle. Mathematicians, on the other hand, tell us that the ratio of the circumference of a circle to its radius is approximately 3.1415926535897093. This, too, is a big number in the sense that the numbers behind the decimal can be expanded indefinitely. So imagining it to be different is also difficult. But these are not comparable acts. It is one thing to imagine the size and

---

2. Aquinas, *Summa Contra Gentiles* II.17. Burrell explains it like this: "the best way of securing the difference between an act of creation, which presumes nothing at all, and an ordinary making—at least on Aristotle's analysis of coming-to-be—is to remind one that there is no motion (or change) involved in the activity of creating. And if no alternation is involved, there is no way of our grasping the activity since literally nothing is 'going on.'" Burrell, *Freedom and Creation*, 40.

composition of the universe to be different than it is; it is something quite different to image the ratio of the radius to the circumference of a circle to be different than it is.

These are distinct and different acts of the imagination because pi is a strictly mathematical term. Imagining it to be different from what it actually is would be like imagining a time or place where 2 + 2 = 5. No one can form a mental image of such a time or place without, so to speak, cheating like a magician who says "abracadabra" and then slips another card into the hat without anyone else noticing.

On the other hand, imagining the number of fundamental particles in the universe to be different than it actually is does not require this sort of "cheating," since the number of particles in the universe is not mathematically determined.[3] Our concept of a bicycle tells us in advance that it must have exactly two wheels. But the only way we can know how many tables are in an auditorium is to look and see since there is nothing about the concept of either "table" or "auditorium" that tells us in advance how many will be present. So too, there is nothing about the concept of a universe that tells us in advance how many particles it must have. The only way to determine the number of particles in our universe is through careful observation. So, imagining the universe to be much smaller—so small that it is composed of only a single particle—is no harder than forming a mental image of a unicorn, i.e., a one-horned, horse-like animal.

Now here is Newton's crucial question: If there is only a single particle in the universe, is it possible for that particle to *move*? Newton thought it was; Aristotle, Aquinas, and Einstein thought it was not. Here's why.

Newton's theory of gravity is a theory about what happens in *absolute* space and time. Newton thought of space and time as "absolutes" because he said that they did not presuppose the existence of anything else; they were thought to exist all by themselves and on their own. Space was conceived to be an infinitely large *empty* container. And time (though this is trickier) was conceived to be a river with *nothing in it* that forever flowed at a constant rate. With these conceptions of space and time, it is not difficult to imagining a *single* particle moving. Even if there is only a single particle, that particle could move "through" absolute space at either a constant or accelerating "velocity" as measured by absolute time.

Many people still think about space, time, and motion in Newtonian terms. And hence, they find it fairly easy to follow Newton's reasoning. Aristotle, Aquinas, and Einstein, however, held a radically different conception

---

3. As we will see in chapter 6, hard-core Platonists would disagree. But consideration of their objections will have to wait.

of space, time, and motion.[4] They all denied the existence of absolute space, and instead argued that space is itself a relative term. In this respect, they thought of "space" as analogous to words like "father" or "taller than." "Taller than" requires two terms to make a sentence. "Tom is taller than Sally" is a sentence; "Tom is taller than" is not a sentence. "Father" also requires two terms. "Tom is the father of Sally" is a sentence; "Tom is father" is not a sentence. So too, Aristotle, Aquinas, and Einstein argued that "space" requires two terms. "There is space between points A and B" is a sentence; "There is space" is not a sentence. So, if "space" is itself a relative term, then unless two things with physical dimensions of height, breadth, and width *exist*, there is no space.

Now everyone agrees that motion is a relative term. X can move closer to Y or farther from Y, but X can't move relative to nothing. Even Newton thought a single particle could only move *relative* to absolute space. Conversely, if absolute space does not exist, then it is impossible to conceive of one thing moving, just as it is impossible to conceive of 2 + 2 = 5.

GOD IS TOO CLOSE TO INTERVENE

So what does all this say about our two different conceptions of God? First, we can only think of creation as a "change" if we also believe in the existence of absolute space, since without absolute space, there is nothing to change. It makes no sense to say that once "space" was empty but now it is not unless "space" somehow exists in and of itself. Second, we can only think of God as occasionally intervening in his creation if both God and the universe exist within the same realm of absolute space and time. Newton thought God could *change* the orbits of Jupiter and Saturn to make them stable only because he thought God, Jupiter, and Saturn all occupy absolute space and time.

But, it makes no sense to conceive of the Author of creation *intervening* in, or making a *change* to, "the realm of nature" because God shares no space or time with anything he creates. This is what it means to say that the Author of creation transcends space and time. And, yet, to transcend creation is the very antithesis of being aloof and distant. Nothing can be more immanent and near to creation than the Creator who sustains its very

---

4. "The creation of the universe out of nothing involves the creation of space and time as well, which means that they are to be regarded as orderly features of empirical processes or events within the universe and not as detached empty 'containers.'" Torrance, *Divine and Contingent Order*, 3.

existence at every moment. As Aquinas says, "existence is more intimately and profoundly interior to things than anything else."[5] To say that God does not intervene in his creation is not to say that he doesn't care for his creation, but that the Creator is "so near" to his creation that the language of "intervention" becomes senseless. Here's why.[6]

Unless one believes in absolute space, the *interaction* between the natural and supernatural realms makes no sense. Only if absolute space exists can we mentally divide it into two realms—a natural realm filled with all physical (dimensional) objects and a supernatural realm filled with dimensionless spirits. Furthermore, both the natural and the supernatural must be pictured as existing *in* absolute space. How else can we imagine some sort of commerce between these two realms?

But Aristotle and Einstein, for philosophical and scientific reasons, respecctively, rejected the ideas of both absolute space and absolute time. They argued that space, time, and physical motion were all *relative* to each other. Space exists where physical objects exist—if there were no physical objects, then neither would space exist.[7] And without absolute space, motion can only be understood as the relative motion between two physical objects. Therefore, time must also be relative because it can only be conceived of as a measure of physical motion—if there were no physical things to move, then time itself would not exist.[8]

---

5. *Summa Theologica* I.8.1.

6. "As one might also put it, the continued existence of anything other than God depends on God as a causal agent, but not as one who causes by acting on anything. God, so we might say, cannot make any difference to anything. And this will not be because he is feeble or distant. It will be because he is present to everything as making it to be for as long as it exists." Davies, "Modern Defense of Divine Simplicity," 556. Or as David Burrell puts it: "What do we know [about how God acts]? At once very little yet a great deal. Aquinas offers us a handy formula: there is no difference between God's conserving activity and God's creating, other than the proviso that creating presumes nothing at all to be already present (ST 1.101.1). In other words, all of God's activity partakes of creating: all that God can do is to create; God does not 'fiddle' or 'micro-manage.' If we add to this Thomas's theorem that the 'proper effect of the universal cause of all things is things' existing' (ST 1.45.5), then God's activity in the world is ever an instance of or a consequence of bestowing existing (*esse*)." Burrell, *Freedom and Creation*, 68.

7. "Physical objects" is here being used broadly to include electromagnetic and gravitational fields.

8. "There would have been no time if there had been no creation to bring in movement and change." Augustine, *City of God* 11.6. Or as Barth puts it, "Time is the form of creation in virtue of which it is definitely fitted to be a theatre for the acts of divine freedom." *Church Dogmatics* II.1, 456.

Aquinas reached the same conclusion. "Time is properly the measure of motion; eternity is properly the measure of existing as such."[9] But being a Christian, he had another reason for rejecting the ideas of absolute space and time. Aquinas (following Aristotle) assumed that nothing is in our intellect that is not first in our senses. We are, after all, rational *animals*, and like all animals our initial understanding of the world must *begin* with input from one or more of the five senses. While angels can intuitively understand the world without sensual images, humans are not angels. But we are not *merely* animals. Though our understanding always begins with what we can see, hear, feel, taste, or smell, it does not end there. Having intellects, humans can *understand* that which cannot be *imagined*. As we argued in the previous chapter, humans can understand what a chiliagon is and we can understand what "tomorrow" means, but it is impossible to form a mental image of either. And according to Aquinas, the same is true of the Author of creation. We can pray to him and we can worship him, but we must never try to *imagine* him. That's why Moses was given the second commandment.

So our first point is this: the idea of God as a supernatural being who occasionally intervenes in the realm of nature comes from an Enlightenment (Newtonian) conception of God. Yet, as we argued in the first three chapters, science itself has moved beyond a mechanistic conception of the world. So why should we continue to conceive of God as one who occasionally intervenes in his creation to do what "nature" is incapable of doing by itself?

Besides, such an Enlightenment conception of God places an unnecessary stumbling block in the path of many very intelligent people. St. Paul likens the church to a body. It is neither right nor helpful for the feet to tell the eyes how to see; or conversely, for the eyes to tell the feet how to walk. So too, it is neither right nor helpful for Christians to tell scientists how they should be doing their work. It's like the eyes giving instruction to the feet on how to walk.

Our second point is this: the idea of God as divine Author is a more biblically and philosophically defensible than the Enlightenment conception of God as divine Craftsman. While authors and craftsmen are both, in some sense, creators who make things happen, in another sense, they create in very different ways. Craftsmen make things out of other parts of their own world. Craftsmen are as much a part of the physical world as are the tables and chairs they make. Authors, on the other hand, are not a part of the world they create. This is especially true of science fiction writers, but it is also true of novelists or playwrights. In one sense, all the characters

---

9. Aquinas, *Summa Theologica* I.10.4.3.

in *Hamlet* (with the possible exception of the ghost at the beginning) and Shakespeare all inhabit the same temporal and spatial world. But in another sense, they live in quite different "worlds." Hamlet lives in the feudal world of twelfth-century Denmark; Shakespeare lived in the world of sixteenth-century Elizabethan England.

And lest we think that there is still some sort of temporal and spatial continuity between their worlds, remember that Shakespeare lived four centuries *after* the character he created. While we can understand what it means to say that a mother was very young when she gave birth to her first child, we cannot understand what it means to say that a mother gave birth *before* the mother herself was born. Yet we have no difficulty understanding how it is that Shakespeare created or "fathered" characters who "lived" before Shakespeare himself was born. We can do this because we do *not* assume a spatial or temporal continuity between authors and their characters.

Contrast this with the craftsman/product relation. Such a relation demands some sort of spatial and temporal continuity. The table that a craftsman makes can't exist prior to the birth of the craftsman. And typically a craftsman has some sort of physical contact with his product, though today the physical continuity may be only indirect, as when a highly skilled craftsman programs a machine to do the physical cutting and shaping.

But God is not a cutter and shaper. St. Paul says that God "calls into existence the things that do not exist" (Rom 4:17). Craftsmen always work on that which already exists. Authors, on the other hand, come much closer to creating worlds and characters that did not previously exist.

DUAL-CAUSATION

In the last chapter, we had much to say about the problems caused by the assumption of mono-causation. Now we are in a position to flesh out the alternative—dual-causation.

Conceiving of God as a Craftsman or as an Intelligent Designer who works in an empirically detectable fashion assumes a philosophically truncated understanding of causation.[10] Ever since Galileo's experiments with inclined planes, moderns have tended to think of causation on the model of billiard balls. On this model, one ball can make another ball move only through physical contact. Not only does this model of causation assume

---

10. For an excellent review of how contemporary science has expanded the truncated understanding of causation bequeathed to us by the Enlightenment see Dodds, *Unlocking Divine Action*, ch. 4.

physical continuity, it also assumes that the cause must temporally *precede* the effect.

Prior to the Enlightenment the idea of an "efficient cause" (i.e., that which makes something happen) was much richer and more inclusive. Back then it meant something like "the responsible agent." The master architect, for example, was said to be the cause of a cathedral for which he was responsible. Yet no one thought that the master architect physically cut and placed each and every stone in the cathedral. Nor did being the responsible agent imply that the cause must temporally precede the effect. When a cathedral stands upright because of the flying buttresses at its sides, it is the buttresses that are responsible for holding up the cathedral, not vice versa.[11] Yet, the temporal relation between the buttresses (cause) and the cathedral standing (effect) is one of simultaneity—they are erected at the same time—it is not one where the cause temporally precedes the effect.[12]

So while billiard ball causation is an example of mono-causation, responsible-agent causation is an example of dual-causation. If a cue ball causes an eight ball to move, then ipso facto some other ball did not cause the eight ball to move. That is what we mean when we say mono-causation. But if a master architect was the responsible agent for the building of a cathedral, then that in no way denies the existence of many other workers who participated in the actual cutting and placing of the stones. Dual-causation allows for the existence of *both* primary and secondary causation.

Notice, too, that the assumption of mono-causation is crucial for the "gap" and "complexity" arguments we considered in the last chapter. The existence of supernatural actions is "empirically detectable" *only* when no wholly scientific explanation is possible. The assumption of the gap and complexity arguments is that if science can explain something, then the God hypothesis is null; but conversely, if science cannot explain something, then the God hypothesis is necessary; and hence, God's actions are said to be "empirically detectable."

Mono-causation is also assumed whenever miracles are conceived of as supernatural interventions that change the natural course of events. For

---

11. "Since men are accustomed to think about acts of production of the type that involve physical change, they do not readily grasp the fact that an agent cause need not precede its effect in duration." Aquinas, *On the Eternity of the World*. Quoted in Bourke, *Aquinas' Search for Wisdom*, 174.

12. One reason, at least for Christians, that we mustn't assume that causation requires temporal succession is that it would make the relations in the Trinity unintelligible. The classic creeds always describe Jesus as the Son of God who was begotten, not made, that is, while the Father "begets" (or in Barth's language "establishes"; see *Dogmatics in Outline*, 44) the Son, there was never a time in which God the Father existed without God the Son. And the same is true of the Holy Spirit.

example, when a child is born we may *metaphorically* speak of the "miracle of life."[13] But this is not the sort of event that gap and complexity theorists point to as evidence of an Intelligent Designer. Instead, they point to events like the sudden turning of water into wine or walking on water; there is no scientific explanation for such occurrences. Without the assumption of mono-causation, it would not be possible to argue that *since* there is no physical cause for water suddenly turning to wine, or for Jesus being able to walk on water, there *must* be a supernatural cause.

But Aquinas, Barth, and the Bible do not think in terms of mono-causation. Instead, they think in terms of dual-causation,[14] or as Aquinas would say, in terms of primary and secondary causes. The master architect is the primary cause of a cathedral, in the sense that he directs and is responsible for all that takes place. Yet, at the same time, there are many secondary causes—stonecutters, mechanics, window glazers, etc.—who participate in, and make real contributions to, the building of a cathedral. When the Bible says that God "calls into existence things that are not" and then goes on to "set his people free," it is not saying that a supernatural Craftsman made a *change* to absolute space and then, many years later, physically *intervened* to set his people free. Instead it is saying that God is the *responsible agent* for both the universe's very existence and the freeing of the Israelites from Egyptian bondage.[15]

Notice what the Bible says in Exodus: "The LORD drove the sea back by a strong east wind . . . and the waters were divided" (14:21). If we imagine that modern-day meteorologists were present at the exodus, it would in no way detract from the miraculous nature of God's action if they explained

---

13. Interestingly, the event that Barth consistently (and insistently!) points to as the paradigm of a miracle is one which is also quite common—a sinner placing his or her faith in Christ alone. Every conversion of a sinner is a miracle, says Barth, because without the gracious work of the Holy Spirit no one would ever place their hope in Christ's atoning death and resurrection. We will say much more about this in subsequent chapters.

14. For the use of the term "dual-causation" in connection with Barth, see Hunsinger, *How to Read Karl Barth*. Barth's own term was "the divine accompanying." *Church Dogmatics* III.3, 90. Likewise, Mayr uses the same term in a biological and "scientific" context. See *What Makes Biology Unique?*, 30.

15. Barth puts it like this: "But in the case of a miracle God is not different from what He is otherwise. The power in which God is Lord over all created powers is in itself one and the same power, whether God uses and manifests it for us in the usual or in an unusual way. . . . According to the testimony of the Bible, it is not a matter of setting up a second *ordo extra ordinem* [extraordinary order], or the establishing of a special world of miracle in and alongside the remaining world of nature and history. . . . Miracle reveals the richness and comprehensiveness of the divine ordering of things, but not that God sets aside or destroys His own order." *Church Dogmatics* II.1, 539–41.

what happened in terms of a particularly strong weather front. Affirming that God was the responsible agent (primary cause) of the Israelites' freedom is not—on the model of dual-causation—to deny that a particularly strong and fast-moving weather front was the secondary cause of Israel's freedom.

Recall how we began the previous chapter with Isaiah's words describing what happened when the Assyrians were camped outside of Jerusalem: "Then the angel of the LORD set out and struck down one hundred and eighty-five thousand in the camp of the Assyrians" (Isa 37:36). If we imagine that a modern-day epidemiologist was present, is there any reason to assume that they would not also be able to explain the sudden death of the Assyrian soldiers in terms of a sudden outbreak of cholera or some other disease? And while Isaiah makes no explicit mention of the secondary causes through which God worked, the ancient Hebrews certainly understood the deadly effects of "camp disease."[16] So here again, to argue that it was *really* cholera that killed the Assyrians (and not the hand of God) presupposes a theory of mono-causation, i.e., that if cholera was the physical cause of the Assyrians' death, then God wasn't.

Finally, consider the story in the New Testament that St. Luke tells of Paul and Silas sitting in an imperial prison when "suddenly there was an earthquake, so violent that the foundations of the prison were shaken; and immediately all the doors were opened and everyone's chains were unfastened" (Acts 16:25). Here Luke makes explicit reference to the earthquake that broke open the doors of the prison. Yet it is also clear that Luke is assuming a theory of dual-causation, where it is God who is the responsible agent behind the freeing of Paul and Silas, while the earthquake is only the secondary cause he used to achieve his ends. The miracle remains, even if it was the earthquake that *physically* opened the doors. Only if we *assume* an Enlightenment theory of mono-causation has the miracle been "explained away."[17]

---

16. Though Isaiah 10:16 does *explicitly* say that Yahweh "will send wasting sickness among his [Assyria's] stout warriors."

17. Once the notion of dual-causation is named and made explicit, it will be found throughout the Old and New Testaments. Here are some of the other passages from Isaiah where God is the primary cause and humans are real secondary causes: "Ah, Assyria, the rod of my anger, the staff of my fury!" (10:5). "Thus says the LORD . . . who brings forth chariot and horse, army and warrior" (43:16–17); "Thus says the LORD to his anointed, to Cyrus, whose right hand I have grasped, to subdue the nations before him and ungird the loins of kings" (45:1). Elsewhere, Isaiah describes God as using the forces of nature to bring about his intended results, e.g., "For I am the LORD your God, who stirs up the sea so that its waves roar—the LORD of hosts is his name" (51:15). Psalm 65 is full of similar language: "You still the roaring of the seas, the roaring of their waves, and the clamor of the peoples." In 2 Samuel 24:15–17 and Numbers 25:9 God is described as using pestilences and plagues to bring about his goals. In Amos 9:1 God

So why do so many modern Christians assume an Enlightenment conception of God that defines miracles as supernatural *interventions*? As we have alluded to several times, the assumption seems to be that if God never intervened, then that would mean that he was an aloof and uncaring God. But this objection misunderstands the Creator/creation relation. The reason we shouldn't think of miracles as God's interventions is *not* that God is too far removed from his creation. Instead, it is the exact opposite—God is so near, so interior, so much the primary cause and responsible agent for *everything* in his creation that it makes no sense to think that he *occasionally* intervenes. How can one who is present *at every moment* intervene? How can a playwright intervene in a play when he is responsible for *everything* that happens? Fred can *intervene* in Sally's life because Fred and Sally are two independent people. But what sense would it make to say that Fred *intervenes* in Fred's own life?

And when we move from the question of miracles to the act of creation, the idea of mono-causation becomes even more problematic. God is the creator; all Christians affirm this. But true creation—the calling into existence of that which does not exist—makes no sense if one assumes a theory of mono-causation *unless* one also assumes the existence of absolute space and time. If God exists alongside of, or even within, absolute space and time, then it makes sense to say that at $time_1$ nothing physical existed, that at $time_2$ God chose to create, and then at $time_3$ physical stuff existed where it previously had not. But if space and time do not exist *until* God creates, then the temporal sequence of the previous sentence ($time_1$, $time_2$, and $time_3$) makes no sense. Again, we must move beyond an Enlightenment conception of creation.

The problem with thinking of creation in these specifically Newtonian terms is that it invites all sorts of questions that should not be asked. First, there are the purely scientific questions about what it *means* to say that two events occur at the same time in different regions of space. The problem here is that our best scientific observations and theories demonstrate that nothing can travel faster than light. (This is the light cone problem we mentioned in chapter 1.) Second, there are the philosophical questions about what it means to treat nothing ("empty and boundless space") as if it were something into which other things were placed. Talk of "nothing" (absolute space) as being "something" is at best problematic.

---

says to those who do evil thinking that they can hide from God, "I shall command the serpent and it shall bite him." In Deuteronomy 8:18 God reminds his covenant people that it is he who "gives you power to get wealth." Likewise, in the New Testament, "for every house is built by someone, but the builder of all things is God" (Heb 3:4).

Finally, assuming that God creates *in* space and time (as opposed to literally creating space, time, and everything contained within them) invites all sorts of theological questions which should not be asked. Is the color blue heavier or lighter than the color red? The only good answer to such a question is to reject the premise. So too, we should reject the premise if asked: "What was God doing *before* he chose to create?"; "Does God know *before* a person acts what she will do?"; "If God knows beforehand what a person is going to pray for, then why bother praying?"

"Before" God created, there was no physical stuff, hence there could be no motion, and without motion there is no time. And while God knows events that happen *in* time (e.g., that Fred does A before he does B) that does not mean that God himself is in a *temporal* relation with his creation.[18] The fact that I see that a ball is blue doesn't mean that my eyes are blue. So too, that fact that God "sees" the sequence of events *in time*, doesn't mean that he is "in time." No, the relation between temporal objects and God is always and only one of Creator and creature. And the fact that God gives all his good gifts "from eternity" doesn't mean that prayer is superfluous.[19] Some of his good gifts he gives *because* of prayer. And remember, the "because" relation need not be a temporal relation—The cathedral stands upright *because* of the buttresses, even though the buttresses were not in place *before* the cathedral stood. (We will flesh this argument out much further in chapter 9.)

In sum, God's act of creation exhibits a power far surpassing anything scientists could ever imagine. Yet, we must always remember: not only did God create "out of nothing," but his act of creation *changed* nothing. What does this mean? How can it be understood? How can a power surpassing anything known to science *change* nothing?

Here we must heed the admonition of Robert Boyle, frequently called the father of modern chemistry:

> When I say that spirit is incorporeal substance . . . if he should answer, that when he hears the words incorporeal substance, he imagines some aerial or other very thin, subtle, transparent body, I shall reply, that this comes from a vicious custom he has brought himself to, of imagining something whenever he will conceive anything, though of a nature incapable of being truly represented by any image in the fancy [imagination]. . . . Because

---

18. "God's will is altogether unchangeable. All the same note that to change your will is one matter, and to will a change in some things is another." Aquinas, *Summa Theologica* I.19.7.

19. Do our prayers, acts of worship and charity, etc. "make a difference to God"? Clarke writes, "Difference (could have been otherwise, this rather than that) does not logically imply change (*this* after *that*)." Clarke, *Philosophical Approach to God*, 134.

the use of imagining, whenever we would conceive things, is so stubborn an impediment to the free acting of the mind, in cases that require pure intellection, it will be very useful, if not necessary, to accustom ourselves not to be startled or frighten with every thing that exceeds or confounds the imagination, but by degrees to train up the mind to consider notions that surpass the imagination and yet are demonstrable by reason.[20]

GOOD REASONS ARE NOT ALWAYS CONVINCING REASONS

As chapter 4 ended, there may have been a few howls of incredulity at our conclusion that without a divine In-former, science would make no sense. Thus far we have been in partial agreement with the New Atheists. Because God has so frequently been modeled after a superhuman Craftsman or an Intelligent Designer who occasionally intervenes to supply what science cannot, it is understandable that some scientists and philosophers might be incredulous, and even a little angry, at those who argue that science presupposes God.

Nonetheless, we will not shy away from our claim that the success of the scientific enterprise is itself a *good* reason to believe in a divine In-former, though now we will add that *good* reasons must not be construed to mean *convincing* reasons. Having good reasons to believe in either God or black holes is not the same as being able to convince people that either God or black holes exist. Earlier we said that many people know how to ride a bicycle without understanding any of the physics that make bicycle riding possible. Similarly, good reasons can exist even if most people don't understand what those good reasons are.[21] We will begin with a true story.[22]

20. Quoted in Edwin Burtt, *Metaphysical Foundations of Modern Physical Science*, 183–84.

21. Barth says something similar to this in the "Light of Life" section in *Church Dogmatics* I.3.1, 137 (emphasis added): "The simple point is that the creaturely world, the cosmos, the nature given to man in his sphere and the nature of the sphere, has also as such its own lights and truths and therefore its own speech and words. That the world was and is and will be, and what and how it was and is and will be, thanks to the faithfulness of its Creator, is declared and attested by it and may thus be perceived and heard and considered. Its witness and declaration may be missed or more or less dreadfully misunderstood. But it is given with the same persistence as creation itself endures thanks to the faithfulness of its Creator. *It is given, therefore, quite irrespective of whether the man whom it addresses in its self-witness knows or does not know, confesses or denies, that it owes this speech no less than its persistence to the faithfulness of its Creator.*" See also Barth, *Christian Life*, 120–23.

22. I first ran across this story in Weigel, *Witness to Hope*. A couple of years later

During the Cold War era, one of the Solidarity movement's popular placards protesting the Soviet Union's domination of Poland read: "For Poland to be Poland, 2 + 2 must always = 4." The placard made explicit the point of a popular joke at the time that went like this:

The Communist Party boss asks: "How much is 2 + 2?"

The Polish worker responds: "How much would you like it to be?"

The placard and joke illustrate an important point: It is relatively easy to coerce a verbal *statement*; though it is pretty much impossible to coerce *belief*. It would be fairly easy for those with sufficient power to make a worker *say* that 2 + 2 = 5; but only a fool thinks that he has thereby made the worker *believe* that 2 + 2 = 5. There are no *good reasons* to believe that sometimes 2 + 2 equals 5, even if people can be coerced into *saying* that 2 + 2 = 5. The converse is also true—good reasons to believe X may well *exist*, even if very few (or even no one) *say* that good reasons exist.

Now we are not suggesting that "good reasons" exist in some sort of spooky, eternal, immaterial realm prior to and independent of a person's formulation of those reasons. All we are assuming is that "good reasons" are something that people *discover*; they are not created or invented. For example, Galileo argued that his telescopic discovery of mountains on the moon provided good reasons to reject the older Aristotelian belief that celestial objects were perfect spheres composed of a quintessential element. Some of his contemporaries, however, did not believe this because they suspected that the mountains Galileo claimed to "see" on the moon were really the distorted images *made* by the telescope. When *reasons* or *evidence for* a hypothesis are fabricated by a scientist (or generated by the tools in the scientist's laboratory), then everyone understand that these "reasons" or "evidence" are not *good* reasons and evidence.

We can illustrate what it means to think of good reasons existing apart from what people believe with a common science fiction plot. It goes like this: "A long time ago, Copernicus, Kepler, Galileo, and Newton discovered good reasons for believing that the earth really moves around the sun at thousands of miles per hour. But a few centuries later, the scientific revolution which they initiated taught people how to make an atomic bomb by turning matter into pure energy. There were, however, no corresponding advances in the humanities teaching people how to live in peace. So one thing led to another, and with the exception of a few isolated people in the Australian outback, all humans died in a nuclear war. After several

---

the story was confirmed by one of my own students, herself a Pole, who as a teenager witnessed firsthand Solidarity's success.

generations, a 'second Galileo' arose and argued: 'You know, even though all appearances are to the contrary, I believe there really are good reasons to believe that we are hurtling through space at thousands of miles per hour around the sun.'"

And like the first Galileo, he *said* that there were good reasons for a moving earth *prior* to anyone actually knowing what those good reasons were. Now whatever we make of the first Galileo's claim to have proved that the earth really moves,[23] the second Galileo's claim that there are good reasons to believe the earth moves is clearly true, *even if no one of his generation knows what these good reasons are.*[24]

Now let's develop our science fiction story one step further. Suppose this race of "new humans" is beginning to die off from some waterborne illness. Out of compassion, intergalactic visitors come to earth to *reveal* a simple and cheap test for determining whether or not a water supply is contaminated. It only involves taking a readily available red liquid and placing a drop of it in the water. If nothing happens, the water is safe to drink. But if the water turns green, it is contaminated. Here's the crucial question: Suppose the entire race of "new humans" is red/green colorblind. Did the compassionate intergalactic visitors really *reveal* a solution to the problem of contaminated water? As we will see, it depends on what you mean by "reveal."

Here's a final case. Oliver Sacks is a famous neuroscientist who has written several books for a popular audience, including *The Man Who Mistook His Wife for a Hat*. In his most recent book, he reveals that he, along with about two percent of the population, is face blind, that is, he cannot recognize faces without contextual clues, like hair styles, location, vocal clues, etc. I'm pretty sure that I am one of this two percent as well. Here's why. One day, I was walking to my office at school and I passed within a foot of a "student" walking the other way. We made eye contact so I smiled and continued to my office. A second later, I heard the "student" yell out "Dad!" My married son, who I see weekly, was "out of context," and hence, I did not

23. We must remember, Galileo has at least seven different reasons for saying that the earth really moved—at least six of them we know today were wrong. See my *Life, the Universe, and Everything*, ch. 2, for details.

24. Everything that exists, says Aquinas, has the transcendental properties of unity, goodness, and truth. Many contemporary analytic philosophers have objected that "truth" can only meaningfully be predicated of propositions. And though we will admit that it is awkward to say of a table, electron, or any other *thing*, that it is true, it is not meaningless. Saying that "An electron is true" simply means that the thing itself provides good reason to believe that it exists, *independent of what any person believes or doesn't believe about electrons*. We will flesh this argument out in much more detail in chapter 10.

recognize him. So when I first smiled at this "student," did I *see* my son? If "see" means that I was on the receiving end of *good perceptual evidence* for believing that my son was at the college where I teach, then I suppose the answer is Yes. If "see" means that I *believed* my son was at the college where I teach, then the answer is No.

An analogous phenomenon occurs with the divine In-former argument presented in the last chapter. Defenders of the argument insist that it presents "good reasons" for believing *that* God exists. Critics of the argument point out that such "arguments" almost never change people's minds about the existence of God, or make them "see" what believers "see."

What's required to settle such disputes is a distinction between a "good reason" and a "convincing argument." Consider again the science fiction story about "contaminated water." Suppose the story continues like this: After showing them how to perform a simple chemical test to determine if water was contaminated, they went on to perform sophisticated operations on some people to restore their color vision. The words of "Amazing Grace" would literally be true of them—"I once was blind, but now I see." The simple test for contaminated water does not change; what changes is a person's ability to see the evidence for what it already was.

Or again, when my son passed within a foot of me at my college, did he provide additional evidence when he called out, "Dad!"? The best answer is both Yes and No. For the 98 percent of the population who are not face blind, passing within a foot of your son and making eye contact is all that is necessary for believing that your son is nearby. But for 2 percent of the population, it's not sufficient. And even for this 2 percent, hearing the exclamation "Dad!" is not exactly additional evidence; it's more like a sudden "gestalt" shift. It is not as if the exclamation "Dad!" when added to what I had already seen provided an additional piece of evidence that, when added to my previous visual impression, allowed me to *infer* "That's my son I just passed." No, what happened is that I now recognized my son whom I just saw in the hall—"I once was blind, but now I see."

In the next section we will connect this idea of a "gestalt" shift that allows a person to "see" reasons and evidence for what they really are with the idea of dual-causation. Doing so can help resolve a long-standing dispute about the proper place of purely philosophical arguments for the existence of God (i.e., "natural theology") in the Christian faith.

AN EXCURSUS ON "NATURAL THEOLOGY"

Aquinas famously began his five-volume *Summa Theologica* with his "Five Ways" to prove the existence of God, and Barth famously began his even longer *Church Dogmatics* by proclaiming the "analogy of being" (i.e., what he took to be the metaphysical foundation of Aquinas's proofs[25]) to be "the invention of the Antichrist."[26] So it is not surprising that many philosophers and theologians would read Aquinas and Barth as bitter antagonists when it came to questions about the "natural knowledge" of God. But this is starting to change. Today many philosophers and theologians, at least with respect to the natural knowledge of God, are reading Aquinas and Barth as comrades in arms in the battle against an Enlightenment conception of God.[27]

Our goal in this last section is not to rehearse the exegetical arguments or the history of the controversy. It is only to demonstrate that if we begin with a robust understanding of dual-causation, then there will be no contradiction between Aquinas and Barth. Aquinas claimed that Aristotle had philosophically demonstrated the existence of a divine In-former apart from any access to biblical revelation. Barth claimed that saving knowledge of God is impossible apart from the grace of God revealed in Jesus Christ. These are distinct propositions and there is no contradiction in affirming both.

Dual-causation always presupposes different levels of explanation, one of which is the distinction between reasons and causes. Suppose someone asks: "Why does Fred believe that in a right triangle $A^2 + B^2 = C^2$?" At least two different kinds of answers might be given. First, we could give Fred's

---

25. Two qualifications are necessary. First, Barth is conflating Aquinas's understanding of analogy with later theologians' understanding, especially Cajetan and Przywara, a contemporary of Barth. As T. F. Torrance says, "Barth became more aware of the subtle dangers of Augustinian thought . . . in its notion of grace which through its ingredient of Neoplatonic participation in the divine could be used to bridge the gap between God and nature. It was, of course, this element in the thought of Przywara and others that had been allowed to corrupt the conception of analogy found in St Thomas Aquinas, and set Barth off in a wrong slant against it." Torrance, "Natural Theology," 122–23. No human being, Barth thought, could "participate" in the being of God. The irony, as we have seen, is that Aquinas would wholeheartedly agree. Second, Barth's antipathy toward "natural theology" softened considerably as he matured. "On the contrary, I would gladly concede that *nature* does objectively offer a proof of God, though the human being overlooks or misunderstands it. Yet I would not venture to say the same of natural *science*, whether ancient or modern." Barth in a letter to Carl Zuckmayer (May 7, 1968). Quoted in Rogers, *Thomas Aquinas and Karl Barth*, 206.

26. Barth, *Church Dogmatics*, preface, xiii.

27. For example, Rogers, *Thomas Aquinas and Karl Barth*, and Hauerwas, *With the Grain of the Universe*.

reasons. For example, perhaps he had learned a geometrical proof. Second, we could describe the causal factors that led to his belief. For example, perhaps he lived in a state which required all high school students to take a geometry class.

Or again, suppose Fred is alone in a fairly small room with nothing in it except a black cat lying silently in the corner. Imagine too that the room is pitch black with absolutely no light. After a couple minutes, someone turns on the light. Immediately Fred sees the black cat in the corner. If someone asks "Why does Fred believe there is a black cat in the room?", we can, and must, give two different kinds of answers. First, we can give Fred's reasons, i.e., he believes that there is a cat in the room because he sees it. Second, we can describe the cause of his belief, i.e., someone turned on the light.

Finally, suppose we ask, "Why did Aristotle believe there was a divine In-former?" Once again, there will be at least two distinct kinds of answers. First, there are Aristotle's reasons that we outlined in chapter 4. And, here, the only thing that we will add is to note that none of his reasons made any reference to biblical revelation. If Bob is asked, "Why do you believe that in a right triangle $A^2 + B^2 = C^2$?", he might simply say, "Because I read it in a book" or "Because my teacher said so." Whether these are good or bad reasons is beside the point. The only point here is that when Aristotle argued for the existence of a divine In-former he never said anything like, "Because it said so in the Bible." How could he, since he had no access to biblical revelation?

But there is also a second answer to the question "Why did Aristotle believe in a divine In-former?" That second answer says something about the *causes* of his belief. Unfortunately, here we know very little about what those causes might be, though certainly being a student of Plato was one of the causal factors. Yet, a complete explanation of the causal factors of Aristotle's belief in a divine In-former is going to include much more. And for a Christian theologian like Aquinas those causal factors, at the very highest of levels, are going to include the fact that God created Aristotle with a good brain, placed him in a situation where he had the means and time to study, and ultimately sustained his existence at every moment of his life. It is customary to call these sorts of causal factors "common grace" since they extend to all of creation.[28]

---

28. Here are some passages from Barth on the theme of common grace. "The simple point is that the creaturely world, the cosmos, the nature given to man in his sphere and the nature of this sphere, has also, as such its own lights and truths and therefore its own speech and words. . . . However corrupt man may be, they illumine him, and even in the depths of his corruption he does not cease to see and understand them." *Church Dogmatics* IV.3.1, 139. And again, "Grace is the secret behind nature, the hidden

Returning to our original question—"Is there natural knowledge of God?"—we must now make another distinction to eliminate another crucial ambiguity, namely, what is meant by "natural knowledge." First, "natural knowledge" might refer to that which is philosophical, not theological. That is, it doesn't rely on biblical authority. Second, "natural knowledge" might refer to that which is wholly internal to the knower. That is, the knower is solely responsible for his or her knowledge; there is no one else to whom credit is owed; no help came from without. A paradigm of such knowledge would be an inventor or discoverer, for example, Pythagoras sitting down by himself and working out his geometric proof.

In this second sense, "natural knowledge" of God (or anything else) is strictly speaking impossible. True, we can imagine Pythagoras sitting all by himself simply thinking about triangles and then formulating his proof. But the language that he "thought" in, and that he reported his discovery in, is something that "came from without." And, at least according to Aquinas, so is his very existence! "Natural knowledge" in this second sense, whether it be of God or anything else, is something that Aquinas could never endorse.[29] Common grace is going to be part of the causal explanation for all beliefs, including Aristotle's belief in a divine In-former.[30]

Finally, there is a third ambiguity concerning the natural knowledge of God. Are we talking about a divine In-former who Aristotle could only know as the responsible agent behind the essential natures that makes science possible? Or are we talking about the God who was incarnate in Jesus Christ reconciling the world unto himself?

To illustrate the difference, let us amend the story about Fred, the black cat, and a dark room. Suppose now that the black cat he sees is not just any old cat, but that it is Penelope, the lost cat of Sally the billionaire who has offered a huge reward for Penelope's return. Let us also assume that Fred is homeless, hungry, and without hope of ever fulfilling his dream of earning

---

meaning of nature. When grace is revealed, nature does not cease to exist." Ibid., II.1, 509. Finally, "But there is in nature more than nature. Nature itself becomes the theatre of grace, and grace is manifested as lordship over nature, and therefore in freedom over against it." Ibid., II.1, 509.

29. "And we may characterize Thomas's natural knowledge of God, just where it makes use of cosmological arguments, as one that depends for its effectiveness on attitudes of justice and gratitude that only grace working through nature could supply." Rogers, *Thomas Aquinas and Karl Barth*, 213.

30. George Hunsinger also argues that Barth's primary criticism of natural theology is its tendency to become "an expression of illusory self-sufficiency in matters of theological truth. It is a rampart in our defense against the miracle of grace.... Natural theology assumes that we have some sort of independent and autonomous leverage with respect to grace." *How to Read Karl Barth*, 97.

a college degree. Having the lights turned on, by itself, will neither feed nor house Fred, much less make a college education a realizable dream. But it is a different story if a couple of minutes after the lights are turned on a voice announces—"That's Penelope, the billionaire's lost cat." The lights caused Fred to see a black cat; but it was the voice that caused Fred to see Penelope. And with this new knowledge came a new hope.

Here we have a simple way to make Barth's point, namely, for Aristotle to know that a divine In-former exists is quite different from knowing that Jesus Christ is Lord and Savior of all, and it is only the second sort of knowledge that brings hope. Turning on the lights so that Fred can see the black cat gives Fred no hope. Hope only comes when Fred hears the announcement that it is Penelope who is in the room.

And equally important to Barth is the fact that Fred must *hear* the announcement. Barth insists that revelation is always an *event*; it is not an abstract set of propositions residing in the Bible. "Tool," "Instrumento," and "Werkzeug" all convey the same concept. Likewise, "The cat is Penelope" and "*Die Katze ist Penelope*" both convey the same proposition. So, if the announcement had been made in German, then the same *proposition* would have been uttered. But if Fred understands only English, then the *effect* on him would not have been a newfound hope. In other words, for Barth, the announcement must be more than a true and meaningful proposition; it must be a proposition that *causes* Fred to understand the full significance of the cat in the room. (Precisely *how* God causes Fred's new hope is the topic of chapter 9.)

Once again, there is nothing substantive to which Aquinas would here object, though there is a purely verbal difference in the way Aquinas and Barth make the same point. This verbal difference has to do with the difference between "revelation" used as a verb and the same word used as a noun. For example,

- "Fred *revealed* (verb) the true nature of his feelings to Sally."
- "Fred's memoirs contain many shocking *revelations* (noun)."

Barth uses the term "revelation" in both ways, but each must be kept distinct. Barth sometimes speaks of Jesus Christ as God's revelation. When he does, Barth is using "revelation" as a noun. But when he insists that God's revelation is always an *event* initiated by the Holy Spirit that enables a sinner to recognize Jesus for who and what he truly is, Barth is using the term as a verb. Aquinas, on the other hand, typically uses the term "revelation" as a *noun* to refer to Scripture. So when he speaks of a "natural" or "purely philosophical" knowledge of God he is *only* speaking of the kind of knowledge that does not assume as one of its premises the truths about God that are only found in the Bible. For example, no person needs access to a Bible to know that sodium reacts violently with water or that in a right triangle A² + B² = C². So too, Aristotle didn't need a Bible to understand that if the violent reaction between sodium and water is more than a mere correlation, then there must be a divine In-former.

On the other hand, when Aquinas sought to make the point that without God acting as the primary cause, no person *on his own power* can come to a saving knowledge of Jesus Christ, he would typically speak of God's grace.[31] So where Barth uses the term "revelation" as a verb, Aquinas would speak simply of grace.

We can sum this up in the following chart.

	Divine In-former	Jesus Christ
Reason to believe	1. Philosophy	2. Revelation
Cause of belief	3. Common grace	4. Saving grace

When at the beginning of his *Summa* Aquinas provides "Five Ways" to demonstrate the existence of God he is arguing that there are good philosophical *reasons* to believe in a divine In-former. When Barth begins his *Church Dogmatics* by denouncing the "analogy of Being" as the antichrist, he is denouncing the assumption that there is some path to hope and salvation apart from God's revelation that *causes* belief in Jesus Christ.[32] (Again, we will say much more about *how* saving grace works in chapter 9.) In short, when Aquinas says that there is "natural knowledge" of God, he is talking about the first box. When Barth says that there isn't "natural knowledge" of God, he is talking about the fourth box. Between these two there can be no contradiction because they are talking about apples and oranges—the first concerns *reasons to believe*; the second concerns the *cause of belief*.[33]

---

31. Aquinas affirms that the assent of faith "is from God who interiorly moves us through grace" and that while faith depends on the will, it must be "prepared by God through grace" to make an act of faith. *Summa Theologica* II-II.6.1.3. See also II-II.2.9.3, II-II.5.2.2.

32. Aquinas would not disagree. "After discovering the decrees of the Council of Orange, and their affirmation of the necessity of God's grace for even the beginnings of faith, Aquinas modifies his theology accordingly. He seems to have concluded that his earlier account downplayed the role of grace, since in his earlier account the will seems to assent to God's revelation on its own natural power, and not by any prompting of God's grace. In the *Summa*, therefore, Aquinas emphasizes the activity of God in the will as well as in the intellect. He affirms that the assent of faith 'is from God who interiorly moves us through grace' and that while faith depends on the will, it must be 'prepared by God through grace' to make an act of faith. [*ST* II-II.6.1.3, see also II-II.2.9.3, II-II.5.2.2]." Lombardo, *The Logic of Desire*, 151.

33. T. F. Torrance comes to substantially the same conclusion. "Just as when we are

In the next chapter we will flesh out the difference between belief in a divine In-former and belief in Jesus Christ. In Aquinas's terms, we are talking about the distinction between the "preambles to faith" and "articles of faith."[34] In Barth's terms, we are talking about the distinction between "religion" in general and Christianity in particular. Or as Barth says, "religion as a human attempt to justify and sanctify himself before a willful and arbitrary God" and "the church as the true religion to the extent that through grace it lives by grace."[35] Here we are up against what academics like to call the "scandal of particularity."

---

justified by the grace of God in Jesus Christ our natural goodness is set aside, for we are saved by grace and not by our own works of righteousness, without there being any denial of the existence of natural goodness, so here, in the epistemological relevance of justification by grace, our natural knowledge is set aside, for we know God through his own grace and not by our own efforts of reason, without there being any denial of the existence of natural knowledge." "Natural Theology," 126.

34. *Summa Theologica* I.2.2.
35. *Church Dogmatics* I.17, 280.

—6—

In Defense of Particularity

Philosophy and science deal with the universal and general; history deals with the particular and specific. The central event of Christianity is historical—the life, death, and resurrection of Jesus, through which God reconciled the world unto himself. As Barth never tires of repeating, good theology describes ("reports") what God has done; it never invokes universal generalizations to explain God's actions. As the Author of creation, God is free to write any drama he so chooses.

"Theoretical physicists are Platonists," said one of their own about his profession. He then explained that their hope and goal is to one day demonstrate that the entire universe is "generated from a few mathematical truths and principles of symmetry, perhaps throwing in a handful of parameters like the mass of the electron." Unfortunately, he says, fulfillment of this dream is looking more doubtful today than it was a few decades ago.[1] While the confidence of physicists has waxed and waned over the last century or two, the dream of discovering the mathematical truths that *explain* everything dates back to a century before Plato to the time of the Pythagoreans. And as we saw in chapter 2, it reappeared in Descartes's vision of logic as the sole and sufficient guide to all truth.

---

1. Lightman, "Accidental Universe," 35–40. See Ritchie, *Studies in the History and Methods of the Sciences*, chapter 1, for a historical explanation of this use of "Platonist."

These philosophies have a strong attraction to the abstract and the universal and an even stronger distaste for the particular. And this distaste is not hard to understand: the irreducibly particular defies explanation and calls into question our mastery of our own destiny. Though the unpredictability of a tennis ball bouncing down a rocky road may have little effect on one's destiny, the ten-cent nut that brought to naught the rescue of the Iranian hostages and the flight of the arrow that shattered the peace between the Trojans and Rutulians had a huge effect on people's destiny.

Aquinas certainly appreciated abstract and universal philosophical principles, but he was too much of a philosophical realist to believe that reality can be explained by logic alone. As we argued in chapter 2, logic tells us nothing about what *is* the case; it only tells us what *is not* the case. Barth was even less appreciative of the abstract and universal than Aquinas.[2] But on these matters, the differences between Aquinas and Barth were far less than their agreement that the Christian faith is centered on what was done by a *particular* man, in a *particular* time, and in a *particular* place. This man was Jesus, and the resurrection is what he did.

So while philosophy and science have their place in the stewardship of God's good creation, the central claim of Christianity is historical, namely, that God was in Christ reconciling the world unto himself.[3] As Barth never tires of repeating, good theology simply *describes* ("reports") what God has done.[4] It never tries to *explain* why God does what he does—doing so would ipso facto limit the freedom of God.

PREAMBLES TO FAITH

To illustrate the difference between philosophy and Christianity, Aquinas asks us to consider two friends walking down a country road. Far ahead they see someone coming toward them. It is clear that it is a person, not

---

2. "And so the Bible is not a philosophical book, but a history book, the book of God's mighty acts, in which God becomes knowable by us." Barth, *Dogmatics in Outline*, 38.

3. "When we recognise that the Christian faith and the Christian message is directed to all men, that it proclaims the God who is the God of the whole world, we must also see that the way to the general, universal truth that embraces the whole world and all men, is the way of particularity, in which God, in a way which seems strange and arbitrary, is the God of Abraham, Isaac, and Jacob." Ibid., 74.

4. "Theology is the record of this [salvation] history. It must not degenerate into a system [i.e., a deductive algorithm]. It must always be related to that history. It must always be a report. It must not strain after completeness and compactness. Its aim must simply be to make the right report." Barth, *Church Dogmatics* III.3, 295.

a deer or a bear. But they have no idea *who* it is. Whether the person is a friend or foe can only be known if the person decides to reveal himself by shouting out "It's me, Peter."[5]

Aquinas told a story to distinguish between the "preambles to faith" and the "articles of faith." Using ordinary vision the two friends can see that another person is coming. But their vision is unable to distinguish between friend and foe. It is only the self-revelation of the person approaching that can answer the second question. Ordinary vision (philosophy) provides the "preambles to faith"; God's self-revelation (theology) provides the "articles of faith."

Crudely put, the "preambles to the faith" tell us *that* God exists;[6] the "articles of the faith" tell us that God's existence is *good news*. Living in the West, this crucial difference is frequently forgotten. With its long Christian past, today Westerners automatically assume that "God" refers to something that is good and loving. But this was certainly not the case when Paul wrote to the Romans. Outside of Christendom, "God," or more typically, the "gods," referred to a very mixed bag—powerful, yes; awesome and fearful, yes. But was "God" (or the "gods") loving and good? That was a completely different question.

When ancient Romans looked at the world, like St. Paul, they understood that God's "eternal power and deity has been clearly perceived in the things that have been made" (Rom 1:20). Yet that was hardly a comforting thought. Of course kings and rulers and deities were powerful, but it was a power everyone understood to be a two-edged sword. With the proper petitions and gifts, those with great power might be persuaded to dispense a great blessing; but with improper petitions or gifts there was also the threat of great harm, even if the impropriety was completely inadvertent.

This is why the great Roman poet Lucretius found a receptive audience for his poem praising the benefits of atheism. Since there are no gods, he said, we can live our allotted days on earth in peace and tranquility, confident that when we die there is no possibility of further pain or sorrow, because then we will no longer exist. There is no immortal soul nor is there a God or gods who might punish us for any offense against their dignity. And if people find the thought of their existence coming to an end distressing or depressing, Lucretius reminds them that they were not distressed or depressed *prior* to their birth. None of us are distressed or depressed knowing that we were not around for our great-grandparents' wedding. Why should

---

5. Aquinas, *Summa Theologica* I.2.1.1.

6. Remembering, that is, all the qualifications we added in chapter 4 to the term "exists" when predicated of God. And we will add further qualifications in chapter 10.

the thought that we will not be around for our great-granddaughter's wedding be any more distressing or depressing?

Romans would never quibble with William Paley's observation that there is much in the created universe that is good and beautiful,[7] but they would dismiss with scorn Paley's claim that the observable goodness and beauty of nature points to a *good* and *loving* God. Was Paley simply oblivious to pain and sorrow, filth and ugliness? Could he not see that nature was "red in tooth and claw"? Had he never cried out at the painful death of an innocent child?

Nor would a Roman be impressed if Paley had only claimed that *on balance* this world contains more good than evil. How or who is able to quantify the goodness and beauty in nature to weigh it against the evil and ugliness? Does the beauty of a hundred orchids surpass the pain of a toothache? Such questions are ridiculous on their face. But even if we grant for the sake of the argument that there is "more" good than evil, how does that make a case for a good and loving God? When a student gets 51 percent of the questions right on a math test we don't say that he is *good* at math. Why should a God who makes a universe with a 51/49 percent balance of good over evil be thought of as a *good* God?

Neither St. Paul nor Aquinas nor Barth would disagree with the Romans—the *goodness* of the Creator is not something we discern by studying nature. Until or unless the person coming down the path reveals *who* he is we can have no idea whether he is to be welcomed as a friend or feared as an enemy. No abstraction about the ratio of good to evil in the world can answer *particular* questions about who God is.

RELIGION IN GENERAL OR CHRISTIANITY IN PARTICULAR?

Fifty years ago a famous skeptical philosopher laid the following challenge before a group of Christian philosophers:

> Now it often seems to people who are not religious as if there was no conceivable event or series of events the occurrence of which would be admitted by sophisticated religious people to be a sufficient reason for conceding "There wasn't a God after all" or "God does not really love us then." Someone tells us that

---

7. The full title of Paley's book, which begins with the famous "Watchmaker argument" for God, is: *Natural History: Or, Evidences of the Existence and Attributes of the Deity, Collected from the Appearances of Nature*. Needless to say, the "attributes" of God Paley claims to have discovered in nature were all good.

> God loves us as a father loves his children. We are reassured. But then we see a child dying of inoperable cancer of the throat. His earthly father is driven frantic in his efforts to help, but his Heavenly Father reveals no obvious sign of concern. Some qualification is made—God's love is "not a merely human love" or it is "an inscrutable love". . . .We are reassured again. But then perhaps we ask: what is this assurance of God's (appropriately qualified) love worth, what is this apparent guarantee really a guarantee against?[8]

In response, one philosopher said, "I wish to make it clear that I shall not try to defend Christianity in particular, but religion in general—not because I do not believe in Christianity, but because you cannot understand what Christianity is, until you have understood what religion is."[9] Here is a classic example of Enlightenment thought favoring the abstract and universal over the concrete and particular.

The respondent then goes on to explain that religion is essentially a *private* affair concerning a supernatural or "spiritual" realm. Religious and nonreligious people, he said, don't have different beliefs about the realm of nature. We all believe that the earth revolves around the sun and that birth always ends in death. It is just that religious and nonreligious people have a different set of attitudes or feelings about these laws of nature. Religious people believe there is a spiritual realm, not open to scientific investigation, where a caring God resides. Whether or not this God is all-powerful and able to prevent *all* suffering, especially the suffering that is caused by humans, is an open question. But it is not an open question that God cares for his creation and that when religious people pray they receive a spiritual blessing and sense of inner peace.

Nonreligious people don't share this peace and comfort; all they can see is what can be observed by the methods of science. To understand Christianity, said this philosopher, you must first learn to "see" the world through the eyes of a religious person. Then you will find that the essence of Christianity, when stripped of its first-century cultural myths, is all about an attitude of love and care, and we can learn this from any of the world's great religions.

Aquinas and Barth see things quite differently. The central claims of Christianity are essentially *public* and they are about *particular* historical events. The Apostles' Creed that Christians have publicly confessed for over 2,000 years says, "I believe in Jesus Christ, born of the virgin Mary, who

---

8. Flew, "Theology and Falsification," 98–99.
9. Hare, "Theology and Falsification," 99.

suffered under Pontius Pilate, was crucified, dead and buried, and on the third day rose from the dead." The death and burial of Jesus are concrete historical events no different from Julius Caesar's crossing of the Rubicon. So too, they are public events that can be investigated using the standard methods of the historian.

The virgin birth and the resurrection, though, are trickier. The Christian philosopher we just considered is but a single example of those who have argued that since virgin births and resurrections violate the laws of nature, there is nothing historians can say one way or the other about such alleged "events." And they put "events" in scare quotes for good reason. Since their focus is religion in general, not Christianity in particular, they argue that *true* religion has nothing to do with the truth or falsity of historical events. Whether or not Mary really was a virgin or Jesus was bodily resurrected are irrelevant questions for the abstractly religious person. Even if these events really happened, what possible significance would they have to a person born in China or India? What's important, they say, is not the *bodily* resurrection of Jesus, but the *spiritual* resurrection embodied in the disciples' newly discovered sense of meaning and significance after the death of their master. And this sort of spirituality is equally available to *all* people.

Aquinas and Barth would have nothing to do with this sort of "spiritualization" of central elements of Christian doctrine. With St. Paul, they would say that without the bodily resurrection of Jesus, Christians are the most miserable and pitiful of persons (1 Cor 15:19). If it were not for the resurrection, they would agree with the skeptical philosopher we began with: "What is this assurance of God's (appropriately qualified) love worth, and what is this apparent guarantee really a guarantee against?"

Remember, according to the biblical authors, Aquinas, and Barth, it is *not* nature that declares the goodness of the Creator.[10] It is only God's self-revelation, his calling out, which gives us reason and cause to believe, in the face of pain and suffering, that in fact God is good. St. Paul says, "God shows his love for us in that while we were yet sinners Christ died for us" (Rom 5:8). St. John says, "By this we know love, that he [Jesus] laid down his

---

10. "How do we know that the overcoming of evil is resolved and even accomplished in the eternal will of God, and that the evil which opposes this will is nothingness? We know it quite simply because we have before us the conflict which takes place between them in Jesus, in His encounter with the world. We know it because we take seriously the manner in which the conflict is waged in Him as the source of our sure and certain knowledge of this matter. In other words, we know it because we try to be consistently Christological in our whole thinking on the subject. Jesus! And we cannot avoid using such words as 'conflict' and 'event' to describe what is before us. To say 'Jesus' is necessarily to say 'history,' His history, the history in which He is what He is and does what He does." Barth, *Church Dogmatics* IV.3.1, 179.

life for us" (1 John 3:16). St. Peter adds, "By God's great mercy we have been born anew to a living hope through the resurrection of Jesus Christ from the dead" (1 Pet 1:3). And "the resurrection" does not refer to an abstract and universal truth of philosophy, but to a concrete and particular historical event.

MIRACULOUS INTERVENTION OR SIGNS AND WONDERS?

Modern skeptics argue that science demonstrates that the virgin birth and the bodily resurrection of Jesus are violations of the laws of nature and therefore they never happened. Most modern Christians respond in one of two ways. As we have just seen, some Christians argue that it is not the bodily resurrection that is important. Rather, it is Christ's *spirit* which lives on because *spirit* cannot be killed by a cross. Other Christians (like the ones considered in the previous chapter) argue that since God created the laws of nature, he is equally free to suspend them, intervene, and bring a dead body back to life if he sees fit.

Though our approach is much closer to the second, it is also significantly different. In the previous two chapters we argued that God must *not* be thought of as simply the biggest, best, and most powerful *thing* in the universe. A God who first created the universe, and then withdrew to let it run on "its own steam" might occasionally choose to intervene. But the Author of creation is not like that. Between God and the created order there is "an infinite qualitative distinction." God, and only God, exists on "his own steam"; everything else is absolutely and totally dependent, at every moment, on the sustaining power of God. As we have already argued, the God who is the Author of creation can no more *intervene* in his creation than Shakespeare can *intervene* in one of his plays. The problem is *not* that God and Shakespeare are too far removed or lack the power to intervene in their respective creations; but that they are both are too close, too intimately involved with their creations, to make the idea of their intervention *make sense*. As a friend, I might intervene in your life to prevent you from doing something really stupid, and conversely, you might do the same for me. But what sense does it make to say that I might *intervene* in my own life?

"Intervention" presupposes that something has a life of its own, that it is fully capable of carrying on under its own power. But this is precisely what Aquinas and Barth deny. Nothing in the created world, they argue, is capable of "carrying on" by itself.[11] God not only creates, but also sustains

11. Barth puts it like this: "But in the case of a miracle God is not different from

everything that exists. Even our own faith, says the author of Hebrews, is not something that we "mustered up on our own." No, it is God who is the "Author and finisher" of our faith (Heb 12:2).

In an interventionist understanding, miracles are a product of mono-causation. It is precisely the fact that an event has no natural cause—only a supernatural cause—that makes it a miracle. On the other hand, when miracles are considered through the lenses of dual-causation, the miraculous nature of some events is not eliminated, but it is, so to speak, raised to a higher level. It is not the fact that an event is "scientifically" inexplicable that makes it a miracle. Rather, it is the fact that an event, considered in the whole of the historical narrative in which it occurs, becomes a "thin place" and a *sign* of God's purposes and intentions. When humans turn ink on paper or electrons on a computer screen into a word, they do not first "suspend" the laws of nature. So too, when God communicates to his people with a "sign and wonder" (the more typical biblical expression for "miracle"), God is not required to first "suspend" his previously enacted laws before the event can become a *sign*. Remember, there are no "laws of nature" (i.e., humanly predictable outcomes) for the vast majority of what happens in God's good creation.

Imagine a time machine in which a skeptical philosopher, Thomas Aquinas, and Karl Barth are all transported to first-century Palestine. Their assignment, along with nine other honest jurors, is to decide Joseph's legal

---

what He is otherwise. The power in which God is Lord over all created powers is in itself one and the same power, whether God uses and manifests it for us in the usual or in an unusual way. It is certainly not the function of biblical miracles to present to men a special divine omnipotence, a higher one, exercised and used in a series of exceptions. On the contrary, their function is to remind men by sign, by visible illustrations of His Word, that God is omnipotent (as He calls us into His Kingdom by His Word), and therefore that the omnipotence of such, or with their sum or substance, as we are constantly inclined to think in view of the usual course of events. We are to remember that we are not subject to them or bound to them, but that they are His subjects and servants, and therefore that God is Lord over the usual course of events which we constantly misinterpret. It is to point us to this that God's revelation is accompanied by miracles.... Miracle reveals the richness and comprehensiveness of the divine ordering of things, but not that God set aside or destroys His own order." *Church Dogmatics* II.1, 539–40. And again, "From the knowledge of the simplicity of God, it follows as a matter of course that His relation to the world cannot on any account be understood and interpreted as a combination, amalgamation or identification of God with the world. From the same standpoint there are also no effluences, emanations, effusions or irruptions of God into the world, in virtue of which, apart from God Himself, there are in a sense islands or even continents of the divine in the midst of the non-divine." Ibid., II.1, 446. And Aquinas, with his characteristic brevity, put it like this: "God cannot grant to a creature to be preserved in being after the cessation of the Divine influence: as neither can He make it not to have received its being from Himself." Aquinas, *Summa Theologica* 104.1.

suit against Mary. Mary's defense attorney produces several witnesses to prove beyond a reasonable doubt that she had neither motive, means, nor opportunity to fornicate. The evidence is so strong that all twelve jurors agree—Mary is not a fornicator, and hence, they deny Joseph's lawsuit.

However, by itself, this story says nothing about the theological *significance* of Mary's giving birth as a virgin. The skeptical philosopher, for example, might quite coherently argue like this: "Yes, the evidence shows beyond a reasonable doubt that Mary is no fornicator. But we live in a world where the march of science is continually uncovering new, purely naturalistic explanations for what previous generations believed were miraculous interventions by God. In Aquinas's day no one knew about parthenogenesis, those rare, but now scientifically verified, cases where sexually reproducing animals give birth without a sperm being introduced by a male. True, this has never been observed in any genus higher than reptiles, but there is no theoretical reason this cannot happen in mammals. So what we have in the case of Mary is not a miracle, but the first legally proven case of parthenogenesis in humans!"[12]

This is a perfectly coherent story, but unless we assume a philosophy of mono-causation, "science" has not thereby "explained away" the virgin birth. And if we start instead with a philosophy of dual-causation and we place this wondrous event in its larger historical context with all its rich particulars, then it becomes a "thin place" where the Creator reveals something of *who* he is. Having choreographed a thousand-year history for a particular people and thereby creating in them the expectation of a messiah whose wondrous birth would be a sign for all who have eyes to see, can there be any good reason, or anything unfitting, in God bringing to completion his purposes by choreographing the first case of mammalian parthenogenesis in human history?[13]

12. The inspiration for this story comes from Richard Dawkins (one of the leading "new atheists"), who considers a report of someone witnessing a stone statue of the Virgin Mary waved her (its?) hand. Rather than proclaiming that the report *must* be false, Dawkins says, "But if, by sheer coincidence, all the molecules just happened to move in the same direction at the same moment, the hand would move. If they then all reversed direction at the same moment, the hand would move back. In this way it is possible for a marble statue to wave at us. It could happen. The odds against such a coincidence are unimaginably great but they are not incalculably great." *Blind Watchmaker*, 160.

13. There is a passage early in the *Church Dogmatics* in which Barth seems to preclude this possibility. Barth writes, "In other words, if we are clear that with the Holy Spirit God Himself is declared to be the author of the sign of the Virgin birth, then we know that in acknowledging the reality of this sign we have a priori renounced all understanding of it as a natural possibility, even when we are tempted to do so by considerations so inviting as that of *natural* parthenogenesis, for example." I.2, 198, emphasis added. This passage is admittedly troublesome for my reading of Barth. However, if

Yet a second question remains. If we reject an "interventionist" understanding of miracles, then doesn't that commit us to a "spiritualist" understanding? Remember the philosopher of the previous section who argued that the nonreligious "must first learn to 'see' the world through the eyes of a religious person." On this understanding, miracles are quite ordinary events: The leader of a band of disciples is killed by his enemies while witnessing to God's love. Though the master's body behaves just as the laws of nature say it must—it lies motionless in the tomb where it was buried, and though the disciples are momentarily disheartened—in three days a new spirit of faith and hope overwhelms them, enabling them to proclaim their master's vision of God's great love throughout the world with great skill, vigor, and courage.

On the "spiritualist" understanding of miracles, what's public and open to historical investigation—a man's body lies motionless in the tomb—is of no theological significance. But on the third alternative that we are defending, for an event to be a sign of God's purpose it must be *public* and its significance, at least in part, is determined by the ordinary canons of *historical* investigation.

We will begin to make our case by considering Isaiah 37. Hezekiah wants to make a treaty with the Assyrians since he is sure that his small army is no match for the army of the invading superpower. Isaiah disagrees and claims to have the "word of the Lord." Then, when the massive army of the Assyrians is camped outside the wall of Jerusalem, we read: "The angel of the lord set out and struck down one hundred eighty-five thousand in the camp of the Assyrians when morning dawned" (Isa 37:36).

All Christians would agree that this was a "sign and wonder" for Hezekiah to keep the faith. But what exactly does it mean? In one sense, questions about the sudden death of 185,000 Assyrians or whether Mary gave birth as a virgin are no different from any other event in the past. And though no historical event is open to the kind of logical or experimental verification demanded by idealists or positivists, we must not forget that many *different* disciplines ask questions about *particular* events in the past. Lawyers try cases to determine paternity; anthropologists try to determine if peculiar marks on bones were made by humans; geologists try to date ancient ice floes; paleontologists try to determine if Archaeopteryxes had feathered wings; and of course, the majority of the questions asked by evolutionary biologists are all historical questions, many of them concerning *particular*

---

we place emphasis on the qualifier "*natural* parthenogenesis," then Barth's point could be that invoking the scientific discovery of parthenogenesis does not *explain away* the virgin birth. That is, God as the "author of the sign" refers to the *primary cause* of the virgin birth, irrespective of the *secondary causes* that God may have used.

events.[14] When we consider the incredible range of "historical" disciplines, we see that the only *method* that these disciplines share is the commonsense method of searching for an answer that accounts for the most data, with the fewest inconsistencies, in a way that "makes sense." It is simply not credible to claim that they all follow "*the* scientific method." In short, we are back to the three Cs of comprehensiveness, consistency, and coherence that we discussed in chapters 2 and 3.

But in another sense, theological questions go beyond the *merely* historical disciplines. It is possible (even if unlikely) that archaeologists might one day discover physical evidence proving that 185,000 Assyrians died suddenly outside the walls of Jerusalem during the reign of Hezekiah from an outbreak of cholera. That would, so to speak, establish that a *wonder* had occurred. But was it also a *sign* from God to Hezekiah or was it just a coincidence? This is a question not for archeology, but for theology. However, before addressing this question in the last section of this chapter, we need to consider the claim that Jesus was dead on Friday and alive on Sunday.

DEAD ON FRIDAY BUT ALIVE ON SUNDAY

A single straw can break a camel's back and a difference of degree can become so great that common sense views it as a difference in kind. The resurrection of a body that has been dead for three days is a case in point. Perhaps a strong east wind did part the Red Sea; perhaps 185,000 Assyrians did die suddenly from cholera; perhaps Mary was the first case of human parthenogenesis—in all these cases it makes sense to think that the Author of creation choreographed the secondary causes to achieve his purposes. But the claim that Jesus was dead on Friday and alive on Sunday is a backbreaking straw. So we must, many would argue, place the resurrection of Jesus in a category by itself where God acts directly, instead of through secondary causes. Here it seems there is no alternative to mono-causation—*either* God intervened to suspend the "laws of nature" *or* Jesus' resurrection was purely spiritual. Yet, even here a third alternative emerges once we commit ourselves to a thoroughly realistic philosophy that is content to leave some events *describable* without ever pretending that they might one day be *explainable*.

---

14. Examples of such *particular* questions considered by biologists include: "When a biologist tries to answer a question about a unique occurrence such as 'Why are there no hummingbirds in the Old World?' or 'Where did the species *Homo sapiens* originate?'" See Mayr, *This Is Biology*, 64.

Anyone who reads Barth will be struck by how frequently he uses the term "abstract" pejoratively. When he does so, he is implicitly criticizing a tendency toward the kind of philosophical idealism that places its faith in "logic." Rather than beginning with universal and wholly formal concepts (the principles of logic and mathematics) and then deducing conclusions about what *must* have happened, Barth insists that theology must always begin with concrete particulars and remain content with understanding *what* God has done without ever pretending to understand *why* God acted as he did.

This difference between an idealist and a realist approach to a problem is not limited to theologians. Frequently scientists who are involved in the search for extraterrestrial life ask: "What are the necessary and sufficient conditions for life?" This is the sort of question that philosophical idealists might ask since it assumes that *all* life must share certain essential characteristics (just as mathematicians assume that there is only one correct answer to all sums). Philosophical realists ask a very different question. They ask, "What are the necessary and sufficient conditions for life *as we know it*?" Here no assumption is made one way or the other about the possibility of *life* taking on forms utterly foreign to anything we have observed on earth.

Realists are like science fiction writers. Both are struck by the incredible diversity of life here on earth. They then extrapolate and create stories about life in other galaxies that is made out of silicon or even life that becomes embodied in gigantic clouds of methane. (True science fiction fans could add many more examples.) Those with platonistic tendencies, on the other hand, are struck by the commonalities of life on earth—it is all carbon-based and it all uses the same double-helix-shaped molecule to pass information from one generation to the next. They then extrapolate that *all* life must have this same set of necessary and sufficient conditions.

It is hard to imagine how this dispute could ever be resolved scientifically. Nor will this dispute ever be resolved philosophically. Whether we begin to philosophize about *things* like plants and animals or begin to philosophize about *ideas* and abstract archetypes is a choice we all make. Here to talk of "proof" necessarily begs the question. A chain of deductive arguments cannot be infinitely long. So wherever it begins, it will begin with an assumption. For realists, that assumption is something like "I know plants and animals exist because I see them"; for idealists, that assumption is something like "I know that I exist as a thinking being because logic demands it."

We have committed ourselves to realism. So we say nothing about the necessary and sufficient conditions for life as an abstract universal; we speak only about life as we know it. And here is what we know. First, a necessary condition for life as we know it is not being crucified by Romans centurions.

Second, the life of God, or even of angels, is not "life as we know it." Third, the resurrection of Jesus is *not* about life as we know it. Lazarus was resuscitated and returned to life as we know it, presumably to one day die again; Jesus was resurrected and inaugurated the *new* life of the kingdom of God, never to die again.[15] Prior to the crucifixion Jesus had life as we know it; after the resurrection he had a new kind of life that can *only* be understood analogically (see chapter 2).

Again, if "natural" and "supernatural" are nouns that name two distinct realms, then the idea of new life as the life of a "spiritual body" is indeed puzzling. If something is a spirit, then it has no body; and if something has a body, then it is not a spirit. But if we think of "spiritual" as describing *how* the body is powered, the way we distinguished in chapter 4 between wind-powered and steam-powered ships, the idea of a "spiritually-powered body" involves no contradiction. In the present life, our bodies are subject to decay and corruption; but in the new heaven and new earth, we will have redeemed bodies, no longer subject to decay and corruption.

Life with a spiritually-powered body will have both continuities and discontinuities with life as we now know it. We will recognize it when we see (or have) it—and we will one day even be able to describe it—but this new life will never be something that we are able to explain in advance. (Though we might add that the inexplicability of new life is currently not much greater than inexplicability of life as we know it.) We can recognize life when we see it, but we cannot predict in advance what even life here on earth will look like or where it might be found. Who, for example, could have predicted that we would discover life miles beneath the ocean in total darkness, deriving its energy from thermal vents, totally independent of the photosynthesis that grounds all other life?

One way to represent the continuities and discontinuities of life and new life is to return to the progression of geometrical figures from triangles to squares to pentagons to icosagons (20-sided regular polygons) all the way up to chiliagons (1000-sided regular polygons). As we argued in chapter 4, in such a series there is both continuity and a definite progression. We know the direction we are moving. So, if we take a final step, and move from a chiliagon to a circle, we will not be changing *direction*, but we will be making a *leap*. We have introduced a discontinuity, yet not in an arbitrary fashion. The initial sequence is clearly pointing in this direction. Circles

---

15. "It is surely in the light of this ontological salvation that we are to understand the so-called 'nature miracles,' as well as the resurrection of Jesus from death, for they represent not a suspension of the natural or created order but the very reverse, the recreation of the natural order wherever it suffers from decay or damage or corruption or disorder through evil." Torrance, *Divine and Contingent Order*, 116.

have no sides, and neither do lines, but the "leap" in our sequence from a chiliagon to a circle "makes sense" in a way that a "leap" from a chiliagon to a one-dimensional straight line would not. Yes, we are, so to speak, taking a "leap of faith," but it is not a blind leap. And there is nothing in logic itself that guarantees a safe landing. But, then, there is nothing in logic that guarantees the conclusion in *any* piece of inductive or analogical reasoning.

Likewise, the resurrected life in a new heaven and new earth will be both surprising (because of its discontinuity with life as we knew it), and yet it will somehow "make sense" (because of its continuity with life as we knew it). So, yes, Jesus' resurrection is an event with discontinuities that surpass God's choreographing the death of 185,000 Assyrians or Mary's giving birth as a virgin. However, if we place it in its historical and theological context, it is more than a senseless wonder. It is also an intelligible sign.

WHAT TURNS A "WONDER" INTO A "SIGN"?

In chapter 3 we discussed the notion of an ad hoc hypothesis. Any scientific theory, no matter how silly or strange, can logically be saved from falsification with an ad hoc hypothesis. For example, even though we see the tops of ships sailing into port before we see the bottoms, Flat-earthers are not *logically* compelled to give up their theory. All they need to do is add an auxiliary hypothesis, namely, that light is bent in the presence of a strong gravitational field. And there are no purely logical criteria for distinguishing between auxiliary hypotheses that are legitimate and those that we dismiss as ad hoc. It takes considerable familiarity with the details of a scientific theory to make good judgments about when we should or shouldn't reject a hypothesis as ad hoc. Without a detailed understanding of the particular virtues of Newton's theory of universal gravity, it would have been quite reasonable to reject it out of hand since it predicts the collapse of the universe into a single, solitary lump. What saved Newton's theory was not a single, undeniable fact or observation. Rather, it was Newton's ability to weave so many particular observations into a single unified story.

So too, the individual reports of Mary, Peter, John, and finally Paul to have seen the risen Christ, considered by themselves, are mere wonders, inexplicable historical "data," that make no sense. Why should we believe that these otherwise reliable witnesses were not hallucinating, lying, or perhaps simply perpetuating a hoax?

There are two inadequate answers, both of which have their roots in David Hume, an Enlightenment philosopher with strong skeptical tendencies. The first argument concerns the *reality* of miracles. The argument goes like this: "Yes, we *know* they were hallucinating, lying, or perpetuating a hoax because we have universal testimony against miracles." In effect, this is an a priori argument against *wonders*. But as has frequently been pointed out, such reasoning is viciously circular—we only have universal testimony against miracles if we already know that the testimony of the thousands upon thousands of people who claim to have witnessed a miracle is untrustworthy.

But there is a second argument that must be taken more seriously. In effect, this argument doesn't deny that miracles occur; it only denies that we can know what the miracle *means* or *signifies*. Suppose, for example, we grant that five hundred people testified to have witnessed the resurrected Christ (1 Cor 15:6). Suppose we also grant that psychologists know of no other case where five hundred otherwise normal people have the same "hallucination" at the same time. Suppose too that no sociologist can explain why five hundred people would tell the same lie when there is nothing to be gained. And suppose finally that no historian can point to another example of such a massive cover-up remaining undiscovered for more than a few years. Nonetheless, says Hume, we have equally strong evidence that dead people do *not* come back to life after three days—just think of the millions, even billions, of dead people we have observed who have stayed dead! Thus, either way, we have a miracle. What we can never know is *which* one of these historically unprecedented events was the real "miracle"—was it that a dead man was raised to life *or* was it that five hundred people were all having the same "hallucination" at the same time or that five hundred people were all telling the same lie *or* that a massive cover-up known to five hundred-people remained undiscovered, etc.? The best we can have in such cases, said Hume, is "proof against proof."[16]

On this second reading of Hume, there is no disputing that a "miracle"—in the sense of a wonder for which there is no natural explanation—in fact occurred. But there is great dispute about what it means. Does it mean that sometimes dead men rise or that sometimes mass hallucination, unprofitable lies, or undetected cover-ups occur? Once again, our answer follows the model laid down in chapter 3 for all "scientific" disciplines: Seemingly inexplicable events become signs with intelligible meaning when they are fit into a comprehensive, consistent, and coherent story that, while not perfect, is better than all competing stories.

Prior to Newton, many astronomers suspected that the earth revolved around the sun, but the motion of such a massive object like the earth without some "mechanical" push was inexplicable. Then Newton came up with a

---

16. Hume, *Enquiry*, 10.1: "On Miracles."

detailed explanation unifying the forces acting on a falling apple with those acting on the planets. Though the idea of "action at a distance" seemed like a throwback to medieval superstition, the elegance of the *whole* story was sufficient to win the day, even if it required God to keep the universe from collapsing in on itself.

So too, to turn the inexplicable reports that Jesus was still alive into a *sign*, we need a compelling story, rich in details and comprehensive in scope. Now to be clear, what follows is *not* that compelling story. Reduced to a few paragraphs, the story surrounding the resurrection of Jesus will never convince skeptics to renounce their belief that dead men stay dead. But the same is true of Newton's *Principia*—no confirmed Ptolemaic astronomer would have been convinced that the earth is really moving through space at thousands of miles per hour by a three- to four-paragraph summary of the *Principia*. The only point of the summary that follows is to indicate the *kind* of story that turns a wonder into a sign.[17]

The story goes like this: Peter, Paul, and many others all heard Jesus teach and preach that *in him* the kingdom of God had begun. However, many were skeptical because the evidence of Roman occupation was visible everywhere. His disciples said, "Yes, but soon Jesus will lead the messianic army that will send the Romans packing just as Yahweh sent the Assyrians packing."

At the same time, while most Jews were bemoaning the Roman occupation, some of the powerful Jews had achieved a modus vivendi with the Romans. Since Jesus was upsetting the status quo, these powerful Jews secretly conspired with the Romans to have Jesus executed. (Notice the dual-causation—it was both Romans *and* Jews who killed Jesus.) For three days, powerful Jews, the Roman occupiers, and the fearful disciples *all* believed that this was the end of the story. But on Sunday things changed. First some women, then two of his male disciples, followed by several others (five hundred by some accounts) all testified that they not only saw, but also touched, the risen Jesus.

Furthermore, they testified publicly. And what they proclaimed was *not* that they had a "spiritual" vision that gave them newfound inner peace. No, they proclaimed and preached that God had vindicated Jesus, that God's kingdom on earth really had been inaugurated, and that all this was accomplished through the resurrection when Jesus triumphed over the forces of Satan, sin, and death. As Paul said, Jesus "disarmed the principalities and powers and made a *public* example of them" (Col 2:15, emphasis added).

---

17. The story I am about to tell is a highly condensed version of the one told by N. T. Wright. He has fleshed it out in great detail in the three already published volumes of his series "Christian Origins and the Question of God."

But the story is not over. We are now in the fifth act of a five-act play. The first act tells of God's good creation. The second act tells of human rebellion against the created order. The third act tells of God's covenant with a *particular* people chosen to be a blessing to *all* people. The fourth act tells of the rebellion of this chosen people and the subsequent sending of God's own Son to do and be the blessing to all nations that the Jewish nation had shown itself incapable of being. So at the end of act four, we have Jesus' death, resurrection, and vindication. Then, at the beginning of act five, the witnesses to Jesus' resurrection are sent out by their risen Lord to proclaim the good news of new life in Christ, *even if it means losing life as they then knew it.*

And while the decisive battle of this war has been won and the victory has been assured, the play goes on. Today we are still living "life as we know it." There are still pockets, maybe even whole battalions, of resistance to be overcome. Yet, Christians yearn for that day when the divinely intended, and assured, blessing of a *new* life becomes universal. That is the hope of both Aquinas and Barth. It is a hope that requires a "leap of faith," but it is not a "blind" leap.

CONCLUSION

We will conclude this chapter with four points.

(1) Scientists tell stories explaining *why* sodium always reacts violently with water. Christian theologians like Aquinas and Barth tell stories explaining *why* Jesus was dead on Friday and alive on Sunday. The stories scientists and theologians tell are obviously different. Scientists (at least physicists and chemists) tell stories about events which are *generally* observed and easily repeatable. Theologians tell stories about nonrepeatable *particular* events. And though the object of their study is different, the questions we ask in evaluating their stories are the same. Is the story comprehensive, that is, does it consider all of the data? Is the story consistent, that is, does it avoid contradictions? And finally, is the story coherent, that is, does it hang together and make sense? And by "making sense" we mean something more than deductive logic; something like the analogical reasoning we described in the second chapter.

(2) Christian theology stands on its own; it does not require an empirically detectable Designer. Nowhere in this story was mention made of supernatural intervention or of the suspension of the "laws of nature." All we've assumed is that history, like the weather, will forever be full of surprises. True, the Enlightenment spoke wistfully about universal "laws of

nature" that would one day explain everything. But as we saw in the first chapter, the march of science has destroyed this dream.

(3) Christians tell their story without any pretension of it being a universally compelling story. Good reasons are not always convincing reasons. Whenever stories have implications for how we live and act, there will always be a gap between motivation and reasons. With sufficient motivation *not* to follow the direction of a story to its conclusion, human ingenuity is always able to find a reason to stop short. Humans will never complete the journey with their own "steam." The problem is universal; the Christian tradition calls it sin, which can *only* be overcome by the utterly free and gracious work of the Holy Spirit. We will say much more about this in the last two chapters of the book.

(4) Finally, the story we have told lays the foundation for a uniquely Christian ethic of grace where the imperative always follows the indicative. This will be the topic of the next chapter.

—7—

The Ethics of Grace

There are two distinct ethical questions: (1) How can I know what to do and (2) how can I do what I already know I ought to do? Enlightenment ethics addresses the first question; it solves moral dilemmas. Virtue ethics addresses the second question; it builds the skills and habits that lead to happiness in this life. To this, Christian theology adds the promise of eternal life and the freedom that comes from knowing that "God is for us." Once we understand all this entails, we will see that the first question pretty much takes care of itself.

WEAKNESS OF WILL

Socrates famously argued that people never knowingly do what is wrong because "doing wrong" always ends up hurting themselves and no one intentionally hurts himself. Therefore, the only explanation for people doing something wrong is that they do not fully understand the consequences of their actions.[1] Once we become convinced that "what goes around comes around," the world's ethical problems will disappear. A generation later, Aristotle was not as quite as optimistic. Weakness of will exists. Today we call it self-destructive or addictive behavior. And even though such behavior

---

1. "No one who either knows or believes that there is another possible course of action, better than the one he is following, will ever continue on his present course." Plato, *Protagoras* 358b-c.

seems irrational—why would people intentionally harm themselves?—we know these behaviors exist because they can be observed, both in ourselves and others. Nonetheless, says Aristotle, it is only "sensory knowledge . . . which is dragged about by emotion."[2] If we *fully* understood the consequences of our actions, Aristotle seems to suggest, we would in fact always act in ways that benefit both ourselves and others.

A few centuries later, even this minimal optimism about reason's ability to control our actions had largely disappeared. St. Paul cried out in despair: "For I do not do the good I want, but the evil I do not want is what I do. . . . Wretched man that I am! Who will rescue me from this body of death?" (Rom 7:19). For Paul the problem was *not* "knowing what to do." Nor did Paul disagree with Socrates and Aristotle that people always "reap what they sow" (Gal 6:7). Rather, Paul saw a cancer growing within his soul, and like all cancers, its end was self-destruction. When cancer spreads throughout the body and kills its host, it thereby kills itself. Cancer's success ends in its own demise. This is absurd, and Paul knows it! He, like everyone else, wants to be happy; he wants to be a successful apostle; and he wants to see Christ glorified. Furthermore, he has no difficulty *knowing* what actions lead to happiness and are glorifying to God. Yet, he finds himself unable to do what he *wants* to do, even though there are no external impediments to his actions. Instead, the impediments are all within.

So too, with Aquinas and Barth the fundamental ethical problem is not lack of knowledge; it is sin, that absurdity in all of us by which we end up seeking our own misery and destruction. And as it is with St. Paul, so it is with both Aquinas and Barth—the ultimate solution to our problem must come from without. Without a Liberator to overpower and conquer the sin within, we are all in bondage and we will all die in bondage. Only if the story we told at the end of the last chapter is true; only if on the cross and in the resurrection Jesus really conquered Satan, sin, and death; only if the work of the Holy Spirit gives us a *new* life in Christ, can (and will) the absurdity of our predicament be resolved. "Who will rescue me from this body of death?" Paul, Aquinas and Barth know of only one answer: Jesus Christ through the Holy Spirit.

So in the *end*, Christian ethics *is* Christian theology.[3] But in the *beginning*, Christian ethics *starts* with good psychology.[4]

---

2. Aristotle, *Nicomachean Ethics* 1147b16.

3. This is especially clear in the structure of Barth's massive *Church Dogmatics* where his ethics is seamlessly woven throughout his theology.

4. In her famous essay "Modern Moral Philosophy," Elizabeth Anscombe makes precisely this point.

GOOD PSYCHOLOGY

Aquinas's *Summa Theologica* is five volumes long and is broken into three parts. The first focuses on God, the second on humans, and the third on Christ as our way back to God. But the longest section by far is the second part, which is itself broken into a first and second part. Now it would be a mistake to conclude that since the part focusing on humans is the longest, humans are at the center of Aquinas's thought. The truth is precisely the opposite. It is because the plight of humans left to their own accord is so dismal that Aquinas spends so much time and energy diagnosing our spiritual and psychological aliments. So in the first section of the second part, Aquinas describes our psychology (i.e., our will, emotions, reason, and habits),[5] and in the second section of the second part, Aquinas describes the *cure* for our broken souls (i.e., the theological virtues of faith, hope, and charity). Then, in the third part, he gives us the medicine (Christ, the church's sacraments, and the Holy Spirit) that will restore us to a right relation with the God who is the only source of lasting happiness.

As many have described it, the argument of Aquinas's *Summa* is one big circle. The story of God our good Creator is told in the first part. The second part tells of humanity's futile rebellion against its Creator. And the third part tells of Christ restoring the broken relation between the Creator and his creatures. That's the big picture. In this section our focus will be limited to Aquinas's description of our psychological condition.

Augustine says there is only one reason to philosophize: to achieve happiness.[6] Aquinas agrees. "Well-ordered self-love," he says, "is right and natural; a self-love by which one wishes for oneself what is suitable."[7] But what kind of self-love is "suitable"? Aquinas answers this question just as a craftsman would answer the question: What's the most suitable tool for doing X? The answer, not surprisingly, depends on what you are trying to do.

---

5. "For Aquinas, ethics is nothing other than the study of human psychology insofar as it flourishes or fails to flourish . . . Aquinas' approach offers a refreshing synthesis of psychology and ethics. In many popular understandings, there is something paradoxical about divine commandments: God gives us desires and then commands us not to act on them. For Aquinas, there is no paradox, because God commands us through the desires he give us. The commandments of divine revelation are ancillary to our natural inclinations; they are signposts to the fulfillment of desire, shorthand conclusions following from the logic of human nature." Lombardo, *The Logic of Desire*, xi.

6. Augustine, *City of God* IX.1.

7. *Summa Theologica* I-II.77.4.1. Barth himself writes that God's command is "desirable and pleasant and true and good and beautiful. In the face of it, the justifiable concern of eudemonism [happiness] need not be displaced." *Church Dogmatics* II.2, 652. Furthermore, "We want to be happy," said Aquinas, "not by free choice but by natural instinct." *Summa Theologica* I.90.10, see also I.19.3, 82.1–2, 83.2, I-II.5.4.

If you are cutting a piece of wood, then a saw is the most suitable tool. If you are pounding a nail, the handle of a saw might do in a pinch, but a hammer is much more suitable. Likewise, if you are looking for a suitable kind of self-love, you must begin by asking: what are humans meant to do? At a higher level, this question is theological. But at a lower level, it is a straightforward question about the essential nature of a human being. And just as questions about the essential nature of sodium should be approached scientifically, questions about the nature of our "soul" (*psyche* in Greek) should be approached psychologically.

As we argued in chapter 2, our "soul" is not *in* us that way that dirt is in a rug. Rather, our soul is the animating principle (or "life within") that enables various kinds of things (plants, animals, and humans) to successfully achieve various kinds of ends. Describing the nature of our "life within" tells us *what* humans are. And once we know what we are, we will know what we are most suited to do.

At this lower level, Aquinas followed Aristotle's lead. Commonsense observations about what humans *do* reveal three basic categories. First, we eat, drink, and copulate just like all other animals. Second, we form friendships of various degrees with other humans. And third, we ask questions about everything, from how to get the last fifty RPM from a motorcycle engine, to what the essential nature of sodium is, to what happens when we die.

Though all of us ask questions about dying, not all of us ask questions about motorcycle engines or the essential nature of sodium. But as a species it is hard to disagree with Aristotle's observation that all people *by nature* desire knowledge.[8] While some of the things we seek to know are required by life itself (e.g., how can we stay warm over a long, cold winter?), many of the things we seek to know transcend mere animal existence (e.g., what keeps the earth in motion and what happens when we die?).

Of course, bears and wolverines, like humans, also want to know how they can survive long, cold winters. And like humans, bears and wolverines have come up with some very clever ways of doing just this, so no one should deny that bears and wolverines are intelligent animals. But we have no evidence that bears and wolverines do astronomy or contemplate their death. This difference between animal intelligence and human intelligence, Aristotle argued, was evidence of a specific human ability called "rationality," which is our defining attribute.[9]

8. Opening sentence of Aristotle's *Metaphysics*.

9. A necessary condition for asking questions about our own death is the power of self-reflection. "[N]o sensitive power reflects upon itself. . . . the supreme and perfect grade of life which is in the intellect, for the intellect reflects upon itself and the intellect

Not only do humans and other animals ask different questions; humans and other animals have different means of acquiring the answers they seek. Bears and wolverines do it by *instinct*; humans do very little by instinct. Instead, we *learn* how to answer our various questions from the *community* into which we are born. Of course, ants and wolves also live in communities. But baby ants do not learn what they need *from their elders*, since their survival is dependent on instinct, or as we would say, it is genetically hardwired. Even wolves, intelligent socializing mammals that they are, do not spend years at the feet of instructors as we do, learning everything from the alphabet to advanced engineering. Instead, they learn by observing and then imitating the actions of other wolves. So, in Aristotelian terms, a second defining attribute of humans is our social nature—without a community of responsible elders, we could not learn what we need to know for survival, nor could we lead a humanly significant life pursuing the true, the good, and the beautiful (which had been considered the highest goal of human life by the ancient Greek philosophers).

Furthermore, the difference between wolf and human society is more than a mere difference of degree. Because a large brain (as far as we know) is a necessary condition for abstract thought, human craniums must be relatively large with respect to the rest of the body. Delaying birth until the body and brain becomes more developed would make the passage of the cranium through the birth canal much more difficult and dangerous. The biological solution to this problem is that humans, compared to other animals, are born about seventeen months premature.[10] Puppies and kittens can move themselves around the day they are born. Newborn human babies can't even hold up their heads by themselves. The only way human babies can survive is with significant assistance from family and friendly members of the community.

Science has also provided an explanation for the easily observed differences between animal instinct and human learning. Aristotle argued long ago that one good way to distinguish between instinct and learning is to determine whether all members of a species solve a particular problem in the same way. Bears all hibernate to survive long, cold winters. Wolverines all have extremely warm fur and have developed sophisticated (and fearless) hunting techniques to survive long, cold winters. And humans have all learned to make clothes and shelter to survive long, cold winters. But the *kind* of clothes and the *kind* of shelters that humans make and use vary

---

can understand itself." Aquinas, *Summa Contra Gentiles* IV.11, 4–5.

10. Mayr, *What Evolution Is*, 249.

tremendously. While some of the variation has to do with the availability of materials, the most cursory study of comparative cultures reveals that much of it has to do with *learned* tastes and preferences.

With this in mind, consider Ernst Mayr, whom we first discussed in chapter 4. He argues that one of the most important biological criteria for ranking humans above all other animals

> is parental care (promoted by internal fertilization), which provides the potential for transferring information nongenetically from one generation to the next. And the possession of such information is of course of considerable value in the struggle for existence. This information transfer generates at the same time a selection pressure in favor of an improved storage system for such remembered information, that is, an enlarged central nervous system. And, of course, the combination of postnatal care and an enlarged central nervous system is the basis of culture, which together with speech, sets humans quite aside from all other living organism.[11]

In short, the necessary information for survival in all nonhuman animals is *genetically* passed from one generation to the next; in humans it is *nongenetically* passed from one generation to the next via a culture made possible by language.

Mayr continues, "Even though we often use the word 'language' in connection with the information transmittal systems of animals, such as the 'language of bees,' actually all of these animal species have merely systems of giving and receiving signals. To be a language, a system of communication must contain syntax and grammar. Psychologists have attempted for half a century to teach language to chimpanzees, but in vain. Chimps seem to lack the neural equipment to adopt syntax. *Therefore, they cannot talk about the future or the past.*"[12]

Aristotelians define the human soul (*psyche*) in terms of two unique traits: (1) rationality, which enables humans to communicate with a language sufficiently rich to name concepts for which there is no image (such as chiliagons, yesterday, or tomorrow) and (2) our social nature, which enables humans to pass on the accumulated knowledge of past generations to future generations. We believe that this definition has stood up quite well to the discoveries and theories of modern biology.[13]

---

11. Mayr, *One Long Argument*, 66.
12. Mayr, *What Evolution Is*, 253, emphasis added.
13. Of course, there is much more to be said on this subject, some of which I discuss in *In Defense of the Soul*.

Moderns might ask, "What does psychology have to do with ethics and morality? After all, it is impossible to ever deduce a *value* from a *fact*." But as we will see in the next section, this is a uniquely modern prejudice.

THE IMPERATIVE ALWAYS FOLLOWS THE INDICATIVE[14]

A generation ago, philosophers were discussing what G. E. Moore labeled "the naturalistic fallacy." This was the alleged fallacy of trying to infer an "ought" (imperative) from an "is" (indicative). In one sense, it is obviously fallacious to argue that since rapists, thieves, and murderers all exist, therefore it is morally permissible to rape, steal, and murder. But in another sense, Moore's "naturalistic fallacy" is itself fallacious.

Moore argued that it was impossible to infer an "ought" from an "is" because he assumed a rigid fact/value distinction. Few of his contemporaries questioned this assumption since it grew straight out of the positivism that was then the dominant philosophy. As we saw in chapter 3, positivists assumed that facts are *objective* because they are scientifically established, whereas values are *subjective* because, like beauty, they only exist in the eye of the beholder. With a single wave of the positivist's hand, all ethical judgments are thereby dismissed as nothing more than an expression of individual's and/or culture's subjective preferences. Moore granted the positivists their premise; however, he argued that moral judgments could nonetheless be objectively justified because (1) "goodness" was a "non-natural" objective property of certain actions and events and (2) all properly educated people had an immediate and direct "intuition" of this "non-natural" property.

Aquinas would certainly have sympathized with Moore's *goal*—and when we talk later about the place of conscience in moral judgments we will see a certain similarity with Moore's notion of an immediate and direct "intuition." But Aquinas, following Aristotle, would never have approved of his *argument*. Moore thought that the term "good" was indefinable. Aristotle, on the other hand, began his treatise on ethics by defining the good as that which all humans by nature seek and desire.[15] Moore thought that it was an "open question" whether or not pleasure was good. Aristotle thought that it was obvious that pleasure is good; the only serious question is whether pleasure is the *only* good. Without pleasures and pains to guide them, no animal would survive, and certainly, in the higher mammals, sexual pleasure is the primary means to ensure the survival of the species. So, since humans are

14. This phrase is one of Barth's favorites.
15. Aristotle, *Nicomachean Ethics* 1.1.1094a.

generically animals, it follows that at least certain kinds of pleasures are good. Not only *do* we seek these pleasures (an indicative), but we *ought* to seek these pleasures (an imperative).

On the other hand, Aristotle would be the first to insist that humans are not *merely* animals. Our social and rational nature must frequently trump our animal desires. And this "must" also follows from the indicative. Because we *are* social and rational, this means that, among other things, adultery will always be wrong—there is never a time or place when sexual relations with a person other than one's spouse is morally acceptable.[16] Why? It was not because Aristotle had read the Ten Commandments. Rather, he simply looked at the indicatives that follow from adultery—a broken marriage that contributes to social decay. Since humans are by nature social animals, and since the primary social unit is the family, Aristotle concluded that adultery contradicts what humans *are*. So, again, an imperative (don't be an adulterer) follows from the indicative (humans are social animals).

Now there are two sorts of contemporary objections to this line of argument. First, the claim that broken marriages contribute to social decay is much discussed by social scientists. And there is some disagreement among social scientists about the nature and strength of the causal connection between broken marriages and social decay. Therefore, some may argue that there is insufficient evidence to justify Aristotle's claim that adultery is a significant contributor to social decay. But even if it turns out that the evidence is insufficient, there is no disagreement about whether this is an empirical question open to the standard research methods of the social sciences. That is, there is no question about the "indicative" nature of the claim (eventually to be proven true or false by social scientists) that broken marriages lead to social decay.

Second, there is the objection summed up in the phrase "existence precedes essence." It was famously coined by Jean Paul Sartre and repeated throughout the '60s. Though the phrase is no longer with us, the idea behind it continues to exert a powerful influence. Sartre's point was to stand Aristotle on his head. Aristotle thought that our essential nature as human beings dictated, in broad outline, what would constitute a well-lived life. Just as humans don't *choose* what kinds of food will nourish the human body, neither do humans *choose* what kind of life will nourish the human soul (*psyche*). True, we can—and some people do—*choose* to limit our aspirations to sensual pleasure, material acquisition, and/or fame. But, Aristotle would argue, we can no more flourish as humans by ignoring our distinctively human calling to form friendships, to create and enjoy things of beauty, and, as far

---

16. Ibid., 2.6.1107a4–17.

as humanly possible, to pursue an understanding of things divine any more than we can *choose* to flourish on a diet of arsenic.

Sartre denies all of this. He argues that human nature is infinitely plastic, which is to say that there is no human nature. The only nature we have is that which we choose for ourselves. Human autonomy is the supreme value, and failure to take *sole* responsibility[17] for one's life is the supreme vice. The only sin is to live "inauthentically" by allowing other people or other institutions (like family, political parties, or churches) to make one's choices.

So how did Aristotle and Sartre reach such diametrically opposed positions? Here Sartre is quite explicit: "Existentialism is nothing else but an attempt to draw the full conclusions from a consistently atheistic position." And the first conclusion that follows is that "there is no human nature, because there is no God to have a conception of it."[18] On the other hand, as we argued in chapter 4, Aristotle was convinced that without a divine In-former, science would be impossible because there would be no essential natures, and without essential natures it is impossible to distinguish between real causation and mere correlation. Since Aristotle was a great fan of science and Sartre was not, it is not surprising that they would come to opposing positions concerning the essential natures of things, including humans.[19]

There is another difference between the way Aristotle and Sartre approach ethics. For Aristotle, the goal of ethics is to find the virtuous mean between two extremes. The reckless man fights at the slightest offense; the cowardly man never fights; the courageous man, on the other hand, fights at the right time, for the right reasons, and in the right way. In other words, the imperative for Aristotle is to employ practical wisdom to find the "golden mean" on the *continuum* between cowardliness and recklessness. Approaching ethics in this way via the virtues (as opposed to a set of rules) greatly diminishes our ethical quandaries.

---

17. Notice again the assumption of mono-causation.

18. Sartre, "Existentialism Is a Humanism."

19. Consider two propositions: (1) "If there is no God, then there are no essential natures" and (2) "If there are essential natures, then there is a God." These are contrapositives and hence they are logically equivalent propositions. Number one is the first premise of Sartre's argument and number two is the first premise of Aquinas's divine In-former argument that we considered in chapter 4. So if Sartre's first premise is true, then so is Aquinas's. The difference between Sartre and Aquinas is that Sartre denies the existence of essential natures, and hence, he logically committed to denying the real difference between causation and correlation. Aquinas, on the other hand, affirms the existence of essential natures, and hence, he affirms the real difference between causation and correlation. With Sartre, there is no God and no science. With Aquinas, there is both God and science.

Yet, such an approach is highly unsatisfying for those who demand that ethics be grounded in precise and unequivocal rules like: "Don't lie." But, if lying is *always* a violation of the moral law, then there is a real quandary for a Christian during the Holocaust who is hiding Jews. What if a member of the Nazi Gestapo asks, "Have you seen any Jews recently?" Is lying in such circumstances right or wrong? Here we have the topic of many late-night college "bull sessions." Much of the impetus (and angst) in these discussions comes from treating it as a "true or false" question where one's answer is either right or wrong. And like any problem involving rigid thresholds, there is no such thing as "partial credit" for coming close.

Aristotelians have no less interest than undergraduates in the question, but they treat it as an essay question where one's grade is determined by the quality of the reasoning behind the answer. Even if one needs 90 points to earn an A, an 89 is still a very good grade and a single-point deficit can certainly be overcome in the future. So, for an Aristotelian, the anxiety level for the well-prepared students on "moral tests" is relatively low.

But in another sense, an Aristotelian approach is much more rigorous. Questions about the permissibility of lying while hiding Jews in Nazi Germany may produce great anxiety for non-Aristotelians for whom there must be a yes or no answer. Yet, on the other hand, they have the luxury of knowing that the question is more theoretical than practical. After all, very few people ever have to make such a decision about whether to lie under such extreme circumstances. In fact, if we think of ethics as a set of prohibitions—don't steal; don't murder; don't commit adultery; don't lie—then days, even weeks, will go by without ever having to make an ethical decision.

Aristotelians don't have this luxury. Every day, even every hour, all of us are making "ethical" decisions; that is, we are making choices that create habits that are making us either more virtuous or more vicious. And since virtue is a necessary condition for human happiness, the habits we are forming every day of our life are never a trivial concern.

Sartre, of course, was not a virtue theorist, and certainly not a Christian. Hence, he never worried that his eternal destiny might hinge on getting the right answer to a true/false question about whether to tell a lie while hiding Jews. However, he famously considered a similar question. Suppose one has to make a choice: should you stay home to take care of your elderly mother or should you join the French resistance and fight the Nazis? For Sartre this is a kind of true/false question. You can't do both; you must do one or the other and the consequences of either are great. It's like being forced to leap over a twenty-foot chasm—missing by an inch is no better than missing by ten feet. One never has the luxury of saying, "I *had* to do that, so I can't be blamed for the consequences." You, and you alone, are fully responsible for your actions.

So Aristotle's virtue ethic and Sartre's existentialism are each quite demanding in their own way. For Sartre, one can never avoid responsibility for the consequences of one's actions by noting that at least their intentions were good. For Aristotle, there are no "moral holidays"; every day and every hour we are inexorably creating habits—some are virtuous, some are not.

Though Aquinas never had to choose between virtue ethics and existentialism, there was a similar dispute in his own time. It was the dispute between those who grounded ethics in reason, broadly understood, and those who grounded it in God's will, narrowly understood. Why are murder, theft, and adultery wrong? Some philosophers argued that these are only wrong because God said they were wrong. Since God is infinite, there are absolutely no limits on his will. If God wants to be "unreasonable," he is perfectly free to do so, since his will reigns supreme. Therefore, like the leader of a gang, if God had so willed it, he might have issued the commandment that to enter the kingdom of heaven (his gang), everyone must commit at least one murder.[20]

Aquinas was unequivocal in his rejections of such a position: "To say that justice depends simply upon the will of God, is to say that the divine will does not proceed according to the regulations of wisdom; and this is blasphemous."[21] Aquinas's reasons are implicit in the arguments we developed previously. God's creation is good because it is an *ordered* creation. Aquinas was fond of the biblical verse "Thou hast ordered all things in measure, and number, and weight" (Wis 11:21). It is this ordering of nature in terms of essential natures which makes it possible for scientists to distinguish between mere correlations and real causes.

God did not *simply* decree that murder, theft, and adultery were wrong; rather, he created a universe in which many effects follow causes in a predictable and humanly discernable fashion. Just as there are laws of nature that allow us to predict that unsupported heavy objects will always move toward the center of the earth, so too, there are moral laws that allow us to predict that murder, theft, and adultery are contrary to human flourishing. God's moral decrees must not be thought of as *external* constraints that limit God's freedom. As one philosopher put it, "To say, therefore, that God is bound by it [the moral law] is merely to say, from one particular

---

20. Duns Scotus and William of Ockham are two primary examples of this position. See Mascall, *He Who Is*, 122, and Pinckaers, *Sources of Christian Ethics*, 248.

21. Aquinas, *On Truth*, q. 23, art. 6.

angle, that God is God."[22] In other words, because of the indicative (i.e., God created humans as rational, social animals), the imperatives against murder, theft, and adultery follow straightaway.

One final point needs to be made about indicatives and imperatives—it concerns what has come to be called the "hedonistic paradox." Humans are created in such a way that we all seek happiness, not misery. So does that mean that "happiness" is something toward which we should direct our actions? In a word: No. We must never make happiness our goal. If we do, we will not achieve it. Happiness is always achieved *indirectly*. "We arrive at happiness through actions," says Aquinas.[23] By pursuing other worthy goals—making a motorcycle go faster, learning to play the piano well, participating in the church's worship of God—happiness will follow. Happiness is the reward for a job well done; it is not the job itself.

Contemporary social psychologists have come to the same conclusion. While positivism was the dominate philosophy for the middle half of the twentieth century, behaviorism was the dominate psychology for the same period. The idea behind behaviorism was that people (and mammals in general) only act to avoid pain or to achieve a reward (such as food, water, or sex). But then psychologists began to look more carefully at the behavior of apes, monkeys, and human babies. And what they observed is that they all have "a basic drive to *make things happen*. You can see it in the joy infants take with 'busy boxes,' the activity centers that allow them to convert flailing arm movements into ringing bells and spinning wheels."[24] What made this surprising, and ultimately contributed to the demise of behaviorism, is that there was no reward for this expenditure of effort other than the joy of a job well done!

CHRISTIAN ETHICS IS CHRISTIAN THEOLOGY[25]

We've just completed what might be called the "preambles" to a Christian ethic of gratitude. And while such an ethic has its *starting point* in the virtue ethics of Aristotle, it doesn't end there. Aristotelian ethics formulate the real secondary causes that lead to a well-lived life *as we now know it*. And while life as we now know it was the whole story for Aristotle, it was not the whole story for Aquinas and Barth. The new life made possible by Christ's

22. Mascall, *He Who Is*, 122.
23. Aquinas, *Summa Theologica* I-II.6, "Introduction."
24. Haidt, *Happiness Hypothesis*, 220.
25. "The propositions of Christian ethics are propositions of Christian dogmatics." Barth, *Church Dogmatics* II.2, 603.

The Ethics of Grace

triumph over Satan, sin, and death is the goal of Christians. How, then, is this achieved?

Once more, we must answer in terms of dual-causation. The primary cause is God's grace. Here, more than any place else, a "scientific" discussion of secondary causation is woefully inadequate. The specifically Christian virtues of faith, hope, and love are utterly beyond the reach of human striving. When they come to a person, they come as a *gift*; they are never an *achievement*. While not denying the part played by the humanly administered and received sacraments, with respect to faith, hope, and love, human secondary causes are utterly insignificant when compared to the primary causation of the Holy Spirit.

But to insist that human secondary causes are (ultimately) insignificant is not to say that they are unimportant. After all, compared to God, everything is insignificant. Even though Paul insists that "it is God who is at work in you to both will and to work for his good pleasure," he begins by exhorting us to "work out your own salvation with fear and trembling" (Phil 2:12–13). Such a verse obviously raises big questions about the compatibility of free will and predestination. We will say much more about this in chapter 9. But for the rest of this chapter, we will stay wholly at the level of human willing and doing. And we will do this by contrasting the ethics of gratitude with an ethic of worthiness.

The clearest statement of the ethics of gratitude is in Saint John's First Epistle: "We love because God first loved us" (4:19). The clearest statement of the ethics of worthiness is found in Immanuel Kant's *Religion within the Limits of Reason Alone*. We begin with Kant.

Kant's famous "categorical imperative" is commonly understood to forbid certain kinds of actions no matter what the circumstances or consequences. Though Kant died two centuries before Hitler, his essay, "On the Supposed Right to Lie from Altruistic Motives," anticipates the stock question of today's quandary ethics that we previously considered: Is it right to lie to the Nazis to save Jews hiding in your basement? He answers with a firm No.[26] Kant is also commonly understood to explicitly rule out personal happiness as a legitimate goal in moral reasoning. If a businessman never

---

26. Kant writes, "After you have honestly answered the murderer's question as to whether his intended victim is at home, it may be that he has slipped out so that he does not come in the way of the murderer, and thus that the murder many not be committed. But if you had lied and said he was not at home when he had really gone out without your knowing it, and if the murderer had then met him as he went away and murdered him, you might justly be accused as the cause of his death. For if you had told the truth as far as you knew it, perhaps the murderer might have been apprehended by the neighbors while he searched the house and thus the deed might have been prevented." "Right to Lie," 2.

cheats his customers *because* he believes that a reputation for honesty is good for business, then the businessman's actions are of no moral worth. "Do the right thing because it leads to success and happiness." This is a hypothetical imperative; it assumes that personal happiness stands above the moral law itself. The categorical imperative, on the other hand, is: Do the right thing—period, full stop, with no exceptions and no concern for personal happiness.

But the story doesn't end there. Kant also sought to limit reason in order to make room for God, free will, and immortality. While each of these transcend human experience, and thus, transcend what can be *known*, he thought they were the necessary postulates (assumptions) for morality. Unless good is ultimately rewarded and evil punished, there is no morality. Obviously, in this life, good frequently goes unrewarded and evil unpunished. So, we must have faith, said Kant, that there is a God who in the next life will reward us for freely choosing to do the right thing, i.e., choosing without the incentive of personal happiness.

What this means, according to Kant, is that we should never *aim* for happiness, but instead, we should aim to be *worthy* of happiness. Whether good acts will *in fact* result in personal happiness is unknowable, according to Kant. We can only *hope* that there is a God who, in the end, will reward our worthiness, since there can be no philosophical or scientific reason to think that such a God exists. But here's the important point: if it turns out that there is a God, then Kant thinks it is simply obvious that this God is *obligated* to distribute rewards and punishment according to a person's individual worth as measured by his or her wholly free and autonomous choices here on earth.

But Aquinas and Barth reject this Enlightenment conception of God. First, Kant's aim to be *worthy* of happiness empties God's *grace* of much (if not all) of its content. And, second, Kant fails to fully appreciate what it means to say that God is the creator of the universe. Instead he thinks of "God" as the supernatural judge who infallibly dispenses rewards and punishments according to individual merit. And though this judge is supernatural, it is clear to Kant that he is univocally bound by the same rules as judges here on earth.

This is in sharp contrast with Aquinas and Barth. They both assume that there is an infinite qualitative difference between the Creator and the created, and hence, all our affirmations concerning God must always be analogical;[27] they are never univocal (see chapter 2). So our descriptions

---

27. "But the object itself—God's truth in His revelation as the basis of the veracity of our knowledge of God—does not leave us any option but to resort to this concept [analogy].... And, pressed again by the true revelation of God, we are pushed on to the

of God must always include both a Yes and a No—Yes, God exists, but No, he doesn't exist like us; Yes, God is good, but No, he isn't good like us; Yes, God is just, but No, his justice isn't the same as human justice. Yes, God is all-knowing and all-powerful, but No, he can't ride a bicycle![28]

On the other hand, Kant's set of categorical imperatives—don't lie; don't murder; don't steal; don't commit adultery—bear a striking resemblance to the second book of the Decalogue. They are even reminiscent of Aristotle's assertion that there is never a right time, place, or person with whom to commit adultery. In such cases, Aristotle says, "The very name conveys baseness."[29] Isn't this convergence of Kant, Moses, and Aristotle a strong argument for the existence of moral absolutes? Yes, but the notion of a moral absolute must be understood correctly.

Barth compares moral absolutes to a "frame" encircling the Christian life.[30] Art schools teach how to draw and paint. But it is unlikely that they begin their instruction with the command: Make sure you stay within the frame of the picture! That goes without saying. And no artist takes pride in the fact that his paint remains wholly inside the frame of the canvas. Nor is it a serious criticism of an artist's skill if, in extreme circumstances—say an earthquake or tornado—some of his paint is "applied" to surfaces outside the frame. Likewise, while adultery is always wrong, not all instances of sexual relations outside of marriage are adultery. A married woman who has been violently raped is not an adulteress—only *wrongful* intercourse outside of marriage is adultery.

And here the word "wrongful" functions in the same way that "ad hoc" functions when talking about auxiliary hypotheses used to save a theory from falsification (see chapter 3). While there are no logical rules that determine when an action is wrongful or when a hypothesis is ad hoc, we have no difficulty recognizing these in *extreme* cases. For example, it is ad hoc if a Flat-earther saves his theory by arguing that light is bent in the presence of a strong gravitational field. Conversely, it is quite legitimate to excuse a

---

word 'analogy.'" Barth, *Church Dogmatics* II.1, 225–26.

28. This sort of "negative theology" is crucial to Aquinas's theology, especially in the first thirteen questions of the *Summa Theologica*.

29. *Nicomachean Ethics* 1107a10.

30. "[T]he Ten Commandments do not contain any direct commands, but only prohibitions or rather delimitations. . . . [W]e must not expect to find here something more or other than a framework and programme of the divine action and corresponding human conduct. . . . The whole history of Israel develops, accordingly, with the framework provided by the revelation of the Law, but not as if this framework were itself the picture: for the latter consists in the special concrete events of divine commanding and forbidding, of human obedience or disobedience, not envisaged in the Law as such." Barth, *Church Dogmatics* II.2, 684–86.

married woman who is violently raped. In such a case, her intercourse with a man who is not her husband is not wrongful. Of course, not everyone is willing to make reasonable judgments about such cases. For example, there are cultures where women who have been violently raped *are* the object of "honor killing." But, then, there are also Flat-earthers who will dismiss contrary evidence as nothing more than a "communist plot"!

However, as we move away from extreme cases and closer to the center, it becomes more difficult to make good judgments about ad hocness and wrongfulness. Is Newton's hypothesis that God keeps the universe from collapsing ad hoc? Again, this is not something that deductive logic can decide. As we argued in chapter 3, there is no logical bridge that connects observations to theories. It was only *after* scientists had undertaken a careful and thorough consideration of all the particulars of Newton's theory of universal gravity that they then concluded that it was superior to the Aristotelian understanding of gravity.[31]

The same is true of Mrs. Bergmeier. She is the woman made famous in Christian circles by Joseph Fletcher's book *Situational Ethics*. After being placed in a POW. camp by the Russian army as they advanced toward Berlin, Mrs. Bergmeier was faced with an extremely difficult choice. Should she remain in the prison camp, separated from her family who had no idea if she was dead or alive, or should she allow herself to be impregnated by a willing guard, in which case she would become a liability and be sent back to Germany? Is this sort of "sacrificial adultery" a case of *wrongful* intercourse? Here we are getting pretty near the center of the continuum and reasonable people are going to disagree: some will say Yes, others No.

Yet, there is a third alternative, namely to reject the question. "In ethics it is not a matter of what somebody ought to do in a hypothetical case, but of what we ourselves ought to do in our own given situation," said Barth.[32] And Aquinas explains why. "But the means to the end, in human concerns, far from being fixed, are of manifold variety according to the variety of persons and affairs."[33] We are not in a position to answer a question concerning Mrs. Bergmeier one way or the other; she is the only one who has sufficient knowledge of the particulars to make such a judgment. A case of

---

31. See ch. 2 of my *Life, the Universe, and Everything*.

32. Barth, *Church Dogmatics* II.2, 654. And with respect to "rejecting the question," Barth says, "Again, the problem of an eventual mitigation of penalty does not fall in the sphere of our investigation, since ethics cannot give direction as to judging, let alone punishing, but only as to the proper approach to what is right or wrong before God." *Church Dogmatics* III.4, 428.

33. Aquinas, *Summa Theologica* II-II.47.15.

conscience[34] such as this cannot be decided by "looking up" the answer in a book of casuistry. (Casuistry is the attempt to deduce a particular conclusion from general moral principles or commands of God, thereby specifying *in advance* what a person should do in particular circumstances.)

Though it is seldom noticed, the story of the good Samaritan is, at least in part, directed against casuistry. To understand the full impact of Jesus' story it is imperative that we remember the verse in Leviticus that its original audience of religious lawyers knew so well: "God said to Moses, 'Speak to the priests, the sons of Aaron, and say to them that none of them shall defile himself for the dead among his people, except for his nearest of kin, his mother, his father, or his virgin sister'" (Lev 21:1–2). The lawyers of Jesus' day treated this as a *general* command from which their conclusion could be deduced. So Jesus made sure that he told a story where the priest and Levite were flawless in their deductions:

1. The man lying on the side of the road may be dead; or worse yet, he may die in my hands if I try to help.
2. He is not my nearest of kin, mother, father, or virgin sister.
3. Therefore, God commands me in Leviticus 21 to pass by on the other side.

While their logic was impeccable, their assumption of casuistry made them unable to hear the *particular* command of God for the *particular* situation.[35]

In a long excursus[36] in *Church Dogmatics,* Barth gives twenty-eight biblical examples of God's *particular* commands, each of which was given *before* God gave Moses the Decalogue in Exodus 20. Then, limiting himself only to the Gospel of Matthew, he cites thirty-one more examples of *particular* commands given to a particular person at a particular place. Here are just a few of God's *particular* commands:

- Commands Abraham to leave the country.
- Commands Sarah to change her name.
- Commands Lot to leave Sodom.
- Commands Moses to remove his shoes before the burning bush.
- Commands the Israelites not to gather manna on Saturdays.
- Commands Joseph to marry Mary.

---

34. "Conscience is nothing other than the application of knowledge to a particular action." Aquinas, *Summa Theologica* I-II.19.5.

35. Barth, *Church Dogmatics* II.2, 664.

36. Ibid., II.2, 673–75.

- Commands Joseph and Mary to flee to Egypt.
- Commands Peter and Andrew to leave their fishing nets.
- Commands a son to leave the burial of his father to others.
- Commands a blind man to tell no one that he was healed by Jesus.

Barth's point in producing such an extensive list is that "we usually think too readily and one-sidedly . . . of universal religious-moral-juridical rules and therefore with legal codes that are valid regardless of space and time." This causes us to forget that "as the Lord of this history, God seems hardly to be interested at all in general and universally valid rules, but properly only in certain particular actions and achievement and attitudes. . . . We must divest ourselves of the fixed idea that only a universally valid rule can be a command."[37] Yes, we must make sure our paint stays on the canvas and within the frame. But if that is all we learn, we will be poor artists. So too, we must never *wrongfully* kill, lie, steal,[38] or commit adultery. But if that's all we have learned from the Bible, we have learned very little indeed!

So how ought we to make moral decisions in hard cases? Barth's answer is that we must listen for the Holy Spirit speaking *to* our conscience. And he is very clear that God's "command is not revealed and given *by* conscience but *to* conscience."[39] The "conscience" is not a decision-making organ, nor is it the primary cause of our decisions; it is only the organ (secondary cause) we use to listen for the word of God.[40] And just as the eyes of geologists must be trained before they can see the subtle differences in various strata of rocks, so too, the conscience of a Christian must be trained before it can accurately hear God's commands for particular cases.[41]

---

37. Ibid., II.2, 672–673.

38. We will devote the whole of the next chapter to fleshing out the idea of wrongfully taking from someone else.

39. Barth, *Church Dogmatics* II.2, 668.

40. "To have a conscience is no more and no less than to have the Holy Spirit. For 'no one knows what is in God except the Spirit of God' (1 Cor 2:11)." Barth, *Ethics*, 477. And "'Violation of freedom of conscience, no matter how well intended, always means that the others upon whom I force myself with the claim of my conscience no longer hear their own." Barth, *Ethics*, 194.

41. "In this field there can be no absolute Yes or No carrying an absolute commitment. One reason for this is that an absolute guarantee of human right and worth cannot be expected from the rule of any idea or the power of any life-form. From one standpoint or another, every idea or life-form will sooner or later prove a threat to man. Hence Christians, looking always to the only problem that seriously and finally interests them, must allow themselves the liberty in certain circumstances of saying only a partial Yes or No where a total one is expected, or a total Yes or No where a partial one is expected, or of saying Yes today where they said No yesterday, and vice versa. Their total and definitive decision is for man and not for any cause. They will never let

First, Christians need to understand that the God of Abraham, Isaac, and Jacob is not a "supernatural" being who makes *moral* judgments the way that human judges make *legal* judgments. Nor is the difference merely that human judges lack all the facts and are sometimes prejudicial in their judgments. It is not merely the infallibility of God's judgments that sets him apart. It is the fact that God is the creator of all that is, and as the sovereign and free creator, he is the lord, king, and judge of good and evil. (We will say much more about the transcendental link between God and good in chapter 10.)

Here, however, we must be clear that Barth is *not* affirming what we saw Aquinas reject earlier, namely, that "if God so willed, He might have commanded that to enter the kingdom of heaven, everyone must commit at least one murder."[42] Being the lord, king, and judge of good and evil is not the same as tyrannically imposing one's own will merely because one has the power to do so. "Power as power does not have any divine claim, no matter how imposing or effective it might be. . . . By deciding for God he [the Christian] has definitely decided not to be obedient to power as power."[43] The well-trained conscience obeys the particular commands of God because it looks to God as the Choreographer of all history. For example, after the fall, public nudity is not good. However, Isaiah had a trained conscience and obeyed when God said at a *particular* time, to a *particular* person for a *particular* reason that he was to prophesize naked for three years (Isa 20:2).

History is a dance that is only performed once. Not knowing what is to come, the dancers must learn to hear and obey the Choreographer as the dance is being performed. Left to their own devices, none of the dancers could know which steps would complement the future moves of the other dancers and which would turn the dance into a clumsy charade. So the good dancers hear and obey, not because the Choreographer has power, but because he knows what moves will follow the moves the dancers

---

themselves be addressed as prisoners of their own decisions or slaves of any sacrosanct consistency. Their Yes and No in this sphere can always be only a relative Yes and No, supremely because if it were more they would be affirming and acknowledging the existence of those absolute or lordless powers, canonizing their deification, and instead of resisting the true and most dangerous enemies of man and his right, life, and worth, offering them the most hazardous and fateful help." Barth, *Christian Life*, 268. Haddorff sums it up like this: "First, there is the conscience. Throughout his various ethical writings, Barth is consistent with the claim that the freedom of conscience depends upon the self's understanding of God's freedom to act and speak through the Word, which releases her from being preoccupied with her own moral consciousness as well as the consciences of others." *Christian Ethics*, 347.

42. See previous note concerning Duns Scotus and William of Ockham.
43. Barth, *Church Dogmatics* II.2, 553.

are presently performing. Though a particular move (prophesizing naked for three years) may appear awkward to the dancers, who can only make judgments in view of what *has happened*, the Choreographer has plans and purposes which, with hindsight, the dancers will one day see to be precisely the correct move—*given what was to come*. Thus, we must learn to hear and obey the commands of God not because God has power, but because God has plans and purposes.

Second, if we are to be able to hear God speaking *to* our conscience, we must place ourselves under the instruction of the church universal. Barth writes:

> The Christian is in the church. He is not just in it externally, accidentally, or incidentally. He is not in it merely in the sense that he might first be a more or less good Christian by his personal choice and calling and on his own responsibility as a lonely hearer of God's Word, and only later, perhaps optionally and only at his own pleasure, he might take into account his membership in the church. If he were not in the church, he would not be in Christ. He is elected and called, not to the being and action of a private person with a Christian interest, but to be a living member of the living *community* of the living Lord Jesus Christ.[44]

The church is to Christian ethics what the family and community are to virtue ethics. As we said earlier, all babies are born helpless because they are biologically speaking about seventeen months premature. At one time, we were all utterly dependent upon the family and community into which we were born. While other mammals are richly "hardwired" with abilities and instincts for survival, we are not. Just as we cannot learn virtue without instruction from family and friends, we cannot learn the ethics of grace without the church.[45]

If a person were born into the kind of good society we'll describe in the next chapter, *even if it knew nothing about Christianity*, then that person could expect to receive instruction in the universal human struggle to overcome the fear of pain (courage) and the temptations of sensual pleasure (temperance). But the Christian has an additional struggle. As St. Paul says,

---

44. Barth, *Christian Life*, 188, emphasis added.

45. "The Word of God is not principally heard in one's individual conscience (as an autonomous faculty of reason and experience), nor in the community of the world (through social enculturation), but in the church, which remains the earthly community where the history of God's reconciliation of humanity, between the resurrection and the *parousia* is taking place." Haddorff, *Christian Ethics*, 353.

we are contending against "principalities and powers" (Eph 6:12). Barth describes these as

> the hidden wirepullers in man's great and small enterprises, movements, achievements, and revolutions. They are not just potencies but the real factors and agents of human progress, regress, and stagnation in politics, economics, scholarship, technology, and art, and also of the evolutions and retardations in all the personal life of the individual. It is not really people who do things, whether leaders or the masses. Through mankind's fault, things are invisibly done without and above man, even above the human individual in all his uniqueness, by the host of absolutisms, of powers that seek to be lordless and that make an impressive enough attempt to exhibit and present themselves as such.[46]

It is only in the church and its sacraments that we are continually reminded that Jesus "disarmed the principalities and powers and made a public example of them, triumphing over them on the cross" (Col 2:15). If this is ever forgotten, the ethics of grace will die.

Most importantly, it is within the church that we are instructed in the *indicatives* of Christian doctrine so that the *imperatives* of grace become obvious. But how, we are tempted to ask, can the imperative for Mrs. Bergmeier become obvious? Isn't it pure folly, or perhaps arrogance, to think that inside the church all moral dilemmas simply melt away?

Not if we understand the most frequent command in the New Testament—Be not anxious!—and the syllogism from which it follows:

1. The imperative always follows the indicative.

2. God is for us.

3. Therefore, be not anxious.

First, by definition, a moral dilemma requires that there be at least two moral rules in opposition. By focusing our ethical reflection on the above syllogism this definitional requirement for a dilemma is eliminated. Certainly there is no biblical injunction to be fearful. Yet, what other command could be in opposition to the command: Be not anxious?[47]

---

46. Barth, *Christian Life*, 216. As Haddorff describes it, "the powers corrupt social institutions that give order and meaning to people's lives and create instead communities of disorder and chaos. It is the *ignorance* of the powers, both in their existence and fallenness, which serves as its greatest potential threat to humanity." *Christian Ethics*, 278.

47. "Be not anxious!—Be not afraid!—the only possibility is either utter obedience or utter disobedience. . . . If God's claim on man is to be comprehended in a word, on

Second, what is true of Aristotelian virtue ethics is all the more true of Christian ethics: our understanding of virtue is always tested in an essay; never by a true or false question. The thing that gives "moral dilemmas" their bite is the assumption that missing the mark (the answer the teacher keyed) by an inch is as bad as missing it by a mile. But God never asks: Mrs. Bergmeier commit adultery—true or false? And neither is it a question that we should ever ask or attempt to answer. But even if it turns out that she missed the bull's-eye of perfect righteousness, she will have only missed it by an inch or so.

Of course, if God is *not* for us, then missing the mark by an inch may be as disastrous as only mustering up the strength to make a nineteen-foot–eleven-inch jump when the chasm is twenty feet wide. Here, the physical consequences are as harsh as if you had missed the mark by ten feet. But if the Christian indicative is true, i.e., if both God's power and will is *for us*, then the eternal consequences of missing the mark by an inch are nil.[48]

Christian ethics, as Barth understands it, always follows a Yes-No-Yes pattern. It begins with the glorious Yes of Jesus' death, shouldering the eternal consequences for all our sins—past, present, and future. Yet, in Jesus' resurrection, God said No to the powers and principalities. So we, too, must say No to the lordless powers and absolutes of this fallen age. But our stand against these powers will be "uneven" at best. And at the worst, we will utterly fail, since we are not Christ, but only *in* Christ. Nonetheless, since God is for us, we can go out and act with confidence, letting God worry about the consequences and remembering that the last word in the ethics of grace is always an eschatological Yes.

The crucial point, says Barth, is that we "think and speak in terms of theses and not principles."[49] A thesis is something that remains to be tested; a principle is a proposition that is assumed to be true prior to its implementation. Principles stand in advance and prior to a person's action "here and now." A thesis, on the other hand, is something that will be *tested* in

---

the one side (predominantly in the Johannine writings) it is that we should abide, and on the other (predominately in Paul) that we should stand." Barth, *Church Dogmatics* II.2, 600. There is no opposition or tension between Law and Gospel because the only command of the Law is to "abide" or "stand" in the Gospel and to "be not afraid."

48. "All our knowledge of the character of the divine command as such, and therefore all our obedience to it, stands or falls with our knowledge of the connexion between the indicative and the imperative in Gal. 5:1: 'For liberty Christ hath made us free: stand fast, therefore, and be not entangled again with the yoke of bondage.' He is relieved of all the care and all the fear of being for himself. . . the command of God can only be the deepest and most radical 'may' of the man who sees that God is not against him, but for him." Ibid., II.2, 593, 597.

49. Barth, *Christian Life*, 268

a person's action "here and now." In obedience to Christ, the Christian is encouraged not to "feel, or think, or consider, or meditate! Not turn it over in your heart and mind! But *do* something brave."[50]

In sum, Mrs. Bergmeier, like all of us, may have said Yes when she and we should have said No. And when that happens, the Author of creation will knock us down and the Holy Spirit will say: "That's not how it is done! Get up and try again."

CHRISTIAN EXHORTATION[51]

All of this means that the characteristic discourse of Christians must always be one of exhortation; it must never devolve into the language of "shoulds and oughts." Only God is the commander with authority to tell individuals what they should or should not do in a particular situation. The difference between telling and exhorting is the status of the one who speaks. Telling someone else what to do presupposes a higher status on a legal or social hierarchy. When a coach has a couple of replacement quarterbacks on the bench during preseason games, he has the status to *tell* the quarterback what to do. But in the third quarter of the Super Bowl, when the first- and second-string quarterbacks have already been injured and sent to the sidelines, the coach needs his quarterback as much as the quarterback needs the coach. Only the language of *exhortation* fits these sorts of situations.

There will always be leaders *telling* followers what to do when it comes to the administration of the church's affairs. But when it comes to making moral decisions, no Christian has the status to tell another Christian what he should or should not do. The moral status of all Christians is the same— we are the worst of the worse; we are pardoned murderers and child molesters! And remember, receiving a pardon does not mean that the person pardoned is free of guilt. It only means that they will not suffer the deserved punishment for their crimes.

To those currently outside the church, the ethics of grace has nothing to say except to stand as a witness to the truth of this indicative, namely, that *all* have been pardoned and set free (about this we will say much more in

---

50. Barth, *Church Dogmatics* IV.2, 540.

51. "*Paraclesis* [earnest exhortation] puts us in a relationship with God that has passed beyond legal justice to mercy. It is the most appropriate mode for the apostle when he is transmitting the doctrine of the Lord's mercy to his disciples, who have become his brothers and whom he addresses with the tenderness of a father. He does not give them orders as if they were servants, for he has already opened their hearts to love. He exhorts them by word and example, as his brothers and friends." Pinckaers, *Sources of Christian Ethics*, 165. See also Corbett, "Paraclesis as Moral Discourse," 89–107.

chapters 11 and 12). To those currently inside the church, the ethics of grace only exhorts others to more fully become all that God has created them to be. And conversely, *not* to want what God has created someone *else* to be! As Barth says,

> Not all human possibilities are the possibilities of all, even though they may seem desirable to all. . . . On the other hand, no one should make less of himself than he is. . . . Again—and this is perhaps the most urgent point—no one should try to be or pretend to be different from what he is. We must be careful not to become enamored of the roles which we see others play even if they seem to be finer and more interesting than our own. We must play our own part, and this alone. A genuine chorister is better than a false soloist, and an honest pupil than a supposed master on his own responsibility; and in any case there are no good or less good roles before God but only the right ones as individually assigned by Him.[52]

---

52. *Church Dogmatics* III.4, 388–89.

—8—

The Politics of Stewardship

Because we are social animals, virtue ethics can never be separated from politics. As Plato said, "the citizen must indeed be happy and good, and the legislator will seek to accomplish this; but very good and very rich at the same time he cannot be." The older Christian theologians concurred. Since God is the primary cause of all wealth, we are only its secondary cause and thus must act as good stewards.

This too changed with the Enlightenment. John Locke argued that when humans "mix" their labor with the land, God ipso facto grants them an individual right to the fruit of their labor, as long as nothing went to waste. However, with the invention of money, the fruit of the land could be transformed into a medium which did not rot (money), and hence, there were no longer moral and theological limits to an individual's acquisition of wealth. Government's obligation to protect private property became absolute. No longer did justice define property; now property defined justice. But Locke's argument fails.

A *Theory of Justice* by John Rawls is one of the most important books of the twentieth century. In it Rawls articulated and defended two fundamental principles of justice: (1) everyone should be granted maximum liberty to do as they please, just so long as they do not infringe on the rights of other people, and (2) inequalities of wealth are *only* justifiable when they work to the benefit of the least favored groups. In other words, Rawls has no objection to "trickle down" economics, if it in fact improves the condition of the poor.

Working out the details of these two principles takes Rawls over six hundred pages of closely argued text, because it is not difficult to envision conditions where the two principles conflict. If a businessman in San Francisco, following all the laws, works seventy hour per weeks to create a successful and highly profitable business, then why should his right to the fruit of his liberty and labor be contingent on his work having improved the conditions of the poor in Los Angles? And though Rawls works hard to reduce the conflicts between these two principles, he acknowledges that it is impossible to eliminate them completely. So in the end, he concludes that these two principles should be "lexically ordered." "This is an order which requires us to satisfy the first principle in the ordering before we can move on to the second.... A principle does not come into play until those previous to it are either fully met or do not apply."[1] In short, liberty trumps equality.

Thomas Aquinas had a very different understanding of the proper relation between liberty and equality because he had a very different understanding of liberty. Rawls assumes that liberty is the freedom to do what you *want*; Aquinas assumes that liberty is the ability to flourish as a human being by doing what you *need* to do.[2] Given Aquinas's definition of liberty, we don't have to decide whether liberty or equality should have priority because in his theory liberty and equality are grounded in the same principle: that of *need*. Everyone has an equal right to that which they *need* to flourish as a human being.

But unlike the radicals of the nineteenth century, Aquinas never suggests that equality of rights leads to the abolition of private property. He explicitly says that private property is good. If all property was held in common, Aquinas argued, the incentive to work would be weakened, order would be disrupted and hence there would be no peace.[3] Yet, in working out his theory of property, Aquinas kept firmly in mind the three philosophical and theological ideas previously defended:

- The Preacher's wisdom that "time and chance happen to *all*" (chapter 1).

---

1. Rawls, *Theory of Justice*, 43. See par. 82 (541–48) entitled "The Grounds for the Priority of Liberty" for his justification of the "lexical ordering" of the two principles.

2. Aquinas's assumption can be traced back to Aristotle. "It is evident that a State is not a sharing of locality for the purpose of preventing mutual harm and promoting trade. Those things must necessarily be present if a State is to exist; but even if they are all present a State does not thereby exist. Rather, a State is a sharing by households and families in a good life, for the purpose of a complete and self-sufficient life." Aristotle, *Politics* 3.9.1280b30–35.

3. *Summa Theologica* II-II.66.2.

- The Author of creation is the primary cause of *everything* (chapters 4 though 6).
- God created us as rational, *social* animals (chapter 7).

These truths set a natural limit on a person's right to accumulate private property because a person's freedom vis-à-vis property was always limited and trumped by the needs of others.

However, with the demise of these ideas, the relationship between justice and freedom vis-à-vis property was reversed. During the Enlightenment the freedom to accumulate unlimited property became an absolute right that trumped all other rights. This chapter will trace the history and review the rationale for this reversal and the triumph of political liberalism.

THE PROMISED LAND

The defining event in Jewish history was the exodus. Here there is no disagreement. Nor is there disagreement that the Bible uses the language of grace to describe this defining moment. The land of milk and honey is a *gift* from God. Yet the meaning and significance of this description has largely been forgotten in our post-Enlightenment age. There are many reasons for our forgetfulness, but one of them is the modern penchant for thinking in terms of mono-causation.

Our predilection for mono-causation is evident when we skeptically say things like: "Sure, the Bible *talks* about God's gift of the land to the Israelites, but in point of fact Joshua led a traditional army with swords and shields to *take* the land from the Hittites, Girgashites, Amorites, etc. This was not a 'gift'; it was war. The Jewish armies conquered and displaced the indigenous people of Palestine just as previous armies had been doing for centuries. To speak of God's 'gift' is a transparent rationalization for a war of aggression, followed by the slaughter of all the men and the enslavement of the women and children; or in some cases, the slaughter of everyone—women and children included."

There is a truth here that we neither can nor should ignore: when God acts through his rebellious creatures, his agents (secondary causes) rarely act with pure and undefiled motives. In succeeding chapters we will say much more about the pain and suffering—much of it at the direct command of God—that Joshua and his army visited upon the first Palestinians.

But in this chapter, we will focus on the flip side of the Promised Land being a gift. Calling the promised land a *gift* means that the Jews must forever acknowledge that the land and its wealth were not the product of *their own labors*. It was not something they earned; it was not something to which they had a right; rather, it was something they were given. "Beware lest you say in your heart, 'My power and the might of my hand have gotten me this wealth.' You shall remember the Lord your God, for it is he who gives you power to get wealth." And the consequences of minimizing this essential truth would be harsh: "And if you forget the Lord your God and go after other gods and serve them and worship them, I solemnly warn you this day that you shall surely perish" (Deut 8:17ff. See also Hos 12:8, 13:6; 1 Cor 4:7).

Moreover, while their Lord and God gave them the land to enjoy, it was not given solely for their *own* enjoyment. As we would say, there were "strings attached." When the land was first promised to Abraham, God announced his intention to bless Abraham's kin *so that* through them "all the families of the earth shall be blessed" (Gen 12:3). If the Jews were true to their calling, they must be stewards of the land, not its owners. And as stewards, they had no right to do with it as they pleased.

This conception of land and the wealth that it produces was overturned by the premier political theorist of the Enlightenment, John Locke.

LOCKE'S THEORY OF PROPERTY

Locke was a Christian, so he would never deny that God is the creator of the land and all its resources. Thus he began by assuming that in its original condition (what he called the "state of nature") land and its produce were given *in common* to all people. Anyone who went to the effort of gathering nuts and berries had a natural (i.e., God-given) *right* to the fruit of their labor just so long as two conditions were met. First, they did not acquire a monopoly in a given area so that there was not "enough, and as good, left in common for others."[4] Second, no one was permitted to gather more than they could use before it rotted and went to waste. To make his point Locke approvingly quotes St. Paul's First Epistle to Timothy: "God has given us all things richly" (6:13). He then explains that this "is the voice of reason confirmed by inspiration. But how far has he given it us? To enjoy. As much as any one can make use of to the advantage of life before it spoils, so much he may by his labour fix a property in: whatever is beyond this, is more than his share, and belongs to others. Nothing was made by God for man to spoil or destroy."[5]

However, Locke believes that all this radically changes with the invention of money. There are two crucial facts about money. First, whether it is sea shells, gold, or dollar bills, all money gets its value from common

4. Locke, *Second Treatise*, pars. 27, 33.
5. Ibid., par. 31.

consent. Though today gold has some intrinsic value from its use in manufacturing electronic and other consumer goods, this is not what *made* it money. No one in Locke's day hoarded gold because they believed that in three centuries it would be used in the manufacturing of iPhones. The only reason people accumulated gold was because other people had *agreed* to exchange it for all sorts of other goods and services. Back then, gold was no different from dollar bills today; both were essentially worthless. It is only because people have *agreed* to freely exchange goods and services for dollar bills that these slips of paper have any value. All money is a kind of promise. If people *give* intrinsically worthless promissory notes in payment for goods and services, then they have implicitly promised to *accept* equally worthless promissory notes in payment for their goods and services. Failure to do so is ipso facto to break a promise.

The second crucial fact about money is that it neither rots nor spoils. This is obvious and needs no explanation.

What is not immediately obvious, and what Locke first demonstrated to the satisfaction of many Enlightenment thinkers, is that the invention of money ipso facto repeals the moral and theological limits to the amount of wealth a person can lawfully accumulate for their own private use. Prior to the invention of money, a person could rightfully protest against the excessive accumulation of wealth since no one has a right to waste God's bounty. If anyone gathered so many nuts and fruits that they spoiled, or if anyone enclosed more land than they could profitably cultivate, then they had affronted God and violated his moral law. But once everyone agreed upon the use of money, which neither rotted nor spoiled, such protests were null and void.[6] In fact, objecting to another person's wealth now became a violation of the tenth commandment—"Thou shall not covet."

So, after the invention of money, Locke argued, the moral and theological prohibition against wasting God's bounty was no longer applicable. As long as a person's private wealth had been justly acquired through their own labor,[7] no one else had a legitimate claim on it. For anyone to infringe upon someone else's private property—no matter how much they owned— was thievery. From here Locke argued that the chief and only legitimate end of all legitimate governments is to protect a person's God-given right to life, liberty, and the unlimited accumulation of property.[8]

---

6. It is worth noting how, in the spirit of the Enlightenment, *people's* agreement is sufficient to modify the divine intent.

7. Though in *Second Treatise,* par. 28, he says that the labor of a *servant* becomes the property of the *master.*

8. Locke, ibid., is occasionally even more extreme in his defense of the unlimited accumulation of private property. "God has no other end," he writes, "but the preservation

However, the second prohibition against monopolizing resources remained. Doesn't the unlimited right to accumulate property violate Locke's own proviso that there must be "enough, and as good, left for others"? If people are permitted to accumulate as much land as they wish for their private use, will not all the good land soon be gone? So doesn't *this* place a limit on the private accumulation of wealth?

In response, Locke inserted a new argument in the fourth edition of the *Second Treatise*.[9] Theoretically Locke agrees that the "enough and as good" proviso *seems* to impose limits to the amount of property that could rightfully be accumulated. But in practice, he argues, those limits are never reached. Privately enclosed and cultivated land, Locke now argued, is at least ten times or probably more like a hundred times, and perhaps even a thousand times, more productive than land which is held in common.[10] By enclosing land for private use, Locke argued, the entrepreneur has so greatly increased the productivity of the land that far from diminishing what is left for others, the entrepreneur has actually increased the total wealth of a nation that is available for others to appropriate through their labor.[11]

What are we to make of this argument? Locke's conclusion is based on the factual premise that enclosed and cultivated land is up to one thousand times more productive than land held in common. It is hard to determine whether this is really true, though if it were, then Locke's argument might be plausible. And given the relatively low population density of seventeenth-century England (especially since he assumed that the land in America was free for the taking by any Englishman[12]), it may have been true that by increasing the productivity of the land, the large landholders ensured that there would be "enough, and as good, left for others."

However, today we live in a world where very little land remains "unappropriated" (even by Locke's standards[13]). So are Locke's arguments still relevant? Many think that they are.[14] While all the world's land has

---

of property" (par. 94). And again, "The chief end whereof [civil society] is the preservation of property" (par. 85).

9. Macpherson, *Possessive Individualism*, 211ff.
10. *Second Treatise*, pars. 37 and 43.
11. We see here that "trickle-down economics" has a long history.
12. *Second Treatise*, par. 37.
13. Locke thought that the land in North America was land held in common by the English and free for all Englishmen to appropriate. He of course knew that "Indians" were scattered throughout the land, but it seemed obvious to him that they had not "mixed" sufficient amounts of their labor with the land to give them property rights for it.
14. Robert Nozicks's *Anarchy, State and Utopia* is the classic case in point.

already been appropriated, these philosophers and economists argue that today's entrepreneurs do not, by and large, need land or its resources to create wealth (and therefore jobs). For example, some entrepreneurs have today greatly increased the GDP by turning mere sand into computer chips, while other entrepreneurs have written computer programs using nothing more than the ideas in their own minds to greatly increase our GDP. So, again, theoretical questions about the accumulation of private wealth *seem* to hinge on purely factual questions. But, in fact, if we take seriously the three ideas with which we began—time and chance, our social nature, and the role of dual-causation—we will see that in a modern economy like ours it is virtually impossible to determine who has appropriately "mixed" his or her labor with God-given resources so as to acquire an *exclusive* right to their use.

But, before we can evaluate the continued relevance of Locke's arguments, we must first distinguish between ethical and political theories that are grounded in the concept of "good" versus those grounded in the concept of "rights."

GOOD LAWS ARE ALWAYS ADAPTED TO THE PARTICULARS OF TIME AND PLACE

Several times we've contrasted continuous series with those that are discrete and easily countable. We've also said that Enlightenment thought favors the discrete and countable to that which is imprecise and understandable only with "good judgment." Here again, we need only contrast Aristotle's dictum, "A wise person only demands as much precision as the disciple in question permits," with Galileo's dictum, "Measure what can be measured and to make measurable what cannot be measured." In political theory these contrasting mind-sets are again evident. Plato and Aristotle assumed that the goal of government was *to promote what is good*; Locke assumed that the goal of government was *to protect individual's rights*.

The most obvious difference between *promoting* what is good and *protecting* individual's rights is that the first is a matter of degree whereas the second is all-or-nothing. The Sears and Roebuck department stores used to label many of their items as "good, better, and best." And, of course, there are innumerable possible grades in between. So when governments seek to promote the good, they are following the Sears and Roebuck model. But when Kant thought about our ethical obligations he insisted that these were *categorical*. For Kant, "doing the right thing" was never a matter of finding the "golden mean" between various ends—all of which were good—but instead, it was a matter of following the categorical imperative without exception.[15]

Locke could not have been clearer that protecting private property rights was a categorical imperative. Several times he says that property rights are absolute. He even goes so far as to argue that while nations at war have the right to kill their opponent's soldiers, they never have the right to deprive the heirs of slain soldiers of their rightful inheritance.[16] Compare this with Aquinas's statement: "It is not theft, properly speaking, to take secretly and use another's property in a case of extreme need: because that which he takes for the support of his life becomes his own property by reason of that need."[17] A greater contrast is hard to imagine. However, these radically different theories of property grew out of one small difference at the beginning of their respective arguments.

Both Aquinas and Locke would agree with St. Paul that there is a law that is written on all people's hearts (Rom 2:15). In this respect both were "natural law" theorists who assumed that the fundamental principles of morality were God-given and universally knowable. Also, they would both agree that if all people have their own property "there will be increased production all round."[18] (Though Locke's attempt to *quantify* this increased productivity would have struck both Aristotle and Aquinas as fundamentally misguided for reasons we will soon consider). Finally, they would both agree that natural law obligates us to respect other people's property.

Nevertheless, there is a fundamental disagreement. Aquinas argued that the laws regulating the acquisition and use of private property are part of *positive* law. Positive laws are those laws enacted by a legitimate government using its best judgment to apply the natural law to particular times and situations. Therefore positive laws acquire their binding force only to the extent that they are well suited to the *particular* circumstances and needs of the people. Locke, on the other hand, argued that the laws regulating the acquisition and use of private property are themselves part of the "laws of nature" and therefore their binding force is *universal*. Remember, according to Locke, no matter where one lives, everyone has a natural right to *kill*

---

15. Think here of the great controversy in the evangelical church that resulted from the publication of *Situational Ethics* and the Mrs. Bergmeier case. As we argued in the previous chapter, the assumption that generated all the controversy was that there was one *right* action in such circumstances and the Christian's job was to figure out what that was.

16. *Second Treatise*, par. 189.

17. *Summa Theologica* II-II 66.7.2.

18. Aristotle, *Politics* II.5. Aquinas's own arguments are found in *Summa Theologica* II-II.66, 2.

invading soldiers, but they have no right to deprive the heirs of invading soldiers of their *property*. But from Aquinas's point of view, treating property law as part of natural law is an example of a "small error at the beginning of something that is a great one at the end."[19]

According to Locke, property laws can be *deduced* from the "law of nature." Reduced to a simple syllogism, his argument looks like this:

1. All people have a *natural* right to their liberty.
2. Liberty gives rise to free labor and to the fruit of one's labor.
3. Therefore, all people have a *natural* right to the fruit of their labor.

The simple elegance of Locke's argument gives it great intuitive appeal. Yet the second premise conceals a crucial problem. Locke fleshes out a person's right to the fruit of his labor as something that arises when a person "mixed his labour"[20] with the land or when he "encloses land" and makes subsequent "improvements."[21] By anyone's standards (much less the exceedingly high standards of precision set by most Enlightenment thinkers) these criteria need clarification. If a person works very hard to extract purple dye from blueberries he has gathered, and then pours an ounce of it in the middle of a very large lake, when the molecules from his dye are equally distributed throughout the entire lake, has he thereby "mixed" his labor with the whole lake and thus obtained exclusive claim to all the fish in the lake? Or has he simply wasted his dye? Or if a person labors to lawfully acquire sufficient chalk to outline a square mile of very fertile land, does the line of chalk constitute an "enclosing" of the land? Or, again, has he simply wasted his chalk? Nowhere does Locke address such questions.

These sorts of difficult questions about how we should interpret Locke's ideas of "mixing one's labor" and "enclosing land" can be multiplied without limit in a modern economy. Suppose I actively farm a piece of land on the edge of a canyon in such a way that no reasonable person would question the fact that I have "mixed my labor" with the land and hence that I have a right to the crops on *my* land. But if a miner, digging a tunnel from land which is still held in common, discovers an extremely rich vein of gold which is one hundred feet under the land I *own*, is the gold mine or his?

Or suppose a group of private pilots purchase a piece of land to build an airport that is five miles outside the city and far away from any existing houses. However, twenty-five years later the city has grown and now houses sit next to their airport. If the homeowners begin to complain about the

---

19. Aquinas, *Being and Essence*, first sentence.
20. *Second Treatise*, par. 27.
21. Ibid., par. 37.

noise the airplanes make when they land and take off, then do the owners of the houses have a legal right to forbid the noisy overflight of these private planes five hundred feet above their land? Do they have the legal right to forbid the overflight of commercial airlines thirty thousand feet above their land? And more importantly, *how* are such questions to be answered? One thing seems clear; they cannot be *deduced* from the "law of nature."

Again, these sorts of objections to Locke's argument do not entail a rejection of private property *in general*. But they do entail, according to Aquinas, that "the distribution of property is not a matter of natural law but of human agreement which pertains to the positive law."[22] Here's an analogy. Natural law permits (or even requires) governments to coercively enforce laws designed to maintain public order. An example of such a law in the United States is that drivers of motor vehicles must always drive on the right-hand side of the road. But in England public order is maintained by driving on the left-hand side of the road. Of course, the English law does not *violate* the natural law; it merely implements the natural law in a way that *best fits* the particular circumstances surrounding roads in England. Likewise, Aquinas argues that "private property is not against natural law but it has been added to natural law by the inventiveness of human reason."[23]

Therefore, wise legislators must seek to write property laws that *best fit* their particular circumstances of time and place. And in doing so, they must never forget the three bullet points listed at the beginning of this chapter: 1) time and chance happen to all, 2) humans are rational *social* animals and 3) all human action is a product of dual-causation. We will consider these in order.

THE CURVE BREAKER AND THE MATTHEW EFFECT

As the Preacher said, "Under the sun the race is not to the swift, . . . nor *riches* to the intelligent, nor *favor* to the men of skill, but time and chance happen to them all."

Contemporary economists have sophisticated mathematical tools for measuring the marginal contributions that are made when new laborers enters the work force. And in the *ideal* world of economists—where markets are perfectly free and knowledge about the markets is open and accessible to all—something approaching Locke's theory of property acquisition takes place. Since each new laborer is free to sell his or her labor to the highest

---

22. *Summa Theologica* II-II.66, 2.
23. Ibid. See also II-II.57.3.

bidder, and since each employer is free to hire laborers at the lowest wage at which they will freely consent to labor, workers will get exactly the wages that their labor is worth and employers will get laborer's fruit at exactly the price that it is worth.

Of course, not all labor is worth the same amount. The labor of a skilled and educated person will fetch more on the free market than the labor of an unskilled and uneducated person. And given the assumption of free and open markets, it is easy to understand why this is the case and how it accords with Locke's theory of property acquisition. However, even if we assume that markets are perfectly free and transparent, the Preacher's principle of "time and chance" has seriously deleterious implications for Locke's theory.

Consider what we will call the "curve breaker." When I was in college, we all knew who the "curve breakers" were. When a professor gave an especially difficult chemistry test and thirty-four out of the thirty-five students in the class earned less than 65 percent, the "curve breaker" was that one student who earned a 99 percent. Without the presence of the curve breaker, when every student misses at least 35 percent of the questions, then the student who earned the highest grade in the class, even though they correctly answered only 65 percent of the questions, is likely to receive a passing grade. But with the curve breaker, all bets are off.

I have been on both sides of the lectern and know from firsthand experience—both as a student and as an instructor—that no matter how "fair" a professor tries to be, the presence of a "curve breaker" affects the grades of all the *other* students in the class. If there are five different sections of Intro to College Chemistry, taught by different instructors, then to be a premed student in the section with the "curve breaker" is a case of very bad luck. If Sally were to earn a 65 percent on an especially difficult test in one of the four sections where a 65 percent is the highest grade in the class, then perhaps the curve will be drawn in such a way that Sally earns a "B" and maybe even an "A" for the test. But if by "time and chance" Sally is registered in the section with the "curve breaker," then Sally's chances of earning a good grade and getting into medical school are seriously compromised.

Now economists, even under ideal conditions, can only measure what *is* the case; they have no way to measure what *would have been* the case. How can you *count* "would have beens" since by definition they don't exist? Intuitively it is easy to agree with Locke that people with more or better education have a *right* to higher wages than those with lesser or poorer education. But when you consider the Sallys of the world, whose educational achievement has a great deal to do with the performance of *another* student (the "curve breaker"), then the connection between "rights" and "rewards" is much more dubious.

Furthermore, in a modern, highly competitive world like our own, there is something in social dynamics called the "Matthew effect." It is analogous to the threshold effect in Newtonian dynamics we discussed in chapter 1. A striking illustration of the Matthew effect comes from the opening pages of Malcolm Gladwell's popular book *The Outliers*.

Canadians love to play hockey and they love to watch the world's best hockey players play. To satisfy their desires they have developed the world's most comprehensive and competitive system of youth hockey teams and leagues. It begins by first discovering and then developing the most talented ten-year-old hockey players in the nation. Canadians are very good at this, which means that it is a system based solely on merit and devoid of the corruption that comes from control by "the good old boys." Why, then, when you look at the rosters of the elite or all-star hockey teams in Canada, are the birthdays inordinately biased toward the first four months of the year—40 percent between January and March verse only 10 percent between October and December? One social scientist said, "In all my years in psychology, I have never run into an effect this large. You don't even need to do any statistical analysis. You just look at it."[24]

The same inordinate bias favoring early calendar year birthdays is evident in the best European soccer players. Of the twenty-one players on the roster of the Junior World Cup finals team for Czechoslovakia, six were born in January, six in February, three in March, one in April, one in May, one in August, and one in September.

In the earlier chapters of this book, we repeatedly said that correlation is not causation. Without a story to *explain* a correlation there is no science. The story told by social scientists to explain this extremely strong correlation was first dubbed the "Matthew effect" by Robert Merton.[25] The name comes from the passage in the Gospel of Matthew that sums up the parable of the talents. "For to every one who has will more be given, and he will have abundance; but from him who has not, even what he has will be taken away" (Matt 25:29).

The key that makes sense of this data is that in Canada and in Europe the cutoff date for youth hockey and soccer leagues is January 1. Since children begin competing for spots on these teams around nine or ten years of age, that means that if Tommy and Bobby are competing for the last slot on

---

24. Gladwell, *Outliers*, 23.

25. For an excellent introduction and summary of the data, see Rigney, *Matthew Effect*.

the team and Tommy was born on January 1 while Bobby is born on December 13, then Tommy will have a 10 percent "maturity advantage" over Bobby. And in children, such an advantage will be huge. And even more significant than this initial advantage is the fact that such advantages are cumulative given the power of thresholds to radically change outcomes.

In chapter 1 we considered Laplace's boast that given sufficient data everything would be predictable. The assumption was that small errors at the beginning of a causal chain would only produce small errors at the end of the causal chain. And in many dynamic systems, like the orbit of the planets, this assumption holds true. What chaos theory demonstrates is that in many dynamic systems, if not most, this assumption is *not* true. As the opening example of this book illustrates, when a tennis ball is bouncing down a rocky road the smallest difference in the initial measurement will have inordinately large consequences in the end.

Likewise, in youth hockey and soccer, once Bobby has failed to make it over the initial threshold, his initial disadvantage of being born on December 13 will not be erased when he turns eleven and once more competes for a spot on the team. When he again competes with Tommy for a spot on the team he will not only be handicapped by a physical maturity disadvantage, but he will also have one year less experience playing on a competitive hockey team with good coaching. So "from him who has not, even what he has will be taken away."

Combine the "curve breaker" effect with the "Matthew effect," and in economics and social dynamics, just like a tennis ball bouncing down a rocky road, it is *not* true that a small difference in the beginning will have a small difference in the end. This has huge effects on the validity of Locke's initial assumption. And it has even greater effects on the plausibility of today's Lockeans. They assume that free and transparent markets will allocate wealth in direct proportion to the amount of labor a person freely chooses to "mix" with the opportunities created by entrepreneurs and the free market. And, if wages and rewards are not precisely proportional, at least there will be only *small* differences. What the curve breaker and Matthew effects demonstrate is that small differences in the beginning can have huge consequences in the end!

Even in relatively simpler times, Aquinas argued that it was a mistake and injustice to attempt to *deduce* property law from the "law of nature." How much more would he object to today's attempt to deduce property laws from *mathematical equations* describing the intersection of supply and demand curves?

But if free markets will not ensure justice for all, then what will? The answer is found in Aquinas's dictum that we previously mentioned: "It is not theft, properly speaking, to take secretly and use another's property in a case of extreme need: because that which he takes for the support of his life becomes his own property by reason of that need." The Thomistic criterion for economic justice is *need*. In the next section we will consider this pre-Enlightenment approach built on the assumption that the Author of creation has in-formed us as rational, social animals.[26]

SUFFICIENT RESOURCES FOR ALL[27]

According to Aquinas, *good* governments pursue policies that guarantee all citizens *sufficient* resources for "a life fit for the dignity of man."[28] The goal is neither abundance nor equality. It is not equality (which is tantamount to the common ownership of all material wealth), "since each one would shirk the labor and leave to another that which concerns the community."[29] Again, Aquinas agrees with Locke—land that is held in common is not nearly as productive as land that is privately owned. But he disagreed with Locke that the protection of private property is the primary goal of good government. Instead, Aquinas agrees with Plato. "The citizen

---

26. "Thirdly, there are inclinations peculiar to man as a rational animal. The desire to know is not something we decide to have; it is there as we are. So too is living with others. Thought experiments of the kind indulged in by John Rawls in *A Theory of Justice*, in which individuals imagine a society they will contract to enter, can have the unfortunate consequence of blurring the overwhelmingly obvious fact that no individual human is born or survives independently of others, nor can he reach fulfillment worthy of the name save in the company of his fellow men. Being social is not a choice; it is a fact of our nature." McInerny, *Aquinas on Human Action*, 120.

27. The contemporary philosopher Harry Frankfurt developed a similar idea without specific reference to Aquinas: "Economic equality is not as such of particular moral importance. With respect to the distribution of economic assets, what is important from the point of view of morality is not that everyone should have the same but that each should have enough. If everyone had enough, it would be of no moral consequence whether some had more than others. I shall refer to this alternative to equalitarianism—namely, that what is morally important with respect to money is for everyone to have enough—as 'the doctrine of sufficiency.'" *What We Care About*, 134–35.

28. There is deliberate irony here. The quote is taken from Locke's *Second Treatise*, par. 15. Here Locke is approvingly quoting "the judicious [William] Hooker." It is hard to say why Locke failed to understand that Hooker's intent was quite the opposite of his own.

29. *Summa Theologica* II-II.66, 2. Aquinas also raises two other objections to common ownership of all material wealth. First, "human affairs are conducted in more orderly fashion if each man is charged with taking care of some particular thing himself"; and second, "a more peaceful state is ensured to man if each one is contented with his own." Ibid.

must indeed be happy and good, and the legislator will seek to accomplish this; but very good and very rich at the same time he cannot be."[30]

The sweet spot of sufficiency lies between the excesses of both equality and abundance. It is determined by the principle that the imperative always follows the indicative (chapter 7). How we *ought* to organize economic and political relations is determined by what we *are*, and we *are* rational, social animals. In chapter 2 we looked at the justification for this claim and indicated our agreement with contemporary social psychologists who argue that we are "hardwired" for both social engagement and activities that are mentally challenging.[31] E. F. Schumacher was correct: "The human being, defined by Thomas Aquinas as a being with brains and hands, enjoys nothing more than to be creatively, usefully, productively engaged with both his hands and his brains."[32]

Like all analogical (inductive) reasoning, determining what humans need for a life of dignity is messy when compared to the deductive simplicity we saw in Locke. Our reason, our social nature, and our animal nature form an integrated whole. We can distinguish them for analysis, but we cannot separate them in reality since each aspect of what it means to be human supports, and in turn is supported by, the other two aspects. When humans are malnourished they do not think well, and when they are not thinking well they are less likely to organize themselves in ways that will produce adequate food and better nourishment. Or, when humans are born into communities that fail to adequately educate their young in the virtues—both intellectual and moral—then the whole community suffers and another downward spiral begins. Truly, the sins of the fathers are visited upon the third and fourth generations (Exod 20:5).

It is not the job of philosophers, but of biologists, social scientists, and psychologists, to flesh out in detail all that humans need to flourish as rational, social animals. So our only objective will be to describe how pre-Enlightenment thinkers reasoned *from* our essential nature (an indicative) *to* a conclusion about what humans need, and hence, to a political conclusion concerning the proper goal of good governments (an imperative).

We'll begin with our social nature. Because we are social animals, individual happiness cannot be found outside a flourishing community or city-state. So when individuals focus primarily on their own material well-being, without giving equal attention to the common good, then great

---

30. Plato, *Laws* V.742.
31. See Haidt, *Happiness Hypothesis*, 291ff.
32. Schumacher, *Small is Beautiful*, ch. 10: "Technology with a Human Face."

personal wealth is self-defeating. Plato outlined a number of reasons he thought this was so.

First, if the distribution of wealth became too skewed, then a unified city-state would no longer exist. In his *Republic*, Plato proposed a political organization that stood Enlightenment thought on its head. Locke assumed that policies that increased the aggregate wealth of a nation were ipso facto good. Plato did not. Once a modest living was possible for all, Plato argued that the accumulation of more wealth was positively harmful. His wise legislators purposefully limited the acquisition of wealth. If anyone possessed more than five times what those at the bottom of the economic scale possessed, any additional wealth would legally revert to the commonwealth.[33]

Today many people would dismiss this "taking from the rich to give to the poor" as the wrongful "redistribution" of property. But this is anachronistic. The verb "taking" assumes that the rich have a prior *right* to their riches and the term "*redistribution*" assumes that property was previously distributed by nature. In other words, the notion of "redistribution" simply *assumes*, prior to any argument, that Locke was correct. Conversely it also *assumes*, prior to any argument, that Aquinas was wrong when he said that it is not theft properly speaking for someone in "extreme need to take secretly" from the rich. The fact that so many moderns are so quick to make these assumptions is some indication of just how strong Locke's influence has been.

But even if we refrain from making these Lockean assumptions, a more practical objection to Plato's principles arises. As one of the interlocutors in Plato's dialogue argued: "If we are satisfied with modest material wealth, how will we be able to defend even what we have against rich and powerful neighbors?" Plato responded that a city-state in which there is great disparity of wealth is not really a single entity. In fact, a highly stratified city "is not one state, but many: two at least, which are at war with one another, one of the rich, the other of the poor."[34]

So if a rich and powerful city-state attacked Plato's ideal republic, its leaders would say to the attacking army something like this: "We know that a few of you are very rich and most of you are not. And you know that our combined wealth, though adequate for us, by the standards of others is by no means great. So attack if you will, but understand this—we will fight as *one* army for the common good, disciplined by the pursuit of virtue, and not corrupted by ease and luxury. And if the majority of you who are attacking break ranks with your rich countrymen and side with us, then we will fight

---

33. Plato, *Laws* V.744; Aristotle, *Politics* II.7.
34. Plato, *Republic* IV.422.

with you and against them. And since we already have all the wealth we need and desire, the wealth of your oppressors will be *all* yours."

Of course, implementing such a national defense policy today would require considerable modifications.[35] But then, Plato also understood that the implementation of the ideal city-state sketched in the *Republic* would require considerable wisdom on the part of actual legislators. It is a given of the virtue ethics tradition that positive laws must *fit* the particularities of time and place. Plato understood fully that there would be significant differences between good laws written for *his* time and place compared to good laws written for *our* time and place. Yet he steadfastly argued that *all* good laws will share a common goal—in this case, maintaining social solidarity.

Plato was not the first to stress the importance of solidarity. The Old Testament is filled with specific provisions for maintaining unity—everything from the Jubilee Year (where every fifty years land would revert back to the landless) to laws ensuring that feasts include "your menservants and maidservants, and the Levites, the aliens, the fatherless, and the widows who live in your towns."[36]

Not only do we need unified communities to defend against external aggression, but we need them for the education of our children in the virtues.[37] Many things humans desire—like food, drink, and sex—have natural limits. There is only so much that a person can eat before he or she becomes stuffed and there is only so much that a person can drink before he or she becomes drunk. And there are similar limits to how much sex is possible before a natural limit is reached. But Locke was right about money. It neither rots nor spoils, so there is no natural limit to our desire for wealth. Thus, we must be *taught* by our elders to distinguish between wants and needs when it comes to money if we—both as individuals and as a community—are going to set reasonable limits for the quest for material wealth. Here we get no help from nature.

Or do we? Enlightenment thinkers argue that every person is their own best judge of what will make them happy. Some people prefer to labor eighteen hours a day, seven days a week to earn as much money as they

---

35. In one sense, Plato's military tactics appear hopelessly outdated. But when we consider the success over the last fifty years of "guerilla armies" fighting to a draw, if not defeating, the world's "superpowers," then Plato's proscriptions appear much less quaint.

36. For the Jubilee Year see Lev 25:8ff. For the inclusiveness of feast see Deut 16:14.

37. "Learning of this kind [training in character] as of other kinds, is what the uneducated, left to themselves, do not and cannot want: 'those engaged in learning are not at play; learning is accompanied by pain' (Aristotle, *Politics* VIII.1239a29)." See also MacIntyre, *Whose Justice?*, 110.

can. Other people prefer to labor less and have more leisure. But whatever a person prefers, the choice must be theirs because only they are in a position to know what will make them happy. In this respect, a person's pursuit of happiness is like pain—no one can be mistaken about their own pain; so too, the Enlightenment assumption is that no one can be mistaken about what brings them happiness. After all, isn't the "pursuit of happiness" a self-evident and unalienable right?

Perhaps it is, though pre-Enlightenment thinkers thought that the achievement of happiness was more important than its pursuit. Thus, they argued that without an adequate education as to *what* a human being is, and hence, what a human being *needs* to achieve their God-given ends, the freedom to pursue one's own happiness is as likely to end in misery as it is in happiness. While no one can be mistaken about whether or not they are in pain, we can be mistaken about the cause of our pain. We might, for example, go to a doctor with such a severe pain in our big toe that we are sure that it is broken. And though no doctor is in a position to question the severity of our pain, he is in a position to question the adequacy of our self-diagnosis. Aristotle, Plato, and Aquinas all had a similar skepticism about the innate ability of individuals to self-diagnose what is necessary for achieving happiness. As even addicts know in moments of self-reflection, what they want and what they need are quite different.

The distinction between wants and needs is not nearly as great or as important in other species of animals as it is for humans. When other animals want food, drink, or sex it is almost always good for them since they have no higher calling. But humans have greater abilities than other animals, and hence, we have a higher calling. As Aristotle dimly perceived,[38] and as the Bible explicitly teaches, the knowledge of God is worth more than the knowledge that leads to great riches. Food, drink, sex, and the pleasure they bring are good. But with these, there can be too much of a good thing. But there is no such thing as too much knowledge concerning the good, the true, and the beautiful. "Whatever is true, whatever is honorable, whatever is just, whatever is pure, whatever is lovely, whatever is gracious, if there is any excellence, if there is anything worthy of praise, *think* about these things" (Phil 4:8, emphasis added). Contrast this with other kinds of thinking.

The thinking that leads to knowledge concerning the acquisition of material wealth can be, and most frequently is, a competitive affair. While it is possible for the makers of computers and the writers of software to cooperate so that both can become wealthier, cooperation is never the last word. Here the hardware and software producers are only cooperating because

---

38. *Nicomachean Ethics* X.7.1177b30.

they are in competition with other hardware and software producers. And by definition, competition means there will be winners *and* losers. But the pursuit of knowledge is only competitive when it is tied to the pursuit of material wealth. In all other cases, the pursuit of knowledge produces winners *without losers*. Just because Fred has discovered a proof of the Pythagorean theorem, that doesn't mean that someone else is poorer as the result of Fred's discovery (unless, again, he succeeds in patenting his discovery.)[39]

And lest we lose sight of the larger picture, it is worth reminding ourselves what is at stake. In the tradition of virtue ethics that grounds pre-Enlightenment politics,[40] what we *ought* to do is determined by what we *are*. And we *are* a rational, social animals. So the fact that we *ought* to pursue knowledge for its own sake follows both from our rationality and from our social nature. As Aristotle said in the opening sentence of his *Metaphysics*, "All people by nature desire knowledge." If rhesus monkeys enjoy solving puzzles for their own sakes; if infants enjoy making things happen for their own sakes (see chapter 7); how much more must mature humans enjoy knowing as much as they can about the universe in which they live?

Nor does the argument end here. The fact that we are *social* animals means that our natural inclination is to *share* our new knowledge with others. The vision of a beautiful sunset is enhanced when we can share that vision with our friends. So too the joy in discovering an elegant mathematical proof of the Pythagorean theorem is also enhanced when it is shared. As we said in the early days of the Internet, "knowledge desires to be free"—since free knowledge tightens the bonds of social solidarity.

However, a qualification is necessary. Yes, we want to share our discoveries with others. But frequently, in part and sometimes in whole, our desire to share discoveries with others is motivated by a desire for attention, fame, and the power that it brings. There is nothing intrinsically wrong with any of these. Power can be directed to both good and bad ends. It can enhance the public good, private wealth, or some combination of the two. And here there is nothing that is intrinsically bad. But to the extent that power increases private wealth at the *expense* of the public good, Thomists have no doubts that it is a sinful human desire where more is never better.

---

39. Whether Locke would argue for or against the patentability of mathematical discoveries is hard to say. But either way, such questions once again cast a long shadow over any attempt to *deduce* property laws from the "laws of nature."

40. In many ways, even our "Founding Fathers" were pre-Enlightenment thinkers. Consider, for example, the virtues enumerated in section 15 of the Virginia Declaration of Rights: "That no free government, or the blessings of liberty, can be preserved to any people but by a firm adherence to justice, moderation, temperance, frugality, and virtue and by frequent recurrence to fundamental principles."

These few paragraphs hardly settle, one way or the other, the fundamental disagreement between Aquinas and Locke. But they make clear the disagreement is about *both* the kind of reasoning appropriate for political arguments and the conclusions reached. Aquinas's reasoning concerns a vast web of interconnected analogical arguments regarding the essential nature of human beings. Locke's reasoning concerns a relatively simple deductive argument regarding what he assumed to be self-evident rights. And from these diverse methods of reasoning, they reach diverse conclusions. Locke's conclusion is that the fundamental aim of government is the protection of private property. Aquinas's conclusion is that the fundamental aim of government is to write positive laws that distribute resources so that all its citizens are able to live "a life fit for the dignity of man." In sum, Locke believes we have a right to what we *earn*; Aquinas believes we have a right to what we *need*.

THE POLITICAL IMPLICATIONS OF DUAL-CAUSATION

In this final section, we will consider the havoc dual-causation wreaks on the Lockean assumption that we can accurately measure what a person has rightfully *earned*.

Consider a situation in which Tom and Dick are both pulling on a rope that they attached to treasure at the bottom of the sea. Neither Tom nor Dick is sufficiently strong to pull up the treasure by themselves. So they enter into a contract. They loop the end of the rope and attach two other ropes, each with a scale to measure the force being applied by Tom and Dick respectively. They then agree to divide their treasure in portion to the amount of work each has done. For example, if the work done by Tom is 55 percent of the total work required to pull the treasure aboard, then he will get 55 percent of the treasure and Dick will get the remaining 45 percent of the treasure. And in this case of cooperation we understand what it means to say that each person gets what he has earned.

However, there is a very different kind of cooperation where two people work together to achieve a shared goal. Remember my friend and colleague who said he was going to make an exquisite pasta dish for dinner and asked if my wife and I would like to join him. Though I immediately accepted the offer, I was very puzzled since my friend is a quadriplegic—how, I wondered, was *he* going to cook for me? When I arrived at his house, it soon became clear how he would do this. After the standard chit-chat, my friend politely began giving me instructions—"Get two cloves of garlic from the pantry, three tablespoons of olive oil, a cup of fresh basil..." It continued like this for about thirty minutes, in part, because many of the ingredients and techniques he employed I had never heard of before, and hence, my friend was forced to give extremely detailed (and to his mind, elementary!) instructions. Yet when we finished, the pasta was truly exquisite.

So here's the question: who made the pasta—me or my friend? While in one sense we "cooperated," it would be wrong to describe this as a case where he and I each did 50 percent of the work. No, in the most important sense, my friend did *everything* because I was only the set of hands he used to prepare the pasta. While my hands did the physical work, they would have been utterly useless without his detailed instructions. Nonetheless, there was a real dignity in what I did, and the words "Well done, good and faithful servant" would have made perfect sense.[41] But in this sort of case, how do we determine who *earns* what?

A Lockean economist might agree that it is more difficult in such a case to determine who has a rightful claim to what than in the previous case of Tom and Dick pulling up unclaimed treasure. Nonetheless, and as we already suggested, Lockean economists argue that a free market is able to determine the relative value of brain and brawn. Needless to say, Thomists will disagree. "Nature" cannot answer questions about whether mixing purple dye in a lake establishes ownership of the lake's fish or outlining a piece of land with handfuls of chalk constitutes an "enclosing" of the land. Equally dubious is the claim that "markets" can establish the true value of mental labor vis-à-vis physical labor. So in attempting to answer questions about who *earns* what in a *particular* situation we are at an impasse. But what about the question itself? Is it an intelligible question that should be answered?

How much does the number seven weigh? Is the color red longer or shorter than the color blue? These questions should be rejected, not answered. In one sense, my friend did everything, since my knowledge of good cooking is nil. But in another sense, I did everything, since I was the only one to make physical contact with the pasta. Unless one believes in "action at a distance," my friend's contribution was nonexistent. Like the number seven, knowledge is not the kind of thing that can be weighed. In the previous example, Tom and Dick were both making the same *kind* of contribution to a cooperative project. But my friend's contribution and my contribution were different in *kind*. Comparing our respective contributions is like the proverbial attempt to compare apples and oranges.

---

41. See *Summa Theologica* I.23.8 reply to objection 2 for Aquinas's own example.

Once more, it is not hard to compare the *price* (extrinsic value) of different kinds of things as determined by a free market. But how do we compare the contributions two different kinds of things make to the *health* (intrinsic value) of an organism when both are necessary, but neither sufficient? Functioning brains and hearts are both necessary for life. But it makes no sense to ask which is of greater intrinsic value. In a sin-cursed world, leaders, soldiers, and producers will all be equally necessary in a healthy society. So how can we ask which is of greater *intrinsic* value?

One final example. When strong, talented, or simply lucky people without a homeland conquer a weaker, less talented, or simply unlucky people with a homeland, who is it that now *owns* the land? To be more specific, let's consider the situation with which we began this chapter. The Hittites had a homeland; the Hebrews did not. According to Locke, the Hittites cannot be said to have a "natural right" to their land vis-à-vis the Hebrews since evidently there was not "enough, and as good, left for" the Hebrews. So did the Hebrew's strength, talent, and/or luck *earn* them a rightful claim on the land? Or at least, did it *earn* them a rightful claim on the land until some other stronger, more talented, and/or luckier homeless people conquered them?

Both Aquinas and Barth would reject these questions. The only person who can be said to *own* the land in any absolute sense is the Author of creation. And who *owns* the strength, talent, and/or luck of the conquerors? In one sense it is the strength, talent, and luck *of the conquerors* that resulted in a successful conquest of the land. But in another, higher sense, it was the strength, talent, and luck of the Author of creation that was transferred to the *management* (not ownership) of stewards. "Beware lest you say in your heart, 'My power and the might of my hand have gotten me this wealth.' You shall remember the LORD your God, for it is he who gives you power to get wealth"

Near the end of his life, Barth began an autobiography that he never finished with this preface:

> What are we, and what do we have
> on this whole earth,
> which has not been given to us,
> Father, by you?[42]

There is no better way to conclude a discussion of the politics of stewardship than with such a rhetorical question.

---

42. Busch, *Karl Barth*, 475.

—9—

Free Will and Predestination

The only way humans can make something happen is through the use of lawful causes. But there are two ways God can make something happen: though the use of lawful causes and by creating a universe where accidental causes are choreographed to produce the desired results. In both cases, God always "gets what he wants." But only in the first case can we say that what God wanted was predetermined and had to happen.

Failure to distinguish between the two ways God "makes something happen" creates an unnecessary opposition between free will and predestination. Though we foolishly seek autonomy, the good news is that God's grace outwits our stupidity.

MAKING SOMETHING HAPPEN

A child can make waves on a still lake by picking up a stone and throwing it. Though the child knows nothing about the laws of Newtonian physics, nonetheless the child employs these laws when she accomplishes what she intended to do. Though precisely what happens in the brain of the child at the instant she decides to make waves on a lake is a little murky, after the nerve impulse reaches the spinal cord, biologists, chemists, and physicists would have no difficulty explaining the sequence of causes and effects that results in waves on a still lake. And the number of different kinds of things that humans can "make happen" is prodigious. It extends from throwing stones to landing a man on the moon. But in every case where a person decides to make something happen, they do so by employing *lawful* causal relations, even if they do not fully understand the natural laws they are employing. This is the only way people can make something happen.

What humans cannot do is to decide to make something happen by employing accidental causes. For example, suppose a tennis ball is at rest on a rock at the bottom of a long rocky road. A person who wants to knock the ball off the rock cannot simply throw another tennis ball in the general direction and seriously expect to move the other ball off its perch. If that is her intent, she would have to make a little groove in the road, and then carefully push the ball down the mountain, once again letting the laws of Newtonian physics do their work. Only then would there be a reasonable expectation of achieving her intended result.

Of course, if a person does decide to move the ball off its perch by simply throwing another tennis ball in the general direction there is a very small chance that she will accomplish what she wanted to do. But notice that we say "accomplish what she wanted to do." We do not say "made it happen." In cases like this, we say that she "got what she wanted," but she got it as the result of luck, chance, fate, the gods, or God.

This distinction between "making something happen" and "getting what you want by luck" is grounded in the distinction we made in chapter 1 between lawful and accidental causes. And this is not a controversial philosophical or theological distinction. As we saw, science itself overturned the Enlightenment assumption that *all* causes were lawful. The Author of creation, however, does not require lawful causes to "make something happen"; he can make things happen through *either* lawful or accidental causes. When God makes the earth revolve around the sun every 365 days he is employing what we call the "laws of nature" to ensure that his will is accomplished. But when God makes waves in a previously still lake by having a bird defecate at the right time and place he is employing what we call "accidental" causes to ensure that his will is accomplished.[1] And here the scare quotes around "laws of nature" and "accidental" are necessary. Either way God chooses to make something happen is equally purposeful and equally certain since God is the choreographer of "accidents."

That is not to say that viewed from *within* the universe there isn't a real difference between lawful and accidental causes.[2] To repeat, the Enlighten-

---

1. "Not all effects subject to providence will be necessary, but a good many are contingent." Aquinas, *Summa Contra Gentiles* III.72.2.

2. "It is true, of course, that although there is no identity of the divine and creaturely operation or *causare* [causing], there is a similarity, a correspondence, a comparableness, or analogy. In theology we can and should speak about similarity and therefore analogy when we find likeness and unlikeness between two quantities. . . . But the concept of *causa* [cause] does not merely describe activities, but acting subjects. And

ment was wrong. The vast majority of things that happen will *always* be humanly unpredictable, even though there are no gaps in the causal chains.[3]

To review the argument in the first chapter, the only way humans can know the world is by causally interacting with it. This means that there will always be physical limits to the precision of our measurement. And since our universe is riddled with thresholds (nonlinear systems), the most miniscule error in our initial measurement can cause huge errors further down the causal chain. And on top of that, at every threshold our predictions will eventually be stifled by the three-body problem. Finally, since the notion of "self-prediction" is conceptually incoherent, no outcome which can be affected by the "predictor" can in fact be predicted.

A divine Craftsman—depending on exactly how the idea is fleshed out—may face the same problems. But the Author of creation, who doesn't *have* existence but *does* existence, and isn't a part of the universe, does not need to "observe" the universe by causally interact with it to know precisely what's going on. As we argued in chapters 5 and 6, "signs and wonders" should not be thought of as events where God changes things by causally intervening here and there to bring about his will. For the Author whose word creates all things, *willing* that something happens, *knowing* that something happens, and *ensuring* that something happens are all one and the same act.[4] As Barth says, "It is not that God knows everything because it is, but that it is because He knows it."[5]

---

between the two subjects as such there is neither likeness nor similarity, but utter unlikeness." Barth, *Church Dogmatics* III.3, 102.

3. Again, accidents are not uncaused events. "Nor does an accident have any determinate cause, but only a contingent or chance cause, i.e., an indeterminate one. For it was by accident that someone came to Aegina; and if he did not come there in order to get there, but because he was driven there by a storm or was captured by pirates, the event has occurred and is an accident; yet not of itself but by reason of something else." Aquinas glosses this last phrase, "another external cause." Aquinas, *Commentary on Aristotle's Metaphysics* V.22.1141.

4. Aquinas put it like this: "But in God, power, essence, will, intellect, wisdom and justice, are one and the same." *Summa Theologica* I.25.1. Barth puts it like this: "The old symbolic way of representing God, a triangle indicating the Trinity, and an eye in the middle of it fixed on the observer, is apposite in a way both terrifying and comforting." *Church Dogmatics* II.1, 549. He then quotes approvingly from Augustine and Aquinas: "In the marvelous simplicity of his nature, it is not one thing to know, and one thing to be; rather knowing is also being" (Augustine, *On the Trinity* XV.13.22) and "It must be said that the understanding of God is his substance." (Aquinas, *Summa Theologica* I.14.4). Barth might also have referenced Aquinas, *Summa Contra Gentiles* I.61.7: "The knowledge of the human intellect is in a manner caused by things. Hence it is that knowable things are the measure of human knowledge; for something that is judged to be so by the intellect is true because it is so in reality, and not conversely. But the divine intellect through its knowledge is the cause of things."

5. *Church Dogmatic*, II.1, 559.

The crucial point is this: the Author of creation, like the author of a work of fiction, is free to write any "book" He chooses. If God decides to choreograph a universe with "accidental" causes so that a bolt of lightning strikes the altar of a particular prophet, at a particular time, and in a particular place, he will have *made* something happen without employing lawful causes. Humans can only do this in works of fiction. In the real world, we are only able to make things happen by employing humanly predictable (lawful) causes. But since God *creates* the real world out of nothing more than his own plans and purposes, he is free to make things happen either with or without lawful causes.

WHAT IS FREE WILL?

There are at least two distinct, nonoverlapping definitions of "free will." Jesus alluded to one when he said, "If you continue in my word, you are truly my disciples, and you will know the truth, and the truth will make you free. . . . Truly, truly I say to you, every one who commits sin is a slave to sin. . . . So if the Son *makes* you free, you will be free indeed" (John 8:31–35, emphasis added). This is the promised freedom that will be fully realized only in the new heavens and new earth, though it is inaugurated here on earth. It is the freedom that comes from being all you were meant to be. It is *not* the freedom that comes from wanting and doing as you *please*, but the freedom that comes from wanting and doing what you *need* to become a fully flourishing human being made in the image of God. In this regard, it is the sort of moral freedom that *begins* with the ethics of virtue and the politics of stewardship that we discussed in the two previous chapters, but is not completed until—with the gracious bestowal of the theological virtues of faith, hope, and love—it becomes promised freedom.[6]

---

6. The essential compatibility between virtue ethics and Barth's ethics is frequently passed over. We, however, agree with Matthew Rose, who writes, "One profitable way of reading the *Dogmatics* is as an inquiry into the nature of the good life. By that I mean Barth is putting forth, in the antique sense of the word, a philosophy, an instruction about the art of living and dying well. Much like Justin Martyr, Clement of Alexandria and Augustine, Barth could be regarded a philosopher in that he interprets Christian teachings as providing a path to a happy and well-ordered life." Rose, *Ethics with Barth*, 91. He then makes reference to several lines from the *Church Dogmatics*: "And let us not forget that theology. . . is also a philosophy" (I.1, 188). God's wisdom is "the philosophy of the created universe and the philosophy of human life" (II.1, 432). "When it wants to speak of God, theology must also make use of philosophy" (I.2, 728). To these we would add additional quotes: "Obedience to the command of God the Creator is also quite simply man's freedom to exist as a living being of this particular, i.e., human structure." Ibid., III.4, 324. And again, God's command is "desirable and pleasant and true and

Here's a quick review and preview of the crucial points. For an addict to get what she *wants* is a kind of freedom, but it is not the kind of freedom that will "set her free." Rather, it is the kind of "freedom" that only enslaves. Plato likens human attachments to gluttony, sensual pleasures, and their more sophisticated refinements to "leaden weights" that drag people down so that they can only focus their attention on that which they can see and touch.[7] Breaking free from these leaden weights begins with the acquisition of the virtues discussed in chapter 7. The promised freedom the Son of God gives begins in the same place, but it extends further. As a boy, Jesus learned the virtue of obedience to his parents. Then, as an adult, he learned faith and obedience to his heavenly Father. Finally, at his resurrection, Jesus became the "first fruits" of a new kind of true freedom. It is a freedom that we can catch glimpses of here on earth. And though we now see through a glass darkly, the promise is that one day our opaque eyes will be healed, and then we will both see and be all we were meant to be.

In the meantime, the initial acquisition of virtue and obedience is never easy and rarely instantaneous. Adam's initial disobedience makes the cultivation of the land difficult. It also makes the cultivation of virtue and obedience difficult. Growing crops takes work because of the curse; developing virtue and learning obedience takes work because we are addicted to sin. In the process of breaking free from our addictions, there is an intermediate state where we successfully resist temptation, though we are only able to do so with a great struggle. We still *want* another drink or another roll of the dice or the last word in an argument or whatever other enslaving sin besets us, even though in some sense we know that these are the last things that we *need*. Wanting to sin, while nonetheless resisting sin's temptation, is certainly an improved condition compared to wanting to sin and succumbing. Yet it is not the best of conditions. Though in this life we will never become completely free from the corrupting power of sin, nonetheless that is the goal. And it is this promised freedom of the gospels that Christians now claim by faith and look forward to with hope.

---

good and beautiful. In the face of it, the justifiable concern of eudaemonism [virtue ethics] need not be displaced." Ibid., II.2, 652. Nigel Biggar also reads Barth as a virtue ethicist. "At this point the Kantian character of Barth's ethic recedes even further, and reveals something basically eudaemonist: we should obey God's command, not out of spineless deference to the capricious wishes of an almighty despot, but out of regard for our own best good, which this gracious God alone truly understands and which he intends with all his heart." Biggar, "Barth's Trinitarian Ethic," 215.

7. Plato, *Republic* VII.519.

And note: this freedom is a gift; it is not an achievement because it comes from without.[8] Some temptations we can conquer from within. Here we can exhort ourselves and others with phrases like "exercise some will power" or "do your duty" or "just *do* it." But some addictions run much deeper. Even after alcoholics haven't had a drink for twenty years, and even after they fully understand that for them alcohol is toxic, they still confess to *wanting* to drink—once an alcoholic, always an alcoholic. No one is free from their addictions until they no longer *want* another drink or another roll of the dice or the last word in an argument or whatever else they lust after. Only when they *want* what they need to be fully flourishing humans will they be free from their addiction. And sin runs even deeper than addictions, which may be genetically hardwired. "For I do not do the good I want, but the evil I do not want is what I do.... Wretched man that I am! Who will deliver me from this body of death?" (Rom 7:19, 24). Only the Son of God, says St. Paul. We cannot achieve freedom through our own efforts. All we can do is to pray for the Son of God to *make* us fully free. Promised freedom comes from without, not from within.

The notion that you can be *made* free is almost unintelligible to most moderns. At best, it strikes most of us as nothing more than an oxymoronic figure of speech. If you are *made* to do or be what you are and do, then is not this the very antithesis of freedom? The historical origin of our skepticism dates back to shortly before the Enlightenment. It is found in the writings of William Ockham (1288–1348). He wrote, "What I mean by freedom is the power I have to produce various effects, indifferently and in a contingent manner, in such a way that I can either cause an effect or not cause it without any change being produced outside of this power."[9]

There are two crucial parts to this definition of free will. First, unlike either moral freedom or promised freedom, both of which are characterized as being able to do what is good or needed, Ockham defines freedom as the ability to act *indifferently*, that is, to do either good *or* bad, right *or* wrong,

---

8. To the question "Whether Man Can Will or Do Any Good Without Grace?" Aquinas says No. One of his arguments goes like this: "Man is master of his acts and of his willing or not willing, because of the deliberation of reason, which can be bent to one side or another. And although he is master of his deliberating or not deliberating, yet this can only be by a previous deliberation; and since this cannot go on to infinity, we must come at length to this, that man's free choice is *moved by an extrinsic principle*, which is above the human mind, namely, by God, as the Philosopher proves in his chapter on *Good Fortune*. Hence the mind of man still healthy is not so much master of its act that it does not need to be moved by God; and much more the free choice of man weakened by sin, by which it is hindered from good by the corruption of the nature." Aquinas, *Summa Theologica* I-II.109.2.1, emphasis added.

9. Pinckaers, *Sources of Christian Ethics*, 242.

that which is needed *or* that which is merely desired. The radical revision in our conception of freedom that Ockham initiated can only be understood if we connect it with the argument of the previous chapters.

Ockham was the first "nominalist." In philosophy, nominalism is the theory that the various categories humans use to refer to various kinds things—rocks, plants, animals, humans, etc.—have no grounding in *nature*. Instead, all words are mere names which, for various reasons, humans *choose* to attach to groups of objects. In other words, Ockham denied the reality of essential natures. In chapter 7 we considered Aristotle and Aquinas's argument that *because* humans are rational, social animals, the virtues of courage, temperance, justice, and practical wisdom are all required if we are to flourish as human beings. Here the virtues are philosophically tied to *what* we are. And we also saw what happened when Sartre broke this connection between what we *are* and what we should *do*. But long before Sartre, Ockham had already broken the tie between being and doing when he denied the existence of essential natures.

So why should we refrain from rape, murder, and theft? According to Ockham, we do so *only* because this is what God commands. Our natural inclination to happiness and the natural path to happiness through the virtues count for nothing to Ockham. We should be "indifferent" to happiness and virtue, said Ockham. He made clear just how indifferent we should be by famously arguing that God might very well have commanded us to *hate* our neighbor. And if God had so commanded, then that's what we ought to do, totally indifferent to the natural consequences that would befall such actions.[10]

So without a natural inclination toward happiness and virtue, what possible reason could anyone have for choosing to obey God? Ockham posited a pure will that resides wholly *within* the person. Every person has a will, and each person's will, wholly on its own, has the power to either cause or not cause something else to happen; nothing "outside" a person's *will* is required—that's what he meant when he defined freedom as the ability of the will to choose "without any change being produced outside of this power." Four centuries later, Kant would follow Ockham and define freedom as the "absolute spontaneity of the will."[11]

---

10. Ibid., 247ff.

11. Kant, *Religion*, 19. Elsewhere Kant said that the only thing "which elevates man above himself as a part of the world of sense" is his "freedom and independence from the mechanism of nature." *Critique of Practical Reason*, 89. Furthermore, the independence of humans' will is complete and unblemished. "A physical propensity (grounded in sensuous impulses) toward any use of freedom whatsoever—whether good or bad—is a contradiction." Kant, *Religion*, 26.

Thus, according to Ockham, freedom is characterized by (1) indifference and (2) autonomy. So depending on whether we are emphasizing the first or the second point, we will call Ockham's alternative to promised freedom either the freedom of indifference or autonomous freedom—though we must be clear that these terms do not name two distinct theories. Their only purpose is calling our attention to the two sides of a single theory. (In philosophical circles, this sort of freedom is called "libertarian freedom.")

And what sort of thing is this pure "will," which makes autonomous choices, independent of the web of causation surrounding a human being? Like Ockham, Aquinas frequently spoke of the "will" as a part of the soul. But unlike Ockham, he would always add that a human being is an inseparable unity of body and soul (matter and form). In his pre-Enlightenment understanding, it made no sense to speak of the "soul" or "the will," apart from the body and all its causal relations, making *independent* choices. To talk about an autonomous soul, from a Thomistic understanding, is as incoherent as talk about an autonomous smile, i.e., a smile apart from a face.

As we saw in chapter 2, Descartes answered questions about the nature of the will by conceiving of a human being as two distinct substances—a material body and an immaterial soul. His dualism would become the philosophical foundation for making sense of Ockham's notion of a fully autonomous "will." To understand the radical break the Enlightenment was about to make, we need to contrast this new conception of an autonomous will with Aquinas's pre-Enlightenment conception of the soul.

According to Aquinas, the soul is *in* the body the way that meaning is *in* a word, not the way dirt is *in* a rug.[12] No one is as silly as to think that a super-powerful electron microscope might one day discover a superfine substance called "meaning" in the gaps between the ink molecules that make up words. Words are not two *things*—"meanings" and ink molecules to which they are attached. Likewise, human beings are not two *things*—a "soul" and the body to which it is attached. When humans act freely, according to Aquinas, it is the *whole* human being that acts freely, not some separable *part*. Humans never exist apart from an insanely complex web of interconnected personal, social, cultural, historical, philosophical, and theological relations, all of which are mediated through both lawful and accidental causes. No soul is an island unto itself.

This is precisely what Descartes denied. In his theory, the will is only free when it is acting *apart* from the body. For Cartesians, the will is *in* the body the way a captain is *in* his ship. Captains control the ships; ships don't control captains. True, in a bad storm a captain may not be able to make

---

12. I flesh this out in much more detail throughout *In Defense of the Soul*.

the ship do precisely what he wants, so the captain is not free to do as he chooses. But when the captain is free vis-à-vis the ship he is acting with full autonomy; i.e., the ship has no causal effect on the captain's decisions. So too, when the "will" is choosing freely, the body has no causal effect on the "will." If it did, then it wouldn't be free, according to Ockham, Descartes, and Kant.

There are at least three crucial differences between promised freedom and the freedom of indifference/autonomy.

First, autonomous freedom is an "all-or-nothing" affair. By definition it requires complete independence of all physical cause. Whenever this condition is met, people are free because it doesn't matter if they choose good or evil. Promised freedom, on the other hand, is a "more or less" affair, since a person's ability to choose good over evil varies on a continuum ranging from rarely to almost always.

Second, the freedom of indifference *includes* the possibility of "choosing evil" as part of its definition of freedom. Promised freedom, on the other hand, *excludes* this possibility. The possibility of "choosing evil" is part of a definition of enslavement to sin; not the definition of freedom in Christ. Barth is explicit: "Disobedience [to God's command] is not a choice, but the incapacity of the man who is no longer or not yet able to choose in real freedom."[13] And again, "Hence the freedom of man is never freedom to repudiate his responsibility before God. It is never freedom to sin. When man sins, he has renounced his freedom."[14] David Burrell, a contemporary Thomist, put it like this: "Creatures are indeed capable of an utterly initiatory role, but it will not be one of acting but of failing to act, of 'refusing' to

---

13. Barth, *Church Dogmatics* II.2, 779.

14. Ibid., III.2, 197. And also, "When man sins, he does that which God has forbidden and does not will. The possibility of doing this is not something which he has from God. That he can put this possibility into effect does not belong, as it often said, to his freedom as a rational creature. What kind of a reason is it which includes this possibility! What kind of a freedom which on the one hand is a freedom for God and obedience to Him, and on the other a freedom for nothingness and disobedience to God! Turn it how we will, if we regard this as a possibility of the creaturely nature of man, we shall always find it excusable because it is grounded in man as such." Ibid., IV.1, 409–10. And again, "Freedom is given to man as every other creature is given its peculiar gift by God. It is his creaturely mode. It is adapted and therefore proper to him . . . This freedom constitutes the being of man and therefore real humanity—the freedom which, in accordance with its origin and responsibility towards it, can be actualized and exercised only in the knowledge of God, in obedience to Him and in asking after Him, whereas in any other freedom man would in some sense be stepping out into the void and could only forfeit and lose himself." Ibid., III.2, 194. Finally, "Disobedience is not a choice, but the incapacity of the man who is no longer or not yet able to choose in real freedom." Ibid., II.2, 779.

enter into the process initiated by actively willing 'the good.' In that sense, we can be 'like unto God,' but only in a self-destructive manner."[15]

Finally, while autonomous freedom excludes *all* physical causes from its definition of freedom, promised freedom only excludes *lawful* physical causes from its definition of freedom. The tragic case of Charles Whitman illustrates this third point. On August 1, 1966, Whitman wrote a suicide note just before killing sixteen people, including the wife he loved:

> I do not quite understand what it is that compels me to type this letter. Perhaps it is to leave some vague reason for the actions I have recently performed. I do not really understand myself these days. I am supposed to be an average reasonable and intelligent young man. However, lately (I cannot recall when it started) I have been a victim of many unusual and irrational thoughts.[16]

When an autopsy was performed a highly aggressive tumor (glioblastoma) was discovered in his brain. This explains what Whitman could not understand: his "thoughts" were not his own because there was a *lawful* relation between a tumor located where it was in Whitman's brain and these sorts of "unusual and irrational thoughts." Because Whitman's "actions" were the predictable effects of such a tumor his "actions" were not truly his own. On this both understandings of free will agree.

But unlike Ockham's autonomous freedom, neither Aristotelian moral freedom nor the promised freedom of the Gospels require that the person's choice be physically uncaused.[17] For Aquinas freedom is an attribute of the whole human, not a separate immaterial part of a human being. Without a physical brain, humans can do nothing. And in a brain, everything that happens has a physical antecedent, because nothing comes from nothing. But as we argued in chapter 1, the fact that something is caused does *not* mean that it is determined, predictable, or mechanistic. Without keeping this absolutely crucial distinction between causation and determinism in the forefront of our minds, moral freedom and promised freedom are unintelligible.[18]

---

15. Burrell, *Freedom and Creation*, 91. Here are Aquinas's own words: "The first cause of the defect of grace is on our part, but the first cause of the bestowal of grace is on God's." *Summa Theologica* I-II.112.3.

16. Whitman, "Whitman Letter."

17. "To be moved voluntarily is to be moved from within, that is, by an interior principle. Yet this interior principle may be caused by an exterior principle, and so to be moved from within is not contrary to being moved by another." Aquinas, *Summa Theologica* I.105.4 ad. 2.

18. Though Barth never makes this distinction explicit, he uses it nonetheless. With respect to knowledge of the tree of good and evil, Barth writes, "The purpose of God in

Charles Whitman's tragic killings were morally excusable because they were *lawfully* caused by a brain tumor. But given the distinction between caused and determined it does not follow that for an action to be truly free it must be independent of *all* physical causes. Both moral freedom and faith's freedom are fully compatible with the kind of accidental physical causation we illustrated at the beginning of chapter 1 with a tennis ball bouncing down a rocky mountain road.

Though having said this, we must guard against a second confusion. Just because there are no lawful causes determining the course of a bouncing tennis ball, that in no way suggests that a tennis ball has moral freedom. Moral freedom has *two* conditions—lack of lawful causation *and* a choice of good over evil. Since tennis balls are not the sort of things which make choices, they lack moral freedom, even though their actions are not lawfully caused.

PREDESTINATION AND EFFICACIOUS GRACE

Predestination, sometimes called election, is the Christian doctrine that human salvation results from God's eternal decree or choice. This doctrine raises at least three questions and/or problems. First, how can humans be truly free if the most important choice anyone makes—to love God or to love the world—has been eternally decreed by God? Second, if all our actions are predestined, then doesn't that make God responsible for our sin? Third, if salvation is a matter of God's eternal decree, then must not the same be true of damnation? The rest of this chapter only deals with the first question. The second and third question will be dealt with in chapters 10 and 11 respectively.

One half of the first question has an easy answer. If "truly free" is *stipulated* to mean autonomous freedom, then free will and predestination can *not* be logically reconciled. However, this does not mean that Christians who affirm autonomous freedom do not affirm *some* version of predestination/

---

granting man freedom to obey is to verify as such the obedience proposed in and with his creation, i.e., to confirm it, to actualize it in his own decision. It is obvious that if this is His will God cannot compel man to obey; He cannot as it were bring about his obedience mechanically. He would do this if He made obedience physically necessary and disobedience physically impossible, if He made man in such a way as to be incapable of a decision to obey. . . . He has created him with the capacity for a confirmation and actualization of his obedience, for a personal decision to obey. This is not to say that God has given him, like a Hercules at the cross-roads, the choice of obedience and disobedience." *Church Dogmatics* III.1, 264–65. And again, "The creature does not belong and is not subject to Him like a puppet or a tool or dead matter . . . but in the autonomy in which it was created." Ibid., III.3, 93.

election. They too affirm that we are "saved by grace." So *something* happens "outside" or apart from our own choices that is necessary for salvation. These Christians typically explain what happens "outside" by distinguishing between efficacious and sufficient grace.[19]

Sufficient grace, they say, is made available to all people by Christ's atoning death and resurrection. Without this no person could be saved. And obviously, Christ's death and resurrection is something that happened "outside" or apart from anything we do or choose. But sufficient grace, by itself, saves no one. It is not efficacious until a person chooses to *receive* this incomparable gift. It is only this "choice to receive" that is autonomous and wholly independent of anything "outside" of each human's immaterial will.[20]

Aquinas and Barth, however, affirm that God's grace is not merely sufficient, it is also efficacious.[21] They do not deny that God's gracious provision on the cross must be received. They only add that the very act of "choosing to receive" is itself a wholly unearned gift from the Holy Spirit. Ockham, Descartes, and Kant would say that if the "choice to receive" came from without, then it is not truly *their* choice. But why is this? Humans really do have arms and legs that they did not create. So too, Christians really do have the gift of faith that they did not create. But just because a person's faith "came from without" does not make it less truly *theirs* than their arms and legs which also "came from without." Or at least, that is how Aquinas and Barth understand St. Paul when he says "For by grace you have been

---

19. The *theological* distinction between efficacious and sufficient grace must not be confused with the *logical* distinction between a necessary and sufficient condition. Unfortunately, by an accident of linguistic history, "sufficient" has come to mean precisely the opposite in theological and logical contexts. In a *theological* context, "sufficient" grace means what in a *logical* context would be termed a necessary, but not a sufficient condition, i.e., Christ's atoning death and resurrection is a necessary, but not a sufficient condition for a person being saved.

20. See ch. 9 of Placher's *Domestication of Transcendence* for an excellent historical exposition of these issues. Therein he explains the notion of sufficient grace like this: "No one can be saved without grace, but sufficient grace is available to all, and therefore what distinguishes the saved from the damned is how they make use of that grace. [Said Arminius,] 'It always remains within the power of the free will to reject the grace bestowed . . . because grace is not an omnipotent action of God which cannot be resisted by man's free will'" (153).

21. "God does not justify us without us, since while we are being justified, we consent to God's justice by a movement of free choice. But that movement is not the cause but the effect of grace. Thus the whole operation belongs to grace." Aquinas, *Summa Theologica* I-II.111.2.2. "It is God who elects man. Man's electing of God can come only second. But man's electing does follow necessarily on the divine electing." Barth, *Church Dogmatics* II.2, 192.

Free Will and Predestination

saved through faith; and this is not you own doing, it is the gift of God" (Eph 2:8).[22]

Disputes about the reality of efficacious grace are often treated as questions about how best to interpret the Bible. Defenders of efficacious grace (predestination without qualification) have their list of biblical passages and defenders of sufficient grace (predestination with qualification) have their own list of biblical passages.[23] And while neither side of the debate is so crassly positivistic as to think that the dispute can be settled by counting verses and seeing whose list is longer, frequently disputes about this matter *seem* as if this is what is going on.

Our suspicion is that a person's interpretation of the biblical debate has a lot to do with prior assumptions about the nature of free will. While there is no disputing the fact that the Bible affirms human's free will, nowhere does it *define* free will. Our further suspicion is that the Bible doesn't do this because it is clearly a pre-Enlightenment document and therefore simply takes for granted a pre-Enlightenment understanding of freedom. But suspicions are speculations and these historical speculations can only be substantiated by going beyond the kind of philosophical and theological investigation we are now conducting.[24]

So for the rest of this chapter our only goal will be to explain the philosophical *compatibility* of promised freedom with an unqualified affirmation of predestination (i.e., a commitment to efficacious grace). Whether free will is best defined in terms of promised freedom or the freedom of indifference is something that can only be decided after considering all three of the questions listed at the beginning of this section.

---

22. Aquinas defines faith as "an act of mind assenting to the divine truth by virtue of the command of the will as this is moved by God through grace." *Summa Theologica* II-II.2.9. And Barth explicitly says that faith's "knowledge of God must also come to us from without." *Church Dogmatics* II.1, 249.

23. Here's a list of some favorite biblical passages for both sides.

Efficacious Grace (Calvinist Texts): Matt 22:14, John 6:37, 44, 64, John 8:47, John 10:26, Rom. 9:10–13, Rom 11:5–6, 1 Cor 1: 26–29, 1 Cor. 4:7, Eph 1:4, Eph 2:8, 2 Thess 2:13, Prov 16: 9, 33, Prov 21:1, Isa 45:7, Lam 3:37–38, Amos 3:6.

Sufficient Grace (Arminian Texts): Gen 22:12, Exod 4:9, Exod 32:14, Ezek 12:3, Ezek 18:23, Jer 3:7, Jer 18:9–10, Jer 26:3, Joel 2:13, Jonah 4:2, John 1:9–11, John 12:32, Rom 8:29, 1Tim 2:4, Titus 2:11–12, Jas 1:13–14, 2 Pet 3:9, 12.

24. Placher's *Domestication of Transcendence* does an excellent of job describing the historical change that took place in the seventeenth century when both Catholic and Protestant theologians were moving away from what I've called "promised freedom" toward what we both call the "freedom of indifference." See also the first chapter of Gregory's *Unintended Reformation*.

THE COMPATIBILITY OF FREE WILL AND PREDESTINATION

One very simple definition of predestination is that God always gets what God wants. And though simple, this is not a simplistic definition since it is precisely what the Reformed tradition means when it speaks of "irresistible grace." *When God elects to save a human being, there is nothing a human can do to foil God's election.*[25] Now it is extremely important that we understand this last sentence for what it *says*, not for what we think it might imply. This statement does *not* say:

- God only elects *some* (not all) humans.
- Since God only elects some humans, He must therefore *damn* others.

These are two separate propositions that must (and will) be considered in the next two chapters. For now, we are only considering the single proposition that *God always gets what he wants*.

One of the examples that Aquinas used more than once to illustrate the compatibility of unqualified predestination and the kind of freedom we are defending goes like this. A master sends two of his servants to the market to make a purchase. Each of the servants has additional business to conduct for their master with the other servant. When they meet in the market they think to themselves: "What a happy coincidence, now we can take care of two items of business at once." What these two servants don't know, and cannot know unless it is revealed to them by their master, is that this "happy coincidence" was in fact planned by their master.[26] To a similar

---

25. Notice that this is precisely what Arminius denies. And notice too that Aquinas is in full agreement with the Reformed tradition, at least in part because here both are drawing heavily on Augustine. When God elects to save "it has a necessity—not indeed of coercion, but of infallibility—as regards what it is ordered to by God, since God's intention cannot fail, according to the saying of Augustine in his book on the *Predestination of the Saints* that 'by God's good gifts whoever is liberated, is most certainly liberated.'" *Summa Theologica* I-II.112.3. Again, "God can change the will with necessity, but he cannot compel it." Aquinas, *On Truth*, 22.8. Barth also approvingly quotes Augustine in respect to God's foreknowledge and human freedom: "The religious mind chooses both, confesses both, and confirms both in the faith of its piety." At the same time Barth rejects Molina's model of God and humans as two who "work together like two men pulling a boat." According to Molina, Barth writes, "The indispensable but not finally decisive circumstances and conditions are given by prevenient grace. But it lies in the will of the creature to make use of them or not and therefore to make the grace operative or not. . . . Yet we have to recognise that the continued existence of the Thomistic counter-theory [to Molina's and the Jesuits' theory of "middle knowledge] means that the door to the Reformation doctrine has not been altogether slammed. It remains an inch open." Barth, *Church Dogmatics* II.1, 568–89.

26. Aquinas, *Summa Theologica* I.22.2. Again, "We must therefore say that what

end, Karl Barth affirms John Calvin when he says that no one is so foolish to believe that God moves humans in the same way that he moves a stone.[27]

Aquinas, Calvin, and Barth are all assuming, as we explained at the beginning of this chapter, that the Author of creation can make things happen in two ways—by employing lawful physical causes (as when unsupported stones fall downwards) and by employing what from the human perspective seem to be wholly accidental causes (as when servants meet by "accident" in the market). Yet, whichever way God chooses to "make something happen" the outcome is equally certain. Humans truthfully say that an unsupported stone *necessarily* falls to the ground. And conversely, humans truthfully say that a tennis ball bouncing down a rocky road *may* have come to rest someplace else or that it *could have been otherwise* or that it didn't *have to* come to rest precisely where it did. But from God's eternal perspective the tennis ball coming to rest precisely as it did and an unsupported stone falling to the ground are equally certain because God always gets what he wants—as Jesus said, even the hairs on your head are numbered.

Today we often speak of "points of view" or "different perspectives" to indicate that we are only talking about opinions, attitudes, or personal preferences. John and Mary, for example, might have very different perspectives on their fiftieth wedding anniversary. From John's perspective as an introvert, having a big party celebrating his fiftieth wedding anniversary sounds like a pretty unpleasant affair. But from Mary's perspective as an extrovert, having a big party sounds like great fun. The fact that John and Mary have stayed married for fifty years suggests that they fully understand that in such matters there are no "right or wrong answers"—instead, each must learn to accommodate the other's preferences and perspectives.

However, when we spoke in the previous paragraph about a human perspective and God's perspective, we were *not* speaking of mere opinions, attitudes, or preferences. Instead, we were making a point of formal logic concerning the medieval distinction between *de dicto* and *de re* predication. "*De dicto*" simply means about the word or proposition; "*de re*" simply means about the thing itself. Here is a very simple example:

- "Red" has three letters.

---

happens here by accident, both in natural things and in human affairs, is reduced to a pre-ordaining cause, which is Divine Providence. For nothing hinders that which happens by accident being considered as one by an intellect.... For example, someone who knows of a place where a treasure is hidden, might instigate a rustic, ignorant of this, to dig a grave there. Consequently, nothing hinders what happens here by accident, by luck or by chance, being reduced to some ordering cause which acts by the intellect, especially the Divine intellect." *Summa Theologica* I.116.1.

27. Calvin, *Institutes* II.5.14.

- Red is my favorite color.

In the first, "has three letters" is being predicated *de dicto* because it is talking about the word "red," not the color itself, whereas in the second, "is my favorite color" is being predicated *de re* because it is talking about the color itself, not the word we use in English to refer to the color.

Yet this very simple distinction between *de dicto* and *de re* predication goes a long way in resolving our current problem. Consider these two "if, then" statements:

- If a stone is unsupported, then *it* necessarily falls to the ground (*de re*).
- If God wills that a tennis ball bouncing down a rocky road comes to rest at a particular spot, then *it* is necessarily true that the ball will come to rest in this particular spot. (*de dicto*).

In the first "if, then" statement, it is the stone itself (a thing) that is said to fall necessarily. In the second "if, then" statement, it is the proposition—"the tennis ball will come to rest precisely at this particular spot"—that is said to be true necessarily. The *de re* statement describe *how* something happens; the *de dicto* statement describes the *way* another proposition is either true or false.[28]

There are three (maybe four) ways a proposition can be either true or false. A contradictory statement is necessarily false; a tautological statement (e.g., all truck drivers drive trucks) is necessarily true. All other statements (the sun always rises in the east) are either contingently true or false, i.e., they depend on how the universe has in fact been created.[29] Finally, for some purposes we distinguish between statements which are absolutely contingent versus those which are relatively necessary. It is absolutely contingent that the earth has a circumference of about 24,000 miles. God could just as easily have created it with a circumference of either 23,000 or 25,000 miles. On the other hand, given the fact that the earth has the mass that it does, then it is (relatively) necessary that unsupported objects accelerate toward the center of the earth at about thirty-two feet per second squared.

We would not be surprised if at this point readers are starting to think about angels dancing on the heads of pins. But we beg for patience. As we said in chapter 2, while we must learn to tolerate *vagueness* in analogical

---

28. "'Everything known by God must necessarily be,' is usually distinguished, for this may refer to the thing, or to the saying." Aquinas, *Summa Theologica* I.14.13.3.

29. "*I answer that*, As Dionysius says it pertains 'to Divine providence not to destroy but to preserve the nature of things.' Therefore it moves all things in accordance with their conditions, so that from necessary causes, through the Divine motion, effects follow of necessity; but from contingent [accidental] causes, effects follow contingently." Ibid., II-I.10.4.

reasoning, *ambiguity* should never be tolerated. The potentially ambiguous word in two "if, then" statements is the italic word "*it*." In the first (*de re*) statement, "it" refers to a *thing*, i.e., a stone. In the second (*de dicto*) statement, "*it*" refers to a *proposition* about a tennis ball bouncing down a rocky road. More specifically, the second bulleted "if, then" statement says that if the antecedent (the "if" part of the statement) is true, then the consequent (the "then" part of the statement) is always true, i.e., it is necessarily true.

The *de re*/*de dicto* distinction is as important to philosophers as parentheses are to mathematicians. If we ask mathematicians "How much is two plus three multiplied by four?", they will ask for clarification. If you asking for the sum of (2 + 3) x 4, then the answer is 20. But if you are asking for the sum of 2 + (3 x 4), then the answer is 14. Until we know where to place the parentheses, the initial question is ambiguous and is impossible to answer.

Likewise, to understand what Aquinas and Barth mean when they say that God always gets what he wants, we must begin by eliminating ambiguities. To do so require three logically distinct "if, then" statements:

- If God wants X, then necessarily God gets what he wants.
- If God wants X, then God will ensure that X occurs by employing lawful causes (e.g., unsupported stones falling to the ground).
- If God wants X, then God will ensure that X occurs by employing accidental causes (e.g., two people meeting at the market).

According to Aquinas and Barth, the first bullet is always true. The second bullet is sometimes true, e.g., when God ordains the law of gravity to ensure that unsupported stones fall to the ground. And the third bullet is sometimes true, e.g., when God choreographs accidental causes to ensure that two strangers meet in the market.[30] And though God could have chosen otherwise, it seems that God chose to create a universe in which the third bullet is more frequently true than the second. That is, it seems that God

---

30. Here's the way Barth makes this point: "In [his freedom] God says Yes to the creature and not No. He says it of himself. He says it without the creature having any right or claim to it. Against our No He places His own Nevertheless. He is free in the very fact that the creature's opposition to His love cannot be any obstacle to Him. He is free, too, in the fact that He cannot be satisfied merely with smashing this opposition . . . He is free rather, and His hand is almighty, in the fact that He can rescue the creature from the destruction into which it has plunged itself by its opposition. He is free in the fact that He can turn it [the creature] in spite of itself to the salvation and life which are the positive and distinctive meaning and goal of His love. And it is that which God elects." *Church Dogmatics* II.2, 28–29. Edith Stein makes this same point more briefly: "Human freedom can be neither broken nor neutralized by divine freedom, but it may well be, so to speak, outwitted" (quoted in Balthasar, *Dare We Hope*, 221).

created a universe in which there are more accidental causes than lawful causes.

And why do Aquinas and Barth think that God more frequently gets what he wants by choreographing *accidental* causes than by ordaining natural laws? First, simply because they were not wearing "Enlightenment glasses" and they had no difficulty seeing that every bounce of a tennis ball bouncing down a rocky road is caused, but it is neither predictable, deterministic, nor mechanistic. And if we do the same and acknowledge the distinction between causation and determinism, we too will observe—both in the world at large and in our own particular life—how frequently "the race is not to the swift, nor the battle to the strong, nor bread to the wise, nor riches to the intelligent, nor favor to the men of skill; but time and chance happen to them all" (Eccl 9:11).

Second, because of the importance of dual-causation we can surmise that God has a preference for working through accidental causes. Dual-causation tells us that existence has many distinct levels—first, the relative distinction between the way humans, animals, plants, and rocks exist, and second, the absolute distinction between God and everything else. God is not *part* of the universe.[31] God does not ensure outcomes the way Hamlet ensured the death of Polonius, i.e., by running him through with his sword. Rather, God ensures outcomes the way Shakespeare ensured the death of Polonius, i.e., by writing a play in which Polonius is killed by Hamlet.

Like Shakespeare, God sometimes creates situations where people act with diminished capacity (think of Charles Whitman's brain tumor). Other times, like Shakespeare, God creates situations where people act with a high degree of freedom. And because authors have the freedom to create characters that act in various ways, college English professors ask questions like: Just how much freedom did Hamlet have when he killed Polonius? Was blindly thrusting his sword through the curtain an indication of Hamlet's diminished capacity? There are probably many good and defensible answers to this question. But there is one answer that no college professor will accept: Hamlet had *no* freedom—he only killed Polonius because Shakespeare *made* him do it.

The problem with this answer is that it confuses two distinct levels of discourse. The English professor's discourse concerns the world in which Hamlet lives and moves and exists, whereas the discourse of the student

---

31. "[A] free action is one which I cause and which is not caused by anything else. It is caused by God.... This is not the paradox that it seems at first sight, for God is not anything else. God is not a separate and rival agent within the universe. The creative causal power of God does not operate on me from outside, as an alternative to me; it is the creative causal power of God that makes me me." McCabe, *God Matters*, 13.

concerns the world in which we and Shakespeare live and move and exist. Shakespeare is not a part of Hamlet's world, and hence, no reference to Shakespeare can answer questions about what happened *in* Hamlet's world. The student has, so to speak, forgotten the "parentheses." Consider the difference between two more "if, then" statements.

- If an author wants X to occur in his story, then it is necessarily true that (X will occur in his story).

- If an author wants X to occur in his story, then in his story (X will occur necessarily).

These statements are superficially similar. In fact, the only difference is that in the first statement "necessarily" is *outside* the parentheses, while in the second statement "necessarily" is *inside* the parentheses. But this is a case where being inside or outside of a parentheses makes all the difference in the world.[32]

In the first statement the "necessarily" falls outside the parentheses, which means that it is making a *de dicto* assertion about the *proposition* inside the parentheses. But in the second statement, "necessarily" falls inside the parenthesis, which means that it is making a *de re* assertion about X. The "necessarily" inside the parentheses explains *how* X will occur. The "necessarily" outside the parentheses explains that the parenthetical statement (X will occur in his story) will *always* be true when the antecedent is true, i.e., when the author wants X to occur.

But, and this is the crucial point, just because an author *always* gets his characters to do exactly as the author intends, that doesn't mean that what the characters do they always do with *necessity*.

The student who says that Hamlet isn't free because Shakespeare *made* him kill Polonius is asserting the rather trivial truth contained in the first bullet. *Of course* authors are free to write the story any way they choose. The professor, however, is asking a very different question. The professor wants to know about the non-trivial truth or falsity of the second bullet. She is asking about what happens *inside the story*;[33] she is not asking about the

---

32. "Although it is important to explain how the divine simplicity itself is to be understood, it is perhaps the implications of that doctrine that will be the most telling in impressing upon us just how radical is the difference between God and Creatures, and what it means to say that his transcendence is nothing less that absolute. . . . This means that, in talk about his causation, the causal operator should always be used externally. For example, not 'God makes the Universe exist' but 'God makes it be that (the Universe exist),' not 'God acts on individual X to bring about F' but 'God brings it about that (X do F).'" Miller, *A Most Unlikely God*, 12–13.

33. "Again it is clear that God cannot interfere in the universe, not because he has not the power but because, so to speak, he has too much; to interfere you have to be

freedom of authors to write or not to write a particular story. And hence, to answer this question we must only look *inside* the story to determine whether X occurred as the result of lawful or accidental causes. If the causes are lawful, then the character isn't free; but if there are no lawful causes within the story that make a character like Hamlet do as he does, then Hamlet is free.

The difference between words being inside and outside parentheses illustrates our frequent insistence that overcoming Enlightenment assumptions requires that we *not* think of God as a *part* of the universe. No matter how many superlatives we attach to God's "existence," we will have misunderstood divine transcendence if we think of God as the most important, most powerful, most glorious "thing" that exists. We must never forget that we literally *do not know* what it means to say that "God exists." The most we can say is that God *does* existence, as awkward as that sounds in English.[34]

The reason we are so insistent about this is that we must, so to speak, move God *outside* the parentheses if we are to understand the relation between free will and predestination. Only then can we understand St. Paul when he says, "Work out your own salvation with fear and trembling, for God is at work in you, both to will and to work for his good pleasure" (Phil 2:12–13). Paul is not speaking paradoxically, nor is he asking us to "balance" two propositions going in opposite directions. He is simply saying that from the "inside" *we* must work, but from the "outside" it is *God* who is doing the work. Or, in the language of the previous chapters, when doing philosophy and theology, we must never think in terms of mono-causation, but instead, always think in terms of dual-causation. Aquinas put it like this: "the same effect is not attributed to a natural cause and to divine power in such a way that it is partly done by God, and partly by the natural agent; rather, it is wholly done by both, according to a different way."[35]

---

an alternative to, or alongside, what you are interfering with. If God is the cause of everything, there is nothing that he is alongside. Obviously God makes no difference to the universe; I mean by this that we do not appeal specifically to God to explain why the universe is this way rather than that, for this we need only appeal to explanations within the universe." McCabe, "A Modern Cosmological Argument," 199.

34. "That God's *energeia*, or Act, inheres in his Being, means that God's Being is in his Act and his Act is in his Being. He is not Being which also acts, but Being which acts precisely as Being, for his Being is intrinsically active, dynamic Being. Hence, there can be no thought of knowing God in his Being stripped of his Act, behind the back of his Act, or apart from his active Reality as God, for there is no such god." Torrance, *Ground and Grammar*, 153.

35. *Summa Contra Gentiles* 3.70.8. See also *Summa Theologica* I.23.8 ad. 2. Barth makes the same point when he explicitly *denies* that God and humans work together as "two men pulling a boat" (*Church Dogmatics* II.1, 569).

One final point. When a professor asks about the freedom of a character in a story, it is insufficient to establish that there were no lawful causes (in the story) which *made* him act. We must also establish that he made a *choice* to act as he did. And to properly be said to have "made a choice" requires that the person understands *what* it is that he or she is choosing.[36] A person who drinks the clear and odorless liquid in his water bottle cannot meaningfully be said to have *chosen* to kill himself, if he had no way of knowing that the water had been secretly poisoned. Choice presupposes reason or understanding; it presupposes that you know *what* you are doing.

Now this raises a difficult and interesting question. If promised freedom requires a true understanding of what one is doing, and if sin is the deadliest of poisons, then how can a person ever be said to *choose* to sin? And if no person truly chooses to sin, then it appears that no one should be blamed or punished for their "sin." Here we have the problem of evil in its most intractable form. It will be addressed in the next chapter. But, first, a word about prayer.

PRAYER AND PREDESTINATION

Predestination frequently gives rise to questions about prayer. If I am already among the elect, then there is no need to pray. And if I am not, then prayer will be useless. Either way, if God always gets what *he* wants, then why should I tell him what *I* want?

A common answer (which is no less true just because it is common) was alluded to in chapter 5. There we said that "the relation between temporal objects and God is always and only one of Creator and creature. And the fact that God gives all his good gifts 'from eternity' doesn't mean that prayer is superfluous. Some of his good gifts he gives *because* of prayer. And remember, the because relation need not be a temporal relation—the cathedral stands upright *because* of the buttresses, even though the buttresses were never in place *before* the cathedral stood.

Now that the distinction between what's inside and outside parentheses has been made we can flesh out further how prayer works. Inside the parentheses Polonius dies *because* Hamlet runs him through with a sword. Outside the parentheses, students of literature may speculate about Shakespeare's motives for writing a play where one character kills another character with a sword. (Was Shakespeare's own father a manic-depressive who

---

36. Or at least it requires this if we reject Ockham's notion of an "indifferent" will that is forced to choose between alternatives when there is no essential difference, and hence, reason is useless.

frequently acted in an impulsive manner?) And then, given Shakespeare's decision to write such a play, literature students can once again move inside the parentheses and discuss the *internal* dynamics of the play that make sense of Hamlet's action.

The same inside/outside logic occurs when we consider Elijah's contest with the prophets of Baal on Mount Carmel. Inside the parentheses we can say that God "sent fire from the sky" to consume Elijah's offering *because* of his prayer. We might even offer an explanation of events inside the parentheses with a series of "becauses." For example,

> Because the prophets of Baal practiced child sacrifice Elijah challenged them to an altar-lighting contest, and because Elijah prayed he won the altar-lighting contest, and because Elijah won the altar-lighting contest all the prophets of Baal were killed.

All this takes place within the parentheses, and each of these "becauses" makes perfectly good sense. But we must not speculate about why the Author of creation chose to create a universe in which the prophets of Baal were defeated *by* Elijah's prayers. And we must certainly not say that God chose to create such a universe *because* of Elijah's prayer. What goes on outside the parentheses effects what happens inside; and what goes on inside the parentheses effects other events inside the parentheses; but what goes on inside the parentheses does not and cannot effect what happens outside. That's how Aquinas and Barth make prayer and predestination *compatible*.

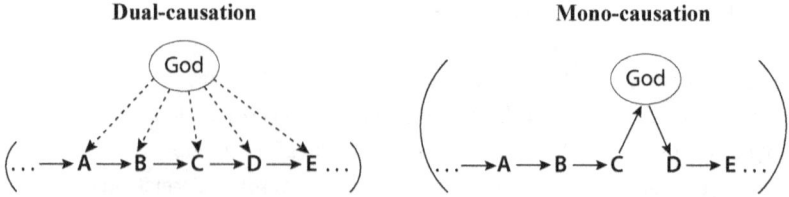

But Aquinas and Barth would also defend a stronger proposition—some biblical prayers *require* predestination, i.e., an understanding of faith as that which "comes from without." Consider the prayer of the father just before Jesus heals his son—"Lord I believe, help thou my unbelief" (Mark 9:24). Or consider Jesus' prayer for Peter "that your faith may not fail" just before Peter is to be "sifted" by Satan (Luke 22:32). Or finally consider one of Aquinas's own prayers:

> Give me, O Lord, a steadfast heart,
> which no unworthy affection may drag downward;
> give me an unconquered heart,

which no tribulation can wear out;
give me an upright heart,
which no unworthy purpose may tempt aside.
Bestow on me also, O Lord my God,
understanding to know you,
diligence to seek you,
wisdom to find you,
and a faithfulness that may finally embrace you;
through Jesus Christ our Lord.
Amen.[37]

None of these prayers make sense if belief/faith is itself an autonomous choice. In all of these cases, someone inside the parentheses is praying to the God outside the parentheses that something else may happen inside the parentheses—for a son to be healed, for a disciple to keep the faith, and for oneself to remain steadfast. The intent is not to change God's mind. Rather, it is to acknowledge that inside the parentheses things happen *because* Christians pray.[38]

Additionally, though prayer does not change God's relation to us, it does change our relation to God. Prayer is what philosophers have called a performative. It is something Christians *do* using words which objectively changes their relation with God. The relation of God to humans will always be one of Creator to creature—that relation can never change. The relation of humans to God can be one of either a rebel to a Lord *or* of a faithful servant to the Lord—that relation changes through prayer.

In this respect, prayer is like a marriage ritual. When the preacher or justice of the peace says "I now pronounce you man and wife," he is using words to do something, i.e., he is *marrying* two people. After he says those seven words the relation between the two people standing before him has changed. Prior to those seven words being said, any sexual relations between the man and woman would be either adultery or fornication. And in some states, if the woman was under a certain age, the man will have been guilty of statutory rape. After the words are said, none of these is true.

---

37. Theology, *Book of Common Worship*, 446.

38. "Divine providence does not merely arrange what effects are to occur; it also arranges the causes of those effects and the pattern by which they occur. Among the many causes influencing human life, the actions of humans are causes of some events. So it is right for human beings to do certain things, not because through their actions they will change the divine disposition but because through their actions they will fulfill certain effects according to the plan of God. We do not pray in order to change God's plan but in order to obtain by our prayers those things which God planned to bring about by means of prayers." Aquinas, *Summa Theologica* II-II.83.2.

And here it is crucial to emphasize that this is a *real* relation that has changed. It is not just a "matter of opinion" that after these words are spoken sexual relations between the man and woman do not constitute adultery or fornication. The change is as real as the change in relation between a car and its driver before gas is put in the tank and after gas is put in the tank. *Before* the gas is put in the tank, the driver can't drive his car, and before these seven words are spoken the man can't have sexual relations with the young woman without becoming an adulterer, fornicator, and/or a person who might be convicted of statutory rape. *After* the gas is put in the tank, the driver can drive his car, and after the seven words the man can have sexual relations with his bride without becoming an adulterer, fornicator, and/or statutory rapist.

But suppose we ask, "Who brought about this objective change in the relation between these two people?" The man and woman who said, "I do" obviously played a role, but in an important sense it is a minor role. Those same words outside the context of a marriage ritual would have no effect on their moral or legal relation to each other. In this case, it is the words of the preacher or justice of the peace that change the moral and legal relation between these two people. But in another sense, even the words of the preacher or justice of the peace play a subordinate role. The preacher or justice of the peace is no magician, able to change the world through his supernatural powers. Instead, his power comes from the whole web of intentional relations that constitute the law in his jurisdiction. In short, here we have another example of dual-causation in action. The objective change in the relation between the man and woman is caused both by the seven words *and* by the set of intentional relations that constitute the law.

Finally, if we are supposing that this marriage ritual takes place in the United States or most other nations in the world today, the relation between the preacher or justice of the peace and the law is a hierarchical relation where the law is the primary cause and the preacher or justice of the peace is the secondary cause. In other words, the law can exist without the preacher or justice of the peace, but the person saying the words—"I now pronounce you man and wife"—cannot exist as a preacher or justice of the peace without the law. It is the law that *establishes* their ability to change the moral and legal relation between people. So too, it is *because* God has established prayer as a performative that it makes a real difference in our relation to both the world and God.

If we think of everything taking place on the same level of reality or if we think of God as existing *inside* the parentheses, then none of this makes any sense. Why would a person pray "I believe; help my unbelief" if they were wholly in control of their own beliefs? But when we understand that not all things exist on the same "level," that "existence" is not univocal, that we merely *have* existence while God *does* existence, then and only then does the father's prayer make sense. On one level the father believes. But he knows that to maintain his belief he needs the faith that can only "come from without,"[39] i.e., that comes from a level of reality that transcends his own.

We already touched on the notion of different "levels" of reality when we described the idea of a "Great Chain of Being" in chapter 2. There we said that existence should be conceived of as a verb. Not only do we say "Fred runs" or "Fred isn't running," we also distinguish various degrees of running, from very fast to very slow. Likewise, Aquinas distinguished various degrees or levels of existence.[40] Plants are alive; they do things that rocks cannot do. Dogs are both alive and conscious of their environment; they do things that plants cannot do. Humans are alive, conscious of their environment, and able to understand what they cannot "see" (like a chiliagon or "tomorrow"); they do things that dogs cannot do. Now at each of these different levels, the "higher" can to some degree understand the "lower" in a way that the "lower" is unable to understand the "higher." Dogs can both see and smell flowers; but flowers can neither see nor smell dogs. Humans can understand *what* dogs are doing when they are following a scent with their nose, even though our noses are way too insensitive to smell what dogs smell. But no dog can understand *what* humans are doing when they are reading a newspaper, and this has nothing to do with the acuity of dogs' vision.

---

39. Barth puts it like this. "The substantiation of our faith and therefore the necessary confirmation of our systematic deliberations and affirmations in respect of the knowledge of God must also come to us from without." *Church Dogmatics* II.1, 249. See also II.1, 212–13.

40. Alexandre Koyre describes what changed in the Enlightenment like this: "The destruction of the Cosmos, that is, the disappearance . . . of the conception of the world as a finite, closed, and hierarchically ordered whole (a whole in which the hierarchy of value determined the hierarchy and structure of being, rising from the dark, heavy and imperfect earth to the higher and higher perfection of the stars and heavenly spheres), and its replacement by an indefinite and even infinite universe which is bound together by the identity of its fundamental components and laws, and in which all these components are placed on the same level of being." *From the Closed World to the Infinite Universe*, 2. Alister McGrath describes the alternative: "The critical realist perspective which informs a scientific theology insists upon the recognition of a plurality of levels within reality, each demanding its own distinct mode of investigation and representation. Ontology determines epistemology. This insight has important implications for any attempt to 'represent' reality. For example, it is necessary to note that each level of reality may demand, not merely its own distinct mode of investigation, but its own correspondingly distinct mode of representation." *A Scientific Theology*, 82.

Now the distance between God's understanding of us and our understanding of God is infinitely greater than the distance between a dog's understanding of us and our understanding of a dog. But when a good dog and his master come to a busy street, the good dog will sit at the command of his master, even though the dog has no understanding of the difference between a red light and a green light. And the good dog does this because in some sense the dog knows that his master has his best interest in mind.

So too, Christians pray for at least three reasons. First, there are times when they can't stop from crying out—"Lord, I believe; help my unbelief." These are the times a Christian is like a person in a state of deep depression who *wants* to do nothing, though at a "meta level" they want nothing more than to engage in those activities in which their old self took such delight. Depression is a state of *wanting* to want, but being unable to want. Similarly, there are times when a Christian's faith is weak and they are powerless to change their condition. These are the times when Christians can take great comfort in the doctrine of election, believing that their faith itself comes from a "meta level" and is not something their autonomous self must muster up.

Second, we pray to change our relation to God. In prayer, we are not only saying that we are Christians; we are *making* ourselves Christian—we have objectively changed our condition from that of a rebel to that of a faithful servant. Barth put it like this: Doctrine "is always impotent until it transcends itself, until it becomes the theology of the resurrection, which means concretely, until it becomes prayer. . . . To the impure all things are impure. . . . It is a faith in which we can only cry and pray that God will help our unbelief."[41]

Third, there are times Christians pray out of obedience to their Lord, who they can no more understand than a dog can understand his master. These are the times we make our requests known to the Author of creation, believing that God (outside the parentheses) has choreographed things on earth (inside the parentheses) so that good things happen *because* we pray.[42] Aquinas puts it like this:

---

41. *Church Dogmatic*, II.2, 763, 768.

42. "People may believe in providence, but how are they to put their belief into practice apart from proclaiming that they have it? According to Aquinas, one answer is 'By prayer.' For by praying, he says we presuppose the working of providence." Davies, *Thought of Thomas Aquinas*, 178. Norris Clarke puts it like this: Do our prayers, acts of worship and charity, etc. "make a difference to God"? Clarke writes, "Difference (could have been otherwise, this rather than that) does not logically imply change (*this* after *that*)." *Philosophical Approach to God*, 134.

> Divine providence does not merely arrange what effects are to occur; it also arranges the causes of those effects and the pattern by which they occur. Among the many causes influencing human life, the actions of humans are causes of some events. So it is right for human beings to do certain things, not because through their actions they will change the divine disposition but because through their actions they will fulfill certain effects according to the plan of God. We do not pray in order to change God's plan but in order to obtain by our prayers those things which God planned to bring about by means of prayers.[43]

Yet, sometimes good things do *not* happen, even though we pray. What then? We'll address this question in the next chapter.

---

43. *Summa Theologica* II-II.83, 2.

—10—

The Goodness of God

How can evil exist if God is good and all-powerful? The question is as old as Job. But the common answer today is as new as the Enlightenment: Evil is the result of our free will, and the good of a free outweighs the pain it entails.

But this is not the response of Aquinas and Barth. They understand evil as a privation. It is the uncreated "impossible possibility" that cannot be explained; it can only be redeemed. And when evil is redeemed, those who have suffered evil will bear no grudge and we who have done evil will turn our eyes to the cross of Christ and joyfully exclaim, "Oh happy fault that merited such a great redeemer!"

Darkness is the absence of light. Evil is the destruction of good. Since both of these definitions tell us what something is *not*, they are only helpful if we first understand what something *is*.[1] It is not hard to understand what light is. We see it every day and scientists define it as a certain frequency of electromagnetic radiation. It is harder to understand what "good" is, at least when we use the term as a general and abstract noun. But when we use "good" as an adjective it is much more obvious what we mean. For example,

---

1. Aquinas fleshes this out: "Like night from day, you learn about one opposite from the other. So you take good in order to grasp what evil means. Now we have accepted the definition that good is everything that is desirable. Well, then, since each real thing tends to its own existence and completion, we have to say that this fulfills the meaning of good in every case. Therefore evil cannot signify a certain existing being, or a real shaping or positive kind of thing. Consequently, we are left to infer that it signifies a certain absence of a good." *Summa Theologica* I.48.1.

we have little difficulty understanding references to a good screwdriver, a good hunting dog, and a good heart (referring to the organ that pumps blood). Each of these things—a screwdriver, hunting dog, and heart—are good when they do what they are intended to do; in this case, drive screws, retrieve prey, and pump blood.[2]

GOODNESS IS A TRANSCENDENTAL

However, no list of good things will produce a proper understanding God's goodness. There are two reasons this is so. First, when we talk about good animals and good biological organs, we are talking about things that have been assigned a function or purpose by God. So they are good to the extent that they are all that they were meant to be. But there is nothing that God was "meant to be." No one has assigned him a function or purpose. He is completely free to do as he pleases. Both Aquinas and Barth insist that God was not under obligation to create anything nor was he somehow compelled to create by his own nature—God is not like a pregnant women who must give birth or suffer the consequences. Instead, God creates wholly out of love and in complete freedom.[3] While God creates good things, that is not his assigned function.

Second, Aquinas and Barth do not adopt the position of some philosophers and theologians who argue that there is a uniquely *moral* sense of goodness that God fulfills.[4] As soon as we try to unpack this uniquely moral sense of the word "good," we run into similar problems. Inevitably "*moral* goodness" is conceived of in terms of rules, duties, and/or obligations. But once again, Aquinas and Barth insist that God is the *creator* of rules, duties, and obligations; God is not the *follower* of rules, duties, and obligations.

---

2. "Once again, it is important to remember that 'good' is generally what Peter Geach calls a logically attributive adjective. Picking up on Geach's point, Bernard Williams notes that such an adjective 'is logically glued to the substantive it qualifies.' In other words, and leaving God aside, we are seriously in the dark when told that such and such is good if we do not know what kind of thing the such and such in question is." Davies, *Reality of God*, 198.

3. "The knowledge of the divine persons [i.e., the Trinity] was necessary for two reasons. The first was to give us the right idea of creation. To assert that God made all things through his Word is to reject the error according to which God produced things by natural need; and to place in him the possession of love is to show that if God has produced creatures, this is not because he needed them for himself nor for any other cause extrinsic to him; but rather through love of his goodness." Aquinas, *Summa Theologica* I.32.1.3. See Burrell, *Freedom and Creation*, 30.

4. See Helm, *Providence of God*, 166–68; Swinburne, *Coherence of Theism*, 179–83; and Swinburne, *Existence of God*, ch. 11.

True, God is faithful and just to keep his covenant promises. But he does not do so out of any *obligation*. The fact that God keeps his promises is not what *makes* him good; rather, God keeps his promises because he *is* goodness itself. As St. Paul says, "God cannot deny himself" (2 Tim 2:13).

The difference between following rules or standards and creating rules or standards can be illustrated by the General Conference on Weights and Measures held in Paris in 1889. This conference defined the meter as the distance between two lines on a particular bar residing in Paris composed of an alloy of 90 percent platinum and 10 percent iridium, measured at the melting point of ice. Until 1960 (when a new standard was established) the distance between these two marks on this particular bar did not *conform* to some standard for being a meter long. Rather, the distance between the marks on this bar was *itself* the standard of what a meter was. So too, God isn't good because he conforms to an exterior standard of moral goodness; rather, God is himself the *source* of all that is good; he is goodness itself.

But what exactly does this mean? First, on the negative side, saying that God is goodness itself does *not* mean that God arbitrarily defines what is good and what is bad; we rejected this theory in chapter 7. The "goodness" of an action flows from its conformity with the nature of things. For example, as we argued in chapter 7, humans are rational social animals. This means that greedy actions will destroy community and thereby make it difficult for individuals to be what they were created to be. Such deeds are evil by nature, not by definition. It is not the case that greed is morally wrong *because* God condemns it; rather, God condemns greed *because* it is contrary to the nature of the creatures that he created.

Second, and on the affirmative side, to say that God is goodness itself means that we must, so to speak, "start from above." We cannot, and must not, start "from below" with human examples of goodness—purifying them of all pride, self-interest, and greed—and then assume that these purified instances of human goodness constitute a defining characteristic of God.

So what is the alternative to "starting from below"? It is found in a statement where Barth approvingly quotes Aquinas: "God does not belong to any category because nothing is prior to God, either ontically [in the order of existence] or noetically [in the order of knowing]."[5] A couple pages later Barth summarizes Aquinas's point by saying that "God is an instance outside of every genus."[6] A "category" or "genus" (these are roughly equivalent) is a part of Aristotle's theory of definition. So unpacking this short, but

---

5. Barth, *Church Dogmatics* II.1, 444. The translation of Aquinas's Latin is from the "Study Edition" of the *Dogmatics* published by T & T Clark in 2009. The actual quote from Aquinas comes from the *Summa Theologica* I.3.5.

6. Barth, *Church Dogmatics* II.1, 447.

dense, piece of philosophy requires that we first say something about how the various parts of a definition work.

The best definitions are always composed of three elements: 1) the species (or term being defined), 2) the genus (or next larger category into which the species *naturally* belongs), and 3) the specific difference (or that which makes the term being defined *essentially* different from the other members of the genus). For example, "house" is defined as "a building intended to be lived in." Here "house" is the species being defined; "building" is the larger category; and "intended to be lived in" is the specific difference that makes houses essentially unlike libraries, concert halls, factories, etc. So as Aquinas says, "The only thing that is defined in the proper sense is the species, since every definition is composed of a genus and difference."[7]

But the definition of any human creation or artifact (like a house) is always going to include some degree of arbitrariness. For example, a person growing up in the 1950s and 1960s may very well define "baseball bat" as a "cylindrical wooden object used to hit baseballs." However, someone growing up today may well define "baseball bat" as a "cylindrical wooden *or metal* object used to hit baseballs." Though some old-time baseball purists vociferously object to playing baseball with metal "bats," no one seriously believes that college baseball (which allows metal bats) and major league baseball (which does not allow metal bats) are essentially different games. "Baseball," being a humanly constructed and defined game, has no essential nature. "Baseball" *is* what its human creators *say* it is. Here the operative principle is: If you make it, then you get to name it (i.e., "define" what it is). There are no "facts of the matter" that determine the legitimacy of playing "baseball" with metal bats, so we can't seriously argue that college baseball isn't *real* baseball because it allows metal bats.

However, Aristotle argued that when we define naturally occurring things that we didn't create—like plants, animals, and human beings—there *are* "facts of the matter" to which we can appeal and must submit. In these cases, nature, not humans, has the last word. And this means that not all definitions of natural species are equally good. No one who defines "animal" as "a physical object weighing less than a thousand tons" has defined what an animal is. While such a definition includes a "species," "genus," and "specific difference," it is not a good definition for at least two reasons. First, there are many physical objects that weigh less than a thousand tons that are not animals. Second, the *natural* genus of animal is not "physical object," but rather "living object," and the *essential* difference between animals and other members of their natural genus is not "weighs less than a

---

7. Aquinas, *Commentary on Aristotle's Metaphysics* V.2.877.

thousand tons," but rather something like "capable of having sensations and self-movement."

Admittedly we have slid over many difficulties. Venus flytraps can move, but biologists do not classify them as animals. And corals do not move, but biologists do classify them as animals. So while these are difficult cases, hard cases make bad law (i.e., norms or rules).[8] And the norm for naturally existing things, which we did not create, is that a good definition must properly "fit" the hierarchies of nature.[9] For example:

- Fred is a human being.
- Human beings are animals that are rational and social.
- Animals are living organisms that move and sense.
- Living organisms are physical objects that reproduce.
- Physical objects are things that exist in space and time.
- Things that exist are . . .

With the exception of the first and last member in this series, the genus in the higher becomes the species in the lower. Now here's the crucial point: in any series of definitions by genus and species the beginning and end of the series will always be *undefined*.[10] "Fred is a human being" is not a definition. Individuals (be they people, dogs, or qualities, e.g., the color red) are, so to speak, a genus unto themselves since they have no specific difference. When we point to a particular person and say "he is Fred," we are not defining Fred by putting him into a larger genus and then specifying how he differs from others things in a particular genus. We can learn *what* a human being is (a rational, social animal) by a definition; we can only learn *who* Fred is by either experience or description. Proper names are always arbitrary. True,

---

8. As Aristotle said, "Nature proceeds little by little from things lifeless to animal life in such a way that it is impossible to determine the exact line of demarcation, nor on which side thereof an intermediate form should lie. . . . In regard to sensibility, some animals give no indication whatsoever of it, while others indicate it but indistinctly. Further, the substance of some of these intermediate creatures is flesh-like [such as the sea anemones]; but the sponge is in every respect like a vegetable. And so throughout the entire animal scale [i.e., the "Great Chain of Being," see chapter 2] there is a graduated difference in the amount of vitality and in capacity for motion." *History of Animals* VIII.1.588b.4–22.

9. Here too we are quickly sliding over significant problems. Lineaus's famous "tree of life" arranged species by observable characteristics. Today, evolutionary biologists order the "tree of life" in terms of biological ancestry. But in both arrangements there is a progression from lower to higher.

10. "For species alone may be defined, since every definition is composed of genus and difference." Aquinas, *Commentary on Aristotle's Metaphysics* VII.3.1327, see also 877.

we can say that "Fred is a human being." That gives us a genus, but there is no definition until we have a specific difference. And remember, in a good definition the specific difference should specify an *essential* difference. If we say that "Fred is a six-foot-tall, black human being" we have *described* Fred, but we haven't *defined* who he is.

At the bottom of the series a similar problem arises. Existence cannot be defined because there is no larger genus in which it naturally fits.[11] A person who has never seen a chiliagon can still know *what* it is. A simple definition will work: "A chiliagon is a thousand-sided regular geometrical figure." With such a definition we know all there is to know about the *essence* of chiliagons, but we know nothing about their *existence*. More specifically, we don't know whether chiliagons do, have, or will exist outside of people's minds. The same is true of black holes. We can know *what* they are before we can know *that* they are. At least a decade before physicists knew whether or not black holes really existed, they had already defined them as an object with a gravitational field so strong that even light was incapable of escaping its pull. And, of course, in one sense this is quite obvious. It is impossible to conduct a search for black holes until one knows *what* one is looking for.

In other words, knowing *what* a concept means (logicians call this the intension of a term) and knowing whether or not a concept refers to anything that really exists (called the extension of a term) are two distinct and different kinds of knowledge. Existence cannot be understood with a definition; it can only be "understood" through experience. And in this last sentence, the scare quotes around "understood" are deliberate and necessary. Since existence cannot be defined, no person can have a *concept* of existence. "Existence" cannot be understood the way plants, animals, chiliagons, and black holes are understood via a definition. Like "Fred" or the color red, experience is required if we are to understand "existence's" reference. Trying to "understand" existence from a mere definition is like a man born blind trying to understand "red."

As both Aristotle and Kant insisted, existence is not simply another category (genus) of things the way life, sentience, and rationality constitute categories for different kinds of things. The reason is simple: the whole point of categorizing things is to distinguish them from other things. But once we reach, so to speak, the largest (i.e., most inclusive) category we can no longer make a distinction between it and something else. As we suggested in

---

11. "For simple notions cannot be defined, since an infinite regress in definitions is impossible. But actuality [existence] is one of those first simple notions. Hence it cannot be defined." Aquinas, *Commentary on Aristotle's Metaphysics* IX.5.1826.

earlier chapters, "existence" is really more like a verb than a noun. Existence is not an attribute of a thing; it is what a thing *does*.[12]

Furthermore, the "doing" that constitutes existence is unique. And here we might even use the redundant phrase "absolutely unique" to stress just how unusual the term "existence" really is. Trees do many things—they turn light, water, and carbon dioxide into carbohydrates, they grow, they drop their leaves and change their colors, etc. But as long as we are talking about a real tree (not an imaginary tree) it is *doing* something even more fundamental—it is existing. Aristotle called this most fundamental kind of doing *actus*, or actuality. Aquinas said that "existence is more intimately and profoundly interior to things than anything else."[13] Josef Pieper, a contemporary Thomist, put it like this: "Anyone who wishes to underline the difference between a real tree and an imaginary one can do no better than to repeat the same phrases: that the real tree exists, that it 'actually is,' that it is 'something real.' Existence cannot be defined: *actus. . .definiri non potent*—so says Thomas in his commentary on Aristotle's *Metaphysics*. This means that at this point in our considerations—without the slightest exaggeration of the actual facts—our thinking has encountered the riddle of being, perhaps for the first time. Perhaps, to put it more sharply, our thinking meets the *mysterium* of being."[14]

---

12. "But *esse*, or 'to be,' is something else and much harder to grasp because it lies more deeply hidden in the metaphysical structure of reality. The word 'being,' as a noun, designates some substance; the word 'to be' or *esse* is a verb, because it designates an act." Gilson, *God and Philosophy*, 63–64. James Anderson puts it like this, "The metaphysical root of the Scotist doctrine of the univocity of the concept of being lies in an essentialist conception of being. This means, at least implicitly, that *ens* is emphasized at the expense of *esse*. Grammatically speaking, *ens* is being considered as a noun, while *esse* is being considered as a verb: the one denotes thingness, the other, act of existence; the one says *that which*, the other says *is*; *ens* signifies being in its essence-aspect, while *esse* signifies the act of existing itself. Being qua *ens* is substantival being; it is the ultimate ground of logical intelligibility, and hence of univocal conception; being qua *esse* is being-in-act; it is the ultimate ground of metaphysical intelligibility, and hence of analogical conception. To make the concept of being 'univocal,' even in a tenuous sense, is to confuse these two orders or aspects of being . . . Being as such is not a logical entity and it cannot therefore be enclosed in our logical univocal frames. This is why no metaphysically sound philosophy is or can ever be 'systematic' in the sense proper to a system of logic or to a 'dialectical' or an idealist ontology. The idea of being is a transcendental-analogical idea. But being itself is not any sort of idea." Anderson, *Bond of Being*, 274, 285. See also Miller, *Most Unlikely God*, 44, and Burrell, *Freedom and Creation*, 203.

13. *Summa Theologica* I.8.1.

14. Pieper, *Guide to Thomas Aquinas*, 136–37. Another Thomistic philosopher, Norris Clarke, put it like this: Existence "is so fundamental that it is impossible to define it by anything clearer, or by setting it off as a class within a wider class, as is done in ordinary definitions, for outside of it there is nothing." *One and the Many*, 26.

The Goodness of God

In Aquinas's own terms, "existence" is a transcendental, i.e., it transcends all attempts at definition because it is a member of no genus. Nonetheless, existence is something we "experience" in some strange sense. And what makes this "experience" strange is that even though it is the most ubiquitous of all experiences, there is a sense in which not even the best philosopher or poet can say anything more about "existence" than to emphatically wave their hands, raise their voice, and repeat words like "it's real" and "it's actual."

But, in another sense, Aquinas thought we could say more about the various "faces" of existence. This "something more" concerned the transcendental properties of unity, truth, and goodness. In the technical terms of the logician, "existence," "unity," "truth," and "goodness" all have the exact same *extension* (i.e., reference), but they each have a different and distinct *intensions* (i.e., meanings). For example, the phrases "President of the United States" and "Commander-in-chief of the US Armed Forces" always refers to the same person, i.e., they have the same extension. However, they have different intensions (meanings) because they highlight different roles. When acting as Commander-in-chief the President is, so to speak, wearing a different "face." So too, everything that exists has three different "faces."[15]

First, everything that exists is in some sense "one thing," even though we cannot define what it means to be "one thing." As we have already said, there is nothing that one table, one baseball game, one angel, one corporation, one essay, and one poem have in common except the indefinable concept of integrity, wholeness, and being undivided. So "unity" is the first transcendental property of everything that exists. "Existence" and "unity" are coextensive (i.e., they have the same extension). Everything that exists has a unity and everything that has a unity exists. Yet, "existence" and "unity" do not have the same meaning (i.e., they differ in intension). While neither "existence" nor "unity" can be defined by genus and specific difference, we "experience" both as distinct "faces" of the same thing.[16]

---

15. "Following Frege (1848–1925), contemporary philosophers distinguish between the sense and the reference of an expression; between, that is to say, the thing that the term denotes, and the way the referent is presented by the expression. One consequence of this distinction is that two or more expressions can be referentially or extensionally equivalent though they have different senses. Aquinas was already familiar with something like this distinction, for he uses it to explicate the idea that truth, being and goodness—what he calls 'transcendentals'—are in reality one and the same. What he means, I think, is that there is one reality at issue, but that it can be identified from different perspectives and that the nature of these perspectives determines, in distinctive and different ways, what is seen from them." Haldane and Smart, *Atheism and Theism*, 133.

16. Aquinas puts it like this: "What has an essence, and a quiddity [whatness]

"Truth" is the second transcendental "face" of all things that exist. But here we must proceed carefully. A transcendental is something that can be "seen," "experienced," or "intuited," but not defined. Yet, in one sense, "true" *can* be defined. Even Aquinas had no quibble with Aristotle's famous definition of "true" as a proposition that says of *what* is that it is and of *what* is not that it is not. Propositional truth is thus a kind of correspondence or agreement between the meaning of a proposition and what actually exists. And since the concepts used in a definition, according to Aristotle, only exist in the minds of human beings, it follows that "true" refers to a kind of correspondence or agreement between the mental realm and the realm of things whose existence does not depend upon human thought. Rocks and plants and animals exist whether or not anyone is thinking about them, but concepts exist only as they are being "thought" by rational minds.[17]

While Aquinas would not disagree with Aristotle's understanding of propositional truth, being a Christian he took Aristotle's definition one step further. According to Aristotle the universe has always existed and always will exist. And while Aristotle freely incorporated the "gods" into his philosophy, none of his "gods" functioned as an efficient cause that created the universe or any of its parts. Aquinas, on the other hand, believed that the universe and everything in it was created by God. So for Aquinas, in addition to propositional truth, there is also transcendental truth. Again, propositional truth is exhibited whenever a *person* thinks and/or says "the cat is on the mat" when in fact the cat *actually* is on the mat. Here the "whatness" (concept) in a person's mind is in agreement with the "whatness" of the real world. But when Aquinas considers the doctrine of creation, he argues that there is a second kind of agreement. Since everything that exists was first conceived in the mind of God that means that there is a further agreement between everything that exists and the mind of God. So rather than saying that truth *only* refers to propositions that agree with reality, Aquinas argued that there is also a second kind of agreement between the mind of God and all things that exist. He called this transcendental truth.[18]

---

by reason of that essence, and what is undivided in itself, are the same. Hence these three—thing, being, and one—signify absolutely the same thing but according to different concepts." *Commentary on Aristotle's Metaphysics* IV.2.553.

17. Of course, philosophical idealists would disagree. But we have already outlined our fundamental disagreement with idealism in chapter 2 and we will say more in chapter 12.

18. "Truth consists in the squaring of intellect and thing, as said above (Q. 16, 1). Now the intellect that is the cause of the thing [the Creator] is related to it as its rule and measure, while the converse is the case with the intellect that receives [the knower] its knowledge from things. When therefore things are the measure and rule of the intellect, truth consists in the squaring of the intellect to the thing, as happens in ourselves. For

The Goodness of God

Even though the idea of transcendental truth is theological in origins, there are still contexts where this idea is reflected in everyday speech. For example, imagine someone trying to unscrew a screw with a dime. A second person comes along and says, "Let me help—I have a real (i.e., true) screwdriver." Or consider field biologists who speak of collecting "true" members of a species, i.e., individual specimens that are "true to type" and without misleading "defects."

So, according to Aquinas, everything that exists first exists in the mind of God. And since God is the almighty Creator who creates out of nothing, everything that exists first corresponds perfectly to the mind of God—nothing that has been created is "defective." Unlike human artists and artisans whose final product frequently falls short of their concept, there is never any "gap" between the mind of God (his plan or knowledge) and the will of God (what he creates).[19] So, again, while "exist" and "true" are coextensive (i.e., have the same extension), they do not have the same meaning (i.e., they differ in intension) because they name distinct "faces" of that which exists.

"Good" is the final transcendental. Again, in one sense, "good" is also definable. Aristotle and Aquinas both defined "good" as that which all people want or desire. And as we saw in chapters 7 and 8, both philosophers went on to distinguish between real and apparent goods. As the result of either poor reasoning or weakness of the will, all of us sometimes act without justice, courage, and temperance. And when we do, our goal is only an apparent good, which in fact will impede, rather than promote, our own happiness. So even though we sometimes desire these apparent goods, they are not truly good. Thus, there is frequently a definable "gap" between our desires and that which is truly good.

But in another sense "good" is also an indefinable transcendental. As we just said, to say of something that it is true means that it is "without defect." And, clearly, when we say something is "without defect" we are also saying that it is good. So notice again what follows from the notion of transcendental truth. Because there is no "gap" between God's knowledge and

---

according as a thing is, or is not, our opinions or our words about it are true or false. But when the intellect is the rule or measure of things, truth consists in the squaring of the thing to the intellect; just as an artist is said to make a true work when it is in accordance with his art." *Summa Theologica* I.21.2. And again, "The divine intellect, therefore, measures and is not measured; a natural thing both measures and is measured; but our intellect is measured, and measures only artifacts, not natural things. A natural thing, therefore, being placed between two intellects is called *true* in so far as it conforms to either." Aquinas, *On Truth*, 1.2. See Pieper, *Silence of St. Thomas*, 53–56.

19. God "in knowing Himself, immediately knows other things." Aquinas, *Summa Contra Gentiles* II.4.5.

God's will[20] (as there frequently is in humans), God can never fail to carry out his intentions. Even with human artists and artisans, their intention is never to make something bad. True, sometimes artists and artisans create things that will be put to a bad use, like a bomb or propagandistic film. Or at other times their goal is not so much to create something good as it is to meet a deadline. And in such cases, they may well make something that is less than good. But God's *ex nihilo* creation was not propaganda (who would he be trying to deceive?) nor was he rushed by a deadline (since "time" didn't exist until God created things that move). Everything that exists is all that God intended it to be. Why? Because there is never a "gap" between God's conception of how a thing should be and how it is. That's what it means to say that creation is good.

So, if "unity" and "truth" are distinct faces of all that exists, goodness must be the third face.[21] That's why Aquinas said "All things are good in so far as they have being."[22] And again, "For all existing things, in so far as they exist, are good, since the being of a thing is itself a good."[23] In sum, "Being good and being true imply one another: we value truth as a good, we perceive goodness as a truth about things."[24]

---

20. "Much would have been gained if Protestant theology on its side had at least held to the Thomistic position without qualification. . . .[that] God's knowledge, will and action cannot be divided. What God knows He also wills, and what He wills He also does." Barth, *Church Dogmatics* II.1, 577-78, see also 551.

21. In Aquinas's own words, "Thus the character of good includes more notes than that of the true and is constituted by a sort of addition to the character of the true. Thus good presupposes the true, but the true in turn presupposes the one, since the notion of the true is fulfilled by an apprehension on the part of the intellect, and a thing is intelligible in so far as it is one; for whoever does not understand a unit understands nothing, as the Philosopher says. The order of these transcendent names, accordingly, if they are considered in themselves, is as follows: after being comes the one; after the one comes the true; and then after the true comes good." Aquinas, *On Truth*, q. 21 art. 3. As one contemporary philosopher puts it: "But Aquinas's concept of being is much broader than our concepts of existence. By 'being,' Aquinas has in mind something like the full actualization of the potentialities a thing has in virtue of belonging to a natural kind; and this is what both 'being' and 'goodness' refer to, though they refer to it under two different descriptions. The expressions 'being' and 'goodness' are thus analogous to the expressions 'morning star' and 'evening star' in referring to the same thing but with different senses." Stump, "Faith and Goodness," 179.

22. *Summa Theologica* I.6.4.

23. Ibid. I.20.2.

24. Ibid. I.5, 11.

THE GOODNESS OF EXISTENCE

While syllogistically Aquinas's reasoning is impeccable, it seems that there is an obvious objection. Cancer cells exist, but who thinks of them as good? This is a valid objection that we will address later. But first we must consider an obvious connection between existence and goodness. Everyone desires their own happiness, and this is good. But to be happy, one must first exist! So to desire happiness is to first desire existence. As Aquinas says, "Now, we have said above that good is everything desirable; and thus, since every nature desires its own being and its own perfection, it must be said also that the being and perfection of any nature has the character of goodness."[25] Many people have wrestled with the rhetorical question: How can a good God exist when there is so much evil? Aquinas's preliminary answer is an equally rhetorical question: How can so much good exist without a God to create it?

But Aquinas also has a less rhetorical response. It begins with a distinction. As we said in the opening paragraph of this chapter, evil is an absence of good, but it is an absence of a particular kind. Some people are blind and all stones are blind, but blindness is only an evil in the case of people. Stones were never intended to see, so there is nothing evil about the lack of sight in stones. Thus there is a threefold distinction between (1) things that exist and are good because they have been created by God (i.e., being); (2) things that don't exist because they have not been created by God (i.e., nonbeing); and (3) privations. A privation is a property or characteristic which something should have, but doesn't. The distinction between mere nonbeing and a privation is necessary because lack of sight in stones (nonbeing) is not evil, whereas lack of sight in a human being (a privation) is evil.

A thought experiment will illustrate the difference between nonbeing and privations. Suppose God creates the universe with a million people who are perfectly content, happy, and productive. Furthermore, suppose that all the other creatures are also perfectly content, happy, and productive. In short, imagine a faultless universe devoid of all evil. Nonetheless, such a universe would not, according to Aquinas, be "the best of all possible universes." The reason is simple: since God creates *ex nihilo*, the term "best of all possible universes" is as meaningless as the term "largest prime number." God does not require pre-existing material out of which he then fashions the universe. So there can never be anything that prevents God from creating a "better" universe with a million and one perfectly content, happy, and productive people. (The fact that we think that a universe with a

---

25. Ibid. I.48.1.

million and one happy people better than one with a million happy people is further confirmation of Aquinas's assumption that existence itself is good.) Yet, at the same time, it would be churlish to blame God for not creating a universe with a million and one happy people because the nonexistence of the millionth and first person is not an evil privation; it is merely a case of nonbeing.[26]

On the other hand, suppose God creates a universe with a million perfectly content, happy, and productive people, and then Fred murders Sally. Now we have a privation—something that was intended to be, but is no longer. Yet Sally's death is a privation of a particular kind. When the Gospels tell the story of a man who was born blind, Jesus explicitly says that this man's blindness was neither the result of his own sin or the sin of his parents. Rather, it was a deliberate act of God to make manifest his own power (John 9:3). In one sense, all people who are born blind suffer from a privation. But a privation suffered is not the same as a privation inflicted.[27] The man born blind suffered from a privation that resulted from a series of natural causes for which no person was responsible. However, Sally's privation (death) was intentionally inflicted by Fred. We will call the first (the innocent man born blind) an instance of evil suffered and the second (Fred murdering Sally) an instance of evil done.[28]

The existence of two different kinds of evil raises two different kinds of questions.[29] We will begin with evil done—Why would Fred, who by sup-

26. Aquinas is a little more subtle. "The universe, the things that exist now being supposed, cannot be better, on account of the most noble order given to these things by God, in which the good of the universe consists. For if any one thing were bettered, the proportion of order would be destroyed, just as if one string were stretched more than it ought to be, the melody of the harp would be destroyed. Yet God could make other things, or add something to those things that are made, and then that universe would be better." Ibid. I.25.6.3.

27. Of course, many would say that the man's blindness was *inflicted* by God, and hence, most difficult and problematic for belief in an almighty and good God. But as will become explicit below, the goal of this chapter is not to *explain* or justify God's action; it is only to *describe* what he has done. Our point here is that any future redemption of Fred and Sally will necessarily be distinct. If Fred is to be redeemed, he will be redeemed for *evil done*. If Sally is to be redeemed, she will be redeemed from *evil suffered*.

28. Davies, *On Evil*, 21.

29. "Aquinas's account of evil also illuminates his view of created appetite. Following Augustine, Aquinas defines evil as a privation of goodness. [*ST*, I.48.1] He distinguishes between two different kinds of evil (*malum*): physical evil and moral evil. Physical evil is nonmoral and refers to material loss or corruption, as when something material passes from existence. Physical evil in general, though not necessarily in any given instance, is willed by God insofar as it makes the movement from imperfection to perfection possible in the realm of material things. Moral evil is found only in rational

position is perfectly content, happy, and productive, deliberately murder Sally? In one sense, a murder in paradise is absurd and unintelligible. If a person is already perfectly content, happy, and productive, there is nothing to be gained by the murder of someone else. The murder of Sally by Fred is a crime without a motive; it cannot be explained—it can only be described. The best we can do is to posit an "attack" of pride or jealousy. Fred, we might surmise—as content, happy, and productive as he was—couldn't stand the thought that his contentment, happiness, and productivity was not wholly his own;[30] he couldn't stand the thought that there was someone (namely, God) *better* than him. So out of sheer spite, Fred acted to destroy part of God's good creation. Since the perpetrator gains nothing, this would be an act of pure vandalism.

Yet this is not much of an explanation. It is not much of an explanation to say that Fred's act was unmotivated. How can a *lack* of motivation be an explanation? But, on the other hand, it is not hard to think of cases (either in our own actions or those of others) where a person's goal is nothing other than the destruction of that which is good. (Think, perhaps, of the Joker in the movie *The Dark Knight*.)

Barth names that which "triggers" acts of pure vandalism "nothingness." Nothingness is a surd and contradiction. "Nothingness really exists [but] it cannot be legitimately incorporated into any philosophical system."[31] Thus, "by its very nature sin defies explanation or understanding."[32] Wolf Krotke describes the problem like this: "in its revolt against creation, it does not pursue a sensible purpose; it aims only to destroy. . . . nothingness 'is' only as something denied by God, that it is determined by God solely to pass away, and that it only exists in actuality in that it rises up against God and God's creation. . . . In the forms of sin, death, and evil, it wants to win room in creation; yet it pulls into ruin the very room that it gains. . . . Nothingness is the antithesis of all positivity and independence, of all constancy and order. God is the abundance of his perfection. Nothingness is only that

---

creatures and consists in the voluntary choice of something disordered and contrary to one's *telos*. This kind of evil is never willed by God [ST I.48-49, esp. 48.5-6, 49.1 ad. 3, 49.2]." Lombardo, *Logic of Desire*, 30.

30. John Searle says something similar about antirealist philosophers: "As I suggested earlier, many people find it repugnant that we . . . should be subject to and answerable to a dumb, stupid, inert material world. Why should we be answerable to the world? Why shouldn't we think of the 'real world' as something we create, and therefore something that is answerable to us. If all of reality is a 'social construct,' then it is we who are in power, not the world." *Mind, Language and Society*, 32.

31. Barth, *Church Dogmatics* III.3, 303.

32. Ibid., IV.3.1, 463.

which is void; it is privation itself."³³ Evil is a parasite. Without good things to twist, pervert, and destroy, there would be no evil.

Now here's the important point. There is nothing evil about a universe with a million perfectly content, happy, and productive people just because a millionth and first person doesn't exist. But there is something evil in a universe intended by God to have a million people, which is then reduced by one. The ability to engage in pure vandalism comes from the power of "nothingness." It is not "nonbeing" nor is it something that exists independent of God, as something against which God is eternally in opposition. Prior to God's creation, nothingness did not exist and it was powerless to attack God. Nor was nothingness a part of creation that God deliberately chose to create. Philosophically, all we can say is that God foreknew the power of nothingness and nonetheless chose to permit it as the "third element" of creation. But theologically we can say more. Barth define nothingness as that which says No to God's grace.³⁴ As the "third element" of creation (being, nonbeing, and nothingness) it only exists "in its own improper way. . . as impossible possibility."³⁵

HOW NOT TO EXPLAIN EVIL

"Any wise guardian," say Aquinas in explaining the most common and most obvious objection to the Christian faith, "wards off harm and evil from his charges as much as he can. Yet we see many evils in things. Either God cannot prevent them, and so is not almighty, or he does not really care for all."³⁶ An equally common and obvious response is to point out that *some* pain and suffering is conceptually necessary for greater goods. If there was no pain and suffering in our world then neither would there be any charity or courage. Or in Aquinas's own words, "there would be no patience of martyrs if there were no tyrannical persecution."³⁷ Here we see what Barth calls the "shadow side of creation." Unlike the mysterious "third element" and the attacks of "nothingness" that flow from it, Barth is explicit that the "shadow side of creation was deliberately created by God to "produce endurance, and endurance produces character" (Rom 5:3–4). Virtually everyone can look back on their own life to instances of pain and suffering, which at the

33. Krötke, *Sin and Nothingness*, 49–51.

34. "The true nothingness is that which brought Jesus Christ to the cross, and that which He defeated there." Barth, *Church Dogmatics* III.3, 16.

35. Ibid., III.3, 351.

36. *Summa Theologica* I.22.2 obj. 2. See also I.3.2. obj. 1.

37. Ibid., I.22.3 reply 2.

time appeared unredeemable, but are now seen as necessary for the virtues they produced. Aquinas and Barth both affirm that "soul making" provides a perfectly good explanation for *some* of the evil we suffer.[38] But they would deny that this is true of all evil. In addition to such relatively benign pain and suffering, there is also what one contemporary philosopher has called "horrendous evils."[39] These are evils of such overwhelming power that the people who suffer them are not led to greater strength and virtue, but instead are led to brokenness and despair. These are evils that do not produce a greater good *here on earth*.

When asked to explain such horrendous evils, the temptation among Christian philosophers, and even some theologians, is to bring in heavier artillery, the big gun of "free will." Perhaps, they argue, these evils are logically necessary for the greater good of "free will." "No one should blame God for the Holocaust," they say, "since it was caused by the free choices of humans. Of course, God could have miraculously intervened by turning poison gas into harmless water vapor. But this would be tantamount to eliminating free will. God was thus faced with two, and only two, options. He could create a universe in which people are truly free to inflict horrendous evils or he could create a universe without horrendous evils because humans where mere puppets in God's hand, lacking a unique dignity and ability to have a personal relation with God." These philosophers conclude that it is impossible to demonstrate that God was less than wholly good because he chose to create a world with true freedom and horrendous evils instead of a world with no horrendous evil, but also, with no truly free people with whom a mutual relation of love could be established.

We call this a "big gun" because it has all the characteristics of an explanation based upon *universal* principles and logic, just the sort of thing that rational Enlightenment thinkers ought to accept. It draws a valid deductive conclusion from a set of self-evident premises and definitions.

1. Freedom is the ability to autonomously choose either good or evil (definition).

2. Autonomous freedom is the greatest of all goods (self-evident premise).

3. Therefore, God cannot be blamed for creating a world with horrendous evils because such evils are a logical consequence of the greatest of all goods, namely, autonomous freedom.

However, neither Aquinas nor Barth take such a philosophical approach. First, because it assumes a definition of free will that they utterly reject. As

---

38. See Hick, *Evil and the God of Love*.
39. Adams, *Horrendous Evil*.

we argued in the previous chapter: (1) God can no more create an independent and autonomous creature than he can create a second God; (2) the ability to choose both good *and* evil is a definition of enslavement to sin, the very antithesis to the promised freedom of the gospel; (3) to assume that true freedom entails that a person must sometimes chose evil wreaks havoc with the theological claim that Jesus was truly human but without sin; and finally, (4) life in the new heavens and new earth will be one where we no longer make choices *between* good and evil, but instead recieve the gift of *true* freedom in which we gladly, delightfully, and without hesitation *only* choose the good.

But in this chapter we are making an additional point. When Aquinas says that evil is a privation or Barth says that evil is an attack of nothingness, they are not attempting to *explain* evil in terms of a greater good. They both agree with Augustine that "To try to understand evil is like trying to hear silence or see darkness."[40] Instead, they are merely *describing* the biblical story of creation, fall, and redemption.[41]

We cannot explain why God permits evil. All we can do is describe it as a perverse and absurd "third category" not caused by God. There is no explanation for all the good that exists other than "the good God created it." So too, there is no explanation for evil other than "the good God permits it." (And notice the deliberate break of parallelism. Aquinas and Barth never speak of "evil that *exists*" except in the paradoxical sense that we might speak of "darkness that *exists*.") Earlier we argued that existence itself is a mystery—thus, the problem of good. The penultimate point of this chapter is that evil is also a mystery—thus, the problem of evil.[42] Yet, we must be clear about how we are using the term "mystery."

---

40. Quoted in McCool, *Universe as Journey*, 86.

41. "Evil is not of itself knowable, because the very notion of evil means the privation of good. Therefore evil can neither be defined nor known except by good." Aquinas, *Summa Theologica* I.14.10.4. The biblical scholar and skilled popularizer N. T. Wright has also recently endorsed this approach to the problem of evil. He writes, "This goes with the account of evil offered by many great theologians, such as Thomas Aquinas: evil is really the absence or deprivation of good, and yet this doesn't mean it's in any way nebulous or vague or not to be worried about. . . . And I think the point to be made, whether by Paul [in 1 Cor. 8–10 where he is discussing food offered to idols] or Aquinas, is that idolatry—and sin in all its forms—causes potholes in the road, causes rungs to drop out of ladders, where we and others need them to be. Evil is then the moral and spiritual equivalent of a black hole." Wright, *Evil and the Justice of God*, 113.

42. C. J. F. Williams once put it like this: "God, then, does not need this world, and there are infinitely many better worlds which he could have created rather than this one. His reason for creating us is far from sufficient. There is, therefore, an analogy between our sinful acts and God's creative act. We are, precisely in our capacity to sin, like God. This should no doubt be said with bated breath, and with every precaution to

WHAT'S A MYSTERY?

There are at least three different ways we use the word *mystery*. First, in its weakest sense, those who insist that everything be explained in terms of "clear and distinct ideas" and/or that which is quantifiably measured, frequently refer to the immediate and undefinable knowledge we have of things like "good analogies," "forms," "existence," and "evil" as great mysteries. Here, of course, they are using the term disparagingly. But we have already spent the first three chapters disparaging the disparagers of these "mysteries" for their scientifically and philosophically dubious assumptions of mechanism, universal quantification, and mono-causations. Needless to say, our use of the term "mystery" will have nothing in common with their use of the term.

In a slightly stronger sense, *particular* events will always be slightly mysterious. We now know that electrical charges always move from negative to positive. Thus, when the difference between the negatively charged ions in the clouds and the positively charged ions on the ground reaches the critical level, a bolt of lightning will fly from the heavens to the earth. There is no mystery here. And if in a particular time, place, or culture people found such phenomena mysterious, only "explainable" in terms of the anger of the gods, then they were acting out of ignorance, though in most cases it was not *culpable* ignorance. However, if in an eighth-grade science class a student answered a question about lightning like this, there may very well exist some degree of culpability. The student *should* have been listening more attentively during class.[43]

On the other hand, consider Peter, who has just discovered the cure for cancer, and is walking down a country road with his friend Paul. But before he explains his magnificent discovery to Paul, Peter is struck and killed by lightning. In such circumstances it is only natural to ask, "Why was Peter, rather than Paul or even the tree besides them, struck by lightning?" Here the profoundly correct answer is: It's a mystery. Though it was

---

avoid blasphemy. It is nothing but an analogy. It is not for a moment to be affirmed that God himself sins—this would be unintelligible, since nothing that could do evil could properly be called God. But what for us is of the essence of sin, knowingly choosing something less good than what we know we could choose, is of the essence too of God's creative activity. Acting without a sufficient reason is, for God, creation and, for God's creatures, sin." Williams, "Knowing Good and Evil," 239–40.

43. Here I am speaking with much hesitation. The idea of "mystery" is sometimes invoked in a way which, while not fully culpable, nonetheless exhibits a kind willfulness. Science, philosophy, and theology are all hard work, and frequently they are frustrating work. To prematurely answer a difficult question in these disciplines with "It's a mystery!" can be more a sign of laziness than humility.

obvious to both Aristotle and Aquinas that individual, particular events are the result of accidental causes (and hence, not open to "scientific" explanation), today we live in a culture where "particularity" has become a scandalous offense against the widespread belief that humans are in control of their own destiny. But as we argued in the first three chapters, while everything that happens in our world has a cause, not all causes are lawful. Hence, not all events are predictable. Much that happens in our world can only be *described* after the fact. Any attempt to plumb the depths further is a mark of hubris.

Finally, there is a third, and even stronger, use of the term *mystery*. In its specifically theological use, a mystery refers to that which is *currently* unintelligible to humans, yet will one day be understood as the glorious work of the divine Choreographer who works all things together for good. Horrendous evils are mysterious in both the second and third sense, but it is the third sense that is essential to understanding the transcendental goodness of God.

But before we flesh out this third sense of "mystery," it is worth noting a parallelism between the way definitions work and a proper invoking of "mystery." At the beginning of this chapter we saw that definitions only work at "mid-level"—the most general of all terms, "existence," cannot be defined; nor can an individual, whether it be a person or a particular quality. Conversely, "mystery," as we are using the term, is properly invoked at only the highest and lowest levels, precisely those levels where definitions are impossible. But for mid-level questions appeals to mystery are misguided.

- Why is there something rather than nothing? (Creation)
- How do nonliving molecules give rise to molecules that are alive?
- How does lightning work?
- Why does God frequently use pain and suffering as a megaphone to capture a person's attention? (i.e., the "shadow side of existence")
- Why does God permit horrendous evils? (i.e., the impossible possibility)

At both the highest and lowest levels there is a mystery that transcends human understanding. Yet it would be wrong to answer any of the three mid-level questions with: It's a mystery! It is not a mystery when Sam has a heart attack after years of overeating, underexercising, and forsaking friends and family in the pursuit of great wealth. And while only those who have the proper relationship with Sam should point this out, there is nothing wrong with them doing so. Likewise, it is not wrong for a science teacher to tell a student who has failed to study that the physical causes of lightning are *not* a mystery. And, finally, it is not wrong for a scientist to spend a career trying to discover the physical antecedents and chemical reactions that give life to molecules, even if biologists and chemists never succeed in their quest to understand biogenesis. Even though God is truly the Lord and giver of life, that doesn't mean that humans will never understand the secondary causes by which he acts.[44]

We will now return to the third, and most important, sense of "mystery" as we are using the term.

"OH HAPPY FAULT!"

In question one of the third part of his *Summa*, Aquinas asks, "Whether, if Man Had Not Sinned, God Would Have Become Incarnate?" Like all analogical reasoning, Aquinas's answer includes both a Yes and a No. Aquinas begins by pointing out that human salvation is "beyond the creature's due" (hence it is a matter of grace) and therefore it is not something that can be understood by philosophical reasoning. He then points out that "in Sacred Scripture the sin of the first man is assigned as the reason of the Incarnation." From this he concludes that the best answer is that "If man had not sinned, God would not have become Incarnate." However, he is equally clear that this is the best answer, but not the *only* possible answer. "And yet the power of God is not limited to this; even had sin not existed, God could have become incarnate."[45]

Immediately Aquinas introduces what is sometimes called a "fortunate fall" (*O felix culpa!*) understanding of the incarnation. "For God allows evils to happen in order to bring a greater good from them; hence it is written (Rom. 5:20): *Where sin abounded, grace did more abound*. Hence, too, in the blessing of the Paschal candle, we say: 'O happy fault, that merited such and so great a Redeemer'!"[46] Here Aquinas is making two important points— one positive and one negative. The positive point is in stark contrast to the "autonomous freedom argument" that we mentioned earlier. Defenders of autonomous freedom argue that the reason sin exists, and hence evil, is that without the freedom to sin humans could not be truly free. But, according to Aquinas, the reason sin exists, and hence evil, is that it makes "fitting" the incarnation. Aquinas argues that the *evil* of sin brings about the greater good of the incarnation. He does not argue, as do the defenders of autonomous

---

44. Here we should remember that it is only *after* Pasteur that biogenesis becomes problematic. In Aquinas's time it was the norm.

45. *Summa Theologica* III.1.3.

46. Ibid.

freedom, that the greater good of free will brings about the evil of sin. For Aquinas "free will" understood as the freedom to do good *or* evil is *not* a "greater good." What's so good about the ability to sin? Don't all Christians long for that day when, "freed" from sinning, they can sing God's praises unimpeded? Aquinas did not try to explain sin in terms of "free will." He only told a story with the glorious ending of the death and resurrection of Jesus Christ, God's only Son, that makes possible promised freedom and is truly good news for all.

Barth makes a similar move. In reference to the story of the fall in Genesis chapter 3, Barth asks whether the creature's disobedience diminishes the glory of God. His response: "The God of Genesis 3 is more living because more definite, than the God of Genesis 1—2. And He has turned more intimately to the creature than before. Something other and greater than mere creation has now taken place. It is so much greater than the dangerous saying is forced to our lips: 'O happy fault, that merited such a great redemption.'"[47] And again, "Is it not the case that now [after the fall] for the first time the reality of the creature emerges as a reality distinct from God and the preserving grace of God as grace that as such waits for gratitude and can only really be received in gratitude? Again our thought may turn to the *felix culpa*."[48]

Of course, since the incarnation is a revealed truth, it cannot be established by philosophical reasoning. Thus, we must acknowledge that there is no philosophical explanation of evil other than it's a mystery of the third level, just as the mystery of existence itself is. Yet for Aquinas there is a theological story to be told in which evil makes "fitting" the greatest of all goods, the incarnation of God in Jesus. As a theologian Aquinas is only *describing* why God became man, while at the same time insisting that God could have achieved his purposes in some other way—"And yet the power of God is not limited to this; even had sin not existed, God could have become incarnate."[49] In this respect, Aquinas is like the scientist who *describes* (i.e., measures) the circumference of the earth, while at the same time insisting that it might have been either bigger or smaller.

Barth's approach is similar. God is constant in his purposes and intentions. He does not create dogs and later decide it would be better if dogs didn't exist. God neither does nor can act contrary to his own purposes and intentions. But sin, by definition, is contrary to God's unchanging intention. God is unable to sin—to do so would be to deny his constancy and this is

---

47. *Church Dogmatics* II.1, 507.
48. Ibid. II.1, 508.
49. Aquinas, *Summa Theologica* III.1.3.

explicitly contrary to St. Paul's point that "God cannot deny himself" (2 Tim 2:13). God is also unable to *cause* one of his creatures to sin. For God to be the cause of sin would be tantamount to inconstancy—creating a human to worship and live in communion with him, and then changing his mind and deciding that this particular person should not be living in communion with him.

Finally, while God is able to create humans who are real secondary causes (and hence, are able to do what they were created to do), God is not able to create humans who can create "out of nothing." Only God creates *ex nihilo*, and since God cannot create another God, God cannot create a human who is able to do what only he can do. A human who could create *ex nihilo* would de facto be a second God.[50] But God can (and did) create humans with the ability to do what he *cannot* do, i.e., to destroy some part or aspect of God's good creation. Of course, for an individual to be able to destroy something, that individual must first exist, and hence, he or she will have been created by God and will be sustained by God at every moment of his or her existence, *even at the moment they are destroying some other part or aspect of God's good creation!* Here Barth is making the same distinction that Aquinas does when he *denies* in one article that "God is the cause of sin" though in the very next article he *affirms* that "the act of sin is from God."[51] All this is what both Barth and Aquinas mean when they say that God *permits* sin, even though he might have prevented all sin.

So how could God have prevented sin? There are at least two ways. First, God could have chosen not to create anything and live in perfect bliss as Father, Son, and Holy Spirit. Second, God could have chosen to create and not permit any of his rational creatures to sin. C. S. Lewis's *Perelandra* is an imaginative attempt to describe such a universe.

Why, then, didn't God choose either of these options? We can all be thankful that God didn't choose the first option. If he had, we wouldn't exist. But why not the second option? Wouldn't a world populated by billions of free creatures who never sinned be an obviously better world than the world in which we now exist? Here we are face-to-face with a mystery of the third level.

But while Calvinists, Arminians, and Thomists/Barthians all embrace third-level theological mysteries, they do so at very different locations. As we will see in the next two chapters, Calvinists invoke "mystery" when they speak of "God's secret decree" electing to save some while damning others

---

50. "For it is not possible that there be two highest goods, since that which is said by superabundance is found in only one being." Aquinas, *Summa Contra Gentiles* I.42, 2. See also Barth, *Church Dogmatics* II.1, 553ff.

51. Aquinas, *Summa Theologica* I–II.79.1–2. See also Aquinas, *On Evil*, 3.1–2.

for no reason other than that is what he has decreed. Arminians, as we saw in part in chapter 9 and will see in more detail in chapters 11 and 12, invoke "mystery" when they attempt to reconcile God's absolute sovereignty and humans' autonomous freedom. Finally, Thomists and Barthians invoke "mystery" when they describe the "impossible possibility" of sin, which God did not create and will one day destroy, though for now it is nonetheless permitted. Much of the argument of the next two chapters will be that it is best to locate the theological mystery where Aquinas and Barth locate it because their location makes the most sense of the Christian virtue of hope.

But for now we can summarize their position like this. God is the primary cause of all that is good, while humans are real secondary causes of many good things. On the other hand, humans are the primary cause of the destruction of good things, while God is the "secondary" cause of this destruction, which he could have prevented. They never invoke "free will" as a mystery that limits God's ability to fulfill his intentions. Augustine prayed, "The good that I do is done by you in me; the evil is my fault."[52] And the converse is something like: "The evil that I do is done by me in you; the good is your gift."

WHAT THE INCARNATION MAKES POSSIBLE

No Christian theology would be complete without an account of what the incarnation makes possible. The author of Hebrews reminds us that "without the shedding of blood, there is no forgiveness of sin" (Heb 9:22).[53] Likewise, it is only because Jesus conquered Satan, sin, and death by his life, death, and resurrection that we have hope in a world beset with horrendous evils.[54]

---

52. Augustine, *Confessions* 10.4, 209.

53. Again, we should emphasize that "without" must not be understood in a univocal way as to imply that God could not save humans in some other way. In the story that the Author of creation chose to write, there can be no forgiveness without the shedding of blood. But does not mean that the Author of creation could not have written a different "book" in which it was true that "without the cutting of hair there is no forgiveness." And we must not be like the churlish book reviewer who de facto criticizes the book he is reviewing for not being the book *he* would have written.

54. "Christian hope puts a spin on our suffering, but it is a different spin than that for which it is commonly mistaken, namely the spin of explanation. Hope does not explain to us why we suffer; indeed, precisely because we hope, we recognize that our suffering lies beyond present explanation. Instead, hope places us squarely in a narrative in which our suffering can be endured and accordingly made part of our life. As we enter this narrative we are given the grace to see our suffering as leading somewhere; as a part of a journey that stretches before us toward a destination that includes sharing in the glory of God." Hauerwas and Pinches, *Christians among the Virtues*, 122.

Previously we distinguished between "evil done" and "evil suffered." Christ's conquest of Satan, sin, and death redeems both of these, but it does so in different ways. For Sally, who "suffered evil," Christ's resurrection makes possible "the new heavens and earth," where God "will wipe away every tear from their eyes, and death shall be no more, neither shall there be mourning nor crying nor pain any more, for the former things have passed away" (Rev. 21:4). So when Sally looks back to that moment of horror just before she was murdered by Fred, she will consider her suffering nil, in one sense no more consequential than a flea bite. Yet, in another sense, she will consider her horror as the honor and opportunity to "suffer with her Lord." For Sally, the "sting" of death is replaced by solidarity with Christ. And if Fred has repented of his evil deed, when Sally meets Fred in the new heavens and earth, she will bear no grudge, seeing him as a "pardoned murderer," in essence no different from herself.

On the other hand, when a repentant Fred looks back on the pain and suffering that he caused, in one sense he will view his actions with pain and horror given the evil that he caused. But in another sense, when he turns his eyes to the cross of Christ he will joyfully exclaims—"Oh happy fault that merited such a great redeemer!" And when Fred meets Sally in the new heavens and earth, his shame and sorrow will be met not with contempt and condemnation, but with, "Come, let us *together* worship *our* Lord and Redeemer."

So while Christ's victory over Satan, sin, and death redeems the evil Sally suffered in one way and the evil Fred did in another way, in fact, everyone in the new heavens and earth will experience the redemption of *both* evil suffered and evil done.[55] We are redeemed from evil done by the pardon made possible by Christ's death, and we are redeemed from the evil suffered by Christ's resurrection.

But a final question remains: What about hell? Suppose Fred doesn't repent of his sin? What then?

---

55. My argument in this last section has been heavily indebted to Adams, *Horrendous Evils*, 167. Stump is profoundly correct when she writes: "Aquinas's idea, then, is that the things that happen to a person in this life can be justified only by reference to her or his state in the afterlife." Stump, *Aquinas,* 461. In short, theodicies must be theological.

—11—

Augustine's Conception of Hell

Though God is a God of love, there are plenty of biblical passages, many in the New Testament, that speak of God's wrath. Ever since Augustine, this has led the majority of Catholics and Protestants to assume that (1) God will send many people to hell (2) where they will suffer terrible pain as (3) an everlasting punishment for their sins. Yet, other biblical passages depict God's wrath as more than retribution, and as also (4) restorative, even showing God's wrath ultimately bringing repentance to all. This chapter looks at these four sets of biblical passages.

Assumptions are most deceptive when they are unnoticed. The Newtonian conception of space and time discussed in chapter 5 is a case in point. The vast majority of my students simply assume a Newtonian conception of space and time, even though they know almost nothing about Newtonian physics. And as we have already seen, this has a large effect on their conception of God, free will, and miracles. Until these assumptions are brought to consciousness, alternatives to Enlightenment theology will be unintelligible.

The same problem arises when thinking about hell. The vast majority of today's Christians, both Catholic and Protestant, simply assume that hell is a place of endless punishment from which there is no escape. What most Christians don't realize is how much their beliefs about hell have been shaped by book 21 in Augustine's *City of God* and paragraphs 97 through 103 in his *Handbook*. There is nothing in the earliest creeds about hell.

Prior to Augustine there were diverse options about hell, but nothing like a consensus worthy of creedal affirmation. But Balthasar argues that the publication of the *City of God* and the *Handbook* "signifies a turning point in Church history insofar as Augustine interprets the relevant [biblical] texts in such a way as to show that he plainly and simply *knows* about the outcome of divine judgment."[1]

We have not forgotten the question of the last chapter: Suppose Fred doesn't repent of his sins—what then? We will address this question in the last chapter. But first it is necessary to devote a full chapter to the Augustinian assumptions about hell that are buried in the deep recesses of our minds, even if we have never read Augustine. As long as these assumptions remain buried, they will inevitably color everything we read in the Bible about the wrath of God, his unfailing justice, and eternal punishment.

One final preliminary. Though Augustine's conception of hell is almost universal among today's Catholics and Protestants,[2] it is slightly questionable to refer to it as the traditional understanding of hell. Christians look to Jesus Christ as their one savior and most complete revelation of God's intentions. So it should not be surprising that "traditional" is a badge many Christians wear with honor, whereas "modern" suggests a movement *away* from the finished work of Jesus Christ. But we must remember, there are almost four centuries separating the writers of the New Testament from Augustine's *City of God* and his *Handbook*. We must remain open to the possibility that Augustine's conception of hell is not the "traditional" conception of hell, but is instead a markedly "modern" reading of Peter, Paul, John, and the rest of the biblical authors.

The structure of this chapter is to first outline Augustine's conception of hell, and then consider some of the crucial biblical passages concerning hell, doing our very best to suppress Augustinian assumptions and read them as a fresh piece of truly good news.

AUGUSTINE'S CONCEPTION OF HELL

The three essential characteristics of hell according to Augustine are: (1) God will send the *majority* of people to hell, (2) where they will *suffer* terrible pain, and (3) once in hell their punishment is *everlasting*.

---

1. Balthasar, *Dare We Hope*, 65.

2. Orthodox theologians, on the other hand, tend to view hell in non-Augustinian terms. In part this is due to the fact that Augustine wrote and read Latin while most of the church in the East wrote and read Greek. Hence, his works never gained the dominant influence that they did in the West.

Concerning the first point Augustine says, "For, as a matter of fact, not all, nor even a majority, are saved."[3] And it is no mistake, according to Augustine, that the majority of people are sent to hell. He thinks this is necessary to demonstrate to the saved that their salvation is wholly by God's mercy and apart from any merit on their part. "But many more are left under punishment than are delivered from it, in order that it may thus be shown what was due to all."[4] And again, "It was right that those who are redeemed should be redeemed in such a way as to show, by the greater number who are unredeemed and left in their just condemnation, what the whole race deserved." Augustine appears to think that this is the only way that the redeemed might be prevented from boasting and "that every mouth might be stopped of those who wish to glory in their own merits, and that he that glories might glory in the Lord."[5]

Calvin was tremendously influenced by Augustine and makes no significant change to Augustine's conception of hell. However, he does begin to speculate about the numerical ratio of the saved and the damned. "The supreme Judge, then, makes way for his predestination when he leaves in blindness those whom he has once condemned and deprived of participation in his light. Of the former effect there are daily proofs as well as many proofs in Scripture. If the same sermon is preached, say, to a hundred people, twenty receive it with the ready obedience of faith, while the rest hold it valueless, or laugh, or hiss, or loathe it."[6] In short, the denizens of hell will outnumber the saved by a margin of four to one.

Concerning the second point, Augustine describes hell as a place "where pain without intermission afflicts the soul, and never comes to an end."[7] He is also confident that the pain suffered in hell is not just psychological. "I find it easier to understand both [the fire and worm] as referring to the body . . . Scripture is silent regarding the spiritual pain of the damned, because, though not expressed, it is necessarily understood that in a body thus tormented the soul also is tortured with a fruitless repentance."[8]

Finally, concerning the third point, Augustine is equally explicit that the damned will suffer *everlasting* punishment. Chapters 2 through 9 of

---

3. *Handbook*, ch. 97.

4. *City of God*, 21.12.

5. *Handbook*, ch. 99.

6. *Institutes* III.24.12. It was Barth who first called my attention to this passage in Calvin. See *Church Dogmatics* II.2, 39.

7. *Handbook*, ch. 92

8. *City of God*, 21.9. Note also the phrase "fruitless repentance." The suggestion seems to be that even though those in hell repent of their sins, nonetheless they remain locked in hell forever.

Book 21 of *The City of God* are an attempt to explain how fire and worms can eternally afflict the bodies of the damned without eventually consuming them and bring their suffering to an end. Thus, Augustine asks, "Whether It is Possible for Bodies to Last for Ever in Burning Fire?"[9] His affirmative response begins by pointing out that there are certain natural substances (e.g., charcoal and diamonds) that are impervious to fire. But even if there were no natural analogies, Augustine argues that "there are many things which reason cannot account for, and which are nevertheless true. [Here] the ultimate reason for believing miracles is the Omnipotence of the Creator."[10] In other words, God works miraculously to ensure that the fire and worms in hell do not prematurely bring to an end the suffering of the damned.

In the *Handbook*, Augustine argues that when St. John speaks of the "second death" in the book of Revelation he is again alluding to the miraculous nature of hell's fire. "When, however, the unhappy are not permitted to die, then, if I may so speak, death itself dies. . . . This is called in Holy Scripture the second death."[11] And in the *City of God*, he describes it like this: "The first death drives the soul from the body against her will: the second death holds the soul in the body against her will. The two have this in common, that the soul suffers against her will what her own body inflicts."[12]

But it is not just to prolong the punishment of the damned that God miraculously ensures that their conscious suffering is never brought to an end. Damnation has a second purpose: to remind the saints in heaven when they look down on the suffering of the damned how great and glorious their own condition. "When reprobate angels and men are left to endure everlasting punishment, the saints shall know more fully the benefits they have received by grace."[13]

---

9. Ibid., 21.2.
10. Ibid., 21.5.
11. *Handbook*, ch. 92.
12. *City of God*, 21.3
13. *Handbook*, ch. 94. The pervasiveness of the Augustinian conception of hell is illustrated by the fact that even Aquinas, who in other places leaves open the possibility that Augustine's conception of hell may not be the final word (see the next chapter), makes this same argument in the Supplement to the *Summa Theologica*, q. 94 art. 1. But we must remember that even though this argument comes at the end of the *Summa*, in fact we are here listening to the teaching of Aquinas from the very beginning of his career. The Supplement was written *after* Aquinas's death, "probably by his companion and friend Fra Rainaldo da Piperno, and was gathered from St. Thomas's on the Fourth Book of the Sentences of Peter Lombard" (Kevin Knight, editor's note to the English Dominican Province Online edition). Aquinas's commentary on Lombard was one of his first publications.

The last half of book 21 considers sundry objections to the idea of everlasting punishment. First, someone might ask: "How can a temporal crime merit everlasting punishment? Where is the justice in inflicting infinite suffering for a finite crime?" In response, Augustine begins by noting that even with human justice there is no correlation between the time spent committing a crime and the time spent in prison atoning for the crime. But more important in his mind is the infinite distance between what Adam was promised and what he chose. All Adam was required to do to receive eternal glory and bliss was to refrain from eating from a single tree. No strenuous effort or great sacrifice was required on Adam's part to receive an infinite reward. Such a disdainful rejection of eternal life, in Augustine's mind, merits nothing less than everlasting punishment.[14]

Second, Augustine considers the objection of those he calls the Platonists, who "suppose that all punishment is administered for remedial purposes." Augustine does not deny that this is true in many cases here on earth. And he even suggest that some form of punishments may take place after death for those who will ultimately be redeemed. However, all *remedial* punishments come to an end at the death of the body, "the last and strictest judgment." After that, all punishment is strictly and solely retributive. The damned in hell are punished solely because they *deserve* to be punished.[15]

He considers the same objection again in chapter 17, only this time he puts it in the mouth of those he calls "tender-hearted Christians who decline to believe that any . . . shall suffer eternally, and who suppose that they shall be delivered after a fixed term of punishment, longer or shorter according to the amount of each man's sin." This time Augustine sarcastically dismisses the objection with a rhetorical question: "Why does this stream of mercy flow to all the human race, and dry up as soon as it reaches the angelic?"[16] If Christian mercy requires that eventually all humans will be saved, then doesn't it also require that Satan himself one day be saved? Augustine takes this to be an obvious "reduction to absurdity" of the tender-hearted Christian's hope.

He takes up this (false) hope of an eventual end to the punishments of hell one final time in chapter 23. This time Augustine's argument rest on the parallelism of the sheep and the goats in Matthew 25:46. "And they [the goats] will go away into eternal punishment, the righteous into eternal life." Once, again, Augustine employs what he takes to be an obvious "reduction

---

14. *City of God*, 21.12
15. Ibid., 21.13.
16. Ibid., 21.17.

to absurdity." If the punishment of the goats will one day come to an end, then the same must be said of the reward of the sheep.

All that remains to complete his conception of an everlasting hell is to consider, and then reject, various ways the damned might be released from hell: the prayers of the saints, the fact that many of the damned had, during their life on earth, taken the sacraments, the fact that many of the damned had once professed faith, and the fact that many of the damned had given alms to the poor.[17]

THE BIBLICAL EVIDENCE

It is impossible to deny the powerful effect Augustine has had on subsequent Protestant and Catholic readers of the Bible. Even so, there are plenty of biblical passages which appear to be straightforward affirmations of Augustine's second and third point, namely, that hell is a place of great suffering and everlasting punishment. For example:

#1. Some people will suffer everlasting punishment.

- "And these will go away into eternal punishment, but the righteous into eternal life" (Matt 25:46).
- "Let no one deceive you with empty words, for because of these things the wrath of God comes on those who are disobedient" (Eph 5:6).
- "These will suffer the punishment of eternal destruction, separated from the presence of the Lord and from the glory of his might" (2 Thess 1:9).
- "And the smoke of their torment goes up forever, and ever. There is no rest day or night for those who worship the beast and its image and for anyone who receives the mark of its name" (Rev 14:11).
- "And the devil who had deceived them was thrown into the lake of fire and sulfur, where the beast and the false prophet were, and they will be tormented day and night forever and ever. . . . and anyone whose name was not found written in the book of the life was thrown into the lake of fire" Rev 20:10–15.

There are also many biblical passages concerning the omnipotence of God. With what seems to many people to be a fairly obvious inference, these passages appear to make Augustine's first point. Since nothing can defeat the purposes of God, the reason people remain in hell forever is that they are *sent* there by God against their own will.

17. Roughly chs. 18 through 27 of bk. 21 in ibid.

#2. Nothing can thwart God's purposes.

- "I know that you can do all things, and that no purpose of yours can be thwarted" (Job 42:2).

- "Our God is in heaven; he does whatever he pleases" (Ps 115:3).

- "'My purpose shall stand and I will fulfill my intention' . . . I have spoken, and I will bring it to pass; I have planned, and I will do it. . . . 'My purpose shall stand, and I will fulfill my intention,' . . . I have spoken, and I will bring it to pass; I have planned, and I will do it" (Isa 45:10–11; 46:11–12).

- "In Christ we have also obtained an inheritance, having been destined according to the purpose of him who accomplishes all things according to his counsel and will" (Eph 1:11).

- Though strictly speaking this is only an inference, the doctrine of creation strongly suggests that God always gets what he wants: "In the beginning, God created the heavens and earth" (Gen 1:1); and "All things came into being through him, and without him [the Word] no one thing came into being" (John 1:3); and "God who . . . calls into existence the things that do not exist" (Rom 4:17).

The fact that God's saving grace is always efficacious seems to provide a second reason for conceiving of hell as a place where the damned are *sent*. As we argued in chapter 9, "*When God elects to save a human being, there is nothing a human can do to foil God's election.*" In his *Handbook*, Augustine is equally explicit: "And, moreover, who will be so foolish and blasphemous as to say that God cannot change the evil wills of men, whichever, whenever, and wheresoever He chooses, and direct them to what is good?"[18] On the power of God's efficacious grace, Augustine, Aquinas, and Barth are in full agreement. Without it, we are back to an Enlightenment conception of God and free will.

Nonetheless, the doctrine of efficacious grace *by itself* does not entail that some people are sent to hell. Augustine's conclusion needs a second premise, namely, that heaven and hell are symmetrically related. There is no reason to suppose that God *sends* people to hell, unless hell is the philosophical and theological "flip side" of heaven. And so it is in Augustine's mind. Since the only reason people make it to heaven is because of God's efficacious grace, Augustine reasons that the converse is also true: the only reason people end up in hell is because God *wants* them there. In Calvinist

---

18. *Handbook*, ch. 98.

terms, election and reprobation are logical corollaries, which many refer to as "double predestination."[19]

Later we will argue on philosophical and theological grounds that heaven and hell are not the "flip sides" of each other.[20] But for now our only rebuttal is to point to a third set of biblical passages directly contradicting Augustine's conclusion:

#3 *God wants all people to be saved.*

- "As I live, says the Lord God, I have no pleasure in the death of the wicked, but that the wicked turn from their ways and live. . ." (Ezek 33:11).

- ". . . God our Savior, who desires everyone to be saved and to come to the knowledge of the truth" (1 Tim 2:4).

- "The Lord is not slow about his promise, as some think of slowness, but is patient with you, not wanting any to perish, but all to come to repentance" (2 Pet 3:9).

---

19. However, Barth's former student, translator, and friend, T. F. Torrance, does not read Calvin like this. He writes, "Calvin himself had taken up a different position, in accordance with which he held with St. Paul that there is not a 'Yes' and a 'No' in God but only the 'Yes' of his Grace which he speaks equally to all, the just and the unjust alike. Hence if it happens that some people do not believe and perish, that can be understood only as an 'accidental' or 'adventitious' result, for Jesus Christ came to save and not to condemn, and it is of the nature of the Gospel to bring life and not death, just as it is the nature of light to enlighten and not bring blindness or darkness. That is to say, we cannot think this matter our on a logical basis, as if there has to be a kind of logical balance between election and reprobation, for in both the activity of God must be construed as Grace alone. It was for this reason that Calvin refused to agree that condemnation or reprobation should be inserted into a Christian confession of faith for it is an irrational and inexplicable happening, contrary to the intention of Christ and his Gospel." Torrance, *Christian Theology*, 136–37.

20. Barth is explicit in his denial of the symmetry of heaven and hell. "We cannot say that God ordains equally and symmetrically as man's end both good and evil, both life and death, both His own glory and the darkening of this glory. . . . The concept which so hampered the traditional doctrine was that of equilibrium or balance in which blessedness was ordained and declared on the right hand and perdition on the left. This concept we must oppose with all the emphasis of which we are capable." However, it is important to note, for reasons that will become clear in the final section of this chapter, that Barth's argument is not grounded in philosophy and/or natural reason. He continues: "But the emphatic nature of our opposition does not derive from any preconceived idea that the love of God prevents His equally willing of both, thus excluding any such symmetrical understanding of double predestination. What right have we to tell God that in His love, which is certainly quite different from ours, He cannot equally seriously, and from the very beginning, from all eternity, condemn as well as acquit, kill as well as make alive, reject as well as elect?" *Church Dogmatics* II.2, 171.

- "He [Christ] has made known to us the mystery of his will, according to his good pleasure that he set forth in Christ, as a plan for the fullness of time, to gather up all things in him, things in heaven and on earth" (Eph 1:8–10).

- "And the city has no need of sun or moon to shine on it, for the glory of God is its light, and its lamp is the Lamb. The nations will walk by its light, and the kings of the earth will bring their glory into it. Its gates will never be shut by day—and there will be no night there. . . . On either side of the river is the tree of life with its twelve kinds of fruit, producing its fruit each month; and the leaves of the tree are for the healing of the nations. . . . The Spirit and the bride say, 'Come.' And let everyone who hears say, 'Come.' And let everyone who is thirsty come. Let anyone who wishes take the water of life as a gift" (Rev 21:23, 22:2, 22:17).

So how can we understand the Augustinian claim that God deliberately *sends* many people to hell, if in point of fact God *wants* all people to be saved? We will consider Augustine's own answer in the next section. But first, we will consider the Arminian response.

From the third set of passages, Arminians conclude that the damned are not *sent* by God to hell; rather, they are in hell solely because of their own "free choice." And many of today's Arminians follow C. S. Lewis and add that "the gates of hell are locked from the inside." In other words, the damned are in hell not only because of the free choices they have made while on earth, but even after they find themselves in hell, they continue to "choose" hell rather than repent of their sins and be ushered into the kingdom of heaven.[21]

---

21. As we already noted, Augustine thought the damned in hell might very well come to see the errors of their ways and repent of their sins. However, he went on to describe it as a "fruitless repentance." So for Augustine, the gates of hell are definitely locked from the *outside*. As Dante famously posted over the gates of hell: "Let he who enters abandon all hope." We emphasize this point since it casts serious doubts on those like Jerry Walls who argue that they are merely defending what the Christian tradition has always taught. In point of fact, by introducing Lewis's notion that "the gates of hell are locked from the inside," Walls has already introduced a significant change to the "traditional" doctrine of hell. This makes highly dubious his argument that the burden of proof falls squarely and solidly on those who would make changes to the "traditional doctrine of hell." Walls, "Philosophical Critique of Talbott's Universalism," 105–24. Walls's "progressive" understanding of hell also moves significantly away from Augustine's with respect to the pain and suffering that the damned must endure. "As I see it," says Wells, "hell is indeed a place of misery but not unbearable misery." In fact, according to Walls, "Only one who fully understood the goodness of God, and had a deep sense of his beauty, as well as of the joy of living in his presence, could truly grasp the horror of being separated from him forever. So, ironically, it is impossible

The Arminian conception of hell is clearly based on an Arminian conception of free will, which assumes that humans must be independent and autonomous agents when they are acting freely. In his book *On Predestination*, Arminius explicitly rejects Augustine's first point that God's "absolute decree" *sends* people to hell. Instead, he says that people end up in hell because of the freely chosen "wages of sin." But on Augustine's second and third point there is no disagreement. Arminius describes hell as a place of "everlasting destruction" where the "everlasting fire prepared for the devil and his angels . . . shall devour the enemies and adversaries of God." Elsewhere he describes the suffering of the damned as "eternal separation of the whole man from God, and his anguish and torture in the lake of fire." And again as "everlasting destruction from the presence of the Lord, and from the glory of his power."[22]

So while Augustine and Arminius have different ideas about how people *get to* hell, there is no disagreement that once they arrive in hell the damned will suffer *everlasting* "anguish and torture."

A BIBLICAL ROUTE TO A NON-AUGUSTINIAN CONCEPTION OF HELL

A non-Augustinian conception of hell agrees with Augustine's first two points, but disagrees with the third. While God *sends* the majority of people to hell, and while those in hell *suffer* terrible pain, the suffering is not *everlasting* because God's purpose in punishing is redemptive and his desire to bring all to repentance cannot be thwarted.

Now there are several routes to such a non-Augustinian conception of hell. The most obvious is a "literal" reading of a fourth set of biblical passages.

#4. *While many (or even all) people will suffer the purifying "fires of hell,"* eventually *all will be saved*.

- "Turn to me and be saved, all the ends of the earth! For I am God, and there is no other. By myself I have sworn, from my mouth has gone

---

for anyone fully to experience the horror of being separated from God." Ibid., 119–20. In short, Walls denies two out of the three essential characteristics of an Augustinian conception of hell, namely, the damned are (1) sent to hell and (2) they suffer terrible pain. The only characteristic of the "traditional" conception that Walls maintains is that (3) hell is everlasting. On the other hand, the non-Augustinian conception of hell that we will articulate and defend in the next chapter affirms both (1) and (2); it only denies (3). This too would seem to make Walls's "burden of proof" claim dubious at best.

22. Arminius, *Predestination,* 153, 381, 413.

forth in righteousness a word that shall not return: 'To me every knee shall bow, every tongue shall swear'" (Isa 45: 22–23).

- "The steadfast love of the LORD never ceases, his mercies never come to an end.... For the LORD will not reject forever. Although he causes grief, he will have compassion according to the abundance of his steadfast love; for he does not willingly afflict or grieve anyone" (Lam 3:22, 31–33).
- "And I, when I am lifted up from the earth, will draw all people to myself" (John 12:32).
- "Repent... so that he may send the Messiah appointed for you, that is, Jesus, who must remain in heaven until the time of universal restoration that God announced long ago through his holy prophets" (Acts 3:21).
- "Therefore just as one man's trespass led to condemnation for all, so one man's act of righteousness leads to justification and life for all" (Rom 5:18).
- "For God has imprisoned all in disobedience so that he may be merciful to all" (Rom 11:32).
- "for as all die in Adam, so all will be made alive in Christ... [so] that God may be everything to every one" (1 Cor 15:22–28).
- "... so that at the name of Jesus every knee should bend, in heaven and on earth and under the earth, and every tongue should confess that Jesus Christ is Lord, to the glory of God the Father" (Phil 2:10–11).
- "... and through him [Christ] God was pleased to reconcile to himself all things, whether on earth or in heaven, by making peace through the blood of his cross" (Col 1:20).
- "Then I heard every creature in heaven and on earth and under the earth and in the sea, and all that is in them, singing. 'To the one seated on the throne and to the Lamb be blessing and honor and glory and might forever and ever!'" (Rev 5:13)
- "Lord, who will not fear and glorify you name? For you alone are holy. All nations will come and worship before you, for your judgments have been revealed" (Rev 15:4).

Augustine was not unaware of these passages. Nor did he fail to see their implication. Instead, he argued that in these passages "all" doesn't mean "all people"; instead it means "all different *kinds* of people." Because his argument

Augustine's Conception of Hell

is so strikingly rhetorical (audacious?) and so frequently repeated, we will quote him at length.

> In any case, the word concerning God, "who will have all men to be saved," does not mean that there is no one whose salvation he doth not will—he who was unwilling to work miracles among those who, he said, would have repented if he had wrought them—but by "all men" we are to understand the whole of mankind, in every single group into which it can be divided: kings and subjects; nobility and plebeians; the high and the low; the learned and unlearned; the healthy and the sick; the bright, the dull, and the stupid; the rich, the poor, and the middle class; males, females, infants, children, the adolescent, young adults and middle-aged and very old; of every tongue and fashion, of all the arts, of all professions, with the countless variety of wills and minds and all the other things that differentiate people. For from which of these groups doth not God will that some men from every nation should be saved through his only begotten Son our Lord? Therefore, he doth save them since the Omnipotent cannot will in vain, whatsoever he willeth. . . . Our Lord also useth the same manner of speech in the Gospel, where he saith to the Pharisees, "You tithe mint and rue and every herb." Obviously, the Pharisees did not tithe what belonged to others, nor all the herbs of all the people of other lands. Therefore, just as we should interpret "every herb" to mean "every kind of herb," so also we can interpret "all men" to mean "all kinds of men."[23]

The non-Augustinian response by Yale philosopher Keith DeRose is itself strikingly rhetorical and in recent years has also been frequently repeated. So it too will be quoted at length.

> Suppose some slippery character is being investigated, and hands over to investigators several files relating to the case under consideration. The slippery character then says that he's handed over all the files about the case. It later turns out that, as the slippery character knew full well at the time of his statement, he's held on to over half of the files. Suppose his reaction to this revelation is: "Well, I handed over several files from each of the 10 major categories into which they fell. And I didn't just pick the least damaging files to hand over. Rather, I picked in a random fashion the files I would hand over from each category, so that each file, regardless of its category, and regardless of how damaging it was to my case, had a chance to be handed over. So,

---

23. *Handbook,* ch. 103.

> you see, I really did hand over all the files—all without distinction, that is; not, of course, all without exception."
>
> This won't fly, precisely because "all" just can't mean anything like what the "all without distinction" crowd [Augustinians and Arminians] says it sometimes means. My reaction, at least, is not that this fellow was being deceitful merely in using one sense of "all" while it has another good sense. He's worse than that: There's no good sense of "all" that would make true his miserable lie. No, "all," when it's used properly, always means all without exception. Quite simply, "all" means all.[24]

Even though we believe DeRose's response is pitch-perfect and decisive, by itself it doesn't negate the prima facie force of those biblical passages we considered under the heading *"Some people will suffer everlasting punishment."* Augustine zeroed in on the conclusion of the parable of the Sheep and the Goats, as will we. Jesus summed up the parable with the terrifying sentence: "And they [the damned] will go away into eternal punishment, but the righteous into eternal life" (Matt 25:46). Here the symmetry between heaven and hell seems to be explicit. As Augustine argues,

> If both destinies are eternal, then we must either understand both as long-continued but at last terminating, or both as endless. For they are correlative—on the one hand, punishment eternal, on the other hand, life eternal. And to say in one and the same sense, life eternal shall be endless, punishment eternal shall come to an end, is the height of absurdity. Wherefore, as the eternal life of the saints shall be endless, so too the eternal punishment of those who are doomed to it shall have no end.[25]

In other words, Augustine argues that if hell comes to an end when the redemptive purposes of God are achieved, then so too the lives of the saints in heaven must one day come to an end. But a heaven that comes to an end is not really heaven, argues Augustine. So if you believe in a real heaven that never comes to an end, you must also believe in a hell that never comes to an end.

The weakness in Augustine's argument is that it simply *assumes* that "eternal" (*aionios*) must refer to a *quantity* of time rather than a *quality* of life. The glory and joy of life in the new heavens and earth is *not* that it will never come to an end. As some cynics have said, an everlasting life like the one we now have would itself be hell. Whether the cynics are correct about this, they are certainly correct that an unending life beset with addictions,

---

24. DeRose, "Universalism."
25. *City of God*, 21.23.

petty jealousies, and other debilitating sins is hardly a glorious hope. No, the Christian hope is for a new *kind* of life, an abundant life (John 10:10), where sin's curse has been redeemed and where we no longer "see through a glass dimly" (1 Cor 13:12). Of course, since death came through sin, and since Christ's death and resurrection has redeemed us from the wages of sin, the life of the new heavens and earth *will be everlasting*. But it is not heaven's *duration* that makes it an abundant life.

So what should we say about *eternal (aionios)* punishment? Gregory MacDonald puts it like this. "The translation of *aionios* has been the subject of numerous studies in recent years, but there seems to be a strong case for maintaining that it means 'pertaining to an age' and often refers not just to any age, but to 'the age to come' (cf. Heb 6:2; 9:12). Thus 'eternal life' may be better translated as 'the life of the age to come' and 'eternal punishment' as 'the punishment of the age to come.'"[26] Such a translation of *aionios* breaks the symmetry of eternal life and eternal punishment. And taking seriously Augustine's own understanding of efficacious grace adds further reasons to break the assumed symmetry of heaven and hell. Remember, Augustine himself asked rhetorically: "who will be so foolish and blasphemous as to say that God cannot change the evil wills of men, whichever, whenever, and *wheresoever* He chooses?" (emphasis added).[27] By employing an Augustinian (which is also a Thomistic and Barthian) understanding of efficacious grace, we thus arrive at a non-Augustinian understanding of hell. "Eternal *(aionios)* punishment" is the punishment in the age to come that *always achieves its goal*, namely, a true understanding of sin, and hence, a true freedom that ends in repentance.[28]

As the author of Hebrews says, "for the Lord disciplines those whom he loves, and chastises every child whom he accepts" (12:6). St. John concurs when he says of God "I reprove and discipline those whom I love" (Rev 3:19).[29] Now discipline involves suffering. And unfortunately, with human parents, teachers, and coaches, the discipline does not always achieve its intended results. But God is not simply the biggest, most powerful, and best

---

26. MacDonald, *Evangelical Universalist*, 147–48.
27. *Handbook*, ch. 98.
28. Oliver Crisp made a similar argument in "Augustinian Universalism."
29. In addition to these explicit biblical passages, we should also consider all those passages contrasting the fleeting duration of God's wrath with the everlasting duration of God's mercy. "For his anger is but for a moment; his favor is for a lifetime" (Ps 30:5); "For a brief moment I abandoned you, but with great compassion I will gather you. In overflowing wrath for a moment I hid my face from you, but with everlasting love I will have compassion on you says the LORD, your Redeemer" (Isa 54:7–8); "The Lord is merciful and gracious, slow to anger and abounding in steadfast love. He will not always accuse, nor will he keep his anger forever." (Ps 103:8–9)

thing that exists. God is the Author of creation whose desires can never be thwarted, even by the rebellious will of the most hardened sinner. Nor are the results of God's discipline limited to merely outward obeisance. A tyrant can force a defeated army to bend their knees, but mere force only produces compliance, never obedience. A merely compliant captive says in effect: "You have defeated me in battle, and with my body and mouth I must do as you say, but my heart will forever resist your tyranny." A fully obedient son says in effect: "I understand that you only desire what is best for me, and while I cannot see that good as clearly as you, I nonetheless place my life fully in your hands knowing that you have choreographed a glorious future for me."

And finally, as we argued in chapter 9, the Author of creation is able to do this without ever violating our freedom because true freedom is *not* the autonomy to choose between good *and* evil. No, true freedom is the ability to *always* choose the good with joy and alacrity. The truly good news of the Bible is that the Hound of heaven *never* relents. Even death will not bring the pursuit to an end (see Rom 5:15, 8:37, 11:15, 14:9, and 1 Pet 4:6).

Some evangelicals will worry that this sounds far too close to a Catholic doctrine of purgatory. Perhaps, but precisely *how* or *when* the Hound of heaven catches his prey is not the real issue. We know that Hitler was a bad man. We also know that Hitler killed himself with a bullet to the head shortly before he could be captured by the Allies. What we can't know is what Hitler was thinking and doing in between the time he pulled the trigger and the time the bullet killed him. Of course, by our normal standards, that is a very, very short period of time. But by astronomical standards it was sufficient time to increase the size of the universe from a geometrical point to a universe billions of miles in diameter. How much can happen in a very short time depends on whose standards of time are being assumed. But as St. Peter says, "with the Lord *one day is like a thousand years*" (2 Pet 3:8). So the time between Hitler's pulling of the trigger and the time he was killed is more than enough time for the Hound of heaven to graciously work and bring him to repentance.

Other Christians who have unconsciously imbued an Augustinian conception of hell will worry that we are trivializing the choices we make here on earth: "it is appointed for mortals to die once, and after that the judgment" (Heb 9:27). But there is nothing here that we wish to deny—after death *does* come judgment; after death we will "pay" for all our sins. All that we deny is the Augustinian assumption that at the moment of death God's desire for redemption and repentance suddenly turns *solely* to a desire for retribution.[30] But what biblical reasons are there for assuming that "judgment" refers *only* to retribution? At the death of a sinner the sentence pronounced by the all-knowing Judge is a *perfect* judgment. It is a penal sentence *individually* crafted in such a way that it will bring the guilty to contrition, reparation, and repentance.[31] Of course, merely human judges can never achieve perfection in their judgments, and hence, they will never be able to restore the soul of the guilty to its pre-fallen order. But God is not a merely human judge. No, God is the Author of creation, who in Jesus Christ has conquered Satan, sin, and death, thereby ensuring that one day a post-fall world will be restored to its pre-fallen order.[32]

So far we have argued that there are *possible* interpretations of the relevant biblical passages that result in a non-Augustinian understanding of hell. But now we will take the argument one step further and argue that we *must* interpret the relevant biblical passages in such a way that they do not result in an Augustinian understanding of hell. Here our argument closely follows Jan Bonda. Reduced to its simplest form, the argument goes like this: We cannot assume that "eternal (*aionios*)" in the New Testament or "everlasting (*'olam*)" in the Old Testament always and only refers to a temporal period of unending duration *without creating needless contradictions in the biblical story*.[33]

A most striking example of a needless contradiction resulting from a univocal interpretation of "eternal" (*aionios*) is Romans 16:25. Here Paul sums up his argument in Romans: "Now to God who is able to strengthen you according to my gospel and the proclamation of Jesus Christ, according to the revelation of the mystery that was kept secret for long ages but is now disclosed" (16:25). The "secret" to which Paul is referring is that the Jews have been "cut off" to bring in the Gentile, thus making the Jews jealous and thereby resulting in the salvation of "all Israel" (11: 26). Previously the Jews' rejection of Jesus as their true Messiah had been a cause of deep distress to

---

30. Notice too that an Augustinian reading of this verse also counts against Lewis's notion that "the gates of hell are locked from the inside." If God's mercy ends at death, then the gates of hell are locked by God from the outside.

31. Of course, in hell "reparation" cannot refer to the payment of money to the offended party. But it can refer to something like the asking of forgiveness from the party unjustly injured.

32. "In the Biblical world of thought the judge is not primarily the one who rewards some and punishes the others; he is the man who creates order and restores what has been destroyed." Barth, *Dogmatics in Outline*, 135.

33. Bonda, *One Purpose of God*, 211–19. It is perhaps worth noting that Bonda himself traces his own understanding of God's one purpose (i.e., his purpose to bring *all* to repentance and then salvation) to Barth's reading of Romans 9—11 in *Church Dogmatics* II.2, 222–26, 235–56, and 294–336.

Paul. "I could wish that I myself were accursed and cut off from Christ for the sake of my own people" (Rom 9:2). And presumably, Paul was not the only Jewish Christian distressed and puzzled by the unbelief of most of their brethren. Why would God seemingly harden the hearts of so many Jews? And what does this say about the everlasting covenant made with Abraham and his descendants? This is the "mystery that was kept secret for long ages." But then, Paul receives a direct revelation from God that "all Israel" will be saved, which he joyfully proclaims in Romans 9 through 11.

For God to have kept his final goal a "secret" for long ages, and then, at the right time, to reveal the secret to Paul, may raise some questions—Why now? Why not earlier? Why not produce the final result without putting Paul and countless others through such deep distress? But there is no contradiction in Romans 16:25 as it has been translated in the New Revised Standard Version and countless other translations. The Greek translated as "for long ages" is "*aionios*"! If "*aionios*" must always refer to an unending duration, then Romans 16:25 would have to read "Now to God who is able to strengthen you according to my gospel and the proclamation of Jesus Christ, according to the revelation of the mystery that was kept secret *forever* but is now disclosed." But a mystery that is to be kept secret *forever* cannot, on pain of direct contradiction, be "now disclosed."

More significantly, because it speaks directly to the *purpose* of God's wrath, is the use of "everlasting" by the Old Testament prophets. Jeremiah describes God's wrath against Judah as a fire "that shall burn forever" and as one that "shall not be quenched" (17:4, 27). A little further on he says that God will make them "an everlasting disgrace" (25:9, cf. 18:16, 20:11, 23:40). It would be easy to conclude here Jeremiah is teaching that God's wrath against Judah will never come to an end. But if we insist on a univocal understanding of "everlasting," how are we to make sense of Jeremiah's prophecy that the day is coming when "No longer shall they teach one another, or say to each other, 'Know the Lord,' for they shall all know me, from the least of them to the greatest, says the Lord; for I will forgive their iniquity, and remember their sin no more" (31:34)? If we assume that "everlasting wrath" must always and only refer to an endless duration, then we have a flat contradiction within a single book of the Bible.[34] But if we assume that "everlasting wrath" refers to the kind of wrath that achieves its intended results *without fail*, then the problem disappears.

A similar problem arises in Isaiah's prophecy that "the palace [in Jerusalem] will be forsaken, the populous city deserted; the hill and the

---

34. Not to mention the contradiction with Paul's proclamation that all Israel will be save in Romans 11:26 and alluded to in 16:25.

watchtower will become dens *forever*, the joy of wild asses, a pasture for flocks" (Isa 32:14, emphasis added). If "forever" always and only means "endless duration," then a contradiction appears in the very next verse: "until a spirit from on high is poured out on us, and the wilderness becomes a fruitful field" (Isa 32:15).

But avoiding contradictions is not the only reason to assume that "everlasting" should not reduced to *quantitative* terms referring always and only to an "endless duration of time." There are also numerous biblical passages where "everlasting wrath" itself takes on a *qualitative* character indicative of a wrath that achieves its intended results. We already mentioned Hebrews 12:6 and Revelation 3:19. Now we will add a few more. In Isaiah the prophet says "The Lord will strike Egypt, striking and healing; they will return to the Lord, and he will listen to their supplications and heal them" (19:22). Jeremiah, who has experienced firsthand affliction and homelessness as "wormwood and gall," nonetheless understands that "the Lord will not reject forever; although he causes grief, he will have compassion according to the abundance of his steadfast love." (Lam 3:19, 3—32) In the Old Testament, Sodom was virtually synonymous with God's wrath and the utter destruction of unrighteousness. However, the prophet Ezekiel describes God's covenant people as morally equivalent to the Sodomites, or even worse: "you acted more abominably than they, they are more in the right than you" (Ezek 16:52). But then God says: "I will restore their fortunes, the fortunes of Sodom and her daughters and the fortunes of Samaria and her daughters, and I will restore your own fortunes along with theirs, in order that you may bear your disgrace and be ashamed of all that you have done, becoming a consolation to them" (Ezek 16:53-54).[35]

Yes, it is a terrible thing to experience the wrath of God. And Yes, God's wrath is a form of retribution. Otherwise, why should one be "ashamed of all that you have done"? Until a person freely acknowledges that his or her sins

---

35. See also Titus 2:11, Mark 9:49. The second is especially pertinent to our purposes since it immediately follows Christ's quoting of Isaiah's description of hell as a place "where their worm never dies, and the fire is never quenched." Sounds like Augustinian hell! But then Jesus says "For *everyone* will be salted with fire" (emphasis added). We leave to biblical scholars to provide a definitive interpretation of Christ's intention in juxtaposing these sentences. One possibility suggested by Bonda is this: the fire itself never dies, but the fire's work of refining and purifying is eventually completed (*One Purpose of God*, 212ff.). Barth describes God's wrath like this: "It judges men absolutely. It utterly abandons them. It burns them right down to faith." *Church Dogmatics* II.2, 487. And "It was His wrath as the purifying fire of His mercy, of His free and unmerited but (for all its unexpectedness) real and active grace, of His faithfulness to the world and His people and men." Ibid. IV.2, 182, see also IV.2, 225. The virtue of such an exegesis is to explain how *everyone* can be salted with fire even though *everyone* does not burn endlessly in hell.

are being *justly* punished, there can be no repentance. And this is not merely a truth of experience. Rather, it is a truth of logic. "Repentance" *means* that a person takes responsibility for what he has done and voluntarily submits to the retribution his actions *deserve*. Repentance is not a "get out of jail free" card. Barth describes the wrath of God like this: "It is a stern, burning, destroying wrath. . . . The imprisonment into which man is flung by God . . . is of itself and as such unconditional and unlimited. . . . The only possibility which it leaves to the one handed over is that . . . he should appeal to God, not to try to change His mind about . . . His sentence or to halt the execution of His judgment, but to implore Him . . . that even as the Judge He will not cease to be his God, . . . that the last word for him might still be His Word and the last work upon him His work."[36]

Yet, while repentance requires that one voluntarily submits to retribution, there is nothing in the notion of retributive punishment that prohibits the *additional* elements of reconciliation and restoration. True, human judges are frequently (perhaps always?) unable to so perfectly match the punishment to the crime and thereby bring about both reconciliation and restoration.[37] Hence, for human judges the only criterion in sentencing criminals is that they are getting no more and no less than they *deserve*. If the punishment also brings about reconciliation and restoration, then so much the better. But if human judges make these their *goal*, then, as C. S. Lewis argued, there will be no limit to the pain, suffering, and deprivation that criminals will be forced to endure.[38] And since human judges can never perfectly match the punishment to the crime, the criminal will always be able to truthfully say of some part of their punishment: "But I don't deserve *this*."

The Author of creation, on the other hand, can and will perfectly match the punishment to the crime. And as we have seen in the previous biblical passages, his ultimate intent is to bring about repentance, reconciliation, *and* restoration. By ensuring that the retribution is perfectly just, the

---

36. Barth, *Church Dogmatics* II.2, 486. Elsewhere he says, "'God is merciful to us' does not mean 'that He becomes soft, but that He remains absolutely hard.'" Ibid. See also ibid., II.2, 212, 560. God's wrath is "purposeful wrath." Ibid., IV.1, 537. And his condemning law is shown to be an instrument of God's love. Ibid., II.2, 753.

37. As I write this sentence the world is celebrating and commemorating the death of Nelson Mandela. I am old enough to remember firsthand almost ever commentator predicting a "bloodbath" when Mandela assumed power. But it was not so. Instead, Mandela, Bishop Tutu, and others organized the tribunals of "Truth and Reconciliation." What they accomplished was miraculous. But how much more miraculous will the results be when the Author of creation establishes his tribunal of "Truth and Reconciliation"?

38. Lewis, "Humanitarian Theory of Punishment."

person being punished can never honestly say: "Why am I suffering *this*?" Only when sinners from the depths of their hearts acknowledge that they deserve *all* that they are suffering—when, as Barth says, those delivered to the hands of a wrathful God pray that "the last work upon him [be] His work"—then, and only then, has the repentance that leads to restoration begun. A *qualitatively* eternal fire is one that is not quenched until it achieves this purifying purpose.[39]

---

39. However, we must not assume that it is by punishment *alone* that God restores sinners. "If we can and must say that God is beautiful, to say this is to say how He enlightens and convinces and persuades us . . . God has this superior force, this power of attraction, which speaks for itself, which wins and conquers, in that fact that He is beautiful." Barth, *Church Dogmatics* II.1, 650.

—12—

God's Gracious Wrath

Broadly speaking, there are three distinct ideas about how the Christian story ends. The majority claim to know that many will be damned for eternity. But a few argue in direct opposition and claim to know that all will be saved. Finally, a few argue that while all people will eventually be saved, this is something for which we can only hope and pray. By conceiving of free will as the promised freedom a person has when Jesus makes them free (see chapter 9), Aquinas and Barth give us good reasons to hope and pray that God's gracious wrath will eventually bring all to repentance.

Chapter 10 on the "goodness of God" and what difference the incarnation makes concluded with the question: "What about hell? Suppose Fred doesn't repent of his sin? What then?" We are now in a position to answer this question. And while our answer will follow the lead of Barth and Aquinas, in this final chapter I am much more concerned with articulating a philosophically and theologically defensible answer than I am in correctly interpreting Aquinas and Barth. In Norris Clarke's words, this chapter is a "creative retrieval" of their arguments.[1]

Barth says, "One thing is sure, that there is no theological justification for setting any limits on our side to the friendliness of God towards humanity which appeared in Jesus Christ."[2] Aquinas says, "we can desire,

---

1. Clarke, *Creative Retrieval*.
2. Barth, "Humanity of God," 64. And elsewhere, "We are not called upon to bear

God's Gracious Wrath 245

with respect to God, that He who exists forever great in Himself, may be magnified in the thoughts and reverence of all men. *This is not to be dismissed as impossible.*"[3] Yet neither Barth nor Aquinas claim to *know* that all will be saved; they only argue that no person can *know* that most, or even *some*, will not be saved.[4] Thus we are obligated to hope and pray that all will be saved.

SIX ESCHATOLOGIES

In this chapter, we will consider six possible responses[5] to the question: In the end, will all be saved? The six are as follows:

---

the suffering of rejection [damnation] because God has taken this suffering upon Himself. And if it is the case that in believing in the divine self-giving in Jesus Christ we can and should believe in the divine predestination, then we can believe in our own non-rejection and the non-rejection of all men." *Church Dogmatics* II.2, 168, see also IV.3, 477.

3. Aquinas, *Compendium*, 2.8, emphasis added. Eugene Rogers also finds support for reading Aquinas as a hopeful universalist in Aquinas's commentary on Paul's letters. "In other words, *this* passage [Gal 2:20] at least presents only the positive will of God to save, and mentions no will of God, positive or negative, to condemn to reprobation, and it supports those who interpret Thomas as holding only single predestination. Thomas has the resources—which this passage displays—to affirm only God's justice in judging, and will to save. He sees no need to affirm the case of a negative outcome, unless he regards himself as otherwise constrained by scripture. In this passage he is free from such a constraint. To take sin seriously does not require him to affirm that God damns, but that God alone can save." Rogers, *Aquinas and Barth*, 83. Even in light of such passages, I fully acknowledge that reading Aquinas as a hopeful universalist is something of a stretch. But on a related question—Will all those who have never heard of Jesus be damned?—Aquinas is unambiguous: "If, however, some were saved without receiving any revelation, they were not saved without faith in a Mediator, for, though they did not believe in Him explicitly, they did, nevertheless, have implicit faith through believing in Divine providence, since they believed that God would deliver mankind in whatever way was pleasing to Him, and according to the revelation of the Spirit, to those who knew the truth, as stated in Job 35:11: 'Who teacheth us more than the beasts of the earth.'" *Summa Theologica* II-II.2.7.3. And again, "Those who are unbelievers though not actually in the Church, are in the Church potentially. And this potentiality is rooted in two things—first and principally in the power of Christ, which is sufficient for the salvation of the whole human race; secondly, in the liberty of choice." Ibid., III.8.3.1. And as one contemporary Thomist says, "To confirm the unity of the whole Christian tradition on this point we have but to express in metaphysical terms, that to seek God is to have found Him already." Gilson, *Spirit of Medieval Philosophy*, 276. See also Rogers, *Thomas Aquinas and Karl Barth*, 229.

4. See Jüngel, *Karl Barth*, 44–45.

5. In the last thirty years, at least among evangelicals, a seventh response has gained respectability. It is popularly called annihilationism, though many of its proponents prefer to call it conditional immortality. This position both affirms and denies that all

1. Natural reason makes it clear that God loves all people, so we can *know* that all will be saved.

2. The Bible makes it clear that God is both willing and able to save everyone, so we can *know* that all will be saved.

3. The Bible makes it clear that God is both willing and able to save everyone, *however*...

   a. while we have good biblical reasons to *believe* that all will be saved, and even in some sense to know that all will be saved, in another sense this cannot be *known* until we see God face-to-face;

   b. as Kierkegaard said, "All the others will be blessed, that is certain enough—only with me may there be difficulties";[6]

   c. because sin is a surd its effects on the future salvation of any and all is unpredictable;

   d. because God is supremely free we are never in a position to say what he *must* do with respect to the salvation of any or all;

   e. for all these reasons, we must openly acknowledge that our position makes no sense in the univocal language of the Enlightenment.

4. Biblical reason makes it clear that God wants *all* to be saved, and though God cannot *ensure* such an outcome since humans possess autonomous (i.e., libertarian) freedom, nonetheless there is no contradiction in assuming that all creatures will freely choose to place their

---

will be saved. It denies that all will be saved because it affirms that at the final judgment many (the unrighteous) will be utterly destroyed in both body and soul. In this sense will there be many who will not be saved. But since the people who are not saved will be annihilated (or at least, not blessed with immortality), there will come a time when all who *exist* are saved. I happily acknowledge that annihilationism provides a plausible reading for the biblical passages we previously listed under the heading, "Some will not be saved." There is nothing prima facie wrong about reading passages describing "eternal destruction" as referring to a death that is final, i.e., one from which there is no return. Also in its favor is its insistence that humans are not *naturally* immortal, but instead, that immortality is a gift bestowed only by God. There is nothing in "nature" itself that makes the soul immortal. This is a commendable move away from a Platonic (i.e., dualistic) reading of Scripture that has been so prevalent in evangelical circles. However, this position still denies the efficacy of grace since it affirms that a person's "free will" can finally frustrate God's intention of saving all people. But as we argued in chapter 9, this conception of "free will" is both a needless concession to the Enlightenment with its assumption of mono-causation and the very antithesis of the freedom *from* sin which is promised by Scripture. So from our perspective, annihilationism is not a distinct seventh position, but simply a variation on the two Arminian positions (#4 and #5) we consider in the text that follows.

6. Quoted in Balthasar, *Dare We Hope*, 88.

faith in Jesus. Hence, we can hope and pray that all will freely choose to accept Christ and be saved.

5. The Bible makes it clear that God wants all to be saved, however, because humans are autonomously free, there is nothing God can do to ensure that all will be saved. Since there is abundant biblical evidence that many will be eternally damned, we should *not* hope and pray that all will be saved.

6. The Bible makes it clear that God is able to save everyone, however, he decrees the everlasting damnation of many to demonstrate his holy justice, and thus, we must *not* hope and pray that all will be saved.

The first two positions are species of unqualified universalism. Positions three and four are species of hopeful universalism. And positions five and six are categorical rejections of universalism.[7]

I believe that a strong case can be made exegetically for placing Barth in the third category. And while this would be much more difficult to justify in Aquinas's case, nonetheless his conception of promised freedom makes possible a strong defense of the third position.[8] So even though Aquinas, at the very end of his life, only hinted that he was moving in this direction, nonetheless I take him as an ally in the defense of what I call "the hopeful universalism of promised freedom."

THE FIVE "HOWEVERS"

Now let me flesh out each of the five "howevers" that distinguish the hopeful universalism of promised freedom from the second position, or what is sometimes called either "necessary universalism" or "biblical universalism."

1. Our position explicitly adopts a nonfoundationalist theory of knowledge. As we argued in the opening chapters of this book, we can confidently say of a large and significant portion of our beliefs that we *know* them to be true, even though prior to the end of history we can never know

---

7. John Hick is perhaps the most prominent contemporary defender of the first position. Some have argued that Barth belongs in the second category, e.g., Balthasar in *Karl Barth,* 163, and Berkouwer in *Divine Election,* 229. And Oliver Crisp has twice argued that either Barth is an unqualified biblical universalist or his position is incoherent. But Crisp has also argued that if we look more to the "spirit and not the letter" of what Barth says, he may be interpreted as falling into the fourth category ("Letter and the Spirit," 53–67). The fourth position is also implicit in an essay by Eric Reitan, "Human Freedom and the Impossibility of Eternal Damnation." The fifth category would include all Arminians and the sixth all Augustinians/Calvinists.

8. See footnote 3.

where we were mistaken. In the language of contemporary philosophy, we are assuming an "externalist" theory of knowledge. This means that there is no "internal" criterion of knowledge. We cannot look inwardly at our psychological states to determine if our beliefs are really true. Someone can psychologically be absolute confident that what they are saying is true, and yet turn out to be mistaken. Nor is it any better when we turn to our collective consciousness. Late nineteenth-century physicists famously (infamously?) boasted that they understood all there was to know about our physical universe—and then came Einstein and Bohr!

As we have frequently said, in one important respect the Enlightenment was nothing more than an attempt to live by Descartes's dictum: "I should withhold my assent no less carefully from opinions that are not completely certain and indubitable than I would from opinions that are patently false."[9] Descartes turned inward and only considered the purely logical and mathematical truths that he knew independent of any external experience. And his empiricist critics, Hume and Locke, turned inward and only considered their private impressions (that which they saw *by*) independent of any external reference (that which they *saw*).

And in one sense, both these foundationalist projects makes perfect "logical" sense. There *is* something logically contradictory about defining knowledge as justified, true belief and then saying "I *know* X, though of course I might be wrong." How can a person, without self-contradiction, say both (1) "My belief is justified and true" and it is possible that (2) "My belief is not true"? Whenever such a possibility actually arises, then the self-contradiction becomes explicit. Yet, this is precisely what all nonfoundationalist theories of knowledge affirm. And while we have made this point before, we mention it again to be explicit that whatever degree of confidence we have in our biblically grounded belief that all will eventually be saved, our "claim to know" is not one that would satisfy a foundationalist's definition of knowledge.

2. "All the others will be blessed, that is certain enough—only with me may there be difficulties." Kierkegaard was speaking "existentially," "from the heart," and undoubtedly pastorally. Perhaps he was even speaking in favor of approaching evangelism with a carrot as opposed to a stick. While I deny none of this (in fact, I affirm it with alacrity!), my point here is to simply remind the reader of the conceptual argument in chapter 1 concerning the incoherence of "self-prediction." Would Mr. Job follow Mrs. Job's advice to "curse God and die"? God certainly knew what Job would do. And if we grant for the sake of the argument that everything we know about quantum mechanics, chaos, "light cones," the three-body problem and logistic maps is wrong, then Mrs.

---

9. Descartes, *Meditations*, Meditation 1, (59).

Job might "in principle" know absolutely everything about her husband's current brain states that is required to validate a prediction of his future actions.[10] Nonetheless, Job himself would not, and *conceptually could not*, know what he was going to do until he actually did it.[11] Any attempt by Job to predict what he was going to do by looking inward at his own beliefs, dispositions, and attitudes (brain states) would initiate an infinite regress, making him like a swimmer trying to catch his own waves. Thus, there will always be at least one person who we can never *know* will be saved, namely, ourself.

Of course, to many Christians the assurance of their future salvation is as doctrinally fundamental as their denial of universalism. So to argue that a Christian can never *know* that they themselves will be saved is hardly going to be persuasive.

To this sort of objection I would respond that "knowledge" must itself be understood analogically. It is one thing to *know* that in a right triangle $A^2 + B^2$ always equals C^2; it is another thing to *know* that one's spouse has been and will be faithful to his or her marriage vows. And it is still something else to *know* that Jesus is the savior of my soul. As Barth said, "We can *trust* a person, and in the case of this person [Jesus] we must do so unconditionally and with final certainty. . . . But we cannot *grasp* a person, and especially not this person, in the sense of conceptual apprehension and control."[12] Christians can confidently entrust their souls to Jesus; but it is in Jesus, not their own deductions from biblical propositions, that their confidence resides.

The kind of confidence a Christian can have is similar to the confidence a person sitting on a jury can have. Suppose the DNA evidence and the testimony of credible witnesses overwhelmingly point to the defendant's guilt. And further suppose that the jury member is herself convinced beyond any reasonable doubt that the defendant is guilty. So she votes to convict with a clear conscience. Nonetheless, given the magnitude of the consequences—imagine it is a capital murder trial—she hopes and prays that she has made the right decision and that the defendant really is guilty of the crimes of which he is charged.

---

10. And as we argued in chapter 1, even this highly optimistic assumption about what Mrs. Job "in principle" can know about her husband's current brain states ignores the fact that Mrs. Job can't know her own future actions. Thus, she cannot know whether her own actions—for example, *telling* Mr. Job what she predicts he will do—will make her initial data obsolete.

11. One of the best articulators of the conceptual incoherence of self-prediction written from an explicitly Christian point of view is D. M. MacKay. *The Clockwork Image* and *Human Science and Human Dignity* are both highly readable presentations of the argument intended for a popular audience. His Gifford Lecture, published as *Behind the Eye*, includes his final articulation of the argument.

12. Barth, *Church Dogmatics* IV.3.1, 176.

If "knowledge" is a univocal term, which has the same meaning when applied to a person's guilt or innocence as it does when applied to the sides of a triangle, then this person's hope and prayer are irrational and/or incoherent. It makes no sense to hope or pray that the next right triangle one comes across will have a hypotenuse equal to the square root of the sum of the squares of each side. Yet, to all non-Cartesians who understand that "knowledge" is an analogical term, this person's hopes and prayers make perfect sense. Even though in one sense the jury member *knows* that the defendant is guilty, in another sense, she understands her own fallibility, and hence, that what she "knows" could turn out to be false. Yes, we can be confident of our own salvation, and even "know" that we are saved. But it is not the sort of knowledge that would satisfy Enlightenment criteria. Instead, is it the sort of "knowledge" that makes the prayer—"Lord I believe, help thou my unbelief!"—perfectly intelligible.

Here's a second example. Suppose a person says in the morning, "The phone number on the billboard is the *same* phone number we saw yesterday on the cab." They then say in the afternoon, "The person we sat next to on the bus is the *same* person who served us breakfast yesterday." It is quite clear that the criteria for being the *same* phone number and the criteria for being the *same* person are not the same! The "same phone numbers" must have exactly the same numbers arranged in exactly the same order. The "same person" does not have the have exactly the same number of hairs on her head arranged in exactly the same order. So too, the criteria for *knowing* the Pythagorean theorem and the criteria for *knowing* that a person is trustworthy are not the same.

Here's a final, more personal example. I know how to walk. Successfully traversing a hundred yards on an obstacle-free sidewalk is something I've done a thousand times, and thus I have excellent reasons to suppose that the next time I attempt to do so I will once again be successful. Yet, suppose I'm offered a hundred dollars to walk a hundred yards on such a sidewalk—the only difference is that there is a 1,000-foot cliff on each side. Given my fear of heights, it's *psychologically* unlikely that I would take such an offer even though *epistemologically* I know I should. Of course, if my wife's life depended on me taking such a walk, I would certainly do it, but I would first *pray* for success!

In one sense, a person can be "absolutely confident" about one's own salvation. But, in another sense, one can and *must*—each and every day—hope and pray that their final confession will be, "Lord, I commend my soul to your hands." Anything else would be a presumptuous confidence in one's own abilities.[13]

---

13. Aquinas fleshes out these differences under the question, "Whether Man Can Know That He Has Grace?" in *Summa Theologica* I-II.112.5. There Aquinas grants that at particular times and for particular purposes God gives a special revelation to an

3. Sin is an irrational surd. By definition it is impossible to understand. That's why we argued in chapter 10 that sin cannot be integrated into any theological system. Advocates of the hopeful universalism of promised freedom keep this point in the forefront of their mind.

When people sin, they are deliberately and knowingly choosing to do what is wrong. And remember, for Aquinas morality is not ultimately about "following rules." Rules exist for the young and irresponsible as a kind of "training wheels" to help them grow into fully flourishing human beings. However, when responsible adults sin, rules are of little use since they already *know* that their actions will diminish their own happiness! "I do not do the good that I want, but the evil that I do not want is what I do" (Romans 7:19). This is absurd! How can creatures who by nature desire their own happiness deliberately and knowingly chose their own unhappiness? Aquinas said, "No cause that is of itself active in character can be assigned to evil as such."[14] In this sense, evil is uncaused, and hence, unintelligible.[15]

---

individual, but this is the exception, not the rule. And the reason certitude of one's own salvation is the exception, not the rule, is that we can never know with certitude an effect unless we also know with certitude the principle (i.e., cause) from which it follows. But since God is the principle of our salvation, and since God's essence cannot be known with certitude, it follows that neither can our own salvation. But, on the other hand, a person can inductively reason from an effect back to its most likely cause. Thus, the hope and delight persons have in God, when their worldly circumstances give them no grounds to hope or delight, justifies the inductive conclusion (Aquinas calls it a "conjecture") that God's efficacious grace is its most likely cause.

14. *Summa Contra Gentiles* II.41.7. Aquinas continues, "Consider, too, that anything brought into being outside the scope of the agent's intention has no essential cause, but happens accidentally, as when a person finds a treasure while digging with the object of planting things. But evil in an effect cannot arise except beside the agent's intention. . . . Evil, therefore, has no essential cause, but occurs accidentally in the effects of causes" (Ibid. II.41.8). Oliva Blanchette explains, "Evil is per accidens in that it occurs when agents fail to attain their appropriate end or the good which is intended per se. Even if we try to think of causes of evil, there is no order between them as causes of evil, but only dis-order, and hence no possibility of a first cause among them. *Perfection of the Universe*, 116. In "Knowing Good and Evil," C. J. F. Williams puts it like this: Since "there is no such thing as a best possible world, every creative act of God must be the choosing of something in the knowledge that it would be possible to choose something better (238). . . . His reason for creating us is far from sufficient. There is, therefore, an analogy between sinful acts and God's creative act. We are, precisely in our capacity to sin, like God. This should no doubt be said with bated breath, and with every precaution to avoid blasphemy (239). . . . But what for us is of the essence of sin, knowingly choosing something less good than what we know we could choose, is of the essence too of God's creative activity. Acting without a sufficient reason, is for God, creation and, for God's creatures, sin" (240).

15. David Burrell speaks of the "surd of sin." "The questions which arise in the wake of so powerful an analysis have rather to do with what the tradition has called 'predestination.' If it is always possible for God to move the human will, and to do so without coercing it, why are not all persons saved? What appears to stand as an absolute limit

Of course, in another sense, talk of an "uncaused action" is itself unintelligible. Thus Barth is forced to turn the absence of a cause (no-thing) into "something" by calling it *nothingness*—that incredibly strange, third ontological category, that is somehow located *between* existence and non existence. Descriptively we've already said all we know how to say about nothingness in chapter 10.[16] Here our only point is to once again call attention to what the Bible calls the foolishness of sin and what we have called the absolute stupidity of sin. "Foolishness" and "absolute stupidity" can be *noted*, but they can never be *explained*.

Of course, Arminians have attempted to explain sin—either Adam's or our own—in terms of free will. But given their definition of free will in terms of "indifference" (see chapter 7), their attempt to *explain* sin quickly dissolves. What sense does it make to say that the *reason* Adam chose to disobey is that he was endowed by his Creator with the ability to be indifferent to choosing good or evil? If Fred is presented with two alternatives *toward which he is indifferent*, then there can be no intelligible explanation of why he "chose" one rather than the other. While materialist philosophers and scientists think that such a "free choice" can be explained in terms of antecedent brain states, Arminians by definition rule out these sorts of purely physical explanations. Ultimately all explanations of sin in terms of "free will" end up endorsing Kant's description of human freedom as "inscrutable," "utterly inexplicable," "inconceivable," and "absolutely incomprehensible."[17] These are not explanations of sin; they are acknowledgements that sin has no explanation.

---

to God's gracious power is what we have called human refusal. Yet since it is a non-action rather than an action, it cannot be a part of God's intent. So predestination and reprobation are not parallel activities of God, as though one could speak of positive and negative predestination." Burrell, *Freedom and Creation*, 157.

16. In one of the later drafts of my manuscript, I noticed an unintended pun. In chapter 11 the heading over the set of biblical passages is: "Nothing can thwart God's purposes." When I wrote this heading my intention was to say that no person's *free will* can thwart God's purposes. And, of course, Arminians who deny my reading of these passages read it in the same way. What I now see is that there is an alternative reading: "Nothing (i.e., "nothingness") *can* thwart God's purposes." Of course, if both readings are permissible (as I believe they are), then that raises the question: "What's the difference between your position and the Arminians'? Arminians say that human *free will* can thwart God's purposes and you say that *nothingness* can thwart God's purposes. So while your labels are different, the results are the same." The difference is this: Arminians believe that free will is a good thing, and thus, they would *never* hope and pray for God to *overcome* its power. We, on the other hand, *each and every day* hope and pray for God to *overcome* the power of nothingness.

17. Kant, *Religion Within the Limits of Reason Alone*, 17n, 158n, 52n, 133. See also 179.

Either way we are left with a mystery. For Kant and the Arminians it is an utterly mysterious "free will"; for Aquinas and Barth it is the utterly mysterious "impossible possibility" of sin. But the consequences of these two mysteries are not the same. Kantians and Arminians are stuck with absolute incomprehensibility for eternity; Thomists and Barthians can be more optimistic. Here's why.

Kantians and Arminians have no doubt that "free will," as they understand it, is a good thing—it is what gives humans their unique dignity. Some even argue that "free will" is the very image of God in humans. Though they admit that it is mysterious, it cannot be something they hope and pray will one day be conquered, overcome, or utterly destroyed.

Thomists and Barthians, on the other hand, never stop hoping and praying that the "impossible possibility" of sin will one day be conquered, overcome, and utterly destroyed. And their hope and prayer is not a despairing hope and prayer. Rather, it is a hope and prayer that is grounded in the life, death, and resurrection of Jesus. Because Jesus conquered Satan, sin, death they believe that all of us can have a confident faith that one day our own enslaving sins will also be utterly destroyed and that the "impossible possibility" will be no more! As Barth says, "The command of God sets itself against human free will, not because it does not wish man to be really free and happy, but on the contrary, because God does want this, because he cannot really be free and happy in his self-will."[18]

In sum, while Kantians, Arminians, Thomists, and Barthians all *begin* with a mysterious surd, there is a great difference among them. Kantians and Arminians believe that the mystery of "free will" will never go away; Thomists and Barthians believe that with the coming of the new heavens and new earth the mysterious surd of sin will be a thing of the past, existing only in our memories as that which made the incarnation *fitting*.

4. In no way are we limiting God's freedom when we say that sin made the incarnation *fitting*. We cannot deduce the implications of sin, and we certainly could not have predicted that Adam's sin would result in God's becoming man. Aquinas and Barth both insist that God was perfectly free to let us suffer the full consequences of our sins. He was under no obligation to atone for them by the death of his Son. And it is only because of Christ's atoning death that we have good reason to hope and believe God's gracious wrath will succeed in utterly destroying the effect of *all* sin. But this must not be understood as a prediction. Only after we awake with our resurrected bodies will it become clear that our reasons for hoping and praying that

---

18. *Church Dogmatics* II.2, 594.

all would be saved really *were* good reasons. Until then "our knowledge is imperfect and our prophecy is imperfect" (1 Cor 13:9).

Our defense of God's supreme freedom is closely connected to our insistence that sin not be "domesticated." Only this time we are, so to speak, looking from above, i.e., from God's point of view. "If we are to respect the freedom of divine grace," says Barth, "we cannot venture the statement that it [salvation] must and will finally be coincident with the world of man as such (as in the doctrine of the so-called *apokatastasis* [the restoration of all things]). No such right or necessity can legitimately be deduced. Just as the gracious God does not need to elect or call any single man, so He does not need to elect or call all mankind."[19] Therefore, we reject the universalisms of both the first and second varieties since both are making a prediction about what God will do on the basis of what he must do. They both claim to *know* that God will save all because he *must* save all.

Universalists of the first variety argue that any philosophically adequate understanding of God's character entails that God loves all people equally, and hence he *must* treat all people equally. And here the "must" is a *moral* must. A human judge who sentences two people who committed the same crime, with the same degree of culpability, to unequal punishments is by definition unfair, unjust, and morally blameworthy. Likewise, they argue, a God who saves some guilty people while damning other people who are no more guilty is also by definition unfair, unjust, and morally blameworthy.

Our short response is: Yes, God is unfair; No, he is not unjust; and it is incoherent to speak of God being *either* morally blameworthy or morally praiseworthy.

First, concerning fairness. To some people God gives great talents; to other people God gives perfectly average talents; to still others he gives talents that are significantly below average. All humans are equally humans; that's a tautology. All humans are born with unequal talents; that's a virtual truism. But the first is not contradicted by the second. Anyone who believes that God's goodness means that he *must* treat all people equally is faced with a dilemma: either change one's understanding of "fairness" or deny the most obvious facts about the universe God chose to create.

In this connection, Aquinas frequently cited the parable of the householder in Matthew 20. When those who worked all day protested because they were paid no more than those who only worked an hour, the householder responded: "Friend, I am doing you no wrong; did you not agree with me for a denarius? Take what belongs to you, and go; I choose to give

---

19. Ibid. II.2, 471.

to this last as I give to you. Am I not allowed to do what I choose with what belongs to me? Or do you begrudge my generosity?"(Matt 20:13–15)[20]

Second, concerning injustice. Philosophical universalists may grant that in relatively small matters (like whether or not a person is born with a great singing voice) God is not required to treat people equally. But when it comes to matters of eternal salvation and eternal damnation, they argue that for God to treat equals unequally is a matter of great injustice, i.e., not giving a person what he is due. But this argument presupposes that salvation is a matter of justice; that it is something that people earn, merit, or deserve. Again, that is precisely what Aquinas, Barth, and the whole Christian tradition vociferously deny.[21]

Third, concerning God's moral obligations. Once again, the universalist argument presupposes what Aquinas and Barth deny. As we argued in chapter 10, God is transcendentally good, but it makes no sense to speak of him as morally good. A good knife is one that is good for cutting; a good hunting dog is one that is good at retrieving; a good boy is one that is good at doing what his parents ask him to do. But no one is in a position to require anything of God. Nor is God good at cutting, retrieving, or any other *particular* task that might come to mind. God's goodness *transcends* each and every instance of goodness in the created realm. God is not good at doing x, y, or z; rather, God is goodness itself. He is the one who creates the very *conditions* that make x, y, or z possible; but he is not good at meeting his moral *obligations*.

With respect to universalists of the second variety, which we'll call biblical universalists: we agree with everything they say about God's willingness and ability to save all people. We also agree with everything they say against an Augustinian conception of *everlasting* hell. Our only disagreement is that they inevitably end up flirting with a Neoplatonic conception of creation. Pregnant women must give birth or they will suffer grave consequences. And light must emanate from the sun, as it does from all stars. But Aquinas and Barth both insist that there is no sense in which God *had* to create; there

---

20. I flesh this argument out in greater detail in ch.11 of *Life, the Universe, and Everything*.

21. Universalists sometime respond: "True, it might not strictly speaking be *unjust* for God not to save any and all people, but no God who could save any and all people would be *good* if he chose not to do so." Such an argument overlooks the paradoxes of omnipotence. For example, good humans always do their best; but God can never do his best since he is always free to shower more creatures with more of his good gifts. And good parents always do their best to raise their children in such a way that they will be capable of one day flourishing without their support and guidance; but God can never withdraw his support and guidance from his creatures—if he did, they would instantly cease to exist. See ch. 11 of *Life, the Universe, and Everything* for more details.

were absolutely no consequences to suffer had he chosen not to create. In his Holy Trinity God's felicity would in no way have been compromised if there were no theater to reflect his glory.[22] In no sense did God create out of necessity. Creation is only intelligible as an act of pure love and pure grace.

The same is true of salvation. God's love and grace is known by *trusting* a person, Jesus Christ, not by *grasping* an argument, whether it is philosophical or biblical. Of course, biblical universalists will respond that they are simply trusting God to *literally* fulfill his promise when he says things like: "Just as in Adam *all* humans died, so too, in Christ *all* will be made alive" (my paraphrase of Romans 5:18). The difference is this: while hopeful universalists also *trust* God to fulfill such promises, they are not so sure about what "literally" means in this context.

When Moses pleaded with God to forgive the great sin of his people, Moses was trusting in the goodness of God, but he understood that God's goodness may result in his being "blotted out of the book that you have written" (Exod 32:32). When Paul despaired of the salvation of his Jewish brethren, he was trusting in the goodness of God, but he understood that God's goodness may result in his being "accursed and cut off from Christ for the sake of my own people" (Rom 9:2). So too, we must trust in God's goodness. This means that we must trust him to fulfill all his promises. But it does not mean that these promises can be univocally understood as entailing precise predictions about what he will do in the future. As with all things divine, we now see through a glass dimly.

5. Our fifth and final "however" is a kind of summary of the first four. It is the "however" that unequivocally rejects all philosophical idealisms, by which I mean the philosophical disposition to argue like this:

1. A universe in which all things are univocally named and deductively related is the most intelligible of all possible universes.

2. A good God must make the most intelligible of all possible universes.

3. Therefore, our universe is one in which all things are univocally named and deductively related.[23]

The second position, biblical universalism, flirts with this sort of philosophical idealism. It argues that since God always gets what he wants and since God wants all humans to be saved, therefore we *must* infer that all will be saved. Deductively speaking the argument is impeccable. We have no

---

22. The metaphor is Calvin's. See *Institutes*, 1.6.2, 1.14.20, and 2.6.1.

23. C. S. Lewis also warned against this kind of reasoning in *Reflections on the Psalms*, 112.

quibble with its validity. What we reject is its *applicability* to the world God chose to create.

Imagine a Philistine at a garage sale, who sees a buffet built to store and display fine china. It has a flat top, and it is very cheap, so he buys it, puts it in his garage, bolts on a heavy vise, and begins pounding out horseshoes with an eight-pound sledgehammer. While he is pounding out the second horseshoe the corner of the buffet collapses. The Philistine utters a few expletives and then exclaims, "Whoever built this thing sure wasn't much of a craftsman!"

Of course, it is the Philistine who is acting like his namesake, not the craftsman. The point and purpose of a piece of fine furniture is quite different from the point and purpose of a workbench. To ignore this difference demonstrates a lack of understanding. What's required in the construction of a good workbench is not required in the construction of a good buffet. Remember the Aristotelian dictum: "An intelligent and well-schooled person is one who searches for that degree of precision in each kind of study which the nature of the subject at hand admits."

The subject of our study is God. And more specific to this chapter, our study does not concern what God *has* done; it concerns what God is *going* to do. To assume that God's future actions can be deduced from a set of premises—be they philosophical, theological, or biblical—is to search for a degree of precision that is not permitted by the subject of this study. As we have implicitly said several times already, we agree with Barth that good theology is always a *description* of what God *has* done, never an *explanation* of what God *must* do.

So we will openly acknowledge that the hopeful universalism of promised freedom makes no sense in terms of deductive logic. But why should it? Why shouldn't the vast majority of our universe only be intelligible in analogical and nondeductive terms?

As E. L. Mascall once said, "The principle of sufficient reason . . . cannot be simply reduced, as many scholastic and other philosophers have tried to reduce it, to the principle of contradiction. . . . Metaphysics is thus something more than logic: as Mr. Gilson has repeatedly pointed out, it was the basic error of idealists to identify them."[24] And Mr. Gilson himself said, "The varieties and shades of error misrepresenting the proper activity of second causes [dual-causation] are innumerable. It is not a question here of adopting or rejecting any particular solution but rather of taking a position for or against an entire philosophy. Behind each of the doctrines he is refuting, St. Thomas detects the hidden presence of Platonism [philosophical idealism].

---

24. Mascall, *Openness of Being*, 102.

If he rejects them it is because he feels that the philosopher's task is to interpret the real world of Aristotle, not the world of appearances described by Plato. And if he attaches himself firmly to Aristotle's real world it is in order to verify simple good sense, beyond which it is impossible to go."[25]

Mascall and Gilson were making two philosophical points: (1) metaphysics is more than logic and (2) though this is affirmed by realists and denied by idealists, neither the affirmation nor the denial can be proved. Or as Gilson says, "It is not a question here of adopting or rejecting any particular solution but rather of taking a position for or against an entire philosophy." Likewise, our fifth "however" takes a position against an entire theology that treats the Bible as a collection of propositions from which theological conclusions are to be deduced. In doing so, we are making two *theological* points: (1) God chose to create a universe that can only be understood in analogical and nondeductive terms and (2) though this is affirmed by Aquinas and Barth, and denied by Enlightenment thinkers, neither the affirmation nor the denial can be *proved*, i.e., deduced from a set of self-evident premises.

REMAINING POSSIBILITIES

We will be brief with the three remaining eschatologies.

The fourth position is essentially Arminian since it assumes that free will is to be understood in terms of autonomy and indifference. Yet it does not reach Arminius's own conclusion that some (or even a great number of) people will choose to reject God's grace. Instead, it argues like this: since any *single* flipped coin might land heads up, a *thousand* flipped coins might also land heads up. Of course, the odds against this happening by chance are vanishingly small, but it is not impossible. Therefore, given the proper circumstances it would not be wrong for a person to hope and pray that this will happen. And if we suppose that a flipped coin landing heads up is analogous to a person freely choosing to accept God's gift of salvation, then it is also not impossible that *all* people will freely (i.e., autonomously) choose to repent, and hence, there is nothing that prohibits us from hoping and praying that all will be saved. I will call this the superhopeful universalism of pure logic.[26]

---

25. Gilson, *Christian Philosophy of St. Thomas Aquinas*, 181.

26. See Reitan, "Human Freedom and the Impossibility of Eternal Damnation." I am not suggesting that the argument in this paragraph accurately reflects Reitan's argument. I seek only to give him credit for suggesting the coin flipping analogy. However, his argument goes beyond the one I'm considering in this paragraph. Imagine, he says,

The problem with this position is that it pictures God as either uninterested in, or unable to affect, the final outcome of our lives here on earth. True, it makes logically possible a "happy ending" in which all are saved. But if the possibility is in fact realized, it will be a happy ending that comes about literally "by chance." This, however, is not a happy conclusion to those who believe that God both wants and is able to save all people. Getting what one wants by chance is not the same as *doing* what one wants.

Positions numbered five and six both claim to *know* that all will *not* be saved. The fifth, essentially Arminian position argues that God is unable to save everyone since people are always "free" to reject God's grace. The sixth, essentially Augustinian position argues that God is unwilling to save all since doing so would compromise his glory and justice. We have already said most of what we have to say on these two positions. Here we would only add one final argument against the Arminian and Augustinian conception of hell.

Since much of this book has been an argument against anyone who would reduce qualitative differences to measurable quantities, I make this final quantitative argument with some hesitation. Nonetheless, remember the four lists of biblical passages considered in chapter 11: (1) some people will suffer everlasting punishment; (2) nothing can thwart God's purposes; (3) God wants all people to be saved; and (4) while many (or even all) will suffer the purifying "fires of hell," eventually all will be saved. The conception of hell that we are defending only denies the prima facie reading of the first. On the other hand, the Arminians deny the prima facie reading of (2) and (4), while the Augustinians deny the prima facie reading of (3) and (4). In other words, to the extent that such issues are quantifiable (and I fully intend the irony!), the non-Augustinian conception of hell that we are defending is twice as close to "a straightforward reading of the Bible" as the reading of the Arminians and Augustinians is.

---

that we consider the tails side of a coin "bad" and the heads side "good." A thousand coins are placed tails side (bad) facing up, on which is placed a drop of superglue. The box is then shaken. When the shaking stops, a number of coins will now be glued to the bottom heads side (good) up. Further shaking will not dislodge these "good" coins and it will only increase the number of "bad" coins that get stuck "good" side up. Thus, as the shaking continues, we have good reason to believe that eventually all the initially "bad" coins will become and *remain* "good." Simply replace the word "good" with "saved" and you have a deductive argument for the impossibility of eternal damnation. While his analogy wonderfully captures the asymmetry of good and evil that we have been arguing for, as the "impossibility" in his title suggests, this argument is a species of philosophical idealism that we just rejected.

QUESTIONS NOT TO ASK

But we still have not answered the final question: Suppose Fred doesn't repent of his sins? What then?

First we must understand that different kinds of questions deserve different kinds of answers. There are certain questions that cannot be sensibly asked: for example, "Is yellow heavier or lighter than the number 7?" There are certain questions that are rude, for example, calling a friend and asking "What are you doing tonight?" when what you really want to know is if he would be willing to help you with your homework. And finally, there are questions to which at least God knows the answer, but nonetheless, we shouldn't ask. Two such questions are "When will I die?" and "Is hell going to be finally emptied?" We begin with the first.

Try to imagine a world in which all people know with a high degree of certainty the day of their death. Such a world would be radically different from our own, perhaps even unimaginable. Now we must be clear, the point of this exercise is *not* to try to imagine a world in which we are all like condemned prisoners awaiting execution. Such a world may be unpleasant to think about, but it is certainly not unimaginable.

So what's the difference? Simply this: when a prisoner knows he will be executed on June 10, he only knows a sufficient condition for his death; he does *not* know with the same degree of certainty that a heart attack will *not* kill him on June 8 or that a magnitude eight earthquake will collapse the walls of the jail and kill him on June 9. In other words, the arrival of June 10 is a sufficient, but not a necessary, condition for his death. If a novelist or science fiction writer tried to create a world in which everyone knew the day which constituted *both* the necessary and sufficient conditions for their death, they would have to write about a world in which hydrogen bombs exploded over cities destroying every building and killing every animal, insect, and microbe, but only killed those few people for whom this was the predicted day of their death.

God certainly knows the day, hour, and minute that each of his creatures will die. But it is a "paradox of omnipotence" that he cannot communicate this knowledge to others without radically changing everything about the world he in fact chose to create. God chose to create a universe in which we have "the dignity of causality" because we are real secondary causes of much that happens in our world. We grind lenses to make microscopes so that we can learn more about life-threatening bacteria. We study metallurgy and the expansion of gases so that we can build internal combustion engines to power tractors to plow our fields, thereby producing life-sustaining food. We dig mines and lay railroad tracks to deliver coal in the winter to heat our homes so that we will not freeze to death. But in a world in which everyone knew the day of their death, such activities would be pointless—except on a single predetermined day, bacteria could not kill us nor could lack of food or freezing climates. Whether we lived or died would depend on nothing other than the arrival of our appointed day of death.

Could God create such a universe? Perhaps, but it would be a radically different universe, and hence not one about which much can be known. Philosophical idealists like to ask questions about what happens in other "possible universes," and they especially like to ask questions about what happens in all possible universes. Philosophical realists don't ask such questions. Instead, they limit their questions to the only universe they can experience and know much about, namely, our own.

Similar things can be said about theological realists. Aquinas and Barth were content to limit their questions to the universe that God *in fact* created and *in fact* became incarnate in his one and only son, Jesus Christ. Is it true that in all possible worlds God could have created that all people would be saved? Is it, in other words, a *necessary* truth that the God and father of our Lord Jesus Christ must eventually save everyone? Perhaps, but since we don't live in "all possible worlds" and since the world in which we do live is one where God has not chosen to reveal what happens in "all possible worlds," theological realists are content to leave questions about a "possible world" in which Fred does not repent unanswered, because it is unasked.[27]

CONCLUSION

Our conclusion for this chapter is squarely inside the long tradition of negative theology. Aquinas insisted that we can never know what God is, but

27. "God's activity in the world is ever an instance of or a consequence of bestowing existing (*esse*). Again, one would misconstrue matters if one thought of existing as a floor provided by the creator upon which and by virtue of which we then accomplished what is ours to do. That is a common enough picture, not unlike the prevailing deist conception of creation as 'getting things rolling,' a description which eliminates conservation altogether. Again, if existing were the mere position in actuality [as Ibn Sina and Alvin Plantinga think] this picture would be a cogent one, but such a conception of existence—itself generally accepted—effectively denies the perspective of *creatio ex nihilo*, for it must logically presume a fully articulated 'possible world' simply put into action." Burrell, *Freedom and Creation*, 68. And in Barth's words, God "knows the possible as that which has its possibility in and by Him, whether as that which He will raise to reality in its own time, or as that which will always be a possibility from Him and by Him, but only a possibility. And He also wills this possibility as such, whether it is to be realized in the future or not at all. He knows also the impossible, that which from Him and by Him is not possible. He knows it as that which He has rejected, excluded and denied: sin as sin; death as death; the devil as the devil." *Church Dogmatics*, II.1, 551.

only what he is not. We can know that God is not a material body composed of divisible parts. Hence, we say that he is a spirit. We can also know in some analogical sense that God is transcendentally good, since creation is itself good and there can never be more in the effect than in the cause. But because analogies always include both a Yes and a No, we must immediately add that God is *not* good in the way that other things and people are good. Instead, God is goodness itself (see chapter 10).

As the transcendent Creator, not himself part of creation, God is not subject to its rules and regulations. But at the same time, God is nearer to all of us than the best of earthly parents are to their own offspring. It is "in Christ and through Christ and by Christ" that each of us lives and moves and has our very existence. So with St. Paul we can confidently proclaim that nothing can separate us from the love of God revealed in the death and resurrection of Christ. We can also proclaim the efficacy (not the mere sufficiency) of Christ's atoning death and resurrection *for all people*.

But more than this, we *must* make these proclamations. Barth continually railed against gloomy Christians, and there was no one gloomier than Calvin when he reportedly referred to everlasting reprobation as "that horrible decree." Only slightly less gloomy are Calvin's Arminian critics who tolerate an *everlasting* hell because they believe that it is a logical consequence of God choosing to create humans with free will.

That's not to say that cheerful proclaimers of the gospel must never mention gloomy truths. We *all* need to be exhorted to "work out your own salvation with fear and trembling" (Phil 2:12), since some of us (perhaps all of us) will only willingly repent of our cherished sins after we have gone *through* hell—think here of C. S. Lewis's likening pain to "God's megaphone."[28] But immediately after being told the bad news, we need to be told the good news: "for it is God who works in you to will and to act according to his *good* purpose" (Phil 2:13, emphasis added).

And finally, until we move beyond Augustine's conception of hell, I doubt that anyone can be a truly cheerful proclaimer of the good news while believing God's *everlasting* wrath is the logically necessary "flip side" of his promise of eternal life. No, the "flip side" to eternal life is God's *gracious* wrath.

---

28. Lewis, *Problem of Pain*, 91.

Bibliography

Note on Sources: When citing classical sources, so many of which are readily available on the Web with a simple Google search, standard divisions by book, section, chapter, paragraph, etc. are typically used, though sometimes page numbers that correspond to the edition cited in the bibliography are also included. For example, in "Augustine, *Confessions* 10.4, 209," the book and chapter numbers are universal and should appear in all editions of the *Confessions*. The last number, 209, refers to the specific page in the edition of the *Confessions* cited here.

Adams, Marilyn McCord. *Horrendous Evils and the Goodness of God*. Ithaca, NY: Cornell University Press, 1999.
Adler, Mortimer J. *Problems for Thomists: The Problem of Species*. New York: Sheed & Ward, 1940.
Anderson, James F. *The Bond of Being*. New York: Greenwood, 1969.
Anscombe, Elizabeth. "Modern Moral Philosophy." *Philosophy* 33, no. 124 (January 1958). http://www.pitt.edu/~mthompso/readings/mmp.pdf.
Aquinas, Thomas. "Being and Essence." In *Aquinas: Selected Writings of St. Thomas Aquinas*, translated by Robert P. Goodwin, 7–28. Indianapolis: Bobbs-Merrill Educational, 1965.
———. *Commentary on Aristotle's Metaphysics*. Translated by John P. Rowan. Library of Loving Catholic Thought. Chicago: Regnery, 1961. http://dhspriory.org/thomas/Metaphysics5.htm#2.
———. *Compendium of Theology*. Translated by Cyril Vollert. St. Louis: B. Herder Book, 1947.
———. *On Evil*. Translated by Richard Regan, edited with an introduction and notes by Brian Davies. New York: Oxford University Press, 2003.
———. *On Truth*. Chicago: Regnery, 1952–1954.
———. "Principles of Nature." In *Aquinas: Selected Writings of St. Thomas Aquinas*, translated by Robert P. Goodwin, 7–28. Indianapolis: Bobbs-Merrill Educational, 1965.
———. *Summa Contra Gentiles*. Translated by Anton C. Pegis. Notre Dame, IN: University of Notre Dame Press, 1975.

———. *Summa Theologica*. Translated by Fathers of the English Dominican Province. Great Books series. Chicago: Encyclopedia Britannica, 1952.

———. *The Three Greatest Prayers: Commentaries on the Lord's Prayer, the Hail Mary, and the Apostles' Creed*. Manchester, NH: Sophia Institute, 1990.

Aristotle. *History of Animals*. Great Books of the Western Tradition 9. Chicago: Encyclopedia Britannica, 1952.

———. *Metaphysics*. Great Books of the Western Tradition 8. Chicago: Encyclopedia Britannica, 1952.

———. *Nicomachean Ethics*. Translated by Martin Ostwald. The Library of Liberal Arts. Indianapolis: Bobbs-Merrill, 1962.

———. *On the Heavens*. Great Books of the Western Tradition 8. Chicago: Encyclopedia Britannica, 1952.

———. *Parts of Animals*. Great Books of the Western Tradition 9. Chicago: Encyclopedia Britannica, 1952.

———. *Politics*. Great Books of the Western Tradition 9. Chicago: Encyclopedia Britannica, 1952.

———. *Posterior Analytics*. Great Books of the Western Tradition. 8. Chicago: Encyclopedia Britannica, 1952.

———. *Topics*. Great Books of the Western Tradition 8. Chicago: Encyclopedia Britannica, 1952.

Arminius, Jacobus. *On Predestination*. PDF: http://www.ccel.org/ccel/arminius.

Augustine, *Confessions*. Translated by R. S. Pine-Coffin. New York: Penguin, 1961.

———. *Handbook on Faith, Hope, and Love (Enchiridion)*. http://www.newadvent.org/fathers/1302.htm.

———. *City of God*. Great Books of the Western Tradition 18. Chicago: Encyclopedia Britannica, 1952.

Balthasar, Hans Urs von. *Dare We Hope: "That All Men be Saved"? With a Short Discourse on Hell*. San Francisco: Ignatius, 1988.

———. *The Theology of Karl Barth*. Translated by John Drury. New York: Holt Rinehart and Winston, 1971.

Barth, Karl. *The Christian Life: Church Dogmatics Volume IV, Part 4*. Translated by Geoffrey W. Bromiley. London: T & T Clark, 1981

———. *Church Dogmatics*. Translated by G. W. Bromiley, G. T. Thomson, and Harold Knight. London: T & T Clark, 2009.

———. *Dogmatics in Outline*. Translated by G. T. Thomson. New York: Harper & Row, 1959.

———. *Ethics*. Translated by Geoffrey W. Bromiley. New York: Seabury, 1981.

———. "The Humanity of God." In *Karl Barth: Theologian of Freedom*, edited by Clifford Green, 46–66. Minneapolis: Fortress, 1991.

Berkouwer, G. C. *Divine Election*. Translated by Hugo Bekker. Grand Rapids: Eerdmans, 1960.

Biggar, Nigel. "Barth's Trinitarian Ethic." In *The Cambridge Companion to Karl Barth*, edited by John Webster, 212–27. Cambridge: Cambridge University Press, 2000.

Blanchette, Oliva. *The Perfection of the Universe According to Aquinas*. University Park, PA: Pennsylvania State University Press, 1992.

Bonda, Jan. *The One Purpose of God: An Answer to the Doctrine of Eternal Punishment*. Grand Rapids: Eerdmans, 1998.

Bourke, Vernon J. *Aquinas' Search for Wisdom*. Milwaukee: Bruce Publishing, 1965.

Burrell, David. *Aquinas: God and Action*. Notre Dame, IN: University of Notre Dame Press, 1979.

———. *Freedom and Creation in Three Traditions*. Notre Dame, IN: University of Notre Dame Press, 1993.

———. *Knowing the Unknowable God*. Notre Dame, IN: University of Notre Dame Press, 1986.

Burtt, Edwin Arthur. *The Metaphysical Foundations of Modern Physical Science*. Rev. ed. Atlantic. Highlands, NJ: Humanities, 1952.

Busch, Eberhard. *Karl Barth: His Life from Letters and Autobiographical Texts*. Translated by John Bowden. Philadelphia: Augsburg Fortress, 1975.

Callaway, Ewen. "Brain Scanner Predicts Your Future Moves." *New Scientist*, April 13, 2008. http://www.newscientist.com/article/dn13658-brain-scanner-predicts-your-future-moves.html.

Calvin, John. *Institutes of the Christian Religion*. Translated by Ford Lewis Battles. Philadelphia: Westminster, 1977.

Cavanaugh, William T. *The Myth of Religious Violence: Secular Ideology and the Roots of Modern Conflict*. New York: Oxford University Press, 2009.

Clarke, Norris. *The Creative Retrieval of St. Thomas Aquinas: Essays in Thomistic Philosophy, New and Old*. New York: Fordham University Press, 2009.

———. *Explorations in Metaphysics: Being, God, Person*. Notre Dame, IN: University of Notre Dame Press, 1995.

———. *The One and the Many: A Contemporary Thomistic Metaphysics*. Notre Dame, IN: University of Notre Dame Press, 2001.

———. *The Philosophical Approach to God: A New Thomistic Perspective*. 2nd rev. ed. New York: Fordham University Press, 2007.

Copernicus, Nicholas. *Revolutions of the Heavenly Spheres*. Great Books of the Western Tradition 16. Chicago: Encyclopedia Britannica, 1952.

Corbett, John "Paraclesis as Moral Discourse." *The Thomist* 73.1 (January 2009) 89–107.

Crisp, Oliver. "Augustinian Universalism." *International Journal for Philosophy of Religion* 53 (2003) 127–45.

———. "The Letter and the Spirit of Barth's Doctrine of Election: A Response to Michael O'Neil." *Evangelical Quarterly* 79.1 (2007) 53–67.

Davies, Brian. "A Modern Defense of Divine Simplicity." In Brian Davies, *Philosophy of Religion: A Guide and Anthology*, 549–64. New York: Oxford University Press, 2000.

———. "Aquinas, God, and Being." *Monist* 80 (October 1997) 500–520.

———. *On Evil: Thomas Aquinas*. New York: Oxford University Press, 2003.

———. *The Reality of God and the Problem of Evil*. London: Continuum, 2006.

———. *The Thought of Thomas Aquinas*. New York: Oxford University Press, 1992.

Dawkins, Richard. *The Blind Watchmaker: Why the Evidence of Evolution Reveals a World Without Design: With New Introduction*. New York: Norton, 1996.

DeRose, Keith. "Universalism and the Bible: The Really Good News." http://pantheon.yale.edu/~kd47/univ.htm.

Descartes, Rene. *Discourse on Method and Meditations on First Philosophy*. 3rd ed. Translated by Donald A. Cress. Indianapolis: Hackett, 1993.

———. *Meditations on First Philosophy*. In *Discourse on Method and Meditations on First Philosophy*, edited and translated by Donald A. Cress. Indianapolis: Hackett, 1993.

———. *Rules for the Direction of the Mind*. Great Books of the Western Tradition 31. Chicago: Encyclopedia Britannica, 1952.

Dodds, Michael. *Unlocking Divine Action: Contemporary Science and Thomas Aquinas*. Washington, tiDC: Catholic University Press of America, 2012.

Duhem, Pierre. *The Aim and Structure of Physical Theory*. Translated by Philip P. Wiener. Princeton, NJ: Princeton University Press, 1954.

Einstein, Albert. *Albert Einstein: Essays in Science*. New York: Barnes & Noble, 2004.

Fletcher, Joseph. *Situation Ethics: The New Morality*. Louisville: Westminster John Knox, 1966.

Flew, Antony, R. M. Hare, Basil Mitchell, and I. M. Crombie. "Theology and Falsification." In *New Essays in Philosophical Theology*, edited by Antony Flew and Alasdair MacIntyre, 96–130. London: SCM, 1955.

Ford, Joseph. "What is chaos, that we should be mindful of it?" In *The New Physics*, edited by Paul Davies, 348–72. Cambridge: Cambridge University Press, 1989.

Frankfurt, Harry G. *The Importance of What We Care About*. Cambridge: Cambridge University Press, 1988.

Funkenstein, Amos. *Theology and the Scientific Imagination from the Middle Ages to the Seventeenth Century*. Princeton, NJ: Princeton University Press, 1986.

Galileo. *Discoveries and Opinions of Galileo*. Translated by Stillman Drake. New York: Doubleday Anchor, 1957.

Gillispie, Charles Coulston. *Pierre-Simon Laplace, 1749–1827: A Life in Exact Science*. Princeton, NJ: Princeton University Press, 1997.

Gilson, Etienne. *The Christian Philosophy of St. Thomas Aquinas*. Notre Dame, IN: University of Notre Dame Press, 1956.

———. *God and Philosophy*. New Haven, CT: Yale University Press, 1941.

———. *The Spirit of Medieval Philosophy*. Notre Dame, IN: University of Notre Dame Press, 1991.

Gingerich, Owen. "The Copernican Revolution." In *Science and Religion: A Historical Introduction*, edited by Gary B. Ferngren, 95–104. Baltimore: Johns Hopkins University Press, 2002.

Gladwell, Malcolm. *Outliers: The Story of Success*. New York: Little, Brown and Company, 2008.

Gould, Stephen Jay. *The Structure of Evolutionary Theory*. Cambridge, MA: Harvard University Press, 2002.

Gregory, Brad S. *The Unintended Reformation: How a Religious Revolution Secularized Society*. Cambridge, MA: Harvard University Press, 2012.

Gribbin, John. *Deep Simplicity: Bringing Order to Chaos and Complexity*. New York: Random House, 2004.

Haddorff, David. *Christian Ethics as Witness: Barth's Ethics for a World at Risk*. Eugene, OR: Cascade, 2010.

Haidt, Jonathan. *The Happiness Hypothesis: Finding Modern Truth in Ancient Wisdom*. New York: Basic, 2006.

Haldane, J. J., and J. J .C. Smart. *Atheism and Theism*. 2nd ed. New York: Wiley-Blackwell, 2003.

Hauerwas, Stanley. *With the Grain of the Universe: The Church's Witness and Natural Theology*. Grand Rapids: Brazos, 2001.

Hauerwas, Stanley, and Charles R. Pinches. *Christians among the Virtues*. Notre Dame, IN: University of Notre Dame Press, 1997.

Heisenberg, Werner. *Physics and Philosophy: The Revolution in Modern Science.* New York: Harper Perennial, 1962.
Helm, Paul. *The Providence of God.* Downers Grove, IL: InterVarsity, 1993.
Hetherington, Norriss S. *Planetary Motions: A Historical Perspective.* Westport, CT: Greenwood, 2006.
Hick, John. *Evil and the God of Love.* New York: Harper & Row, 1966.
Hume, David. *An Enquiry Concerning Human Understanding.* Great Books of the Western Tradition 35. Chicago: Encyclopedia Britannica, 1952.
Hunsinger, George. *How to Read Karl Barth: The Shape of His Theology.* New York: Oxford University Press, 1991.
Jaki, Stanley L. *Science and Creation: From Eternal Cycles to an Oscillating Universe.* New York: University Press of America, 1990.
Jüngel, Eberhard. *Karl Barth, A Theological Legacy.* Translated by Garrett E. Paul. Philadelphia: Westminster, 1986.
Kant, Immanuel. *Critique of Practical Reason.* Translated by Lewis White Beck. New York: The Bobbs-Merrill Company, 1956.
———. *Religion Within the Limits of Reason Alone.* Translated by Theodore M. Greene and Hoyt H. Hudson. New York: Harper & Row, 1960.
———. "On a Supposed Right to Lie From Altruistic Motives." In Immanuel Kant, *Critique of Practical Reason and Other Writings in Moral Philosophy*, 346–50. Edited and translated by Lewis White Beck. Chicago: University of Chicago Press, 1949. http://www.mc.maricopa.edu/~davpy35701/text/kant-sup-right-to-lie.pdf.
Kenny, Anthony. *Aquinas on Mind.* New York: Routledge, 1994.
Knight, Kevin. Editor's note, Supplement to the *Summa Theologica*. English Dominican Online Edition. http://www.newadvent.org.summa/5.htm.
Koyre, Alexandre. *From the Closed World to the Infinite Universe.* Baltimore: The Johns Hopkins Press, 1957.
Krötke, Wolf. *Sin and Nothingness in the Theology of Karl Barth.* Princeton, NJ: Princeton Theological Seminary, 2005.
Laplace, Pierre Simon. *A Philosophical Essay on Probabilities.* Translated by Fredrick Wilson Truscott and Frederick Lincoln Emory. London: Chapman & Hall, 1902.
Lewis, C. S. "The Humanitarian Theory of Punishment." In *God in the Dock: Essays on Theology and Ethics*, 287–300. Grand Rapids: Eerdmans, 1970.
———. *Perelandra.* New York: Scribner, 1972.
———. *The Problem of Pain.* New York: HarperCollins, 1996.
———. *Reflections on the Psalms.* New York: Harcourt, Brace & World, 1958.
Lightman, Alan. "The Accidental Universe: Science's Crisis of Faith." *Harper's Magazine*, December 2011, 35–40.
Locke, John. *Second Treatise of Government.* Indianapolis: Hackett, 1980.
Lombardo, Nicholas E. *The Logic of Desire: Aquinas on Emotion.* Washington, DC: Catholic University Press of America, 2011.
Lovejoy, Arthur O. *The Great Chain of Being: A Study in the History of an Idea.* Cambridge, MA: Harvard University Press, 1964.
MacDonald, Gregory (Robin Parry). *The Evangelical Universalist.* Eugene, OR: Cascade, 2006.
Machuga, Ric. *In Defense of the Soul: What It Means to be Human.* Grand Rapids: Brazos, 2002.

———. *Life, the Universe, and Everything: An Aristotelian Philosophy for a Scientific Age*. Eugene, OR: Cascade, 2011.

MacIntyre, Alasdair. *After Virtue*. 3rd ed. Notre Dame, IN: University of Notre Dame Press, 2007.

———. *Whose Justice? Which Rationality?* Notre Dame, IN: University of Notre Dame Press, 1988.

MacKay, D. M. *Behind the Eye*. Cambridge, MA: Blackwell, 1990.

———. *The Clockwork Image: A Christian Perspective on Science*. Downers Grove, IL: InterVarsity, 1974.

———. *Human Science and Human Dignity*. Downers Grove, IL: InterVarsity, 1979.

Macpherson, C. B. *The Political Theory of Possessive Individualism*. New York: Oxford University Press, 1962.

Mascall, E. L. *He Who Is*. London: Longmans, 1962.

———. *The Importance of Being Human*. New York: Columbia University Press, 1958.

———. *The Openness of Being: Natural Theology Today*. Philadelphia: Westminster, 1971.

Mayr, Ernst. *The Growth of Biological Thought: Diversity, Evolution, and Inheritance*. Cambridge, MA: Harvard University Press, 1982.

———. *One Long Argument: Charles Darwin and the Genesis of Modern Evolutionary Thought*. Cambridge, MA: Harvard University Press, 1993.

———. *This Is Biology: The Science of the Living World*. Cambridge, MA: Harvard University Press, 1997.

———. *Toward a New Philosophy of Biology: Observations of an Evolutionist*. Cambridge, MA: Harvard University Press, 1988.

———. *What Evolution Is*. New York: Basic, 2001.

———. *What Makes Biology Unique? Considerations on the Autonomy of a Scientific Discipline*. New York: Cambridge University Press, 2004.

McCabe, Herbert. *God Matters*. London: Continuum, 1987.

———. "A Modern Cosmological Argument." In *Philosophy of Religion: A Guide and Anthology*, edited by Brian Davies, 196–201. New York: Oxford University Press, 2000.

McCool, Gerald A., ed. *The Universe as Journey: Conversations with W. Norris Clarke*. New York: Fordham University Press, 1988.

McGrath, Alister. *A Scientific Theology: Theory*. Grand Rapids: Eerdmans, 2003.

McInerny, Ralph. *Aquinas on Human Action: A Theory of Practice*, Washington, DC: Catholic University Press of America, 1992.

Milbank, John, and Catherine Pickstock. *Truth in Aquinas*. London: Routledge, 2001.

Miller, Barry. *A Most Unlikely God: A Philosophical Enquiry Into the Nature of God*. Notre Dame, IN: University of Notre Dame Press, 1996.

Newton, Issac. Letters. http://www.newtonproject.sussex.ac.uk.

———. *Mathematical Principles of Natural Philosophy*. "Rules of Reasoning in Philosophy." Great Books of the Western Tradition 34. Chicago: Encyclopedia Britannica, 1952.

———. *Optics*, Great Books of the Western Tradition 34. Chicago: Encyclopedia Britannica, 1952.

Nozick, Robert. *Anarchy, State and Utopia*. New York: Basic, 1977.

Pasnau, Robert. *Thomas Aquinas on Human Nature*. Cambridge: Cambridge University Press, 2002.

Peacocke, Arthur R. "Chance and Law in Irreversible Thermodynamics, Theoretical Biology and Theology." In *Chaos and Complexity: Scientific Perspectives on Divine Action*, edited by Robert Russell et al., 123–43. Notre Dame, IN: University of Notre Dame Press, 1996.

Pieper, Josef. *In Defense of Philosophy*. San Francisco: Ignatius, 1992.

———. *Guide to Thomas Aquinas*. Translated by Richard and Clara Winston. San Francisco: Ignatius, 1991.

———. *The Silence of St. Thomas*. South Bend, IN: St. Augustine's Press, 1999.

Pinckaers, Servais. *The Sources of Christian Ethics*. 3rd ed. Washington, DC: Catholic University of America Press, 1995.

Placher, William C. *The Domestication of Transcendence: How Modern Thinking about God Went Wrong*. Louisville: Westminster John Knox, 1996.

Plato. *Laws*. Translated by Trevor J. Saunders. New York: Penguin, 1970.

———. *Protagoras*. Great Books of the Western Tradition 7. Chicago: Encyclopedia Britannica, 1952.

———. *The Republic*. Translated by Francis M. Cornford. London: Oxford University Press, 1941.

Polanyi, Michael. *Personal Knowledge: Towards a Post-Critical Philosophy*. Chicago: University of Chicago Press, 1974.

Popper, Karl. "Of Clocks and Clouds." http://www.the-rathouse.com/2011/Clouds-and-Clocks.html.

———. *The Open Universe: An Argument for Indeterminism*. Totowa, NJ: Rowman and Littlefield, 1982.

Putnam, Hilary. *The Collapse of the Fact/Value Dichotomy and Other Essays*. Cambridge, MA: Harvard University Press, 2002.

Rawls, John *A Theory of Justice*. Cambridge, MA: Harvard University Press, 1971.

Reitan, Eric. "Human Freedom and the Impossibility of Eternal Damnation." In *Universal Salvation? The Current Debate*, edited by Robin Parry and Christopher Partridge, 125–42. Grand Rapids: Eerdmans, 2003.

Rigney, Daniel. *The Matthew Effect: How Advantage Begets Further Advantage*. New York: Columbia University Press, 2010.

Ritchie, Arthur David. *Studies in the History and Methods of the Sciences*. Edinburgh: The University Press, 1958.

Rogers, Eugene F. *Thomas Aquinas and Karl Barth: Sacred Doctrine and the Natural Knowledge of God*. Notre Dame, IN: University of Notre Dame Press, 1995.

Rose, Matthew. *Ethics with Barth: God, Metaphysics and Morals*. Farnham, Surrey, GB: Ashgate, 2010.

Ryle, Gilbert. *The Concept of Mind*. New York: Barnes & Noble, 1949.

Sartre, Jean-Paul. "Existentialism Is a Humanism." Translated by Philip Mairet. http://www.marxists.org/reference/archive/sartre/works/exist/sartre.htm.

Schumacher, E. F. "Technology with a Human Face." In *Small is Beautiful: A Study of Economics as if People Matter*. http://www.ee.iitb.ac.in/student/~pdarshan/SmallIsBeautifulSchumacher.pdf.

Searle, John. *Mind, Language, and Society*. New York: Basic, 1998.

Stump, Eleonore. *Aquinas*. London: Routledge, 2003.

———. "Aquinas on the Foundations of Knowledge." In *Aristotle and His Medieval Interpreters*, edited by Richard Bosley and Martin Tweedale, 125–58. Calgary: University of Calgary Press, 1992.

———. "Faith and Goodness." In *The Philosophy in Christianity*, edited by Godfrey Vesey, 167–91. Cambridge: Cambridge University Press, 1989.

Swinburne, Richard. *The Coherence of Theism*. Oxford: Clarendon, 1977.

———. *The Existence of God*. Oxford: Clarendon, 1979.

Taleb, Nassim Nicholas. *The Black Swan: The Impact of the Highly Improbable*. New York: Random House, 2007.

Theology and Worship Ministry Unit. *Book of Common Worship*. Louisville: Westmister John Knox, 1993.

Torrance, Alan. *Persons in Communion: An Essay on Trinitarian Description and Human Participation*. Edinburgh: T & T Clark, 1996.

Torrance, Thomas F. *Christian Theology and Scientific Culture*. New York: Oxford University Press, 1981.

———. *Divine and Contingent Order*. Edinburgh: T & T Clark, 1998.

———. *The Ground and Grammar of Theology*. Charlottesville, VA: University Press of Virginia, 1980.

———. "Natural Theology in the Thought of Karl Barth." *Religious Studies* 6 (1970) 121–35.

Veatch, Henry B. *Aristotle: A Contemporary Appreciation*. Bloomington, IN: Indiana University Press, 1974.

Virgil. *The Aeneid*. Translated by W. F. Jackson Knight. New York: Penguin, 1956.

Walls, Jerry. "A Philosophical Critique of Talbott's Universalism." In *Universal Salvation? The Current Debate*, edited by Robin Parry and Christopher Partridge, 105–24. Grand Rapids: Eerdmans, 2003.

Weigel, George. *Witness to Hope: The Biography of Pope John Paul II*. New York: HarperCollins, 1999.

White, Thomas Joseph, ed. *The Analogy of Being: Invention of the Antichrist or the Wisdom of God?* Grand Rapids: Eerdmans, 2011.

Whitehead, Alfred North. *Science and the Modern World*. New York: Pelican Mentor, 1948.

Whitman, Charles. "Whitman Letter." http://alt.cimedia.com/statesman/specialreports/whitman/letter.pdf.

Wild, John. *Plato's Theory of Man: An Introduction to the Realistic Philosophy of Culture*. Cambridge, MA: Harvard University Press, 1946.

Williams, C. J. F. "Knowing Good and Evil." *Philosophy* 66 (1991) 235–40.

Wright, N.T. *Evil and the Justice of God*. Downers Grove, IL.: InterVarsity, 2006.

———. *Jesus and the Victory of God*. Christian Origins and the Question of God, vol. 2. Minneapolis: Fortress, 1996.

———. *The New Testament and the People of God*. Christian Origins and the Question of God, vol. 1. Minneapolis: Fortress, 1992.

———. *The Resurrection of the Son of God*. Christian Origins and the Question of God, vol. 3. Minneapolis: Fortress, 2003.

Index

Definitions are in **bold** fonts.

absolute space and time. *See* Newton, Isaac
action at a distance, *See* Newton, Isaac
ad hoc, 62, 74, 141
Adler, Mortimer, 31n
Adams, Marilyn McCord, 215n, 223n
aionios, 237
analogy, general, **24–30**, 49, 217, 262
Anderson, James, 206n
annihilationism, 245n
Anscombe, Elizabeth, 128n
Aquinas, Thomas
  analogy, **26–30**, 27n
  causality, xi, 8, 37n, 40, 94n, 175n, 182n, 192
  conscience, 142, 143n
  creation, 76n, 82n, 88, 212n
  existence, 69, 202, 205n, 206, 210n, 211
  evil, 200, 211, 216n, 251
  God, 98n, 209n, 221n
  grace, 107n, 178n, 184n, 185n, 250n
  happiness, 129, 138
  hell, 227n, 244, 245n
  intellect, 32n, 130n,
  knowledge, 75, 175n, 209n
  miracles, 116n
  negative theology, 141n
  philosophy, xvi, 159
  prayer, 195, 199
  preambles to faith, 110–12
  predestination, 186n25, 245n3
  providence, 174n, 175n, 187n, 188n, 195n,
  private property, 152, **158–60,** 164n
  teleological argument for God, 75–80
  space and time, 92
apokatastasis, 254
Aristotle,
  adultery, 134, 141
  education, 167n
  human intellect, 130
  induction, 49n
  men's teeth, 53n
  politics, 152n, 157
  private property, 158, 166
  soul, 132
  stellar parallax, 59
  weakness of will, 128
Arminius, Jacobus, 184n, 186, 233, 258
Arminians, 221–22, 232, 236, 247, 252–53, 259
Augustine,
  evil, 216, 222
  happiness, 129
  hell, 225–29
  predestination, 186n25, 226
  space and time, 91n

Bacon, Francis, 8
Balthasar, Hans Urs von, 189n, 225, 246n, 247n
Barth, Karl
 analogy, 27n, 85n, 103, 107, 140n, 174n
 causality, xi n, 8n, 94n, 95n, 183n, 192
 common grace, 104n
 ethics, xiii, 138n, 141n, 143, 147–50, 176n, 181, 253
 God, 210n
 happiness, 129n, 177n
 existence, 69, 202, 261
 historical revelation, 110n, 114n
 impossible possibility, xv, 200, 214, 218, 222, 253
 miracles, 95n, 115n
 natural theology, 99n, 103–8
 nothingness, 213–14
 parthenogenesis, 117n
 predestination, 184–89, 231n, 245n, 197n
 providence, 174n, 175n
 principalities and powers, 147
 resurrection, 198
 shadow side of creation, 214
 space and time, 91n
 wrath of God, 239n, 242, 243n, 244
Biggar, Nigel, 177n
biogenesis, 219
Bishop Berkeley, 12, 13
Bohr, Neils, 12, 248
Bonda, Jan, 239, 241n
Bourke, Vernon J., 94n
Boyle, Robert, 98
Burrell, David,
 analogy, 27n, 206n
 divine action, 36n, 85n, 88n, 91n, 261n
 human freedom, 181, 252n
 sin, 251n
 supernaturalism, 69n
 Trinity, 201n
Burtt, Edwin Arthur, 99n
Busch, Eberhard, 172n

Calvin, John,
 biblical texts, 185n
 horrible decree, 231, 262
 providence, 187
 secret decree, 221
Carnap, Rudolf, 54n
Carter, Jimmy, 3, 14, 65
casuistry, 143
causation, general, **36–41**
Cavanaugh, William, 69n
chiliagon analogy, 69, 85, 121
Clarke, Norris, 27n, 83n, 98n, 198n, 206n, 244
complexity argument for God, **80–82**
Copernicus, Nicholas, 59ff, 100
Copenhagen interpretation. *See* Bohr, Neils
Corbett, John, 149n
Crisp, Oliver, 237n, 247n
crossword puzzle example, 64
curve breaker example, 160–62

Davies, Brian, 72n, 91n, 198n, 201n, 212n,
Dawkins, Richard, 117n
de dicto/de re, **187–91**
DeRose, Keith, 235
Descartes, Rene,
 clear and distinct ideas, **30–31**, 33, 36, 41, 44, 64
 dualism, 34, 70, 180
 final causes, **36**, 37, 41
 foundationalism, 24, 26, 46, 248
 free will, 184
 gravity, 73
 idealism, 31, 35, 48, 84, 109
 ontological argument, 72n
divine In-former argument, **82–85**
Dodds, Michael, 93
double pendulum, 9, **14–17**
double predestination, 231
dual-causation, x, **93–99**, 116, 139, 157, 170, 190–92
dual-causation, biblical examples, **96n**
Duhem, Pierre, 60n
Durbin, Paul, 26n

Index

Einstein, Albert, 12, 17, 46n, 58, 65n, 89, 248
empirically detectable God, ix, 67n, 74, 80, 94
Existentialism, *See* Sartre, Jean-Paul

fideism, ix
fine-tuning argument, 16, 87
Flew, Antony, 113n
Fletcher, Joseph, 142
fMRI, 7
Ford, Joseph, 17
fortunate fall, 219–22
Frankfurt, Harry, 164
free will, **176–83**
Funkenstein, Amos, 26n

gap argument for God, 74–76
Galileo
 causation, 93
 errors, 101n
 measurement, ix, 77n, 36n, 77, 157
 telescope, 100
Gilson, Etienne, xvi, 206, 245n, 257–58
Gladwell, Malcom, 162
Gould, Stephen Jay, 22n, 62n, 71n
Grace,
 efficacious, 183
 sufficient, 184
 biblical references, 185n
Great Chain of Being, 31–34, 70, 197, 204n
Gregory, Brad S., 25n, 185n
Gribbin, John, 16n, 17n

Haddorff, David, 145n, 146n, 147n
Haidt, Jonathan, 138n, 165n
Hamlet/Shakespeare example, 93, 190–93
Haldane, J. J, 207n
Hare, R. H., 113n
Hauerwas, Stanley, 103n, 222n
Heisenberg, Werner, 13,
Helm, Paul, 69n, 201n
hell, biblical evidence, 229–34, 237n, 241n
Hertherington, Norriss, S. 15n, 60n, 73n
Hick, John, 215n, 247n

honor killing, 142
Hooker, William, 164n
Hume, David, xiii, 38, **122**, 223, 248
Hunsinger, George, 95n, 105n

Ilunga example, 80n
immortality, 35

Jaki, Stanley, 13n, 84n,
Jüngel, Eberhard, 245n

Kant, Immanuel, x, 72n, 139–41, 157, 179, 205, 252
Kierkegaard, Soren, 246, 248
Koyre, Alexandre, 15n, 73n, 197n
Krötke, Wolf, 213

Laplace, Pierre, 15, 16
Laplace's Demon, **5–9**, 14–17, 28n, 44, 47, 74, 163
Lewis, C. S., 86, 221, 232, 239n, 242, 256n, 262,
light cone, 18, 19, 65, 97, 248
Lightman, Alan, 109n
Locke, John, xiii, 151, **154–72**, 248
Lombardo, Nicholas E., 107n, 129n, 213n
logistic maps, **41–44**, 48, 248
Lovejoy, Arthur O., 32n
Lucretius, 111

MacDonald, Gregory, 237
Mackay, D. M., 249n
MacIntyre, Alasdair, 18n, 167n
Macpherson, C. B., 156n
McCabe, Herbert, 190n, 192n
McCool, Gerald A., 216n
McGrath, Alister, 197n
McInerny, Ralph, 164n
Mascall, E. L., 81, 137n, 138n, 257, 258
Matthew Effect, 160–63
Mayr, Ernst,
 Aristotle, 32n, 79
 autonomy of biology, 5n, 39, 40n, 47, 78n
 dual-causation, 95,
 Galileo, 77n
 hummingbirds, 62n, 119n
 language, 71n, 132

seventeen months premature, 131n
Mill, John Stuart, 50–53
Milbank, John, 71n
Miller, Barry, 71n, 191n, 206n
Molina, 186n25
mono-causation, general, ix, **66**, 86, 93–97, 119, 135n, 153, 194
Moore, G.E., 133
mystery, 217–19

naturalistic fallacy, 133
Newton, Isaac,
    absolute space and time, 9, 12n, 17n20, 89, 224
    action at a distance, 61, 73, 124, 171
    God, 15–17, 62, 66, **73–77**, 87, 90
    gravity, 35, 53, 59, 61, 73, 75, 122
    Law of Nature, xii, 2, 67, 86, 173
    mechanistic philosophy, x
    nothing in vain, 82
nominalism, 179
nonlinear events, 2–5, 14–17, 22n, 162–62, 175
Northrop, F. S. C., 13n
Nozick, Robert, 156n

Ockham, William, 58, 137n, 145n, 178–84, 193n

Paley, William, xi, 66, 76, 80, 112
Pasnau, Robert, 32n
Peacocke, Arthur, 76n
Pieper, Josef, 206n, 209n
Pinckaers, Servais, 137n, 149n, 178n
Ping-Pong ball example, 10–11
Placher, William C., 25n, 184n, 185n
Plato,
    economic equality, 151, 164, 166
    freedom, 177
    Great Chain of Being, 32n
    leaden weights, 20, 177
    nature not random, 78n
    philosophical idealism, 258
    political wisdom, 167, 168
    weakness of will, 127n
Plantinga, Alvin, 261n
Platonists, 89n, 103n, 109, 120, 228, 246n, 255, 257

Polanyi, Michael, 65n, 83
Popper, Karl, 18n, 19n, 65n
prayer,
    Augustine's, 222
    hell, xvi, 229, 243
    makes a difference, 87, 98, 98n, **193–99**
    performative, 195–97
    spiritual blessing, 113
predestination, ix, xiv, 139, 183, 251n, 252n
Putnam, Hilary, 54n

quantum theory, 9, **11–14**, 17, 29n, 65

raven paradox, 56
Rawls, John, 151–52, 164n
Relativity theory. *See* Einstein, Albert
resurrection,
    Christ's victory, 124, 128, 148, 220, 222, 237
    historical, 109, 114
    hope, 95n, 177, 184
    miracle, 114, **119–22**
Reitan, Eric, 247n, 258n
Rigney, Daniel, 162n
Ritchie, Arthur David, 53n, 109n
Roger, Eugene F., 103n, 105n, 245n
Rose, Matthew, 176n
Ryle, Gilbert, 12, 21

Sacks, Oliver, 101
Sartre, Jean-Paul, 134–37, 179
Scotus, Duns, 137n, 145n
Schumacher, E. F., 165
Searle, John, 213n
self-prediction, **18–22**, 175, 248, 249n
signs and wonders, **115 - 19**
Stein, Edith, 189n
Stump, Eleonore, 26n, 70n, 210n, 223n

Taleb, Nassim, 14n
tennis ball example, 2–3, 22, 110, 163, 174, 183, 187, 188
three-body problem, 15, 23, 175, 248. *See also* double pendulum
thresholds. *See* nonlinear events
tipping points. *See* nonlinear events

Torrance, Alan, 25n
Torrance, T. F.,
    analogy, 29n
    Barth, 103n
    Being, 192n
    Calvin, 231n
    miracles, 121n
    natural science, 46n, 65n, 85n
    natural theology, 108n
    space and time, 90n
Transcendentals, 201–10
type/token, 20n

univocal. *See* analogy

Veatch, Henry, 40n
Virginia Declaration of Rights, 169n

Walls, Jerry, 232n
weakness of will, **127–28**
Weigel, George, 99n
White, Thomas Joseph, 25n
Whitman, Charles, 182
Wild, John, 78n
William, C. J. E., 216n, 217n, 251n
Wright, N. T., 69n, 124n, 216n

www.ingramcontent.com/pod-product-compliance
Lightning Source LLC
Chambersburg PA
CBHW021655230426

43668CB00008B/627